CONCISE HISTORY
OF
ECONOMIC THOUGHT

CONCISE HISTORY
OF
ECONOMIC THOUGHT

Dr. B.N. Ghosh
Ph.D. (Econ.)
Associate Professor,
Department of Economics,
Punjab University, Chandigarh.

Dr. Rama Ghosh
Ph.D. (Econ.)
D.A.V. College, Chandigarh.
Formerly, Research Associate (U.G.C.)
Punjab University, Chandigarh.

Himalaya Publishing House
ISO 9001:2015 CERTIFIED

First Edition	: 1988	Reprint	: 2012
Reprint	: 1996	Reprint	: 2013
Reprint	: 1999	Reprint	: 2015
Reprint	: 2006	Reprint	: 2017
Reprint	: 2009	Reprint	: October, 2017
Reprint	: 2010	Reprint	: 2019

Published by : Mrs. Meena Pandey for **Himalaya Publishing House Pvt.**
"Ramdoot", Dr. Bhalerao Marg, Girgaon, **Mumbai - 400 004**
Phone: 022-23860170/23863863, Fax: 022-23877178
E-mail: himpub@vsnl.com; Website: www.himpub.c

Branch Offices :

New Delhi : "Pooja Apartments", 4-B, Murari Lal Street, Ansari Road,
Darya Ganj, New Delhi - 110 002.
Phone: 011-23270392, 23278631; Fax: 011-23256286

Nagpur : Kundanlal Chandak Industrial Estate, Ghat Road, Nagpur - 440
Phone: 0712-2738731, 3296733; Telefax: 0712-2721216

Bengaluru : Plot No. 91-33, 2nd Main Road Seshadripuram, Behind Natar
Theatre, Bengaluru - 560020. Phone: 08041138821,
Mobile: 09379847017, 09379847005.

Hyderabad : No. 3-4-184, Lingampally, Besides Raghavendra Swamy Math
Kachiguda, Hyderabad - 500 027. Phone: 040-27560041, 27550

Chennai : New No. 48/2, Old No. 28/2, Ground Floor, Sarangapani Str
T. Nagar, Chennai - 600 012. Mobile: 09380460419

Pune : First Floor, "Laksha" Apartment, No. 527, Mehunpura, Shaniwarp
(Near Prabhat Theatre), Pune - 411 030.
Phone: 020-24496323/24496333; Mobile: 09370579333

Lucknow : House No 731, Shekhupura Colony, Near B.D. Convent Scho
Aliganj, Lucknow - 226 022. Phone: 0522-4012353;
Mobile: 09307501549

Ahmedabad : 114, "SHAIL", 1st Floor, Opp. Madhu Sudan House, C.G. Ro
Navrang Pura, hmedabad - 380 009. Phone: 079-265601
Mobile: 09377088847

Ernakulam : 39/176 (New No: 60/251) 1st Floor, Karikkamuri Road,
Ernakulam, Kochi - 682011. Phone: 0484-2378012, 2378016
Mobile: 09387122121

Bhubaneswar : Plot No. 214/1342, Budheswari Colony,
Behind Durga Mandap, Laxmisagar, Bhubaneswar - 751 006
Phone: 0674-2575129; Mobile: 09338746007

Kolkata : 108/4, Beliaghata Main Road, Near ID Hospital, Opp. SBI Bank
Kolkata - 700 010, Phone: 033-32449649, Mobile: 074390403

Printed by : Infinity Imaging System, New Delhi. On behalf of HPH.

Dedicated

To

Professor P.R. Brahmananda

With a sense sublime of something far more deeply interfused

PREFACE TO THE SECOND EDITION

The entire stock of the first edition of the book has been exhausted in one year. Encouraged by this overwhelming success of the book, we have more painstakingly undertaken the work of revision in the second edition. In this edition, we have thoroughly revised the book, eliminated the printer's devils, inducted additional materials in some chapters and introduced a full new chapter (Ch. 21). This chapter provides the following important topical notes :

1. A Note on the Meaning of Political Economy
2. Salient Features of Classical Political Economy
3. Salient Features of Neoclassical Economics
4. Ricardian Theory of Value and Marxian Theory of Value : A Comparative Estimate
5. A Note on P. Sraffa's *Production of Commodities by Means of Commodities*
6. Ricardian Economics and Sraffian Analysis : A Note
7. Marxian Labour Theory of Value and Sraffian Analysis : A Note
8. Classical Model of Economic Growth : A Mathematical Note

Apart from these changes, several new things have been incorporated in this edition. We have incorporated new materials in the SECTIONS on *Say's Law of Market, Marxian Theory of Profit, Lenin's Theory of Imperialism* and *Classical Growth Theories*. Two new diagrams have been introduced in the analysis of *Physiocracy* and *Glut Controversy*. *Marxian Reproduction Schema* has been completely recast. We have also added Appendices of *American Economic Thought, Post Marshallian Development* and *Post-Keynesian Developments*.

We reasonably believe that the book would be more useful now to the readers. Any suggestion, however, for the improvement of the book would be highly appreciated.

Chandigarh   **AUTHORS**

PREFACE TO THE FIRST EDITION

History of Economic Thought is not purported to be an old story of the dead authors. So long as the past is given to interact with the present, history of thought will remain essentially a living subject in the economic universe of discourse. The students of economics need to be acquainted with the works of the great authors of by-gone days.

However, it is always not possible, owing to many constraints, such as' restricted library facilities, non-availability of good books and journals, and facility of time, to go through the original writings of the great authors. Thus, there is ample justification for a good textbook in the *History of Economic Thought.*

Surprisingly enough, although the subject has been introduced as a compulsory paper in many universities, there still appears to be acute scarcity of standard and balanced textbooks which can satisfy the requirements of present-day university students. No doubt, there are ample good books on the subject. However, some of these books are unbalanced and do not cover the syllabi of Indian universities. For instance most of the foreign books do not discuss *Indian Economic Thought.* In the same way, many of the available books do not delineate with analytical rigours the economics of the old authors. Again, some books do not contain all authors and writers and some books are of elephantine shapes and prove to be too lengthy for students.

The present book is designed as a textbook of *History of Economic Thought.* It outlines the major contributions of almost all the important economists of all recognised schools. The informations and facts are summarised but not at the cost of any point. Our discussion is essentially precise, selective, to the point and examination-oriented. The book makes use of the latest informations available from journals and periodicals, and explains and illustrates with diagrams and mathematics wherever required. The book can serve well as a standard textbook for the Honours and Postgraduate students of various universities where *History of Economic Thought* is taught as a subject. In many ways, the present work is a differentiated product on the subject of History of Economic Thought.

The book is divided into six constituent parts. *The Pre-Adamite Thought* discusses economic thought from ancient period to the days of Physiocracy. Part Two of the book outlines the *Development of Classical Political Economy.* It also includes the critics and contemporaries of Classical School. Part Three deals with *Reconstruction of Economic Science.* In Part Four, *Modern Economic Thought* is discussed. It includes Institutional, Welfare and Keynesian Schools. Part Five of this book deals with *Indian Economic Thought.* Development of some of the economic theories has been discussed in Part Six of the book. We have also added a *Select Bibliography* for the benefit of the students.

While writing this book, we have incurred intellectual indebtedness to many. Their names are given in the body of the book in the form of footnotes and also in the *Bibliography*. We express our gratitude to the following authors from whose works the present book rather draws heavily : Mark Blaug, Joseph A. Schumpeter, Robert Lekachman, J.W. McConnell, Lewis H. Haney, Gide and Rist, Eric Roll and Ekelund and Herbert. We are also indebted to many of our friends and colleagues for various external effects. The list of their names is too lengthy to be mentioned here. We remain thankful to all of them for inspiring us to write this small volume. However, the usual caveat does, of course, apply, and we fully realise the loneliness of the error-mongers.

Chandigarh   **Authors**
1988

CONTENTS

Introduction

Meaning, Nature and Scope of Economic Thought

History of economic thought is sometimes regarded as the old ideas of dead authors. There is some kernel of truth in this statement. However, there are many ways of looking at the subject of history of economic thought. Economic thought can be regarded as a collection of highly subjective, opinionated and personal economic ideas of great economists. History of economic thought may also include opinions of the different schools of economic thought. It is the sum-total of all opinions concerning economic discipline, specially with respect to public policy on different economic issues at any given time and place.[1] Economic thought may reveal class relation, production, distribution, value, economic growth development and a host of many other aspects concerning the economic life of a society. History of economic thought traces the historical change of attitudes towards different economic variables.[2] History of economic thought is an account of the development of economic ideas and also a study of their impact on economic institutions and human activities. It has been rightly pointed out that a history of economic thought is a critical account of the development of economic ideas, searching into their origin, inter-relations, manifestations and effects.[3] History of economic thought is concerned with the history of economic ideas which are placed in order on the basis of origin. Since human beings have always thought about economic problems for their day-to-day existence, economic thought can be ragarded as old as the history of mankind.

History of economic thought is a systematic compilation of economic ideas of human beings which aim at analysing some economic problems, or explaining the origin and mechanism of some economic institutions. History of economic thought also contains plans, programmes and speculation about institutions and their future development. History of economic thought is a systematic, chronological and critical study of the economic ideas and sources of some of these ideas.

---

1. J.A. Schumpeter, *The History of Economic Analysis,* p. 35.
2. *Ibid*, p. 39.
3. Haney, *History of Economic Thought*, p. 4.

History of Economic Thought and Economic History

These two are distinctly different branches of the mainstream economics. Their subject-matters are different. Economic thought is a subjective account of economic ideas, whereas economic history is an objective analysis of the development of the economic system in its various ramifications. Economic history is devoted to the study of agriculture, industry, banking, trade and commerce and so many other economic institutions and phenomena. Economic history deals with facts, but economic thought deals with economic ideas. However, these two areas of economics are closely related in the sense that economic history influences economic thought, and economic thought influences the course of economic history. It should be noted that ideas influence environment and environment influences ideas. Therefore, there is no contradiction between these two branches of economics.

History of Economic Thought and History of Economic Analysis

History of economic analysis is concerned with the development of the science of economics. A science is very loosely defined as a body of systematic knowledge. The *differentia specifica* of science is that it is a system of falsifiable hypotheses. Karl Popper in his monumental work, *The Logic of Scientific Discovery,* has specified the criterion of distinguishing between science and metaphysics.[4] A truly scientific hypothesis must be capable of being falsified. However, Schumpeter observed that any scientific theorising starts with a vision which is subjectively introspective but which supplies the apparatus of thought for the analytical paradigm of theory. Economic knowledge is, in the first instance, theoretical. However, a problem-solving normal science can be looked upon as a rule, and a revolutionary science which throws out a paradigm after repeated refutations and replaces it by another, is an exception in the history of science. According to Kuhn, a science progresses through a protracted period of refinement, in the course of which there may be a sudden change-over from a ruling paradigm to an entirely new one. It would be better for a young science like economics to reject Popperian summary judgement in favour of Kuhnian slow but steady process of enquiry and improvement through which new and better paradigms may be made available to economists.

Lakatos admits of the possibility of a change in the status of a science from regressive to progressive and *vice versa*. Lakatos observes that a single hypothesis or theory can never be successfully verified: rather one should try to verify a group of interconnected theories and auxiliary statements. It would be more purposeful if we can evolve theories having more and better empirical content.

Economics started its paradigm in 1776 with *The Wealth of Nations* of Adam Smith. But it was not a precise science. Economics has become a science since 1870 with the Neo-classical and Marginal Schools who sup-

---

4.   Karl Popper, *The Logic of Scientific Discovery,* Hutchinson, London, 1935.

plied the necessary analytical tools for the falsification and verification of different hypotheses. The science of economics or history of economic analysis has to be analytical. It has to have certain laws and principles and has to study causal relations. Economic science is based on distinct methods and techniques, with the help of which facts can be analysed and interpreted for the purpose of policy prescription. Economic science or the history of economic analysis is analytical and objective, and seeks a transition from good to better and better to best. In other words, it is progressive. But history of economic thought is subjective, descriptive and cannot specify progress or regress. Up to the year 1870, economic thought could not develop any analytical apparatus which could entitle economics to be considered a science. The ancient thinkers did not have scientific economic thought. Their thought was mixed with religion, politics, philosophy, and so on. This is evident from Plato's *Republic*, Kautilya's *Arthashastra* and so on.

Economic was established as a separate discipline, accompanying the first paradigm, during the period of Adam Smith. Thus, whereas the history of economic thought is as old as the history of mankind, the history of economic analysis is necessarily recent. History of economics is only a part of the history of economic thought which indeed covers a very long way since ancient times. History of economic science is "the history of the intellectual efforts that men have made in order to understand economic phenomena or which comes to the same thing, the history of the analytic or scientific aspects of economic thought."[5] However, economic analysis cannot altogether neglect the historical development of thought process on which the direction of economic analysis will depend. Analysis does, of course, separate out personal and subjective inclinations.

Scope of History of Economic Thought

The scope of history of economic thought is very broad indeed. It includes all human ideas relating to economic problems. Economic thought is a record of economic thinking of different authors from the ancient time to the present day. The ides on economics have to be traced from customs, traditions, institutions, laws, practices and so on of a particular community prevailing in a particular period of history. Economic ideas are nothing but the reflections of the contemporary economic conditions. The modern ideas are nothing but refined versions of the old ideas. Gray has rightly pointed out that old doctrines never die, they only fade away to come back again in an appropriate environment.[6]

Economic thought is concerned with the interpretation of production, distribution, value, growth, trade, development, commerce, industries and so many others related to economic matters and problems.

---

5. Schumpeter, *op. cit*, p. 3.
6. Alexander Gray, *The Development of Economic Doctrine*, p. 13.

The scope of economic thought relates to the different periods of economic history such as the Greek period, the Medieval period, the Roman period and Modern period. However, these periods can also be sub-divided into a number of periods such as the ancient economic thought, the classical economic thought, the neo-classical economic thought, Marginalist thought, thoughts of historical writers, economic thoughts of school-men, Marxian thought, Austrian thought, Keynesian thought and so on. The history of economic thought is a record of economic thoughts of different schools. The periodisation of economic thought may be based on a number of considerations. Economic thought also includes the various approaches adopted by the economic historians from time to time in the study of economic problems.

Influences and Motives in the Study of History of Economic Thought

The motives in the study of history of economic thought were analysed by Schumpeter in his *History of Economic Analysis*. Economists are quite naturally involved in social, political and other problems which are contemporary in nature. All these problems and issues influence, to a great extent, economic historians. It should be noted that economics started its career from the mind of a philosopher. Similarly, many people from diverse occupations enriched economic analyses and discussions. For example, Quesnay was a physician by profession, who entered into economics and analysed the circulation of wealth in the same way as the blood circulation in the human body. Wieser was a sociologist like Marx. Adam Smith, who was the father of economic science, was a philosopher, who interpreted the economic philosophy of *natural order* and *optimism* in terms of economic analysis. The ancient economists were concerned with the concept of morality which was introduced in economic analysis. The ancient writers thought that interest payment was an unjustifiable act. Among the ancient people, usury was prohibited because interest charging was not considered legitimate. The school-men analysed economics in terms of *just prices* and standard wages. Thus, it can be shown that human motives and circumstances are very influential in shaping economic ideas.

On the same issue, economists have agreed to differ on many occasions. For example, David Ricardo wanted to abolish the Corn Law because he was against the landlords. He went so far as to say that the landlord class was a parasite class and rent was an unjust payment and a form of unearned income. T.R. Malthus had exactly the opposite views regarding all these, including the Corn Law controversy. Classical political economists broadly agreed on the existence of a class conflict in society. This was very explicitly recognised by Ricardo. Karl Marx was a critic of capitalism and his analysis was in favour of the development of socialism. The Neo-classical marginal writers wanted to introduce some new technique of economic analysis for giving economics the status of a science. The historical school introduced a so-called superior technique of analysing economic phenomena. List's economic thought was based on nationalistic consideration because during his time industries in his country needed protection. Thus, we find that economic thought process is considerably influenced by the motives of the writers. It is well known that Milton Friedman's analysis was bound up with the staunch libertarian political and social ideas. But it is not necessary that personal motive hinders the objectivity of economic analysis.

John Calhoun wanted to defend slavery and secure greater power for southern interests. For this purpose, he devised a new theory of representative government, the theory of concurrent majority.[7] Calhoun's objective may be questioned but the point is that a total disregard of his ideas based on motives will not be proper because his theory is extricable from those moves. Looked at this way, the concept becomes neutral which may be used innocently. Thus, motive always does not distort reasoning or fact. This is true also for Ricardo and Marx on questions of rent and business cycle respectively. Be that as it may, the emotional content of theories and theorists should not be allowed to hide the value of the analytical superstructure.[8]

Why Study History of Economic Thought?

There are a good number of reasons for studying the intellectual development of economics, besides the simple fact that it is very interesting. The following are the main reasons and significances for the study of history of economic thought:

1. A study of the historical aspect of economic analysis gives us the power of rethinking about the foundations of the theoretical ideas which are accepted today in economics.

2. A study of thought helps us to know the achievements, the failures, the capabilities and the limitations of different theoreticians and of different theories.

3. A knowledge of the past is helpful for reducing the probability of errors which the earlier writers committed in the past. This is very important since economics is based on a fragile empirical foundation.

4. A study of thought broadens the horizon of our knowledge and perspective. Schumpeter calls it an appreciation of the ways of the mind. Such a study provides a crucial insight into our ability to analyse problems.

5. New ideas may help us in solving the same or similar problems in our time.

6. It provides a mental discipline and satisfies our curiosity about economics, about a particular school of thought and also about the solution of different problems which our ancestors thought about.

7. A study of history of economic thought gives us a sense of relativity with reference to different theories, *i.e.*, which theory was conditioned by

---

7. Ekelund and Hebert, *A History of Economic Theory and Method,* p. 9.
8. *Ibid.*, p. 10.

what circumstances. The concept of relativity, thus, known, provides a sense of realism in analysis.

8. It is possible to know, by a study of history of economic thought, the chronological growth of different economic theories. We can know the origin of various theories in economics by a thorough study of history of thought. In this process, it is also possible to know the differences of opinion and philosophy in the development of theories in economics.

9. Economic thought provides the readers with a broad basis of comparison between different theories and also between different authors. We can know the progress we have attained and the failures we have faced. Professor Haney says: "Standing at the highest point yet reached, after centuries of economic thought and looking back over the path of truth, strewn with fallacies and truisms though it be, the student feels his judgement broadened, and well-balanced and reasonable conservatism, or a wise progressivism, may fill his mind."[9]

10. A study of thought stimulates the readers to assess correctly the implications of the problems of their time with reference to the old doctrines. In other words, the students can develop a sense of objectivity in outlook.

11. History of economic thought reveals a certain kind of continuity in economic thought. It also points out some amount of unity of purpose in the growth of economic ideas over the years. It can be appreciated that human beings have always tried to find out the solutions of different problems and have also tried to go from error to truth.

12. It reveals the various phases of growth of the subject and the fundamental factors responsible for different types of ideas.

APPROACHES TO (METHODS OF) THE STUDY OF HISTORY OF ECONOMIC THOUGHT

The central problem of economics is not, perhaps, the epistemology, but probably the difficulty in formulating the right approach. Wicksteeds *The Commonsense of Political Economy* records that the general principles which regulate our conduct in business are identical with those which regulate our deliberations, our selections between alternatives, and our decisions. This is the reason why we must take our ordinary experiences as the starting point for approaching economic problems. With him, economics fundamentally becomes a logic of choice. However, there is in the logic of choice a prediction of what Hayek has called "the patterns of outcome". The logic of choice represents the methodological boundaries of economic analysis to Hayek.

Becker and others of Chicago tradition argue that the economic approach is still applicable at the level at which we seek to determine what we value. No wonder that economists usually start their analysis with given individual values and explain little about how these values change. The

---

9. Haney, *op. cit.*, p. 6.

methodologies of economics have changed from *the logic of choice to a science of prediction.* Economics as a social science has traversed a long way from prediction to control, but the externally derived criteria cannot peacefully exist with a methodological framework of the logic of choice. From what has been adumbrated earlier, a number of points can emerge. Firstly, the methodological boundaries of economic analysis are not fixed on any particular analytical plane. The discipline of economics operates on several planes: logic of choice, abstract science of behaviour and predictive science. Obviously, therefore, one can discern many methods which are applied in economic analysis. However, there is no unique method of analysis that the science of economics can utilise for all the time. But the trend of science is to use more and more of empirical method.

In the present century, mainstream economics adopted some methodological principles that seemed to resolve the long-standing debate between theorists and empiricists. Logical empiricism combines pure theory with empirical testing of propositions derived from the theory to achieve what appeared to be a firm basis for scientific economics. However, it must be noted that methods which were more intuitive than systematic some two decades back are now undergoing careful metamorphosis. Some of the major methods of economic analysis are outlined below:

1. Philosophical Approach. In this approach, a particular operational philosophy is taken up by the author and it is developed fully throughout the analysis. Marxian method may be cited as a case in point.

2. Deductive, Theoretical or A Priori Method. This method was applied by the classical economists. Deductive method of reasoning aims at arriving at a particular conclusion from the universal propositions. The Austrian school depended on deductions for laying the foundation of pure theory.

3. Inductive, Empirical or A Posteriori Approach. In economics, empirical approach has been followed by many economists. Hutchison and Samuelson believe in the empirical testing of each axiom and every proposition of a theory. The institutional school also followed empirical methods of analysis. The Historical school was in favour of historical method which is an extension of inductive procedure. In induction, we pass from particular to general propositions.

4. Marginal or Micro Approach. This approach to the study of economics was popularised by the Marginalist school. Micro approach was also applied by the Neo-classical school.

5. Macro or Aggregative Approach. This is also known as the Keynesian approach. Keynes developed an aggregative approach for the study of income, output and employment of the whole economy in macro perspective.

6. Positive Approach. This approach is concerned with the development of theory which is value free. Economics is considered as a positive science by Robbins and others. The Austrians also developed a positive or pure theory. In such an approach, things are explained as they are.

7. Normative Welfare Approach. This approach analyses economics in terms of maximum social welfare. Such an approach has been followed by Pigou, Pareto, Hobson and others. This method considers things in terms of 'what should be' and not 'what actually is'.

8. Historical Approach. This method has been followed by the Historical school. It says that the method of study should be based on history. This method is another version of inductive method. This has been followed by the Historical school and also by Marx, among others.

9. Institutional Approach. This method of study gives importance to institutions and their activities in the development of an economy. This approach was popularised by American institutionalists of which T. Veblen was the leader.

10. Absolutist Approach. In this approach, the main aim is the development of economic theory and tools of analysis. This approach is followed for the scientific theoretical development of economics. It is concerned with the development of absolute theorising without any reference to time, place and circumstances.

11. Relativist Approach. This approach considers theorising with reference to time, place and circumstance. (For Absolutist and Relativist Approaches in detail, see the next section.)

12. The Method of Logical Positivism. This method is a synthesis of two methods—deduction and induction. It is now increasingly recognised that analytical (deductive)studies must be corroborated by empirical (inductive) studies. This method was followed by the Neo-classical school of economic thought.

ABSOLUTISM VS. RELATIVISM

The absolutist theory is concerned with the intellectual development of the subject. It is a journey from error to truth. According to this method of study, economic theories can be ranked in terms of better or worse. Such an approach leads to the development of economic theory which may be the reverse of the existing theory or it may be on a different basis altogether. However, the dramatic shift of economic theory from micro to macro and also from a science of wealth to a science of welfare cannot be explained away be merely the Absolutist philosophy. Schumpeter argues that the nature of scientific economics is autonomous; it remains unaffected by philosophy and history. Absolutist notion of economic analysis is concerned more with logical consistency and theorem than with the time, place and circumstances under which a theory is born.

In contradistinction to the Absolutist notion, relativism is concerned with everything that is a faithful reflection of contemporary conditions. In this approach, each theory is justified in its own context. No theories can be ranked according to the philosophy of relativism. Relativism observed that economic ideas are nothing but rationalisation of class or group interest. In this connection, the readers can refer to Eric Roll's *History of Economic Thought* (1939) and W. Stark's *History of Economics in Relation to social Development*. Of course, relativism does consider the internal coherence of a theory; but it also pays attention to theory's congruence with historical and political environs. In fact, relativist approach is a fusion of history of economic thought with history of political and moral philosophy. It must be noted that knowledge of history is essential to understand a theory in economics, as a Relativists say. Relativist theory is more or less a time-bound empirical reflection. However, according to Viner, relativism frequently amounts to a kind of white-washing with historical necessity.

The Relativist will argue that no theory in economics is universal. Economics deals with a universe where data are freakish and are not universally valid.[10] It is the nature of economic science that it involves phenomena which change from time to time and from place to place. The theory which is crucial at one time and place may turn out to be totally irrelevant and useless at another time and place. For example, a theory which had a reasonable degree of validity during the early decades of the nineteenth century in the British economy became totally irrelevant to the same economy by the second half of the century.[11] "In economics, unlike in the physical sciences, theories have grown laterally rather than in a hierarchical order. They are to be understood with reference to special contexts; to designate an economic theory as 'general' is somewhat overambitious. If we study economic history, we find that different schools and theories were concerned with different relevant problems. For instance, Classical questions centered on progress and poverty. The Marginal revolution concentrated on the relative prices and resource allocation. Keynesian economics was similarly provoked by the great depression of the thirties. Thus, we find the relativity of economic theories.

It has to be appreciated that most of the current debate in the history of economic thought is based primarily on the methodological problem. The absolutist position in economics is like a parade of theoretical ideas or a progression of thought to achieve the truth which is the ultimate desideratum. The Absolutists focus on the development of abstract concepts and theories. On the other hand, the Relativists are drawn more towards the development of ideas and give an important role to the amalgam of philosophy, sociology, politics and other important developments. Their theories are conditioned by time, place and circumstances. The Relativist approach relies heavily on history and the history of social and political thought, whereas the Absolutist approach focuses mainly on the development of analytical ideas *per se*.[12]

---

10. A.K. Das Gupta, *Epochs of Economic Theory*, p. 2.
11. *Ibid.*, p. 3-4.
12. Ekelund and Hebert, *A History of Economic Theory and Method*, p. 4.

The Relativists place emphasis on environment for the development of economic theory. Some relativist writers attach great importance to external effects for the development of economic theory. The reader can see in this connection the book by Leo Rogin, *The Meaning and Validity of Economic Theory*, for example. There appears to be some truth in Fetter's view that "the more closely one associates economic thought with technical analysis, the greater is one likely to consider the effect of economic thought on history, and less the effect of history on thought."

An Absolutist position will not accord a high ranking to the medieval economic thought. The discussion on utility and value by the Scholastic writers is supposed to be fragementary and unsatisfactory. However, in a Relativist framework, the medieval economists may be exonerated for their unsatisfactory insight into the analysis of market, because at that time, a highly developed market mechanism did not exist. A Relativist may argue that the Scholastic argument of economic phenomena in terms of justice is a correct explanation. Nevertheless, some people may argue that the School-men failed to appreciate the growth of market economy. In course of time, human philosophy and desideratum underwent gradual changes. By the sixteenth century, the motive of profit maximisation became an important goal of human life and the market economy got predominance.

When all is said and done with regard to the approaches of history of economic thought, one must not forget to mention explicitly that the best approach to economic thought and theory does not appear to be either a Relativist approach or an Absolutist approach, but it is somewhere in between. The distinction between two approaches has been overemphasised. Judgement, however, always enters into a evaluation of a theory, whether it is a labour theory of value or a cost of production theory of value. This is precisely the reason why the Absolutist and the Relativist can continue on the validity of a theory. Regarding the issue whether one wants Absolutism or Relativism, it must be noted that the correct decision depends on the purpose of a theory. If a theory is to explain a contemporary situation, a Relativist approach seems to be important. However, if a theory is to present simply theorising or intellectual development, Absolutism is the proper answer. If two theories develop side by side at the same time, just as the utility and labour theories of value, one has to examine the internal logic of a theory. Thus, one cannot refrain from being an Absolutist. However, for the intellectual growth of the subject as well as for the solution of contemporary problems, we need to have a synthesis of both Absolutist and Relativist theories. Thus, what is required is a kind of theory which is logically consistent as well as empirically sound.

ORIGIN AND GROWTH OF ECONOMIC THOUGHT

Historians believe in the continuous and cumulative nature of the history of economic thought. A system of economic thought is evolved in response to certain questions which are generated during a particular time period. As and when the circumstances change, the questions and emphasis also change in sympathy. However, it is very difficult to say whether one type of thought is an improvement over the other type or not, because there is no universal criterion to test it. But, there may be progress from a lower level of abstraction to a higher level of abstraction in a particular line of analysis. The entire universe of the history of economic thought can be regarded as consisting of some *epochs*. The epochs stand for the periodisation of economic thought. For the convenience of analysis, periodisation of economic history is very essential but it is at the same time very difficult too, because it can be done by a number of different criteria without any common outcome. Without going into the morass of controversy, periodisation can simply be done with reference to the criterion suggested by Kuhn in his *Structure* of *Scientific Revolutions*. According to Kuhn, a problem-solving normal science can be regarded as a rule and revolutionary science is an exception in the history of science. A science is based on paradigms. A science progresses through the change of paradigms, in the course of which there may be a sudden change-over from a ruling paradigm to an entirely new paradigm. On this basis, a distinguishing and a distinct paradigm of economic science can be identified as a period in economic history. Considered this way, there are the following five main periods in economic history. It should be remembered that these periods are not the same as historical periods in terms of time.

PERIODISATION OF ECONOMIC HISTORY ON THE BASIS OF PARADIGMS

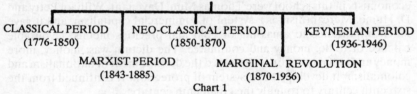

CLASSICAL PERIOD (1776-1850)   NEO-CLASSICAL PERIOD (1850-1870)   KEYNESIAN PERIOD (1936-1946)

MARXIST PERIOD (1843-1885)   MARGINAL REVOLUTION (1870-1936)

Chart 1

Another very broad classificatory scheme can be made in terms of schools of economic thought. A school is a group of thinkers or adherents or followers of a particular system of ideas. There are many such schools in the history of economic thought. The growth of history of economic thought in terms of schools can be seen from Chart 2 on p. 13. While reading the chart, a note of caution is required. The chart does not indicate the names of all the economists belonging to a school. We have simply referred to one or two leading names of a particular school of thought. It must be noted that there are some authors who belong to more than one school at the same time. Therefore, some amount of overlapping is possible in such a classificatory schema. For instance, Pareto belongs to the Mathematical school. He is also a member of the Welfare school. Similar is the case with Walras and so many others.

The growth of economic thought is indeed a chequered one, and hence, interesting. *Economics* is derived from a Greek word, *Oeconomicus* which means the practice of household management. Thus, the genesis of economics can be traced back to the Greek school of economic thought which is a part of the Pre-Adamite thought. The Pre-Adamite thought consists of Greek economic thought, Roman economic thought, Medieval economic thought, Mercantilism and Physiocracy. The Pre-Adamite thought started from approximately 427 B.C. and continued up to 1776. The main representatives of the Greek school of economic thought were Aristotle and Plato. They considered the economic problems of the city-state. They regarded economics as a subject of household management and discussed the importance of division of labour, money, property, slavery system, property relations and the possibility of communism.

The Roman economic thought was represented by Cicero, Varro, Cato and Seneca. These philosophers favored the barter system and condemned usury, and allowed a fixed rate of interest. They also favored small-scale farming. They considered demand and supply as the price determining factors. In the Medieval period, economic thought progressed through St. Thomas Aquinas, Schoolmen Baxter and so on. These writers prohibited the practice of usury and gave the theory of *just price*. They depended on the moral philosophy for the explanation of economic phenomena. Trade was permitted only if it helped the household economy of the society. Aquinas regarded private property in total agreement with the natural law. Thomas Aquinas can be regarded as the first originator of the *labour theory of value*. The Medieval philosophers attacked unjust payment and monopoly.

Next came in the chronological order *Mercantilism*. The leading economists in this school were Thomas Mun, Davenant, William Petty and D. Hume. Mercantilism is a system of commercial capitalism, and it gave much importance to amassing of gold and precious metals, favourable balance of trade, money and commerce. The dictum was: money, more money and still more money. It helped the development of nationalism and colonialism. It developed as a system of protection. It continued from the sixteenth century to roughly the eighteenth century.

In the middle of eighteenth century, another system of economic thought known as the *Physiocratic system* developed first in France. The renowned members of this school of economic thought were Quesnay, Turgot and Mirabeau. Physiocracy gave importance to the *natural order, analysis of net product* and the *circulation of net product*. Physiocratic writers emphasised the importance of agriculture. According to them, it was the only productive occupation. This school was also in favour of a single tax on agriculture. It found the interdependence of the various sectors of economy.

Next in the temporal order comes the development of *Classical Political Economy*. Classical people were primarily concerned with the progress of the economy. The Wealth of Nations of Adam Smith can be regarded as an essay on economic development. The first paradigm of classical thought started with Adam Smith in the year 1776 when his epic, the *Wealth of Na-*

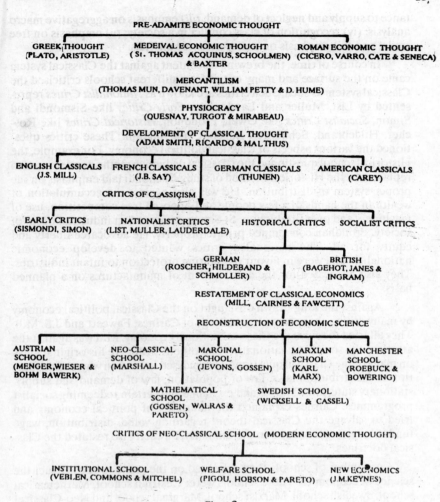

PRE-ADAMITE ECONOMIC THOUGHT

GREEK THOUGHT
(PLATO, ARISTOTLE)

MEDEIVAL ECONOMIC THOUGHT
(St. THOMAS ACQUINUS, SCHOOLMEN)
& BAXTER

ROMAN ECONOMIC THOUGHT
(CICERO, VARRO, CATE & SENECA)

MERCANTILISM
(THOMAS MUN, DAVENANT, WILLIAM PETTY & D. HUME)

PHYSIOCRACY
(QUESNAY, TURGOT & MIRABEAU)

DEVELOPMENT OF CLASSICAL THOUGHT
(ADAM SMITH, RICARDO & MALTHUS)

ENGLISH CLASSICALS
(J.S. MILL)

FRENCH CLASSICALS
(J.B. SAY)

GERMAN CLASSICALS
(THUNEN)

AMERICAN CLASSICALS
(CAREY)

CRITICS OF CLASSICISM

EARLY CRITICS
(SISMONDI, SIMON)

NATIONALIST CRITICS
(LIST, MULLER, LAUDERDALE)

HISTORICAL CRITICS

SOCIALIST CRITICS

GERMAN
(ROSCHER, HILDEBAND &
SCHMOLLER)

BRITISH
(BAGEHOT, JANES &
INGRAM)

RESTATEMENT OF CLASSICAL ECONOMICS
(MILL, CAIRNES & FAWCETT)

RECONSTRUCTION OF ECONOMIC SCIENCE

AUSTRIAN
SCHOOL
(MENGER, WIESER &
BOHM BAWERK)

NEO-CLASSICAL
SCHOOL
(MARSHALL)

MARGINAL
SCHOOL
(JEVONS, GOSSEN)

MARXIAN
SCHOOL
(KARL
MARX)

MANCHESTER
SCHOOL
(ROEBUCK &
BOWERING)

MATHEMATICAL
SCHOOL
(GOSSEN, WALRAS &
PARETO)

SWEDISH SCHOOL
(WICKSELL & CASSEL)

CRITICS OF NEO-CLASSICAL SCHOOL (MODERN ECONOMIC THOUGHT)

INSTITUTIONAL SCHOOL
(VEBLEN, COMMONS & MITCHEL)

WELFARE SCHOOL
(PIGOU, HOBSON & PARETO)

NEW ECONOMICS
(J.M. KEYNES)

Chart 2

tions, was published. The development of classical thought, initially, started with the works of Smith, Ricardo and Malthus. The classical tradition, however, was continued by many economists including J.B. Say of France, Von Thunnen of Germany and Carey of America. At the cost of some error, the Classical period can be denoted as the period between 1776 and 1850. John Stuart Mill can be regarded as the last representative of Classical economics during whose time the Classical economics rose to its zenith and also experienced its downfall. The basic characteristics of the Classical eeonomics were: *(i)* primacy of capital accumulation; *(ii)* importance to supply and neglect of demand; *(iii)* emphasis on aggregative macro analysis; (iv) recognition of class conflict in a society; *(v)* emphasis on free trade; and *(vi)* emphasis on policy-oriented analysis.

In course of time, the brewing discontent against the Classical system came on the surface and many critics from different schools criticised the Classical system as such. Such critics are known as *Nationalist Critics* represented by List, Muller and Lauderdale, *Early Critics* like Sismondi and Simon, *Socialist Critics* like Owen, Proudhon, *Historical Critics* like Roscher, Hildebrand, Schmoller, Bagehot, and Ingram. These critics questioned the various aspects of Classical political economy. For example, the Historical school questioned the Classical deductive method and wanted to replace it by the Historical method of study. Sismondi laid emphasis on the proper system of distribution. He was also against the accumulation of wealth in the hands of a few people and opposed free competition, use of machinery and over production. St Simon envisaged an industrial order of society. Proudhan condemned private property. He advocated liberty and equity for all. The nationalist critics wanted to develop economic nationalism and were in favour of granting protection to infant industries. They also advocated for the development of manufactures on a planned basis.

Against the long-drawn onslaught on the Classical political economy by many critics, there came the writings of Carines, Fawcett and J.S. Mill. They all tried to revive the Classical political economy. Mill was against the attack of the socialists, nationalists and others. Mill gave his original ideas on many of the Classical questions. He analysed in his own way, the production and distribution laws, law of population, law of demand and supply, stationary state, law of wages and exchange and certain redeeming socialist programmes. Cairnes explained the neutrality of political economy and tried to salvage the Classical theory regarding value, distribution, wage fund theory, free trade and so on. Similarly, Fawcett also restated the Classical doctrines.

A number of schools then appeared on the scene to reconstruct the science of economics. These schools were: Austrian school, Mathematical school, Swedish school, Marxist school, Marginal school and Neo-Classical school. The Austrian school, whose members were Menger, Weiser and Bohm Bawerk, emphasised the deductive method of economic analysis. They also refined the theories of value, capital, interest and so on. Their analysis was based on subjective evaluation. This school developed in the middle of the nineteenth century and continued up to the first part of the twentieth century.

The Mathematical school was represented by Gossen, Walras and Pareto. Gossen made original contribution to the development of Marginnalist school. Walras became famous for his general equilibrium system of analysis of price, and Pareto made substantial contribution to the development of the theories of welfare economics, income distribution and so on.

Pareto also contributed to the development of indifference curve analysis. The Mathematical school was developing between the mid-eighteenth century and the early years of the twentieth century.

The Swedish school was represented by Wicksell and Cassel. Wicksell made his contribution to the theories of capital, interest, business cycle, saving and investment and money. Cassel analysed price and he also gave his original theory of the determination of exchange rate on the basis of purchasing power parity.

The Manchester School of economic thought was represented by Roebuck and Bowring. It helped in the development of free trade and put into practice the principles of Classical political economy.

The Marxist school can be subsumed under the classical school but since Karl Marx introduced a distinct paradigm in the analysis of capitalist economy and also in the development of socialist economic thought, he indeed constitutes one prominent school of thought. His period can be specified between 1843 and 1885.

The Marginalist school occupies a period between 1870-1936. The Marginal school was represented by Gossen, Jevons and also Walras. In America, the marginal principle was applied by J.B. Clark. The marginal revolution was mainly concerned with the introduction of a new method of analysis in terms of Marginal technique. The Marginalists gave emphasis on the relative prices, resource allocation, distribution pattern and the development of micro-economics. Marshall followed largely the Marginal principles and helped the development of micro-economics further. He made synthesis between the demand and supply for the analysis of price. Thus, Marshall combined Classical economics and also the basic principles of Marginalism. He was the leader of Neo-Classical school of economic thought which occupied the period 1850-1870.

In course of time, reactions started against Neo-Classical economics, and a number of schools appeared on the scene. These schools were: Institutional school, Welfare school and Keynesian school. The main representative of the Institutional school was Thorstein Veblen who became famous for his analysis of the *Theory of the Leisure Class* in which he explained the hollowness of the upper class in a society. He advocated the importance of the study of institutions for explaining the functioning of an economy. For him, the entire material civilisation was a scheme of institutions. He also opined that economics is an evolutionary science. As an institutionalist, Veblen believed that economic institutions were the mainspring of economic changes.

The Welfare school is represented by Hobson, Pigou and Pareto who outlined the basic principles and ways for the attainment of maximum social welfare.

J.M. Keynes constituted the New school of economics (1936-1946). He analysed the economy in macro perspective for understanding the problems connected with income, output and employment, with a view to fighting depression of the thirties. His was indeed an economics of depression. He introduced some insights which were conspicuously contrary to those of the Classical political economy.

Part One
Pre-Adamite Thought

Part One
Pre-Adamite Thought

1

Ancient Economic Thought

The *Ancient Economic Thought* is not based on any systematic paradigm. In ancient times, economic thought was not organised. It was scattered and haphazard, lying here and there in an unorganised manner. Economic thought in ancient times could be gleaned from the writings of historians, archaeologists and anthropologists. Economic thought during this period was mixed with ethics and philosophy. The economic thought of the ancient times was not scientific. It was drawn from many sources including legends, folklore, myths and so on. The main reasons for the insufficient growth of economic thought was mainly due to the infancy of economic science itself. In fact, economics did not then grow as a full-fledged subject of study. No systematic thinking on economics, therefore, could be had during the ancient times. There were some thoughts on some topical economic problems. Economic thought during this period was mixed up with politics, sociology, metaphysics and history. The economic thought of the ancient period can be discussed under different schools of thought, such as, Hebrew school of thought, Greek school of thought, Roman school of thought and the Medieval economic thought. These are briefly discussed below:

HEBREW ECONOMIC THOUGHT (2500 B.C.-150 B.C.)

The Old Testament of the Bible discusses the Hebrew economic ideas. The ideas developed during the Hebrew period are more or less similar to the ideas of modern capitalism, as considered by Eric Roll. The Hebrew economic thought is based on metaphysical and ethical considerations. During the Hebrew period, agriculture was given the most important place in society. Agriculture, of course, was traditional. There were two classes of people: the privileged and the under-privileged. The royal families used to lead a life of enjoyment. There was also the existence of a slave class. Land was the important form of property. Trade and commerce were not developed. There was the dignity of labour. The slavery system was sanctioned by the Moasaic Law. In the Hebrew period, the family system was patriarchal in nature. The wages of the labourers were paid in kind. For most of the people, agriculture was the primary occupation. A part of the land, however, was kept fallow. The Hebrew society was based on the concept of justice. Corruption was punishable, whereas honesty was rewarded. There was the discouragement of speculative activities. Almost everything regarding the transactions in the market was laid down in principle. Money came into vogue. It facilitated exchange in the market. However, the market was not developed and organised. Money was in terms of bullion. Trade and commerce were not fully developed, but King Solomon gave sufficient incentive for the development of trade and commerce. The Hebrew women were experts in weaving and spinning. There were special arrangements to help the poor people by granting them *tithe* as was permitted under the law of the land. There was no tax system in the Hebrew society. The King could get the services of the labourers for the public works programme. No interest was allowed on loans, and trade and commerce were regulated by laws. The people were advised to lead a life of idealism by giving up corrupt practices and dishonesty.

GREEK ECONOMIC THOUGHT (427-322 B.C.)

The Greek economic thought considered the science of economics as the science of home management, and secondly, also as the art of wealth-getting and wealth-spending. The first one was called *Oeconomicus* and the second one was called *Chrematistics*. The Greek philosophers combined economic reasoning with general philosophy of the management of state and society. However, economics was not treated as an independent discipline. The Greek economic thought was developed mainly by the three writers: Plato, Aristotle and Xenophon.

Plato (427-347 B.C.)

Plato's ideas on economics arose in his book, *The Republic*. Plato advocated the importance of *division of labour* in economic activity. The division of labour arose from the natural differences in human beings. Plato's interest was mainly in the development of the economy and of output. He was also interested in the increase of efficiency. Plato also advocated for the increasing amount of *specialisation* in production. Such a specialisation brings with it the necessity of making exchanges. Plato conceived of two types of classes: the guardians and auxiliaries. According to Plato, the guardian class should not work for profit or accumulate property. However, only the lowest classes, farmers and artisans, were allowed to work for profit and accumulate property. Exchange and trade were an integral part of the social organisation during the time of Plato. Money was not only a medium of exchange but it was also a standard of value. Money facilitated trade and commerce. According to Plato, specialisation is the root of all economic progress. Plato supported property communism. Plato can be regarded as a pure collectivist. Plato thought that the ownership of private property will lead to a number of benefits which will outweigh the costs. Plato considered *slavery* as a permanent and necessary institution in the history of mankind. But he wanted good treatment to the salves.

Aristotle (384-322 B.C.)

The most important contribution of Aristotle to the development of economic thought was his ideas on the meaning and nature of economics. According to him, *Oeconomicus* aims at the management of the household economy and *Chrematisptics* is concerned with wealth-generation and spending. He was in favour of the household economy as it was a natural one. Aristotle's books, *Politics* and *Ethics*, contain his economic thinking. Aristotle was against Plato's idea on property communism. He was also a supporter of the *slavery system*. Aristotle considered value-in-use and value-in-exchange. He was the economist who made such a distinction for economic analysis. Aristotle was against the payment of a high rate of interest (*usury*). Money was a useful way of facilitating exchange. Money was a medium of exchange and also a unit of account. He also thought that money can act as a store of value. Aristotle was in favour of private property, and he was against the joint use of property. He condemned monopoly. He was against the payment of high rate of interest because it is unnatural and it leads to an unnatural accumulation. Regarding private property, he advanced three important arguments[1] in its favour; (*i*) private property increases efficiency by giving incentive; (*ii*) it promotes social peace; and (*iii*) individual moral character building requires private property.

Aristotle wanted the maximisation of average wealth, given the constraining natural law. However, there seems to be a contradiction in the analysis of Aristotle. On the one hand, he wanted to maximise economic wealth by granting the right to private property and on the other hand, wanted to restrict accumulation and interest. Be that as it may, Aristotle's major contribution was the conceptualisation of economics in the form of microeconomic household management.

Xenophon (440-355 B.C.)

The main economic ideas of Xenophon are contained in his book *Cyropaedia*. This book contains a good discussion on the division of labour. He has also discussed about the management of the domestic economy. He was in favour of agriculture. He was of the view that mines can be an important source of wealth for the development of a nation. He urged for the organisation of joint-stock companies. He also recommended a large population for the propserity of Athens. According to Xenophon, merchants and shipowners were considered highly valuable citizens because they brought wealth to the city.

ROMAN ECONOMIC THOUGHT

The Roman economic thought was meagre and not original. It was mainly derived from the Greek economic thought. It was against money-making. It had a high regard for agriculture. The Roman thinkers were in favour of cultivation of small plots of land. Large-scale farming (*latifundia*) was not favoured by the Roman thinkers. The Roman writer, Pliny, was in

---

1. Ekelund, Jr., and Hebert, *A History of Economic Theory and Method,* p. 23.

favour of using gold as money. However, there was a marked change in attitude regarding slavery during the Roman period. The slaves were considered inefficient. The Roman thinkers also questioned the naturality of the institution of slavery. There were many Roman economic thinkers, such as Cicero, Seneca, Pliny, Cato and Verro. *Cicero* was in a favour of wholesale trade and agriculture but he was opposed to usury. *Seneca* believed in the existence of a *natural order*. This is perhaps the source from which the Physiocrats borrowed the concept of natural order. Seneca considered money as the root of all evils. He also recognised the importance of utility for the determination of exchange value of a commodity. He also had faith in the division of labour. *Cato* thought agriculture to be the most important profession. *Pliny* wrote on the use of money and its importance in the development of a nation. He condemned *usury*. He wrote about the superiority of gold as a medium of exchange. *Columella* was in favour of small-scale farming, and pointed out the superiority of free labour over the slave labour. According to him, the utilisation of slave labour was responsible for the decline of Roman agriculture. *Verro* was an industrial economist. He advocated the institution of reward and punishment in the process of industrial production. He said that the labourers should be given incentives for the growth of industrial production. He was in favour of the use of hired labour instead of using the slave labour because the slave labour was less productive.

MEDIEVAL ECONOMIC THOUGHT

The Medieval writers are also called Doctors or Scholars. These writers are moralists. The Medieval thought was based on moral questions of right and wrong, justice and natural law. The Medieval writer, St. Augustine, recognised utility and desire as the two important components of value. The Schoolmen used subjective and objective factors for the determination of value. However, even the objective calculations were based on normative methods. The most important single writer who was responsible for the development of Medieval thought was St. Thomas Aquinas.

St. Thomas Aquinas (1225-1274)

According to Aquinas, value is nothing but the *just price (Justum Pretium)*. The price should include the cost of production, risk and carriage charges. It is really unjust to sell in the dearest market and buy from the cheapest market. Aquinas also supported the division of labour in society. He said that all occupations were valuable, and agriculture alone is not superior. Aquinas condemned usury. But he was in favour of providing compensation for damages and delay to the lenders. Interest was regarded as a sinful and unnatural payment. However, interest could be paid to the lender of money for any gain foregone on an alternative investment. Although internal and international trade were developing during the period of Aquinas, still he considered trade as something unnatural. Aquinas was in favour of private property because it was consistent with the natural law of the land. But he felt that property should be honestly acquired and be used for the common social benefit. According to Aquinas, a state has to perform many important functions such as the maintenance and building of roads, providing a good system of coinage, weights and measures and for eliminating poverty, apart from maintaining the regular law and order situation.

The Medieval thinkers' discussion on utility and value appears to be very elementary. Medieval thinking was based mainly on morality and ethics. Most of the views of these writers were not original. They were borrowed from the Greek and Roman economic thought. Their ides on value were normative. They did not have the insight of the problems of a market-oriented economy. Most of the Medieval thoughts can be rationalised on the basis of Relativist notion. These Schoolmen failed to appreciate the advance of the market system. [2] Gradually, however, economic thinking went in favour of trade and commerce and profit. There was a marked shift away from the Medieval theology and a new world of economic thought soon ushered in. It is pointed out that the Medieval concept of *just price* was the beginning for the development of *labour theory of value*. It was indeed a great Medieval contribution.

---

2. *Ibid.,* p. 28.

2
Mercantilism (1500-1750)

WHAT IS MERCANTILISM?

Mercantilism is a system of commercial capitalism or merchant capitalism which was introduced in different parts of the world during the period 1500-1750. It continued up to the period, roughly speaking, when Adam Smith published his *Wealth of Nations* in 1776. The term *'Mercantilism'* was coined by Adam Smith to describe the loose system which dated roughly from the beginning of the sixteenth century. Mercantilism includes a group of widely-dispersed writers on many important issues like trade and commerce, money, employment and so on. These writers shared some common interest and concern but they did not have a common tool of analysis. There appears to have been little cohesion among the mercantilist writers in the sense that they did not have a commonly-accepted body of ideas.[1] However, in spite of the differences, they had some broad agreement over certain basic issues of their times. They showed several unifying ideas. They had certain ideas having central tendencies. In the discussion of this chapter, we will confine only to the broad generalisations of the mercantilist writers. We will not take into account the differences of the individual writers.

Mercantilism had different meanings and connotations in different countries. In Germany, mercantilism was called *Cameralism;* in France, it was called *Colbertism* and in England, the system was called *Mercantilism.* It is a set of doctrines advocating the accumulation of gold and silver, favourable foreign trade balance, increase in state power and the prosperity of the nation. It is also defined as the economic counterpart of political nationalism. It is a system of restrictive trade practices and is called a system of *protectionism.* According to Heimann, mercantilism is the ideological justification of commercial capitalism. Mercantilism, in fact, is the start of the political economy of capitalism. It is during this period that Sir James Steuart brought out his book, *Principles of Political Economy,* in 1760. This was the first book on political economy. Thus, mercantilism can be regarded as a force which gave birth to the system of political economy. Mercantilist writers are, mainly, Sir Thomas Mun, J.B. Colbert, A. Serra, S.J. Child and S.J. Steuart.

---

1. Ekelund and Hebert, *op. cit.,* p. 29.

FACTORS RESPONSIBLE FOR THE GROWTH OF MERCANTILISM

Many factors are responsible for the growth of Mercantilism. They can be discussed below:

1. Economic Factor. Towards the end of the fifteenth century, economic changes were taking place in the European countries. The domestic self-sufficiency was giving way to the development of a system of exchange. The market economy was developing rapidly. Agriculture was being replaced by trade and commerce. It was necessary to expand the use of money. In fact, the feudalism was being replaced by commercial capitalism. The feudal society was rapidly breaking up, and commercial system was gradually evolving. All these required a commercial system using money.

2. Political Factor. The political organisation which was loose in the past, came to be replaced by a strong nation state. In such a state, law and order situation had to be very strong, and the protective and regulatory function of the state became very essential. Feudalism was superseded by the formation of nation states in many countries. These countries required a strong government. Political philosophers like Machiavelli and others stressed the importance of a strong national state and Jean Bodin advocated for a benevolent monarchy. Thus, what was demanded was a unified national state under a strong king. In many countries, strong kings came to occupy the thrones. Some of these kings were Tudor King and Louis XIV. The mercantilists required protection under strong kings.

3. Religious Factor. The religious factor also became important for the growth of mercantilism. The Reformation movement revolted against the supremacy of the Roman Catholic Church and the authority of the Pope. A new religion, known as Protestantism, appeared on the scene. This religion was against the earlier Catholic religion. The new Protestant religion allowed the acquisition of material goods and property. Money became important in human life along with the prospect of thrift and material efforts. The new religion was in favour of complete liberty and freedom of the individuals. The Protestant religion became very strong in course of time and it was embraced by the merchants.

4. Cultural Factor. Cultural factor was no less important in the growth of mercantilism. The cultural change in those days was propagated by the *Renaissance*. This movement taught that men are free on this earth and they can create and enjoy well according to their sweet will. They need not bother about the so-called heaven. Emphasis was given to the creative human activities, acquisition of wealth and trade and commerce. The Renaissance movement was against the dictates of Medieval theology. The new movement taught the importance of materialistic outlook and acquisitive spirit. In fact, mercantilism was a reaction against the moral and idealistic attitude of the Medieval period.

5. Scientific and Technological Factor. Inventions and discoveries facilitated the rise of mercantilism. Many important explorers invented a new world like the United States. There were also the discoveries like the mariner's compass, printing press, and the like. Columbus discovered America in 1492. Gold and silver mines were also discovered in the new world. People became adventurous and were in search of new lands for trade and commerce. The atmosphere was quite suitable for growth of mercantilism.

6. Intellectual Factor. In many countries, intellectual development on new lines became visible. The new philosophers like Erasmus, Bacon and others, new artists like Leonardo da Vinci and Michael Angelo, the new scientists like Galileo, Kepler and others introduced the new area and concept of knowledge which was challenging to all the concept and thought. For example, Sir Thomas More's *Utopia* challenged the existing basis of the state. In fact, European countries during the sixteenth century were a new brave world which emerged from the dark Middle Ages. In all directions, there were new activities, a new spirit of enterprise and a new subject to explore. The mercantilist idea was advocated by many of these new intellectual writers. Thomas Mun openly campaigned for the growth of mercantilism.

All the above factors combined to help the growth of mercantilism which was a new adventure in the direction of the commercial/merchant capitalism in the European countries.

BASIC PRINCIPLES AND POLICIES OF MERCANTILISM

There are many basic principles and policies of Mercantilism.

The following are, however, the broad ones :

(i)   The desire that the state must be made very strong.

(ii) Money is wealth and capital. There should be amassing of money in the form of gold, silver and precious metals, which can determine the strength of a nation.

(iii) Foreign trade must be encouraged so that a country can have favourable balance of trade through the earning of export surplus. Every country should try to export more and import less. This is a way of getting the inflow of gold and silver by a nation.

(iv) All exporting industries are to be encouraged and imports are to be discouraged.

(v)   A country should give more importance to the development of manufacture and trade.

(vi) There would be a strong government for giving protection to the merchants and for maintaining law and order situation.

(vii) Colonies could be useful both as a market for exports and as sources of supply for raw materials.

(viii) Colonies could only be feeders to the mother country. All colonial trade should be a monopoly for the mother country.

(ix) A country should have its own ships for the purpose of trade.

(x) The wages should be low so that the production cost and the prices can be kept low. These will help the growth of export.

(xi) Population growth should be encouraged. People are the real wealth of the country.

(xii) Mercantilism favoured the increase in state power and wealth.

(xiii) A slowly rising price level is helpful to the producers and also for giving incentive to production. It can lead to additional revenues.

(xiv) Mercantilists were concerned with increasing the employment potential of a nation.

(xv) The mercantilist writers were in favour of a lower rate of interest as it will give incentive to invest and produce.

(xvi) Mercantilism favoured a multiple tax system.

(xvii) Mercantilist writers were against the medieval *just price*. They advocated a system of market value.

(See also *Heckscher's Views on Mercantilism* in the next section.)

HECKSHER'S VIEWS ON MERCANTILISM:[2] PLENTY OR POWER?

Heckscher has examined the various views on mercantilism by writers like Adam Smith, Schmoller, William Cunningham and so on. Adam Smith has considered mercantilism as a type of commercial policy and as a system of protection. According to Schmoller, mercantilism was essentially a policy of economic unity which is to a large extent, independent of particular economic tenets. William Cunningham considered mercantilism as a force, striving after economic power for political purposes.

Heckscher found a confusing note in the above views. The confusion arose between the ends and means of economic policy. Mercantilism is a system of *national economic unity*. For avoiding confusion on trade between different countries, the creation of a national customs system was found to be necessary by Heckscher. Mercantilist policy involved the substitution of a scheme which would give the whole territory the benefits that each town had tried to arrogate to itself. The national policy could create a consistent national system or regulation of internal trade and industry in town and country. Thus, mercantilist policy was based on a *national policy*.

According to mercantilist statement, the subject of state is a means to an end. The end is the *power of the state itself*. The mercantilist conception of what was to a country's advantage centered on two closely allied aspects of economic life. *These two aspects* were the supply of commodities and the supply of money. Mercantilism gave importance to a money economy. The mercantilists wanted to get maximum gain for the country. This could be

---

2. E.F. Heckscher, "Mercantilism," in H.W. Spiegel's *The Development of Economic Thought*, pp. 31-42.

done by stimulating production and by increasing the competitive power of the country. The real gist of mercantilist doctrine was: Wealth consists in money, or in gold and silver. Therefore, mercantilists insisted upon an excess of exports over imports. The distinction between bullionists and mercantilists is very clear. The bullionists wanted to prohibit the outflow of bullion, whereas the mercantilists brought forward a theory of the balance of trade. Most mercantilists were favouring a sort of inflation in the economy. Mercantilists believed in protectionism.

According to Heckscher, mercantilism involves a general view of society: a new order of materialism in place of Medieval idealism and morality. If we analyse the view of Heckscher on mercantilism, we come across the following thoughts:

(i) Mercantilism is a *system of power*. It is not so much a system of plenty, as believed by Adam Smith. However, Heckscher did not dispute the point that was raised by Adam Smith by pointing out that mercantilism is a system of plenty. Rather, Heckscher seems to have agreed with Smith when the former has said that it is a system of commodity production.

(ii) Mercantilism is a *system of increasing commodity production*. This is required for reaping greater gain in terms of more favourable balance of trade. This also gives a country more competitive power in the international market.

(iii) Mercantilism is out and out a *monetary system*. This is specially necessary when the economy becomes an exchange economy where money is used not only as a medium of exchange but also as a unit of account. Mercantilism gave stress on the accumulation of treasure.

(iv) Mercantilism represents a *national system of regulation of trade and commerce*. Such a regulation is both internal as well as international.

(v) Mercantilism is a *system of national economic unity*. National unification is required for both country and town, and also for the domestic and the international traders. It organises the different people and institutions along a uniform line. Mercantilism aims at the unification of nation states.

(vi) Mercantilism is a *system of defending the country* and strengthening the country both economically and politically.

(vii) Mercantilism is a *system of protection*. It supports protection to different types of industries for their proper growth and expansion, so that these industries can contribute to the earning of a favourable balance of trade by exporting more than before.

FOREIGN TRADE AND SPECIE FLOW

The mercantilist writers were in favour of having a favourable balance of trade which could be earned by exporting more than import. It should be noted that a balance of payments must always balance over time, because it is only a book-keeping identity of debit and credit. But a balance of trade need not be in balance. The surplus in the balance of payments which was emphasised by the mercantilist writers, was the excess of exports, both visible and invisible, over imports.[3] This surplus will come to the domestic country in the form of gold inflow. In fact, the mercantilists were thinking of the current account in the balance of payments.

Foreign trade was regarded as very important in the mercantilist system. It is evident from the title of Thomas Mun's book: *England's Treasure by Foreign Trade.* Viner observed that there was nothing wrong in emphasising a favourable balance of trade.

Why Foreign Trade?

The mercantilist writers have emphasised favourable trade balance (export over import) for the following main reasons :

1. To make the country economically stronger through the excess of treasure and wealth than can be earned through foreign trade.

2. Foreign trade is the means to purchase cheaper raw materials from the international market.

3. Foreign trade is also a means for selling out the domestic output in the form of export. It is an outlet for the finished goods of the domestic economy.

4. The mercantilists were eager to earn money and wealth through foreign trade. Money in the form of gold and silver and other precious metals was very valuable to the mercantilists. Money was equated to capital or wealth. Foreign trade was a means to acquire more and more money from the foreign countries.

5. Foreign trade surplus was regarded as an index of economic welfare.[4]

6. The mercantilists wanted to acquire bullion through foreign trade. They knew very well that bullion will have a favourable effect on the price level of the commodities. They pointed out that a gently rising price level was very favourable for the growth of industries, trade and commerce.

7. The inflow of bullion may also reduce the rate of interest. This is very essential for increasing investment, output and employment.

8. One of the main objectives of mercantilism was to create more and more employment opportunities for the people of the country. This could be made possible by a favourable balance of trade which will have several employment-creating effects.

9. The mercantilists believed that a country can be great only at the cost of others. They were interested in making their own country relatively stronger than the neighbouring countries.

How to Attain a Favourable Balance of Trade?

The mercantilists followed a number of policies in order to maximise the net gain from foreign trade. The main strategy is to increase the produc-

---

3. M. Blaug., *Economic Theory in Retrospect,* p. 12.
4. *Ibid.,* p. 12.

tion of exportable commodities in the domestic economy, and reduce the import of articles from foreign countries. Output in the domestic economy can be maximised by the following methods:

(*a*) Land resources may be more fully utilised and fallow lands may be brought under cultivation.

(*b*) More and more employment opportunities should be created in the country so that the unemployed human resources are utilised for the purpose of increasing production which can be exported.

(*c*) Better methods and techniques of production should be introduced in the production process.

(*d*) For the purpose of increasing production and employment, the mercantilists advocated a system of a low wage level.

(*e*) The colonies can be used for supplying raw materials to the mother country. The colonies can also be used as a market for finished products.

(*f*) There may be an occupational shift of population from low productivity jobs to high productivity occupations.

Trade Regulations and Policies : Export-Import Policy

(*i*) The mercantilists were in favour of exporting goods and services, particularly, they were interested in the export of finished products. Export of raw materials was not favoured.

(*ii*) Raw materials are to be imported from foreign countries.

(*iii*) Certain types of imports such as imports of luxuries are to be totally banned.

(*iv*) The mercantilists did not favour the export of bullion.

(*v*) They had a *fear of foreign goods,* and they were not allowed to import foreign finished products.[5]

(*vi*) A country was allowed to import semi-finished goods and then to process them for the purpose of export.

(*vii*) It was advisable to carry on foreign trade with the country's own ships.

(*viii*) Banks are to be established and the use of credit instruments is to be facilitated.

(*ix*) Food import is to be restricted, and food should be grown in the domestic country by improving the agricultural sector.

(*x*) The government should register mortgages, sales and other commercial transactions.

(*xi*) A colony should not be allowed to enter into foreign trade directly with another country. All commodities should come to the parent country wherefrom they are to be exported again.

---

5.   Heckscher, *Mercantilism,* Volume II, p. 117.

(xii) Some industries should be given subsidy. These industries are shipping, fishing and so on which are taking part in the export trade.

(xiii) Imports from other countries are to be reduced to the minimum.

(xiv) Primary importance must be given to the development of export industries and then the emphasis should be given to the development of agriculture and other allied industries.

Great importance is attached to the state as the centre of all economic activities. The control and regulation of the government are essential for the attainment of the most favourable balance of trade. In this connection, the protectionist policy of the mercantilist system may be discussed. The mercantilist system was, as discussed earlier, a system of protection. It recommended *protection* for a few different reasons: *(i)* Protection may be granted to the strategic industries. These important industries which are strategic for the nation both in terms of their export contribution and also in terms of their contribution to economic development, can be earmarked by the government of the country. *(ii)* Protection may also be granted to the weak but promising industries which are at the infant stage of growth. *(iii)* Protection may also be granted to the defence industries which are considered to be so essential for the country. *(iv)* The policy of protection should be guided by the consideration of self-sufficiency. Those industries should be given protection which are helpful for generating self-sufficiency and self-reliance for the country. *(v)* Protection may also be given to the industries which are engaged in producing import substitutable and export-promoting goods, and at the same time, are absorbing the unemployed and the underemployed labour resources of the economy.

From all this, it appears that the mercantilist writers were well-informed and well-balanced in their ideas on the different aspects of foreign trade economics, including the principles of protection. However, there appears to have been no clear explication of the theory of balance of payment, as it is used in modern times.[6] The single most important concern of the mercantilist writers was that the nation's resources be used in such a manner as to make the state as powerful as possible, both economically and politically. In their scheme of things, money was very important for foreign trade. This was perhaps the reason why mercantilist writers gave vent to the desire of *hunger for money*. However, the lofty ideal of the achievement of a favourable balance of trade is bound to be only temporary. Thomas Mun clearly pointed out that the inflow of bullion is sure to lead to a rise in the price level of domestic articles. In that case, the possibility of export promotion appears to be bleak and self-defeating. Another reason for which the mercantilist writers are blamed for their self-centeredness is the fact that their foreign trade policy directly impinges on the growth of other countries. The mercantilist writers wanted to sell in the dearest market and purchase from the cheapest market. This can easily lead to the *beggar-thy-neighbour* policy which is again self-defeating. One country cannot be con-

---

6. Ekelund and Hebert, *op. cit.*, p. 33.

tinuously the gainer in the international market at the cost of others. This was not perfectly realised by the mercantilist writers.

However, there were writers who could very well understand the price-specie flow mechanism and full implications of the effects of increased bullion on the domestic price level. One such writer was John Locke. William Petty was against an indefinite accumulation of bullion. Thomas Mun also understood the effect of bullion on the domestic price level.

However, the mercantilist writers were very pragmatic. They were not building up any analytical engine, but suggested some practical measures so that the country may be made strong through foreign trade.

MONEY, PRICE LEVEL AND INTEREST RATE

The mercantilist writers were in favour of accumulation of more and more treasure for the country. Money in fact was equated with wealth and capital. They advocated the amassing of gold, silver and other precious metals from foreign countries. A country which does not have gold mines must amass gold through foreign trade. The slogan of the day was: *gold, more gold, more wealth and more power*. It must not be forgotten that the mercantilist system was essentially a system of commercial/merchant capitalism which was primarily based on the materialistic notion. Thus, money came to the forefront of all actions. Money was regarded not merely as a medium of exchange but also as a store of value. The following are the reasons for attaching so much importance to money in the days of mercantilism.

(i)   Money is a form of working capital and wealth.

(ii)   Money is a medium of exchange.

(iii) Money is a store of value.

(iv)   Money was a unit of account.

(v)   Money could facilitate trade and commerce.

(vi)   Money was the life-blood of the exchange economy which developed during the period of mercantilism. The importance of money in a market economy which was developing at that time can hardly be exaggerated.

(vii) A system of taxation was developing during the period of mercantilism, where money was very essential for the payment of taxes. Needless to say, taxation in barter system is obviously difficult.

(viii) Money was essential for making payment to the standing national armies and also for purchasing the war materials. Thus, the slogan of the sixteenth century statecraft was: *Money, more money and still more money*.

(ix)   Money was a convenient form of holding wealth in lieu of holding it in the form of commodities.

(x) Money was demanded *per se,* as an alternative form of holding wealth, as there were no immediate and sufficient investment opportunities for all people. It was held against the rainy days.

(xi) The mercantilists felt the scarcity of money in the economy which was standing in the way of development of trade and commerce. Therefore, money was demanded for the expansion of trade and commerce.

(xii) Money could provide the sinews of war.

(xiii) According to some mercantilists, increased money supply can lead to a lowering of the rate of interest which would be very helpful for the expansion of investment, output and employment. The thinking was akin to that of Keynes. In this connection, Sir Josiah Child observed that the low rate of interest is the natural mother of industry, frugality and arts.[7]

(xiv) More money supply, as can be made possible by the inflow of bullion through foreign trade, can be expected to lead to a further development in the realm of trade. Misselden observed that money is the vital element of trade.[8] The fact that increased money supply leads to lower interest rate was recognised by Locke, Petty and Law, among others. The lowering rate of the interest can lead to the expansion of investment for trade and commerce.

The mercantilist writers knew very well that an increased money supply made possible by a favourable balance of trade may lead to creeping inflation. According to them, a falling price level is unfavourable to economic development and expansion. They were rather in favour of a gently rising price level (mild inflation). In this respect, they were more Keynesian and less Marshallian. They advocated mild inflation for a number of reasons. It should be noted that the relation between money supply and price level was known to many of the mercantilist writers. The money supply made possible through a favourable balance of trade can lead to a number of favourable effects on the economy: it can increase income which can increase the level of effective demand in the domestic economy. The fact that a mild inflation can stimulate economic development and prosperity will be evident from the following points which perhaps were considered by the mercantilists writers while advocating the inflow of more and more bullion or money supply:

(a) Mild inflation leads to more and more profit which can lead to more and more incentive for production and investment.

(b) When the profit rate goes up, the rate of capital formation also increases.

(c) It is possible to have technical improvement during a period when the profit rate is higher.

---

7. S.J. Child, *A New Discourse of Trade, Preface.*
8. Misselden, *Circle of Commerce.* p. 28.

(d) Mild inflation creates a condition of buoyancy and boom in the economy.

(e) Mild inflation may lead to a reduction in the rate of interest which is helpful for the expansion of investment and employment.

For all the above reasons, the mercantilist writers might have advocated a desire for an increase in the price level. However, they could not understand that increased money supply may lead to an unfavourable effect on the prices of exportable commodities. They wanted to make good the *scarcity of money* which was felt in many countries, including England and Holland. The mercantilist writers were aware of the rudimentary working of the quantity theory of money as proposed by David Hume. As pointed out earlier, John Locke was well aware of the relationship between money and price level. However, instead of relating the price level with the quantity of money, they related the favourable effect of money supply (M) on the trade of the country. Thus, it was not the quantity theory of money what the mercantilists were emphasising, but instead, they were emphasising the monetary theory of the volume of trade.[9] The quantity theory during the seventeenth and eighteenth centures had the central proposition that money stimulates trade. While developing the view that an increased supply of money leads to a reduction in the rate of interest, the mercantilists upheld the view that there is a monetary theory of rate of interest. The mercantilists, however, were not in favour of keeping the money as idle treasure, rather they thought of money as an important part of active balance for the purpose of circulation and use. However, needless to say, most mercantilist writers failed to appreciate the hidden implications of Hume's quantity theory of money.

WAGES AND EMPLOYMENT[10]

In the Middle Ages, unemployment was a problem. The main measure of stimulating employment was the development of manufacturing industry. The concern about employment was the main motive of the mercantilists. In Germany, under *cameralism,* the government accepted the responsibility of the state to create employment opportunities and maintaining them. This was also the principle adopted in England in 1795. A number of factors such as dear money policy, foreign competition, taxes and regulations were considered to be mainly responsible for unemployment in those days. It was pointed out that a high rate of interest lowers investment, output and income. Mr. Child explained, however, that a high rate of interest will facilitate premature retirement from business. Be that as it may, the mercantilist writers suggested a number of steps for maximising the employment of labour in a country. Some of these steps are discussed below:

---

9.   M. Blaug., *op. cit.,* p. 19.
10.   Schumpeter, *History of Economic Analysis,* pp. 349-350.

(i) **Cheap Money Policy:** Under this policy, the rate of interest will be lowered so that investment will expand and more and more employment can be created by stimulating production.

(ii) **Increasing the Favourable Balance of Trade:** A favourable balance of trade will have a positive multiplier effect on income, output and employment. William Petty says that it is better to produce useless things than not to produce at all. The inflow of money will create many opportunities for expansion. It will raise the price level, which will have a number of goods effects on the economy. In fact mild inflation to be created by the export surplus will have a number of employment-creative effects (see, the earlier section). However, Malynes and Misselden did not accept this view. They pointed out that bullion import will increase trade without rising prices and this may increase employment. Export surplus by itself may expand investment which would be helpful for creating more employment, income and output.

(iii) **Agricultural Development:** Mercantilist writers advised that cultivation should be extended to the unused lands and certain types of import-substituting crops may be grown.

(iv) **Expansion of Industries:** The mercantilist writers advocated for the expansion of industries, including trade and commerce. Thomas Mun observed that poor people should be given employment first. For this purpose, he suggested the development of agriculture and industry (fishing and shipping).

(v) **Wage and Labour Policy:** The mercantile writers were in favour of maintaining a low wage policy. The low wage, however, should be sufficient for subsistence. According to them, the poor people should be given low wages. If they are given higher wages, they will be idle, inefficient, and the labour supply in the economy will fall. This can be shown with the help of the following diagram:

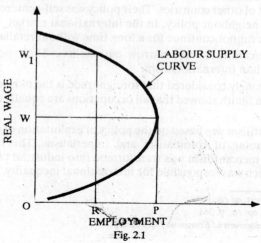

Fig. 2.1

The above diagram shows that if the wage level is OW, the labour supply is OP. When the wage level is increased to OW_1, the labour supply is goes down to OR. This shows that there is the existence of the backward-sloping supply curve of labour. The mercantilists believed in the utility of poverty and in the low moral condition of labourers. All this compelled the mercantilist writers to advocate for a minimum subsistence wage level. They opined that if the wage level is increased, output will decline, and the ability to accumulate specie *via* trade would be similarly reduced.[11] The mercantilist writers wanted to have maximum amount of labour supply in the economy, and at the same time, a low wage level. For this, they advocated a high rate of growth of population which would be able to reduce the wage level through competition and at the same time will provide a maximum amount of labour for the expansion of output for the export sector. They advocated reduction in mortality, reduction in the age of marriage and prevention of emigration and encouragement of immigration. The mercantilist writers could not understand the economy of high wages. They wanted hard work and efficiency from the labourers but did not want to give them the incentive of higher wages. The theory of subsistence wage level which was the basis of exploitation of the labourers to be found in the classical political economy had its genesis in mercantilism.

Critical Appraisal

(i) The balance of trade theory was self-defeating in nature. The mercantilists did not consider the deeper implications of the effect of increased bullion on the price level of the exportable commodities.

(ii) They wrongly thought that wealth consists in gold and silver and other precious metals. They thought that wealth was the same thing as money or bullion.[12]

(iii) The mercantilists regarded wealth as an end in itself.[13]

(iv) The mercantilists advocated the attainment of favourable balance of trade at the cost of other countries. Their policy was self-centered. It also led to beggar-thy-neighbour policy. In the international market, this type of zero-sum game cannot continue for a long time without retaliation.

(v) The mercantilists were narrow nationalists. Their policy was against cosmopolitan internationalism.

(vi) They wrongly considered that foreign trade is the most desirable occupation. Adam Smith showed that all occupations are equally desirable and important.

(vii) Mercantilism was based on the policy of exploitation of colonies. It was the beginning of colonialism and imperialism. The merchant capitalism under mercantilism was transformed into industrial capitalism in later years, which was responsible for international inequality.

---

11. Ekelund and Hebert, *op cit.,* p. 38.
12. See, Schumpeter, *op. cit.,* p. 361.
13. A Gray, *The Development of Economic Doctrines,* p. 79.

(viii) They lacked broad-mindedness and advocated certain narrow policy measures for their temporary gain.

(ix) The mercantilist writers were not in favour of the labouring class. They did not recommend higher wages nor did they understand the implications of the economy of high wages.

(x) "The most misleading doctrine of the mercantilists was the oft-repeated proposition that a country can get rich only at the expense of other countries."[14]

DOWNFALL OF MERCANTILISM

Because of the above criticism, mercantilism could not continue for a long time. The intellectual reaction started against mercantilism since the sixteenth century. The reactions became very prominent during the later years of the eighteenth century. In the seventeenth century, it was found that the European countries wanted state regulation no longer on economic life. The spirit of monopoly and regulation was gradually dying out and in its place was introduced competition in all walks of life. The growth of industries and the onset of industrial revolution changed the character of ownership and control. Commercial capitalism of the mercantilist period was transformed into industrial capitalism and many technological changes were introduced in the process of production. Many changes were also brought into the field of wage legislation. Trade unionism came into existence and the workers became more organised. The Industrial Revolution produced a new philosophy of *laissez faire* and liberalism. In course of time, this replaced the restrictionist philosophy of mercantilism. There was also the growth of economic individualism in many countries of the world. In this atmosphere of change, the wave of mercantilism was gradually swept away. Mercantilism faced its downfall for another reason. It was a narrow and partial way of analysing economic problems. It favoured industry, trade and commerce, and considered agriculture to be almost a non-important occupation. Mercantilism stayed away from the natural laws and rules. This provoked a group of French philosophers to launch another school known as *Physiocracy* in place of mercantilism. However, the mercantilist system was partially revived by the introduction of Keynesian economics in the thirties of this century.

Merits: When all is said and done, it must be appreciated that mercantilism was not supposed to be a scientific analytic system. Its protagonists did not want to build up a theoretical engine of analysis. During the period when the mercantilism grew up, economics did not have the status of a science. Still they understood the basic needs of the country during that period. Mercantilism has to be appreciated with reference to the Relativist approach to the history of economic thought. Most of the confusions are caused when we take into account the general view of the mercantilist school. Some of the mercantilist writers well appreciated the

---

14. E. Heimann, *History of Economic Doctrine.* pp. 34-35.

implications of their practical policies. For instance, John Locke and Thomas Mun observed that wealth consists not in silver and gold but in land, houses and consumptions goods.[15] Similarly, William Petty was against indefinite accumulation of bullion. Mun knew the effect of bullion on the price level and its negative repercussions on exports. They had also an idea of the quantity theory, particularly the effect of money supply on the price level.

Many economists and politicians appreciated mercantilism as an appropriate policy to achieve national self-sufficiency and expansion of state power. Adam Smith indirectly supported mercantilism when he said that "defence is more important than opulence." This was exactly what mercantilism wanted. The mercantilists aimed at building up a strong state, hence, they wanted to achieve the goal even by weakening the economic powers of the neighbouring states. The mercantilist writers were interested in optimum employment in the economy and, for this, they suggested a number of useful steps. The preoccupation of the mercantilists with gold inflows was no childish obsession, but an intuitive recognition of the connection between increased money supply and lower rate of interest.[16] Keynes paid a tribute to the mercantilists for recognising the fact that it is very difficult to give an inducement to investment which is so crucial in economic development.[17] The mercantilists also recognised the favourable impact of mild inflation on employment, income and output.

Since the scarcity of money was a frequent complaint during the period of mercantilism, it was but natural for them to arrange for more money for the expansion of trade and commerce. This is perhaps the reason why they were in favour of more and more money. The economic setting of the mercantilist world made free multilateral trade unworkable and it required a system of bilateral control.[18] Money was also necessary as sinews of war which was apparent in the days of Henry VIII. The mercantilists brought economic questions to prominence, and in doing so, they helped the development of Physiocracy. In the Relativist sense, mercantilist policies were appropriate for that time which wanted to promote a strong nation state in the midst of chaos and disorder of the feudal system. Needless to say, many writers of the mercantilist period adhered to the liberal principles. Keynes indeed found some scientific truth in the philosophy of mercantilism.

15. M. Blaug, *op. cit.*, p. 14.
16. *Ibid.*, p. 14.
17. *Loc. cit.*
18. *Op. cit.*, p. 17.

3
Physiocracy (1750-1776)

WHAT IS PHYSIOCRACY?

Physiocracy is a reaction of a group of Frenchmen against the materialistic, rigid, restrictive and controlled merchant capitalism of the mercantilists. The system of physiocracy developed in France in the middle of the eighteenth century. Physiocracy means the rule of Nature. It is regarded as "a rationalisation of certain specific political aims." Adam Smith considered physiocracy as a *school of agriculture*. The physiocrats considered themselves as *economists*. The physiocrats believed in some natural power which is responsible for human happiness and prosperity. In a sense, physiocracy was a political and social system. The physiocrats put forward a complete system of political economy in which there was the supreme rule of Nature. It was really the movement for going back to Nature and rustic simplicity. The physicoratic school was more coherent and systematic as compared to mercantilism. It was well-organised and more or less orderly. The school was founded by Francois Quesnay.

There were many members of the physiocratic school. The most famous members were : Francois Quesnay, Dupont de Nemours, A.R. J. Turgot, Mirabeau, De la Riviere, Baudeau and Trosne.

COMPARISON BETWEEN MERCANTILISM AND PHYSICORACY

The main points of comparison between Mercantilism and Physiocracy are given in the following chart :

	Mercantilism		Physiocracy
1.	Mercantilism was in favour of trade and commerce.	:	Physiocracy was in favour of agriculture.
2.	Money is wealth.	:	Real wealth is not money but tangible goods and consumable articles.
3.	Mercantilism was concerned with trade and commerce.	:	The physiocracy considered foreign trade as a necessary evil.
4.	Industry is productive and agriculture is unproductive.	:	Agriculture is productive and industry is unproductive.
5.	Supported state intervention.	:	Stood for *laissez faire*.
6.	Mercantilism introduced protection.	:	Physiocracy was in favour of free trade.

7.	Mercantilism emphasised the means and causes of wealth and production.	:	Physiocracy emphasised mainly the distribution of products.
8.	Mercantilism made a lasting contribution to the theories of money and tarde.	:	Physiocracy made a lasting contribution to the general equilibrium analysis, circular analysis and to the scientific development of economics.
9.	Mercantilism was in favour of restrictions.	:	Physiocracy was in favour of liberty.
10.	Mercantilism depended on surplus to be reaped from foreign trade and commerce.	:	Physiocracy also depended on surplus for economic growth, to be reaped from agriculture as net product.
11.	Mercantilists were pamphleteers. The ideas were loose and scattered.	:	The ideas of the physiocrats were more systematic, organised and coherent.
12.	Mercantilism did not believe in Nature.	:	Physiocrats had complete faith in Nature.

FACTORS RESPONSIBLE FOR THE RISE OF PHYSIOCRACY

There are many factors which were responsible for the growth of physiocracy in France. All these factors simultaneously worked for the growth of physiocracy.

1. Continuous Neglect of Agriculture. The agricultural economy of France became stagnant for quite a long time. Colbertism was partly responsible for this. Industrial development was taking place in France at the cost of agriculture. During the period of Colbertism, investments were diverted from agriculture to manufacture, and the changing tastes for manufacture tended to lower the domestic demand for agricultural produce and also its price. Lower prices of agricultural products prevented capital accumulation in agriculture[1] Agriculture suffered due to lack of capital and initiative.

2. Emergence of a Group of Ambitious Agriculturists. In France, a group of ambitious agriculturists and landlords started seriously thinking of the development of agriculture in France. They did not tolerate the suppression of French agriculture by the king. One such ambitious landlord was Quesnay. The on-going agricultural revolution in England influenced very much these ambitious French landowners. They thought that a similar revolution can be brought about in France.

3. Decay of Mercantilism. Mercantilism was already decaying and its policies were severely criticised. People were in search for an alternative system. Already, in Britain, large-scale farming became a success, the knowledge of which was brought to the people of France by the writings of Mirabeau, Montesquieu and others. In fact, people eagerly wanted a system of socio-economic order which can take the place of mercantilism. This system was provided by physiocracy.

4. Subjective Factors. People were not satisfied with the king. After the death of Louis XIV, the people of France got sufficient liberty to ex-

---

1. Ekelund and Hebert, *op, cit.,* p. 52.

press their opinion. This was the beginning of breaking away from the established policies, politics and religion. People wanted something more rational, more simple and more practical, and above all, something which is based on *natural justice*. Thus, naturalism came to the forefront of human action and thought. This demand was satisfied by the new system of physiocracy which essentially was based on the rule of Nature and the natural order.

5. Regressive Taxation. In France, during the reigns of Louis XV and Louis XVI, Taxation was unduly heavy, regressive in character and discriminatory in practice. The nobles and clergymen were exempted from taxation. Most of the burden of tax was borne by the poor peasants and cultivators. The poor farmers had to pay other duties and charges. Taxation was direct and arbitrary. The worst of all taxes was the Salt Tax. The peasants had to pay for the use of roads and bridges. They were also required to pay in terms of personal labour for the construction of public roads. Thus, the poor peasants were economically exploited too much during the periods of Louis XV and Louis XVI. They badly needed a respite from this unjust economic domination.

6. Extravagant Court Life. The life of political administrators was very luxurious and corrupt. There was too much wastage and extravagance. The state coffer was empty. The king had to contract a heavy loan. The burden of royal expenditure was entirely on the common people. Apart from this, heavy expenditure was incurred on wars. The deteriorating economic conditions provided a new ground for new ideas and a welcome change.

7. Existence of Socio-Economic Inequality. France witnessed an extreme form of inequality between different classes of people and between different sectors of the economy. Agriculture was organised on class lines. There were both privileged and under-privileged classes. The common people were underprivileged who wanted an escape from this unwanted situation.

BASIC PRINCIPLES AND POLICIES OF PHYSIOCRACY

The following are the fundamental principles and policies of physiocracy:

(i)   Agriculture is the only productive occupation.
(ii) Industry and trade are sterile occupations.
(iii) Agriculture produces net product (surplus)
(iv) There is a *natural order* which makes life happy and meaningful.
(v)   There is harmony among all classes of people.
(vi) The individual should get maximum liberty.
(vii) State action should be limited to the minimum.
(viii) Trade is a necessary evil, and there should be free trade.
(ix) Value depends on utility. Wealth has value. Value and price are the same things.

(x)   The wage level is at subsistence (iron law of wage).

(xi)   There is interdependence in the economic system.

(xii)   Real wealth lies in tangible and consumable goods.

(xiii) Private initiative must be encouraged.

(xiv)   Distribution of products is very crucial.

(xv)   Money is a medium of exchange.

(xvi)   All that is bought is sold and all that is sold is bought. However, as Say noted, income received is not automatically restored to the income stream.

(xvii) Rent is a perfectly legitimate income of landlords.

(xviii) There should be a single and direct tax on land, as it is the only productive source.

(xix)   Private property is essential.

(xx)   There is the possibility of overpopulation on land.

NATURAL ORDER

The conception of natural order is one of the fundamental bases of the physiocratic system. Natural order supplies the base on which the economic system of physiocracy is built up. Natural order is a philosophical concept. Quesnay built the whole system of physiocracy on the concept of natural order. Dupont de Nemours defined physiocracy as a science of *natural order.*[2] The natural order is designed and ordained by God. Natural order is a permanent, eternal and universal phenomenon. The natural order must not be confused with the state of nature. The state of nature is a savage state, but natural order is in confirmity with the civilised state. The natural order is founded on law and property rights. The natural order implies that human societies are subject to natural laws such as govern the physical world or exercise sway over animal or organic life.[3] The physiocrats conveyed the idea of interdependence of all social classes and of their final dependence on nature through the system of natural order.[4] The natural order is created by God for giving happiness to mankind.[5]

According to Quesnay, the basic objective of economics is to secure the greatest amount of satisfaction with the least possible outlay. This is in confirmity with the system of natural order. When everybody is observing natural order, there cannot be any clash of interest among the different classes of people, and the individual interest and the social interest cannot be in conflict with each other.

According to Dupont, introspective self-examination will reveal the essence of the natural order. It is already existing in society. It is, however, necessary to realise it. The natural order can be applied to the relation of the state to trade and industry. Once the natural order is known, it would be

---

2. Gide and Rist, *A History of Economic Doctrines*, p. 25.

3. *Ibid.*, pp. 26-27.

4. *Ibid.*, p. 27.

5. L.H. Haney, *History of Economic Thought*, p. 178.

followed by everyone through rational behaviour. It must be noted that the natural order is not the same thing as the social order. A social order is created by human beings but natural order is created by God. It is also not the same thing as the state of nature. It is the duty of human beings to first understand the natural order, appreciate its implications and then to bring our lives in conformity with the natural order.[6] The natural order is able to secure for the individual and society the greatest amount of pleasure and happiness.

However, certain institutions are necessary for the working of the natural order. These institutions are : liberty, private property, landed classes, farmers and absolute monarchy. It also requires authority. The essential aspects of natural order were the right to enjoy the benefits of property, to exercise one's labour and to have such freedom as was consistent with the freedom of others to follow their self-interest.[7] Another requirement for the natural order is *laissez faire*. There also must be the removal of all restrictions in the way of freedom of contract, free competition and natural rights. The government should perform only the limited amount of necessary functions. It should try to protect life, liberty and property.

If everybody can realise natural order, there would be heaven on this earth. The natural order is sometimes referred to as the rule of some natural laws. This concept might have been brought from the medieval concept of natural justice. The purpose of such as natural order is to ensure an orderly functioning of the universe of discourse. The natural laws are normative laws for governing the behaviour of human beings on an ideal basis. These laws specify certain ideal rights and duties for human beings to perform. Only rational human beings are aware of such order. The natural order is the ideal order of things. The natural laws can ensure the natural rights to man and these laws govern ideal human action. The natural order does not in any way restrain the liberty of mankind; on the other hand, it stands for greater liberty.

The physiocrats had some pre-established notion about natural order. The natural order is a metaphysical concept which is not capable of being empirically verified. This makes the concept less scientific and more subjective. It is pointed out that natural order is an anticipation of utilitarianism at a time when the society was not prepared for it. The physiocrats considered natural order as something supernatural. It was indeed difficult to naturalise the supernatural. Perhaps it was an attempt to bring about an ideal order of things on the basis of natural justice. Haney has suggested that the physiocratic natural order philosophy was against the materialistic and rigid control of economic life which was enforced under mercantilism.

---

6. Gide and Rist, *op., cit.,* p. 28.

7. Eric Roll, *A History of Economic Thought,* p. 137.

NET PRODUCT (PRODUIT NET)

The concept of net product (surplus) is an important concept in physiocratic analysis. In fact, the concept of surplus later on also became crucial in the analysis of development economics. According to the physiocrats, net product can only be generated in agriculture. Net product is the difference between the goods produced and the goods consumed in the process of production. The net product may be considered either in value terms or in physical terms. In value terms, the question of price becomes very important. When there is a good price (Bon Prix), the amount of surplus is also much large. Thus, one can say that the amount of net product depends on the prevailing market price. Whenever the price level falls, the net product also falls and may even be wiped out.

The physiocrats were in favour of a free trade policy because they thought that free trade will be helpful in raising the prices of agricultural commodities, in which case, the net product would be higher. The concept of net product can be explained with the help of the following diagram:

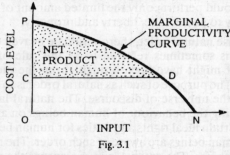

Fig. 3.1

In this diagram, the input applied in agriculture is *ON*. The cost level (average) of input is *OC*. The total product is *OPN*. The total cost of input is *OCDN*. Therefore, the net product or surplus is the dotted portion *CPD*. In fact, net product is equal to the value of output minus the value of input. No other sector, excepting agriculture, is able to produce the net product. This is so because in all other sectors, the cost of production is the same as the value of the total produce. It is in this sense that agriculture could be regarded as the most productive occupation. Agriculture is the chief concern not only of the farmers but also of the entire nation. The physiocrats argued that since agriculture is the most productive sector, it should be encouraged by the state. Dupont observed that the prosperity of mankind is bound up with the realisation of maximum surplus from agriculture. The physiocratic writers favoured a policy of good price for the agricultural products and prosperity. This is so because good price alone can ensure a good surplus. The production of surplus by agriculture is an impact of natural order. The fruits of the earth are given by God. This is mainly the reason why agriculture can create a surplus.

Industry, trade and commerce cannot create any surplus. Thus, industrialists, manufacturers and tradesmen are all sterile or unproductive. But they are not useless. Baudeau observed that "far from being useless, these are the arts that supply the luxuries as well as the necessaries of life and upon these mankind is dependent both for its preservation and for its well being." However, these classes are unproductive in the sense that they do not add anything extra to the stock of wealth. The products of arts are wrought by man who is powerless to create. This implies that God does not help in the production processes of manufacture and commerce to create the net product. Thus, the difference between agricultural and non-agricultural sectors is a fundamental difference based on theology.

It must be pointed out that it is quite probable that the gains in industry and commerce may be more than the gains in agriculture. However, according to the physiocrats, they were gained and not produced. To the physiocrats, production does not aim at the creation of utility, but at generating surplus or net product. By surplus, the physiocrats basically thought of material surplus which can be created by the help of God alone. The power of creating something new was in the hands of God. Man cannot create anything.

The physiocratic concept of net product was based on a political consideration. By showing that agriculture alone can produce a surplus, they wanted to show that landlords are productive and the existing system of feudal landlordism was a highly effective system. Many of the physiocratic writers were themselves landlords, who wanted to retain their position and status. Their idea was to prove that the landlord class was productive and rent was a just payment for the use of land.

The physiocrats maintained that all products were influenced by the market conditions. In such a case, the analysis of net product was connected with the theory of pricing. However, unfortunately, the physiocrats did not have a satisfactory theory of value. Moreover, it could not be said with certainty that the product of the earth differed in any essential respect from the product of industry.[8] According to some, the net product concept is simply a puerile obsession and an optical illusion. It can very well be shown that the non-agricultural sector is also capable of producing the net product. It is rather meaningless to say that non-agricultural classes are sterile and unproductive. It was Adam Smith who showed that all classes of people are capable of producing wealth. It is, however, noteworthy that both Marx and the physiocrats talked about *surplus*. But whereas Marx said that labour alone was capable of producing surplus value, the physiocrats observed that it was land which could generate a surplus. Surprisingly, none of these writers took into account the productivity of capital which is a determinant of surplus.[9] It is also pointed out that the physiocratic notion of net product is absurd. According to them, production is nothing but the creation of gross matter. They could not apperciate that production really means the creation of value and utility. If we consider in this sense, it can be shown that the non-agricultural sector is also capable of producing surplus. The physiocrats believed that the non-agricultural sector could not produce surplus but it can simply replace, modify and transfer wealth which

8. Gide and Rist, *A History of Economic Doctrines,* pp. 34-35.
9. J.A. Schumpeter, *History of Economic Analysis,* p. 238.

is already created by the agricultural sector. However, they have not clearly mentioned whether agricultural sector included mines and other extractive industries or not. The physiocratic idea was that net product was possible due to the bounty of Nature. However, Ricardo, later on, held that net product or surplus is not necessarily due to the bounty of Nature but it is in fact due to the growing sterility of land. Be that as it may, the physiocratic concept of net product is an important contribution. At least, it was able to eliminate the misconception of mercantilism about the true source of wealth.

CIRCULATION OF WEALTH (TABLEAU ECONOMIQUE)

The physiocratic writers not only analysed the generation of net product and wealth but also analysed the distribution of wealth. The circulation of wealth was like the circulation of blood in the human body. The circulation of wealth was analysed by Quesnay who was a physician by profession. The physiocrats considered land as the true source of wealth. In the scheme of circulation of wealth, there are two assumptions: *(i)* the quality of product circulated every year remains the same; and *(ii)* the price level remains constant. According to the physiocrats, Quesnay's *Tableau Economique* is an outstanding contribution in the analysis of distribution of wealth. The distribution of wealth represents a circular flow of wealth among the various classes of people. Thus, is shows some amount of common dependence of one class of people on the other. The physiocrats regarded the economy as fundamentally organic. Their analysis is, in a sense, the first general equilibrium analysis which was applied in the distribution of wealth.

In the distribution of wealth, the physiocrats analysed a *circular flow* of income and expenditure. This is really a macro-economic concept as we use in modern times. In this circular flow of wealth, there are three classes of people; farmers, manufacturers and landlords. The farmers are only the productive class, the landlords are the proprietary class which is partly productive and the manufacturers are the unproductive or sterile class. The net product from agriculture is the true source of all wealth. These classes are represented in the diagram below (see, Ekelund and Hebert's book, *op. cit.* p.53).

CIRCULATION OF WEALTH

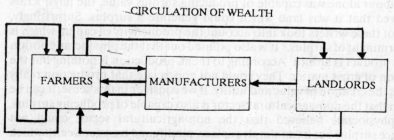

(Each line represents expenditure of one million francs)

Fig. 3.2

The income flows in the diagram are shown clockwise. The net product (or net income) is produced entirely by the agricultural class. The net product may be used to support all the classes in the society. Suppose the total wealth production is of 5 million francs and of this, two million francs will be kept apart for the maintenance and upkeep of the productive class and the livestock during the year. This amount then is shown as payment from the farm sector to the farm sector. It must be noted that this amount (two million francs) does not circulate in the society. Only three million francs will circulate among the different classes of the people. Of the three million francs, two million francs go to the landlords in the form of rent and tax. The remaining one million francs will go to the manufacturers. The payment made to the landlords is the *net product* (surplus). The circle is completed when the landlords spend their income (1 million for food and 1 million for manufactures). The manufacturing class has the income of two million francs (one million francs received from the farmers and one million francs received from the landlords). This amount (two million francs) will go to the farmers for the purchase of food and industrial raw materials required by the manufacturers. Thus, it is interesting to see that agriculture gets back the same three million francs which was already spent away in the beginning. Agriculture gets back two million francs from the manufacturers and one million francs from the landlords (proprietary class). In this process, it is shown that only the agricultural sector products the net product *(i.e.* surplus over cost of production). The same conclusion can also be arrived at through the arrow diagram. One arrow shows the transfer of 1m to the direction of the arrow. The diagram is presented below:

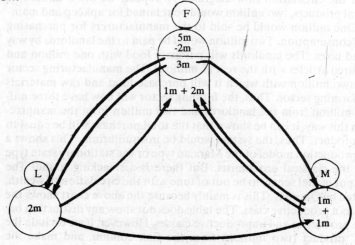

Fig. 3.3

In the preceding diagram, it is shown that out of the total production of 5m in the farming sector (F), 2m are kept apart for consumption and seed, and 3m are circulated: 2m go to landlords (L) as tax and rent and 1m goes to the manufacturing sector (M) as payment for the purchase of non-agricultural goods by the (F) sector. The (L) sector spends 1m for the purchase of food from the (F) sector and 1m for the purchase of manufactured articles from the (M) sector. Thus, the (L) sector is now left with nothing. The (M) sector now has 2m. This entire amount is sent to (F) sector for the purchase of food and raw-materials for the (M) sector. Thus, at the end of the circulation process, the (F) sector gets back the entire amount (3m) which was originally thrown in the circulation process.

The physiocratic concept of circulation of wealth can also be described with the help of input-output table as devised by Leontief.[10] This is shown below:

Table 3.1

Producing Sector	Purchasing Sector		Manu-facturers	Total Products
	Farmers	Landlords		
Farmers	2	1	2	5
Landlords	2(0)	0	0	2(0)
Manufacturers	1	1	0	2
Total Purchase	5(3)	2	2	9(7)

The explanation of the above table has been given earlier in our discussion of the circulation flow diagram. To repeat: Of the 5 million of agricultural products, two million would be retained for upkeep and maintenance. One million would be sold to the manufacturers for purchasing articles of consumption. Two million would be paid to the landlords by way of rent and taxes. The landlords will purchase food with one million and manufactured articles with the rest (1 million). The manufacturing sector will have two million with which it will purchase food and raw materials from the farming sector. Thus, the farming sector will now have three million (one million from the landlords and two million from the manufacturers). In this way, it can be shown that the total purchase will be equal to the total product. Thus, the system would be in equilibrium. This shows a simple reproduction model of the Marxian type or the stationary state type model of the classical economists. But there is a smacking sound. The input-output model seems to be out of tune with the circulation of wealth, as suggested by Quesnay. This is mainly because the above chart shows the landlords as a productive class. The table does not show any distinction between the productive and unproductive classes. However, if we exclude the landlords' product (two million) from the first column, and make the necessary adjustments in the table, as shown by our figures in parentheses,

10. M Blaug, *op., cit.,* pp. 28-29.

then the total product and total purchase can be shown to be seven million. This would, of course, be a case of equilibrium once again.

The circular flow model presented above is extremely interesting as it gives an insight into the policy framework of the physiocratic school of thought. It shows that the agricultural sector can accumulate capital if the tax burden on the farmers is removed. The physiocrats, therefore, prescribed tax reforms. The physiocrats also favoured free trade because that will keep the farm price higher so that the net product would be higher. The removal of all these restrictions along with *laissez faire* will allow sufficient capital inflow into agriculture, and the size of the circular flow will grow over time. The physiocrats also recommended the payment of tax from the net product. Thus, the receiver of the net product (landlords) should alone pay taxes. However, the physiocrats were in favour of private property and the proprietary class. This class made some investment for the improvement of lands. Thus, they were entitled to have a share of the annual produce from land. Landlords were not social parasites. An important feature of the physiocratic scheme of distribution is that it attaches a unique position to the landlords. But the greatest defect of the scheme was that the idlers were praised against the merchants and the manufacturers.

The physiocrats failed to understand the dignity of all types of labour. Their idea of circulation is based on a particular type of socio-economic order. It cannot be generalised. According to many people, their idea of treating the landlords as a productive class does not stand to reason. The treatment of circulation of wealth is a motionless static concept which admits of no scope for development. It is surprising that the physiocrats did not consider labour as a productive agent. However, inspite of many analytical defects of the physiocratic theory of circulation of wealth, it must be admitted that they were the first economists to give a total picture of the circular flow of economic activities and an analysis of general interdependence and general equilibrium.

TAXATION

The physiocrats wanted to simplify the system of taxation. They wanted to put the burden on those who could bear the tax. They favoured a single tax system on the net product. Since the net product was earned by the landlords, they should bear the burden of the single tax. Industry, manufacture, trade and commerce cannot bear the burden of tax because these occupations are unproductive and do not generate any net product. The single tax on agriculture should not exceed 30 per cent of the value of the net product. According to them, the single tax will be sufficient to meet all the fiscal needs of the state. The single tax would be a direct tax and it will be also inexpensive to collect. The most important merit of this tax will be that its burden can be easily borne by the proprietary class. The physiocrats had a fairly good idea about the principles of taxation. They provided really the incentive for Smith's theory of taxation.

TRADE

Trade, according to the physiocrats, is an unproductive occupation. Trade does not produce any wealth but it simply transfers wealth of equal value. Although trade leads to some gain, the physiocrats maintained that one man's gain was another man's loss. The only useful exchange would be the transfer of agricultural products from the producers to the consumers. However, the physiocrats advocated free trade as a challenge to the mercantilist theory. The physiocrats thought that free trade in agricultural commodities will lead to higher prices and higher net product. This will again lead to more capital formation in agriculture. The physiocrats are to be regarded "as the founders of free trade, not because of any desire to favour trade as such but because their attitude towards it was one of disdainful *laissez faire.*"

CRITICAL APPRAISAL

The following criticisms may be levelled against physiocracy:

1. Their theory was drowned in normative statements. This is quite true of natural order doctrine.

2. The physiocrats wrongly pointed out that the manufacturing class is a sterile class. It can be sufficiently proved that this class is a productive class.

3. The physiocrats did not consider labouring class as a productive class. They only narrowly considered land as the only productive agent.

4. While it is possible to show in physical terms that agriculture can produce surplus, it is difficult to show that it will be true under all circumstances in terms of value surplus.

5. The physiocrats failed to produce an analytical theory of value. Of course, they had some notion about value.

6. The physiocrats wrongly considered the landlord class as the (partly) productive class. This is really surprising and is based on a political motive.

7. The net product concept has to be meaningfully related to the price level, in which case it can be shown that under certain circumstances, when price is very low, even agriculture cannot generate any surplus.

8. The physiocrats have placed too much emphasis on the agricultural sector and have neglected the non-agriculture sector.

9. The physiocrats would not appreciate the helpful role of state in the matter of socio-economic development.

10. The physiocrats were extremely individualistic in attitude which led to the formulation of unbalanced policies.

11. Their notion of productivity is not correct. They considered production as the creation of gross matter, and not the creation of value or utility.

12. According to Haney, physiocratic doctrines are full of negative attitudes.

13. Haney has also referred to different types of dualistic attitudes in their economic thoughts, *e.g.,* individualism versus despotism, religion versus rationality, and so on.

DOWNFALL

Many important writers from many walks of life started attacking the philosophy of the physiocrats. Galiani attacked the natural order philosophy. Condiliac attacked the physiocratic notion of productive and unproductive classes. He tried to prove that the manufacturing class was not a sterile class as was depicted by the physiocrats. The kings and despots did not like the idea of physiocracy because it wanted complete liberty and freedom and the enforcement of *laissez faire.* To the detriment of physiocratic writers, when free trade in agricultural commodities was introduced, the after-effect was that the prices of the agricultural produce rose so sharply and high, that the poor people could not afford to purchase the necessary food articles. A situation of conflagration started at many places. There were riots and mob violence which could not be so easily controlled in France. This affair brought a bad name to the philosophy of physiocracy. The industrial class was the bitter critic of physiocracy. From all corners of France, there were attempts to dishonor and disown the philosophy of physiocracy. Although Adam Smith had a word of praise for the physiocrats, still the publication of his *Wealth of Nations* brought some thoughts which went directly against the established notions of physiocratic doctrines. Needles to say, Smith's *Wealth of Nations* presented more acceptable and balanced views about men and mattes. Thus, with the publication of Smith's *magnum opus,* there was a quick downfall of the physiocratic school.

MERITS

In spite of the above points of criticism, the physiocrats have many qualities to draw our sympathy. In a sense, they laid the foundation of modern political economy and stimulated the French Revolution. According to Eric Roll, the physiocrats established proper links with modern economics which went into three directions: national income analysis, general equilibrium analysis and econometrics. They made important contributions to the theory of taxation. Their position in the history of economic thought is transitional between feudalism and capitalism. They were cautious reformers and original thinkers. They were a little oversystematic. However, over systematisation is useful in the early state of a science. According to Schumpeter, the physiocrats made the great bridge through which lay all further progress in the field of analysis. In the same vein, Adam Smith noted that physiocracy with all its imperfections is perhaps the nearest approximation to the truth that has yet been published in the subject of political economy.

Part Two
Development of Classical Political Economy

Part Two

Development of Classical Political
Economy

4

Origin of Classicism

ADAM SMITH (1723-1790)

Although Adam Smith was a bachelor, he is regarded as the father of economic science. The greatness of Adam Smith lies in his effort to systematically and analytically present the facts of economics. He introduced economics as a separate discipline. He was responsible for the introduction of a new paradigm in economics, which is known as the classical paradigm, by unifying the scattered ideas and loose theories of his time. However, even at the time of Adam Smith, economics could not become a science in the true sense of the term. In fact, economics became a science at the end of the classical period, more precisely since 1870, when the neo-classical economics and marginal revolution were introduced in economics to make it more analytical and verifiable.

Wealth of Nations

Smith's book, *An Inquiry into the Nature and Causes of the Wealth of Nations*, which was published in 1776, is not just an ordinary book. It contained the thinking of the whole epoch. There is nothing in this book which can be called purely original. All the ideas presented in this book are already known. Smith simply presented the ideas in a more systematic and analytical manner. It has been rightly pointed out that *"The Wealth of Nations* is the outpouring not only of a great mind, but of a whole epoch". A brief review of the contents of *The Wealth of Nations reveals* its depth of treatment of the subject of economics. Book I discusses the divisions of labour, origin and use of money, determination of prices, wages, profits and rent. Book II contains Smith's theory of capital interest. Book III considers economic development of Europe from ancient times to the eighteenth century. Book IV discusses different systems of political economy, including a criticism against mercantilism. It also discusses the barriers to free trade. Book V is concerned with taxation and fiscal policy of the eighteenth century Britain.

NATURALISM AND OPTIMISM

Like the physiocrats, Smith also believed in natural order. He called his natural order *naturalism*. He derived his view of naturalism from the physiocrats and also from Francis Hutcheson. It should be noted that

Adam Smith was basically a philosopher. He was famous for his *Theory of Moral Sentiment*. The essence of naturalism is that the economic institutions are spontaneous in origin. Optimism says that the naturally created institutions are based on the influence of self-interest and common natural instinct. This, in a nutshell, is the theory of naturalism. The ideas of naturalism and optimism are not separable from each other. Smith's philosophy is based on the idea that whatever is natural must also be good for the society as a whole.

Every individual is motivated by self-interest. Every man, so to say, is the maximiser of gain and minimiser of loss. Therefore, every man undertakes that activity which appears to him to be the most profitable. The entire society is based on this conceptualisation. Everybody wants to make his conditions better. Being guided by such a rationale, when people undertake different activities, the society gets many types of economic institutions. These economic institutions are spontaneous in character. But although the institutions are primarily based on self-interest, they ultimately increase social welfare. It is not from the benevolence of the butcher, the brewer or the baker that we expect our dinner, but from their regard to their own interest. We address ourselves not to their humanity, but to their self-love, and never talk to them about their own necessities, but of their advantages.

Every man is naturally the best judge of his own interest and should, therefore, be allowed to pursue his own way. Adam Smith pointed out that in pursuing his own advantage, every individual is led by an invisible hand to promote an end which was no part of his intention." Smith believed that given the natural order, the interests of different economic units cannot be in conflict with one another. Their interest must be in harmony. This is ensured by the working of the *Invisible Hand*, or automatic adjustment mechanism. If perfect competition prevails, Smith thinks, individual interest and social interest would be compatible with each other. For the working of the natural order or naturalism, there must be liberty, free competition and *laissez faire*.

Smith has given a number of examples of economic institutions which are beneficial in character. For example, *the institution of money* arose as a spontaneous institution; but it removed the difficulties of barter system and facilitated trade, exchange and commerce. Similarly, the demand-supply construct is of spontaneous origin but it does a great service to the market economy by adjusting supply and demand to the price level. The adjustment of price, demand and supply is natural in origin. But it helps to bring about an equilibrium in the market economy. Similarly, Smith's theory of population is also an extension of demand and supply theory of labour. If the demand for labour is very high, labour supply remaining constant, the wage level will rise, and in course of time, people will expand their families and labour supply will consequently go up, and, therefore, wage will come down. The reverse will be the case if the demand for labour is low and the supply of labour is high. The theory of naturalism is also applicable in the case of capital accumulation which is a natural phenomenon. But capital accumulation leads to a great social advantage. Capital accumulation facilitates the task of economic and social development which is very beneficial to all types of people. In the same way, division of labour is a natural institution in the production economy. It arises out of self-interest. But it leads to a number of advantages like increase in output, increase in efficiency, low cost and possibility of invention.

In fact, in pursuing his own interest, every individual is led by the invisible hand to promote the social interest and welfare. As Adam Smith puts it: a man generally "indeed neither intends to promote the public interest nor knows how much he is promoting it. By preferring the support of domestic to that of foreign industry, he intends only his own security; but by directing that industry in such a manner as its produce may be of the greatest value, he intends only his own gain and he is in this as in many other cases led by an invisible hand to promote an end which was no part of his intention."[1]

The natural order is existing in the universe and it guarantees harmony of interests among all classes of people. If there is anything unnatural or undesirable, the Invisible Hand is there to correct it. The forces of perfect competition leads to a few advantages, although it is a natural institution. Perfect competition assures a normal price for the producer, production of a large number of goods and services and the lowest possible production cost. Thus we find that perfect competition leads to a number of advantages for the society. It should also be noted that perfect competition leads optimum allocation of resources. Similar is the case with free trade which is a natural practice or institution. Free trade leads to supply of goods and services at the lowest cost in the international market and also to factor price equalisation.

Smith believed that personal interest leads to the creation of economic institutions but, at the same time, it also ensures greater progress and prosperity of the nation through such institutions. Adam Smith had great confidence in the efficacy of human action. However, he pointed out that there should be certain restrictions on individual actions. For example, the private enterprise to be useful must satisfy the following two conditions: (1) The competition must keep actions within the limit of justice. (2) The entrepreneur must be guided by personal interest.

Criticism

Needless to say, Smith considered mutual interdependence of different sectors and people in the economy. His theory of optimism seems to be correct in the area of production. But in the area of distribution, there is hardly any scope for optimism and harmony of interest. Smith himself has shown that in the field of distribution there is the possibility of a clash of in-

---

1. A. Gray.*The Development of Economic Doctrine* p. 146.

terests, particularly between labour and capital. His theory of optimism is not based on any scientific line of approach. Individual interest and social interest may not coincide with each other all the time. Similarly, the private sector and public sector do not have the same common interest and the same efficiency. The conclusion drawn by Adam Smith with respect to naturalism and optimism is based on an insufficient inductive or empirical study. These are not based on any causal relation or *a priori* theorising. It has been found that with the progress of capitalism, class division in society grows sharper and sharper. Smith is not right when he says that naturalism and optimism can be obtained without the help of the state. In fact, in many cases, state help will be necessary for obtaining optimism and naturalism.

A man is not necessarily activated by the motive of self-interest. Smith's philosophy is over-individualistic. Smith's individual is an *economic man* dominated by self-interest, self-love and shrewd choice. Adam Smith's economics mixes up individual and social points of view. Thus, it will be difficult to build up a theory on such a mixed notion which is essentially uncertain. Lastly, Smith represented the interest of a single class, *i.e.,* the capitalist class. According to him, the capitalist class increases the welfare of society.[2] It is obvious now that Smith's observations seem to be contrary to facts.

Be that as it may, it must be noted that Smith's theory of naturalism and optimism is different and tor, similar on many important respects, from the physiocratic theory of natural order. This is discussed below:

Comparison between Physiocratic Natural Order and Smith's Naturalism

	Physiocratic Natural Order	:	*Adam Smith's Naturalism*
1.	It is a natural law applicable to both life and institutions.	:	It is natural or spontaneous economic institutions.
2.	Natural order maximises happiness.	:	Beneficial in character.
3.	No interference is required.	:	No interference is required.
4.	It may be enforced by authorities or human volition.	:	Invisible Hand guarantees automatic adjustment. No enforcement is required.
5.	Self-interest of human beings is not brought to the forefront.	:	Selfishness is brought to the forefront.
6.	Simply an ideal realisable by cultured and educated people.	:	It is not so. It is a reality.
7.	Liberty, free individual action and *laissez faire* are required.	:	Liberty, free individual action and *laissez faire* are required.
8.	The basis of natural order is property, security and liberty.	:	Smith recognised no such basis.
9.	Natural order is to be discovered.	:	It is existing in the universe.
10.	Natural order is to be revealed, understood and propagated.	:	These are not necessary.

---

2.   Eric Roll, *A History of Economic Thought,* p. 152.

	Physiocratic Natural Order	:	Adam Smith's Naturalism
11.	Possibility of clash of individual interest and social interest. Men should sacrifice self-centrism for social welfare.	:	No clash of interest, excepting in the matter of distribution.
12.	Natural order is tinged with a note of pessimism because of the possibility of wrong working of human beings and institutions.	:	*Invisible Hand* corrects the unnatural and undesired things (optimism). Pessimism is also recognised by Smith.

DIVISION OF LABOUR

According to Adam Smith, division of labour is practically the only factor in economic progress. Division of labour is a system of social cooperation in the production process where every individual is given a job according to his specialisation. Adam Smith has very elaborately discussed the division of labour in his *Wealth of Nations*. In the beginning of his book, Smith analyses the importance of labour in the production process. He says that labour is the true source of wealth. This is the reason why he placed the discussion on labour at the outset of his book. Labour is the cause of wealth and production. This is the main philosophy of *Wealth of Nations*. Labourers enter into social cooperation for production, and the combined effort of these individuals produces the national dividend. Division of labour provides the cooperative efforts necessary for the production of large number of commodities for the satisfaction of all individuals. It is, therefore, a true service for social progress and human welfare. Smith had a very clear idea about the advantages of division of labour which are as follows:

(1) Increase in production is possible.
(2) The worker acquires greater skill through specialisation.
(3) Production takes place at a faster rate.
(4) Specialisation leads to invention.

Smith's division of labour is a true dynamic force. He said that there is increased scope in any nation for increasing productivity through division of labour. It is the logical consequence of the propensity to truck, barter and exchange. A high degree of division of labour leads to a high degree of specialisation which leads to increased efficiency and, thereby, increased productivity. Smith identified the advantages of division of labour with capital accumulation and innovation. However, the factors which limit division of labour are capital stock and the limited extent of the market. Division of labour, in Smith's analysis, is actually technical progress, and, as such, its introduction depends on the opening of new sources of demanded. Smith says that division of labour leads to the invention of machinery which does not displace labour but rather absorbs labour.

Smith's idea that division of labour is limited by the extent of market has been incorporated in the theory of growth, particularly by A. Young and R. Nurkse. They say that underdevelopment equilibrium can be broken if there is balanced industrial development, expansion of demand and market. In modern times, it is observed that inducement to investment is limited by the size of the market, as is evident in every developing country. Division of labour increases the employment of productive workers, and also the total output. Smith observes that increased division of labour must increase production which, for its sake, must depend on markets. The extent of the market must expand with the growth of productivity and output. Development process which is started by division of labour is a cumulative process. When capital stock is sufficient and market is extending, division of labour should be undertaken to increase productivity and national income. Increase in working population and income not only expands the size of the market but will also increase the volume of saving as labour becomes more specialized. As market expands, the incentive to introduce improved method of production increases. These result in further specialisation and productivity increase. In consequence of division of labour, production is multiplied and the society is benefited as a whole. His theory of division of labour is the germ of the economic law of increasing returns, because it points out that as output is increasing, the unit cost would be diminishing. The implication of division of labour was fully brought out by Alfred Marshall.

Although a number of criticisms may be levelled against the Smithian theory of division of labour, still there is no denying the fact that his theory is relevant to the problems of capital formation in less developed countries. The thesis that division of labour is dependent on the extent of market is an important clue to economic progress for an economy which is in the midst of underdevelopment equilibrium.

Smith's originality lies in making division of labour the basis of all economic activities and considers it the true explanation of social production. It is the basis of economic progress in modern times. Smith's emphasis on labour as a source of wealth arose out of his desire to distinguish his ideas from the ideas of mercantilism and physiocracy. Regarding the source of wealth, mercantilism regarded foreign commerce and trade as the only source of wealth, while physiocrats considered agriculture as the mother of all riches. Smith wanted to contradict their mistaken notions.

Smith observed that labour is the source of all wealth. And all classes who work are productive. Smith said that foreign trade and agriculture are ultimately carried on by the labourers. Without labourers, there would neither be trade nor agriculture. According to Smith, the theory of division of labour is a repudiation of all previous economic theories which took only a partial view of production. Smith wanted to take a broader view of production by considering the entire humanity connected together in common labour for production of economic goods. He said that no class of individual, whether farmer or trader, is more important than the other. Every class has its own place and is essential for production. Smith, through his theory of division of labour, pointed out the important fact that production is a total concept and every type of production is equally necessary in a scheme of social production. The views of earlier writers like physiocrats and mercantilists were one-sided and narrow, against which Smith wanted to direct his philosophy of growth of wealth of nations and the result is his celebrated theory of division of labour.

PRODUCTIVE AND UNPRODUCTIVE LABOUR

According to Smith, productive labour is that labour which produces tangible goods having some market value. Unproductive labour, on the other hand, results in the production of intangibles, such as the services performed by teachers, artisans and kings. Adam Smith placed great emphasis on the proportion of productive and unproductive labour in production. Productive labour adds to the value of the subject on which it is applied. But unproductive labour does not add value to anything. Smith, in his analysis of the distinction between productive and unproductive labour, took up a materialistic definition of productivity. This idea was criticised by many writers. According to Smith, productive labour fixes and realises itself in some particular subject which lasts long. The services of unproductive labour are destroyed as soon as the services are performed. In case the ratio of productive to unproductive labour is greater, we can expect a faster rate of capital accumulation. Productive labour can put into motion an equal quantity of labour. This implies that productive labour does not destroy effective demand. Productive labour is perishable in the long run. It is capable of being stocked and stored up for future use.

Smith observes that only durable goods can be congeneal productive labour. Productive labour is engaged in the manufacture of wage goods. The funds which are required for the payment of wages are an increasing function of the volume of productive labour. The larger the size of the fund, the greater will be the riches and the larger would be the size of the market which will determine the rate of introduction of machinery and division of labour.

The unproductive workers do not contribute anything towards the expansion of the stock of wage goods. When an employer employs productive labour, he grows richer but when he employs unproductive labour, he becomes poor. By employing more productive labour, future wants can be satisfied in a better way. The bias for accumulation in Smith's theory of development involves a materialistic bias simply because only material goods can stock labour. Therefore, the production of material goods by productive labour is a bias in favour of saving and accumulation. Productive labour remains very crucial in an economy because such labour is used for investment. The annual produce which replaces capital is never employed immediately to maintain any but productive labour.

Another implication of Smith's distinction between productive and unproductive labour is that the productive labour must reproduce itself. By parsimony, the funds for the maintenance of productive labour can be increased. In such a case, the annual produce of land and labour can also be increased. Smith observes that labour which is productive will command a greater amount of labour than it embodies. Productive labour is stored up and can be effectively used in future. It is better to transfer unproductive labour to productive labour.

The third implication of the distinction between productive and unproductive labour is that the latter workers are disguisedly unemployed or partially unnemployed. They are, in fact, maintained by their relatives. Their marginal productivity is either zero or close to zero. If such workers are given productive employment, the social product will increase. The fourth implication of the distinction between productive and unproductive labour is this that when an unproductive labourer receives his wage, there is no further problem to be considered but when a productive labourer receives his wage, then one has to consider the possibility of selling the commodity produced by the productive labourer. This involves risk, uncertainty and time lags. All these are important for the determination of wages. The productive labourers earn their own income but unproductive labourers are supported by others. This analysis of Smith was very much appreciated by Karl Marx. Whereas a productive labourer creates surplus value, an unproductive labourer cannot create surplus value. Marx credited Smith for finding out such an important truth of the capitalistic economy. Smith's distinction between productive and unproductive labour can be linked with his theory of economic growth. Smith rightly observes that productive labour is able to create capital, increase investment and effective demand. Thus, productive labour can be an important source of creating further productive employment.

ADAM SMITH'S THEORY OF VALUE

Adam Smith's theory of value appears to be confusing for many reasons.[3] Firstly, he had a number of theories of value, such as, demand and supply theory, cost of production theory, toil and trouble theory, labour-embodied theory and labour-commanded theory. Secondly, Smith's treatment of value theory is different in his *Lectures* than that in his *Wealth of Nations*. Thirdly, there appears to be a confusion between the *cause* of value and the *measure* of value. Fourthly, the confusion arises also because of the use of labour-embodied and labour-commanded as a measure of exchange value.

At the beginning of his analysis, Adam Smith distinguishes between value-in-use and value-in-exchange. He has tried to explain the diamond-water paradox in the theory of value but he says that utility cannot be the basis of exchange value. He has not considered the concept of marginal utility. He set out to explain only the exchange value or relative price, and its change over time. He did not compare the exchange ratio of individual

---

3.   See, S Kaushil, "The case of Adam Smith's Value Analysis", *Oxford Economic Papers,*
     March, 1973, pp. 60-71.

units but the whole amount of the two commodities. Therefore, the paradox of value could not be explained. It is said that Adam Smith had a labour theory of value. Adam Smith observes that labour is the real measure of the exchange values of all commodities. According to him, labour embodied in a commodity determines the exchange value of the commodities. Smith goes on to say the it is the *toil and trouble* of acquiring a commodity which entitles it to a value. It appears from the study of *Wealth of Nations* that labour is the source, cause and the measure of exchange value.

When Adam Smith says that labour is the cause of value, he really means by labour, *toil and trouble*. However, *toil and trouble* is not an objective standard measure. Therefore, Adam Smith, considered *disutility* as the common unit of measurement of value. But disutility may be different for different workers for the same type of work. What, then, is the way out? Adam Smith observed that the money value of disutility with reference to a particular work is equalised by competition.

For measuring value, an invariable standard of measurement is required. Adam Smith says that this invariable measure of value is neither gold nor corn nor silver, because the values of commodities go on changing. According to Adam Smith, the invariable measure is the *labour*, because its value remains more or less the same. When the price of a commodity changes, that is a reflection of the market situation and not on the labour content of the commodities. Corn and silver are not invariable in their values, and, therefore, cannot be used as the invariable measure of value for the purpose of inter-temporal and inter-spatial comparison of exchange value.

In order to understand Adam Smith's theory of value, it is necessary to get acquainted with the terms: cause of value, measure of value, labour-embodied concept of value and labour-commanded concept of value. By *cause of value,* we mean the factor which is responsible for value (the source of value). *Measure of value* means the way value is to be computed or measured. *Labour embodied* in a commodity means the amount of labour contained in that commodity. *Labour-commanded concept* means the amount of labour that a particular commodity can command or get in exchange for it in the market. Labour command, needless to say, depends on the market value of a commodity.

Three Models

Adam Smith used three models for the analysis of his theory of value. In the one-sector model, there is only one factor of production (labour). Land is a free gift and capital does not exist. In such an economy, labour embodied in a commodity is the cause of value. Since there is no other factor to measure value, labour alone is the measure of value. If for example, it takes one hour to catch a beaver and two hours to catch a deer then the value of one deer would be equal to the value of two beavers. In a primitive society, where labour is the only factor of production, value is determined by the toil and trouble (disutility). In other words, value is determined by the amount of labour embodied in a commodity. However, in such a society, labour embodied is the same thing as the labour commanded. In a single-sector model, therefore, labour command (= labour embodied) is the measure of value and labour-embodied is also the cause of value, because these two concepts are the same in a primitive economy. The primitive economy is the crude state of society where capital is not used for production. So, in a primitive society, the cause of value is the same as the measure of value, as there is only one factor of production-labour. In a sense, the concept of labour-command is not relevant for one-factor model. The *toil and trouble* theory considers disutility which is a metaphysical concept.

Smith also considered a two-factor model of value. In this case there are two factors: labour and capital. Adam Smith pointed out that capital can be converted into labour in such a case, because capital is stored-up (dead) labour. Thus, in such a case, when capital can be converted into labour, the measure of value is the labour embodied in the commodity. The cause of value in such a case is also labour embodied. This is so because capital element can be converted into labour element. In a three-sector model (or in any multi-sector model), the labour commanded would be different from the labour embodied. The labour-commanded value will include the cost of labour, cost of land and cost of capital. These costs together will be higher than the simple labour-embodied cost. In this case the measure of value will be the labour-commanded measure. And the cause of value would also be the total cost of land(N), labour (L) and capital (C). Wieser, in this connection, has observed that Adam Smith had two theories of value. What he wants to convey is that in a primitive society, Adam Smith's labour-embodied theory of value is applicable whereas in a sophisticated society, the appropriate theory of value is the labour-commanded theory of value. The measures and cause of the different models of Smith's value analysis are given in the following chart:

Adam Smith's Value Models

Nature of Model	Labour Embodied (LE) and Labour-Commanded (LC)	Measure of Value	Cause of Value
One-sector Model (Only Labour)	$L_E = L_C$	$L_E (= L_C)$	L_E
Two-sector Model (Labour-and capital)	$L_E = L_C$ (Capital can be converted into Labour)	L_E	L_E
Three-sector Model (Land, labour and capital)	$L_C > L_E$	L_C	$(L + N + C)$

Although Smith discussed a three-factor cost theory of value, he did not elaborate the determination of factor cost (distribution). The three-factor model of Adam Smith, is based on the concept of natural price or long-run competitive price. In the value analysis of Adam Smith, it is found that really speaking, the labour theory of value is only relevant in a primitive one-sector economy. In a modern economy, where there are many factors of production, the simple labour-embodied theory of value does not apply. Thus, one can say in the modern perspective that Adam Smith did not have any labour theory of value. This is so, because labour-embodied is relevant only in one-factor model and cost of production (labour-commanded) is relevant in a three-factor model which is applicable in modern times.

Adam Smith also speaks of the *market price* and the *natural price*. The market price is the actual price prevailing in the market, which is determined by the forces of demand and supply. If the supply remains constant, an increase in demand can increase the market price, and a decrease in demand can decrease the market price. Similarly, demand remaining the same, an increase in supply will decrease the price, and a decrease in supply will increase the price. The natural price means the long-term price which is exactly equivalent to labour-commanded value of a commodity. The market price may be more than or less than the long-run normal price as shown in the following diagram. However, the market price has a tendency to coincide with the long-run normal price over time. Thus, the market

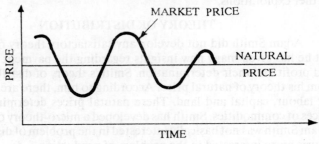

Fig. 4.1

price is a short-run price.

It becomes pretty clear from the analysis of Smith's value theory that Smith never used, not even by implication, the labour-commanded as a cause of value. It is always used as a measure.[4] The concept of toil and trouble has been used by Smith only to establish the validity of labour-commanded measure as the universal invariable measure. Smith also did not use the labour-embodied concept as a measure of value, excepting in the one-sector model.[5] Thus, at the end, it appears from the analysis of Smith's theory of value that labour is not the only source of value nor is it the only determinant of exchange value.[6] There are many other determinants of

4. S. Kaushil, *op.cit,* p. 63.

5. *Ibid.* p. 63.

6. *Ibid,* p. 65.

value such as land and capital. The analysis of Smith's value seems to be more complete in his *Wealth of Nations* than in his *lectures*.[7] It is also clear that Smith had a complete understanding of the interdependence of the commodity and factor markets. Be that as it may, the following points of criticism can be levelled against Smith's theory of value:

1. Smith did not realise the fact that in the absence of distribution theory, the cost of production (labour-command) cannot be known. Hence, his long-run cost of production theory remains to be illogical.

2. For determining the cost of production, it is necessary to show that all factors of production are reducible to some common denominator. He could not clearly show as to how different factors of production can be reduced to labour units.

3. Smith did not have one theory of value, and certainly not the labour theory of value.

4. He says that normal price is determined by the natural price of factors of production. This is question-begging, because it is not known what is a natural price.

5. His primitive economy model is not applicable.

Despite all these, Smith's value analysis has added a new dimension to the labour theory of value and has become a convenient starting point for further explorations.

THEORY OF DISTRIBUTION

Adam Smith did not develop any satisfactory theory of distribution, but he has given many new insights regarding the payment of wages, rent and profit and their determination. Smith's theory of distribution follows from his theory of natural price. According to him, there are natural prices for labour, capital and land. These natural prices determine the natural prices of commodities. Smith has developed a micro-theory of distribution. Adam Smith was not basically interested in the problem of distribution, but he was more interested in the problem of production.

Wage : According to Smith, in a primitive society, wages were determined by the productivity of labour. But in a multi-sector (multi-factor) society, the landlord and the capitalist also share the product of labour. Smith has developed the concept of *wage-fund* theory. The wage-fund provides a theory of wages as well as a theory of capital.[8] In fact, capital accumulation makes it possible to employ labour. The workers are given advances from the wage-fund. The wage-fund provides a rationale for saving, and it also explains wages and profit. The doctrine says that the labourers are dependent on the capitalists for their subsistence. The size of the wage-fund can be increased by the capitalist's saving.

---

7.   *Ibid*, p. 66.
8.   Ekelund and, Hebert, *op.cit.,* p. 68.

Smith has also developed a contractual theory of wages and a subsistence theory of wages. According to Smith, wages cannot go below a minimum level which must be sufficient to maintain the workers. As the size of the wage-fund grows, it can support a large number of labourers. However, when the wage level is higher than subsistence, people feel better off and expand their families so that after some time, the labour market becomes flooded with a large number of new labourers. Under such a situation, the wage level again comes back to the level of subsistence. The size of the wage-fund can explain the size of total wage payment. But the individual or average wage rate is explained by the conditions of demand and supply. By the natural wage, Adam Smith means the subsistence wage. At the subsistence wage, the long-run supply curve of labour becomes perfectly horizontal. However, in the short run, the wage rates may be above or below the long-run equilibrium wage rate. The short-run rate of wage is determined by the forces of demand and supply, and also by contracts. Smith found the possibility of wage differences among different occupations.

Rent : Smith's idea on rent is not well-founded. He was influenced by the physiocratic notion of rent. According to him, the whole of the rent was not due to the investment of capital in land. So, it is found that he also differed from the physiocrats. Smith considers rent as monopoly price. He defined rent as the price paid for the use of land. The sum of annual rent, according to Smith, is usually fixed by a contractual agreement between the landlord and the tenant. Rent is influenced by the location and fertility of land. Smith has also considered rent as a residual payment. It is that part of the annual produce which remains after all the factors of production are paid. Regarding rent-price relation, Smith was not very clear. He regarded rent both as a price-determining factor as well as a price-determined factor. He regarded rent also as gift due to the special natural power of the soil. In connection with rent, Smith has regarded it as a payment for differential advantage, as a reward for the bounty of nature, a monopoly price and a contractual payment. Like the physiocrats, he considered rent as a form of *surplus,* and as an index of social prosperity.

Profit and Interest : Smith did not clearly distinguish between profit and interest. According to him, return on capital was profit, and interest was a part of profit. He says that profit is accumulated by employing the productive workers. He says that profit includes wages for inspection and direction. The value of capital stock regulates profit. Smith considers profit as a remuneration for the risk and uncertainty borne by the capitalist. When a man lends his capital, he receives interest, but when the invests his capital in his own enterprise, he gets profit. The lowest rate of profit must include the compensation for the possible loss. The same is the case with interest. Smith viewed profit as a residual or surplus.

He finds an inverse relationship between profit and wages. When accumulation progresses, profit declines mainly because of two factors: increasing competition among the capitalists and increasing demand for labour leading to higher wages. Smith demonstrated that when the economy makes a transition from progressive to stationary state, profit goes on declining and ultimately, at the level of the stationary state, it becomes zero. Smith considered two theories of interest: real and monetary. An increase in the supply of goods, money remaining constant, will increase the value of money. Profit will fall and interest will decline. Like profit, the rate of interest also falls in the long run. However, he did not consider interest as a separate payment.

Smith's theory of distribution is very much confusing. Smith did not have an integrated theory of distribution. His theory of distribution is slipshod, inconsistent and tainted with physiocratic errors. The originality of Smith's theory of production is conspicuous by its absence in his theory of distribution. According to Gide and Rist, Smith's theory of distribution is the least original of all his works.Smith found a clash of interest between labour and capital in his theory of distribution. Smith said that the interests of labour and capital are opposing: wages and profits move in opposite direction. He advocated a higher share of wages in the national income. However, his theory of distribution is pessimistic where the *Invisible Hand* is inoperative, because it cannot bring harmony of interests among the various classes.

TAXATION

Adam Smith advocated a multiple tax structure. He favoured taxation on all classes of people. He put forward the following four canons of taxation:

(1) The amount of tax should be known and certain.
(2) The taxes should be so determined that they can be collected by the most economical method.
(3) Taxes should be so imposed that people can pay taxes according to their ability.
(4) The taxes should be levied in such a manner in which it is most likely to be convenient to the tax-payers.

Adam Smith considered a progressive system of taxation. He also considered rent as the best source of tax. Tax on land rent is paid by the owner of the land. Tax on land produce is also paid by the landlord. If a tax is levied on a house the incidence falls on both the tenant and the landlord. When a tax is imposed on profit, there is the possibility of shifting the incidence. If a tax is imposed on wages, its incidence is generally shifted to the employer, provided the wage level is at subsistence. A tax on a manufacturing industry will be borne by the consumers of the manufactured articles. In such a case the prices will rise. If a tax is imposed on interest, it is paid by the interest-earner. It should be noted the Smith was against profit taxation. He thought that a tax on profit will discourage investment, output, employment and growth. He was also against taxation on the necessary articles because such a tax will ultimately increase wages. But he recommended taxation on luxury articles.

PUBLIC DEBT

Smith discusses public debt in Book V of *The Wealth of Nations*. He pointed out that for performing the functions of state, the government has to incur some expenditure. To finance these expenditures, the government must have some sources of revenue. The common way of collecting revenue is taxation. However, during an emergency or war, taxation is not enough. Thus, the government has to incur public debt. Public debt is incurred because the government does not follow parsimony. The government can borrow from the public if it has performed its functions efficiently in the past. Whenever the government barrows money, further taxation can be anticipated for the repayment of the debt. Smith did not like this method. He was of the opinion that once public debt is incurred, it gets accumulated. For the repayment of debt, the government imposes taxes during war. This tax continues even during the peace time. Sometimes, the government has to incur new debts in order to pay off the old debts.

Public debt is the transfer of money from the people to the government. According to Adam Smith, public debt does not increase the capital stock of the country, rather it destroys some of the capital of the country. The public debt will have an adverse effect on land and capital which are the two most important sources of revenue. If a tax is imposed on the landlord for the repayment of public debt, the landlords will not be able to make any investment for the improvement of land. In such a case, agriculture of the country will decline. When taxes are imposed on the necessaries of life for the purpose of repayment of public debt, the owners and employers of capital stock find that their revenue goes down, along with rate of return on capital. In such a case, the capital will be shifted to some other country where the return is higher. The industry of the country, in this situation, will necessarily fall, and such a capital outflow will ruin the trade and commerce of the domestic country.

National debt, according to Adam Smith, is never fairly and completely repaid. The practice of repaying the public debt weakens the nation and may ultimately lead to bankruptcy. Many methods can be suggested for the repayment of public debt. Firstly, a popular method is raising the denomination of the coin. However, Adam Smith points out that it will have a very bad consequence. The second method is to adulterate the coin. This operation is also unjust. Thirdly, with the fall in the rate of interest, the funds kept for payment of rate of interest leads to some saving. Out of this saving a *sinking fund* may be created for the payment of public debt. This fund also facilitates the contracting of new debts. When all is said and done, it must be admitted that Smith's idea that public debt is always unproductive does not seem to be valid today. Now-a-days, most governments expand trade and commerce with the help of public debt.

SMITH ON ECONOMIC GROWTH

Smith's *Wealth of Nations* can be regarded as an essay on economic growth. For the purpose of economic growth, Smith gives credit to the principles of division of labour. It is capital accumulation, which keeps the division of labour an on-going process. The main determinants of economic growth are capital accumulation, nature, employment and wealth. The larger the investment of capital the greater is the growth potential of any nation. Capital accumulation enlarges the wage fund which allows the employment of a larger number of productive labour. This increases national output, which when sold, brings larger amount of profit, a part of which can be used for further capital accumulation. In this way, the stock of capital in a country grows over time, supporting more workers and producing more output. There is a chain of causation in the growth process. In the following figure, it is shown that growth starts from the division of labour and continues (clockwise) until the stationary state is reached.[9] The constraint on growth is the increased difficulty of finding out the opportunities of profitable investment outlets, as capital stock enlarges over time.

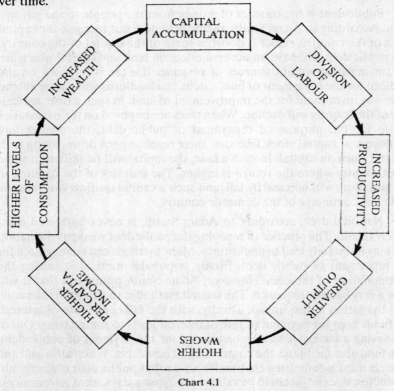

Chart 4.1

---

9.   Ekelund and Hebert, *op.cit.*, p. 74.

Division of labour leads to a number of advantages: increase in skill, reduction in production time, invention of machines and so on. But before division of labour takes place, capital accumulation becomes necessary. This is why, Adam Smith has given much emphasis on saving which is a necessary condition for economic development. If the capital stock increases, it is possible to increase the employment of productive labour. This also results in the production of increased amount of real wealth and revenues. Capital is increased by parsimony and destroyed by prodigality and misconduct. The relationship among capital investment, employment and the generation of surplus is shown in the diagram on below.

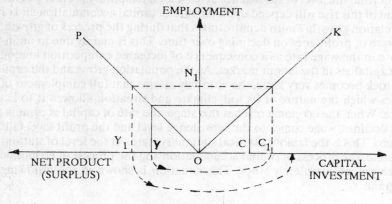

Fig. 4.2

As the diagram shows, as capital investment takes place (*OC*), employment also grows (*ON*) and the net product in the sense of total product minus wage cost (*OY*) also is generated. A greater part of this net product (surplus) is ploughed back as capital investment which further increases employment and surplus. This process goes on for quite some time till the onset of stationary state.

Capital accumulation is very essential for the division of labour. However, according to Smith, it is limited by the extent of market. The division of labour can increase productivity of labour but unless the market is sufficiently large, the total product may not be sold out. In this context, Smith considered the importance of international trade. He clearly appreciated the role that foreign trade played in the economic development of Great Britain.

As development starts, it becomes cumulative. Given the market and capital accumulation, division of labour goes on increasing the level of productivity. The resultant increasing income and the growth of population associated with the growth of income, increases the extent of the market further by increasing the effective demand. This also permits a large amount of saving out of the increased national income. As the market expands and specialisation increases, the ability and the incentive to introduce improvement of art also increase. This type of improvement further leads to specialisation and productivity gains.

In the discussion on economic development, Smith recognizes in a very general way the significance of external economies which lead to a reduction in cost. However, Smith is wise enough to observe that there are limits to growth. This has been explained by Smith in his theory of income distribution. He shows that the wage level in the long run remains at the level of subsistence. During the period of capital accumulation, wages may rise beyond the level of subsistence at least for a temporary period. But the extent of this rise will depend upon the rate of capital accumulation and of population growth. Smith demonstrates that during the process of growth, the rate of profit goes on declining over time. This is mainly due to an increase in the wage rate as a consequence of increased competition among the capitalists in the labour market. As the population grows and the capital stock becomes very large, the economy attains that full complement of riches which the nature of its soil, climate and situation allowed it to acquire. When the economy reaches this stage, the rate of capital accumulation declines, wage comes to the subsistence level and the profit level falls to zero. This is the famous classical stationary state. At the level of stationary state, the process of capital accumulation and the process of economic development completely stops. This situation is shown in the following diagram:

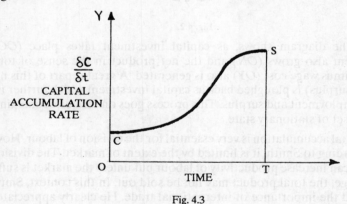

Fig. 4.3

In the above diagram, the economy grown from C to S during the time path, T. After T, stationary state is reached (wage becomes very high, profit level zero and capital accumulation stops). Smith observes that in the stationary state, rent is very high.

Smith's emphasis on capital accumulation in the process of development is the fundamental element which has been followed by many later writers. His concept of stationary state dominated the thinking of the entire classical school. Similarly, his observation that during the process of development, real prices of agricultural commodities rise and. the real prices of manufactured commodities fall, had profoundly influenced the classical economists for a long period of time. Smith was not in favour of governmental interference during the proces of economic growth. He regarded economic development as a gradual and self-perpetuating process.

Smith was of the opinion that productive workers constitute the source of saving potential which is a crucial precondition of economic development. The unproductive workers can be productively absorbed in the economy if capital stock is sufficient. In the Smithian theory of growth, capital accumulation is the prime mover. Accumulation, in fact, is the difference between total production and total consumption. The rate of accumulation is determined by the level of profit which itself is a source from which savings can be made, and it provides inducement to invest. A high rate of capital accumulation will also increase the demand for labour which will not only raise the wage level but will also increase the effective demand. His idea that 'save more and work harder' is the guiding principle for economic development of less developed countries of today. According to V.K.R.V. Rao, the classical theory of development is more relevant to the less developed countries than the Keynesian theory.

Relevance of Wealth of Nations (Growth Theory) to LDCs

Wealth of Nations is an essay on economic growth. It analyses the dynamic forces that determine sustained economic growth. In Adam Smith's analysis, however, allocattive problem occupies a subordinate position. But he demonstrated that in a free market economy, the equilibrium process will lead to an optimum allocation of resources. Free competition, according to Smith, can give rise to a number of advantages. Smith was mainly concerned with the long-run determinants of the rate of growth of social output.

According to Rostow, *The Wealth of Nations* gives a dynamic analysis and policy framework for the underdeveloped countries. Why does production grow over time? Smith says that production grows only due to capital accumulation, and it is the mainspring of all economic progress. Capital accumulation is crucially important for the less-developed countries (LDCs). The basic problem of such countries is the existence of the vicious circle of poverty. This vicious circle can be replaced by a virtuous process of growth by increasing the tempo of capital accumulation. In a less-developed country, as Nurkse observes, balanced growth cannot be achieved owing to the limited market. Smith similarly examined the demand side of the problem by stating that unless the extent of the market is broadened, division of labour cannot be practiced profitably. He also emphasized that capital formation presupposes the willingness and capacity to save. In LDCs, the marginal propensity to save is the crucial determinant of growth. The Smithian prescription of working harder and saving more still holds its sway in backward countries. Smith says that the prospect of development will stimulate an adequate volume of saving.

Smith clearly recognises the fact that the percentage rate of growth of income is an increasing function of saving-income ratio. This seems to be true even today Smith emphasised the importance of wage goods as the basic necessities in the development of an economy. This problem is also relevant in LDCs. To increase the capital stock in such countries, Smith suggested several methods to tax the income of the rentier class, so that a larger amount of surplus may be collected by the government for capital formation. This suggestion is very beneficial to a country like India which has a very skewed income distribution pattern. In terms of Smithian model, one can assign priority to the production of capital goods only if the consumption of luxury goods of some other class is reduced.

Smith shows that agricultural and industrial revolutions go hand in hand. When agriculture is stagnant, industrial development cannot be expected to take place. Smith was of the opinion that agriculture should be developed first and then industrial development can be taken up. This idea is broadly valid in the theory of planning. The expansion of the industrial sector, in many countries is limited by the rate of growth of the agricultural sector. Unless agriculture is developed, sufficient surplus cannot be generated for industrial development. Smith stresses the importance of sectoral balance when he discussed the rural-urban exchanges. He is of the opinion that the gain of one sector does not imply the loss of the other, but still he finds the possibilities of the terms of trade being turned against the rural sector. According to Smith, the corporate spirit and the bargaining power in the countryside are rather weak.

Smith advocates government interference in those areas where the prospect of profit is very low. These areas are the public utilities. Smith's idea here corresponds to our idea of socialist state. Smith maintained that if investment is re-directed from foreign trade to domestic manufacturing and agriculture, the total volume of productive employment may increase.

However, Smith does not assign any dynamic role to the government. In our times, in most of the LDCs, the government has been playing a very crucial role in the drama of development. Smith is concerned not only with the rate of economic development but also with social policy and attitude. He strongly supported public policy programme for capital formation and employment. Be that as it may, his *Wealth of Nations* contains many lessons for the developing countries which are on the path of economic development in our times.

Evaluation

Adam Smith has been able to weave together his own contributions plus those of his predecessors into a systematic and comprehensive treatise. His *Wealth of Nations* is the first full-scale treatise on economics. *The Wealth of Nations* was the groundwork for modern economics. But for this work, the subsequent development of economic thought would have perhaps been impossible. The structure of economic science was firmly set up by him. By reasoning and examples drawn from his observations, Adam Smith persuaded his own generation and intellectually governed the next. It must be admitted that his book did not contain any single idea which was original but it binds together a large number of facts giving new and realistic interpretation. Garner says that Smith has brought a complete revolution in the science of economics. His work was a kind of synthesis. Karl Marx thought that modern economics effectively began with Smith. Smith provided the first paradigm or disciplinary matrix to the science of economics. The *Wealth of Nations* gave a new conceptual system, an ideological slant and a new methodology to economics. The work provided the ruling paradigm for many years to many economists.

DAVID RICARDO (1772-1823)

Ricardian economics, as Schumpeter observes, is difficult to understand, more difficult to interpret and most difficult to make an appraisal. Ricardo was a bird with a different plume. He was a formidable logician and a terribly abstract writer. His *Principles of Political Economy and Taxation* (1817) is written in such an abstract style that on first reading, one cannot feel that the book contains anything understandable. The *Principles of Political Economy and Taxation* is his best known work. Ricardo developed a system of analysis based on abstraction. Ricardo was interested in analysing the problems of political economy rather than in its wealth and progress. He was pre-occupied with the then current problems of England and their solutions. He is one of the greatest representatives of the classical economics and is perhaps one of the most controversial economists of all ages. After Adam Smith, Ricardo is the greatest and most talked-about economist of the classical period. To him, political economy is an enquiry into the laws that determine the division of the produce amongst the classes who are responsible for its production. Ricardo would be remembered for the introduction of a theoretical framework that gave economic thinking a new direction which was unprecedented in the history of economic thought before Ricardo.

NOTE ON METHODOLOGY

Ricardo had a strong analytical mind and logically sound power of thinking. Ricardo built up, so to say, *an engine of analysis*. Blaug has emphasised that Ricardo's appeal rested on his ability to get hold of a wide range of significant problems with a simple analytical model that involved only a few strategic variables which would yield dramatic conclusions of a distinctly practical nature. Ricardo's appeal was both theoretical and practical. He not only provided theory to analyse problems, he has also provided acceptable practical solutions for them. He is still honoured as a great theoretician. Ricardo was educated in the country house rather than in the sophisticated environment of a town. The outcome was that his *Prin-*

ciples turned out to be a very difficult-reading book, both in style and structure.

Ricardo was interested in finding out the laws which govern the distributive shares. His fundamental law of distribution was that wage and profit are inversely related. The methodology which is used by Ricardo is deductive in nature. This is evident in his theory of distribution. Ricardo would build up a theoretical model on the basis of some assumptions which are not very realistic, and would get some useful theoretical conclusions on the basis of deduction. It must be noted, as pointed by Friedman, that the predictive power of a theory is not disturbed even if the assumptions are wrong. This is perhaps applicable in the case of Ricardian analysis.

Ricardo was a very practical man. His analysis was logically perfect but not often empirically true. Ricardo could perfectly combine theory and practice wherever necessary. The methodology which was used by Ricardo however, was abstract in nature. Ricardo had an analytical mind. The analytical method was used by Ricardo in finding out the functional relationship between the involved variables. He also used side by side the empirical method. This is evident in his theory of value, which according to Stigler, is 93% labour theory of value.

Ricardo was concerned with both macro and micro analyses. His relative value analysis is an example of micro analysis. He was also concerned with the macro dynamic behaviour of the crucial variables like wage, rent and profit. His theory of taxation is an example of micro analysis. Ricardo has used macro analysis in his theory of distribution.

Ricardo had a peculiar habit of drawing generalisations without going into the empirical truth of the problem, and of using those generalisations for further studies. This peculiar habit is called the *Ricardian vice*. These vices are present in the writings of Ricardo. One such vice is the dictum that profit depends on the price of wheat.

Ricardo had a very flexible mind. He would very often change his conclusions whenever he came across new facts. This is evident in his theories of value, machinery and so on. However, this is not an altogether unusual habit for a scientific mind. A theory in science is discarded or modified whenever new facts emerge. Ricardo, however, failed to take into account the institutional assumptions. Ricardo studied the class conflict in the economic system and this part of Ricardian economics is liked by Marx.

Ricardo studied economic system as a progressive transformation to a stationary state. The stationary state is a tool of analysis—a conceptual construct. It is not a reality. Be that as it may, Ricardian analysis is not meant for ordinary readers because of the analytical rigour and inexorable logic that characterised his writings. Given the assumptions, Ricardo would set up a simple one-way relation to that in the end, the result would come up as a tautology, and tautologies give rise to Ricardian vices. When all is said and done, it must be admitted that Ricardo was an economist with unparalleled analytical insight.

RICARDO'S VALUE ANALYSIS

Throughout his life, till his last days, Ricardo retained doubts about the adequacy of his theory of value. Ricardo's theory of value contains many Smithian legacies: (1) labour theory of value; (2) natural and market prices; (3) use value and exchange value: and so on.

Ricardo was never satisfied with his value analysis. He has used three types of values: *(i)* Value relevant for scarce commodities; *(ii)* Value relevant for reproducible commodities; and *(iii)* Market value and normal value. This can be conveniently shown in the following chart:

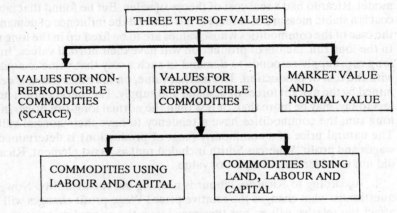

Chart 4.2

Ricardo starts his analysis of value with reference to value in use and value-in-exchange. According to Ricardo, utility is a precondition of value but it is not its explanation. He says that utility is essential if a commodity is to have exchange value; but utility cannot be a measure of value. Commodities possessing utility derive their exchange value from two sources: scarcity and the quantity of labour required to produce them. There are certain commodities which are non reproducible rare commodities, such as Van Gogh's paintings in which case, the supply is fixed and the value is determined by the intensity of demand. These are scarce commodities.

In the case of ordinary reproducible goods, value depends on the amount of labour necessary to produce them. If a commodity is produced by labour and capital, Ricardo would say that since capital can be converted to labour (capital is dead labour or stored-up labour), value would ultimately depend on the labour-content of the commodity. However, if the commodity is produced by the joint effort of land, labour and capital, the value of the commodity will depend on the cost of labour embodied in the commodity plus the cost of labour which represents the cost of capital after conversion of capital into labour. It should be noted that in the Ricardian formulation of value, rent does not enter into price. Therefore, value would be determined by the cost of labour and the cost of capital. But ultimately, it is the cost of labour which matters most. Ricardo shows that labour creates value in capitalist as well as in primitive conditions of production. Ricardo resolves the whole cost of production into labour terms. Ricardo used the labour-embodied theory of value because it leads to the nearest approximation to truth for measuring the relative value.

Ricardo was considering the relative value analysis. In cases where different factors of production are used, Ricardo used the cost of production of the factors production. But he came to the conclusion that labour is still the best single measure of value even in the case of a multi-sector model. Ricardo had a real cost of theory of value. But he found that labour cost is a stable measure of value. He has ignored the influence of demand in the case of the commodities whose values are to be fixed up in the long run. In the long run, factors of production will have their normal values. In the long run, supply responds to demand in such a way that value is equated with the cost of production. The market value, on the other hand, is determined by the market forces of demand and supply. The market price, needless to say, may be more than or less than the normal long-run price. In the long run, the commodities have a tendency to have their normal values. The natural price of a commodity (cost of production) is determined by wages and profit. Whereas Smith included rent as a cost element, Ricardo did not consider rent as a part of value.

According to Ricardo, labour is nothing but the disutility. Now, the question is: what changes the relative price? Wage-profit changes will not affect the relative values, but they may affect the normal price or the absolute price. Even if the relative price is changed as a result of wage-profit change, the effect would be insignificant. When wages rise, some prices will fall relatively, and others will rise. In the Ricardian scheme, rise in wage(W) lowers profit(P) and fall in 'P' lowers the value of capital intensive goods *vis-a-vis* labour-intensive goods. Thus, capital-intensive goods will receive stimulus. Thus, the average period of production is lengthened. This is Hayek's *Ricardo Effect*. All this shows that relative value can be influenced by the changes in the distribution pattern of national income (*i.e.,* in wages and profit).

Ricardo had a flexible mind. He always wanted to make some changes in his labour theory of value. He modified his views regarding the labour theory of value in the third Edition of his *Principles of Political Economy and Taxation*. The following were the modifications introduced in the Third Edition of his *Principles:*

(1) He introduced capital as a factor of production.

(2) He took into account the varying proportion of labour and capital.

(3) He took into account the cost of production.

(4) He introduced labour having varying qualities.

(5) He wanted to have an invariable measure of value.

Ricardo had all along a weakness in favour of labour theory of value. He was of the opinion that the labour theory of value can be valid in spite of the existence of different factors of production, if the following conditions are satisfied:

(i) The ratio of fixed capital to labour remains the same in every type of production.

(ii) All fixed capitals are equally durable.

It should be noted that if the fixed capital-labour ratio differs, value will also change. The higher the capital-labour (C/L) ratio, the higher would be the value, and the lower the C/L ratio, the lower would be the value. Similarly, value may also be different if the fixed capital differs in turn over rates. Thus, it can be clearly seen that Ricardo appreciated the importance of time element in the theory of value much before Marshal Ricardo had to face a number of difficulties connected with the labour theory of value. However, he was able to eliminate the difficulties one by one and demonstrated the fact that ultimately, it is the labour which is a very dominant single factor responsible for value. The problems encountered and the solutions suggested by Ricardo are shown in the following chart:

Problems with Value Theory

Sources of Problems	Problems	Ricardo's Solutions
Labour	(i) Quality difference of labour.	Adjusted by the market forces in course of time.
	(ii) Efficiency differentials of labour	Necessary or customary average labour to be used
	(iii) Differences in kinds of labour	Can be reduced to standard form
Capital	(i) Durability differences (time is taken as a factor)	Time element enters into value.
	(ii) Differences in the ratio of fixed capital and circulating capital (time is taken into account).	Time element enters into value.

After considering the difficulties with respect to capital as a factor in the theory of value, Ricardo wrote to McCulloch that after the best consideration, he thought that there are two main causes which may lead to a change in the relative values of commodities: (i) the relative quantity of labour required to produce the commodities and (ii) the relative time taken to produce the commodities. The question regarding fixed capital comes under the second category. The difficulties with respect to labour qualities, efficiencies and kinds have been solved by Ricardo more or less satisfactorily, as shown in the above chart. However, in spite of taking into account the importance of time element, Ricardo stoutly defended the proposition that it is the quantity of labour which is still the best single measure of value. He clung to the labour-quantity explanation and minimised the importance of his own modifications.

In a multi-sector model, value is determined by the labour cost and profit (capital cost). The difficulty introduced by the element of profit did not pose any real difficulty for Ricardo. He said that profit can be eliminated from the cost of production because it has only a very marginal effect (six to seven per cent) on value. Under perfect competition, the rate of profit also tends to be the same in all industries. Therefore, profit does not pose any real problem. Similarly, labour quality differences can also be eliminated by saying that they do not disturb the value of the same commodity at different time periods. As has been shown earlier, Ricardo pointed out that labour quality variation is already adjusted by the market forces in a free market economy. Therefore, after eliminating all these disturbing factors in the way of labour theory of value, Ricardo peacefully concluded that in the matter of relative value, the real difference is empirically made by the labour-content of the commodity. In this way, owing to overwhelming importance of labour in the matter of value of a commodity, which is found to be empirically valid, Ricardo came to evolve an empirical labour theory of value. In fact, labour cost according to Stigler (*American Economic Review,* 1958), in the Ricardian labour theory of value comes to nearly 93% of the total cost, the rest nearly 7% is accounted for by the profit element. Thus, Stigler rightly christens Ricardian theory of value as 93% labour theory of value. It must be admitted that Phillips in his Phillips curve analysis has also found recently that a large part of the value of commodity is represented by the labour cost (wage). He has calculated it to be more than 80%. In view of this, Ricardian labour theory of value does not seem to be out of tune at a time when the use of fixed capital was not so high as it is now.

Empirical Labour Theory or Analytical Labour Theory?

It appears from the above that Ricardo had an empirical labour theory of value. He did not have any analytical labour theory of value as pointed by Stigler. His theory was not analytical because an analytical theory is invariably based on functional relationship among the involved variables. Ricardo could not show any such analytical relationship of labour alone on any functional basis. Analytically, labour is the only one factor of value; there are many other factors which have equal claim on value. From analytical standpoint, Ricardo based his value on the real costs of labour and capital. But from an empirical standpoint, Ricardo showed that the relative quantities of labour used in the production process are the dominant determinants of relative values. He preferred to base the principles of his deterministic system on a single, dominant variable (*i.e,* labour) instead of a number of less important variables. In the words of Ricardo, "I shall consider all the great variations which take place in the relative value of commodities to be produced by the greater or less quantity of labour which may be required from time to time to produce them."

Ricardo, in the last edition of his Principles, emphasised that labour-embodied is the most practicable measure of value. However, he wrote to McCulloch: "I am not satisfied with the explanation which I have given of the principles which regulate value. I wish a more able pen would undertake it."

Invariable Measure of Value[1]

Ricardo was in search of an invariable measure of value. Needless to say, for properly measuring value, the yardstick of measurement must remain constant (invariable). According to Ricardo, the quantity of labour can serve such an invariable measure of value. It must be noted that the values of commodities would be different under the following two mains situations: *(i)* when the capital-labour ratios are different in different industries; *(ii)* when the wage-profit ratio changes in the economy. Ricardo tried to find out an invariable measure of value which can be applied under all circumstances. Ricardo found his invariable measure from within the causal system of his value analysis. He noted that to be an ideal invariable measure of value, the following conditions must be satisfied:

(1) The commodity which is to be used as an invariable measure must have the average capital labour ratio in its production everywhere.

(2) The same amount of labour produces such a commodity.

(3) The average period of production of such a commodity remains the same everywhere.

Needless to say, there is no commodity in the world which can satisfy the above three conditions. Ricardo selected gold as the standard commodity which can be used for the invariable measure of value. However, he was not completely satisfied with this commodity because it had many problems which will prevent it from becoming an ideal standard measure. Therefore, he had to make the following assumptions:

(1) A year's time is regarded as the average time of production for gold as well as for corn. Thus, in a sense, these two commodities are found to be identical.

(2) It is assumed that all capital is circulating capital and the turnover period of all capital is once a year. The circulating capital is nothing but the wage cost (bill).

(3) Wage is spent on the wage goods.

(4) There is only one type of wage good, i.e. corn.

In this way, Ricardo could generalise his corn model which could be made applicable to the entire economy. So, the national product can either be measured by corn or by gold. No difference will be made because both these commodities are embodying labour.

---

1. M. Blaug, *op. cit.*, pp. 100-105.

Ricardo did not consider Smith's concept of toil and trouble (disutility) as the invariable measure. Ricardo realised that it is impossible to find out a perfect invariable measure of value. But he then wanted to find out the second best commodity which can be used as an invariable measure of value. This commodity was gold. Ricardo in his *Essay on Profits* used corn as the invariable measure. It was more or less satisfactory in a hypothetical one-sector, one-commodity model.[2] This one commodity was corn. So, there was no difficulty. But he soon realised that in a multi-sector model, corn was not a sufficient and perfect invariable measure of value. The *corn measure* was, therefore, discarded by Ricardo. Ricardo, then devised labour content measure for converting and measuring all commodities in terms of the common labour-content units.[3] With this measure, Ricardo could proceed in measuring the behaviour of the relative factor shares in a multi-sector framework.[4] Needless to say, Ricardo could never find out an invariable measure of value, but he always tried to have one. It is indeed impossible to have a standard invariable measure of value free from all defects. Even in our times, economists are constantly hunting to catch this Heffalump of invariable measure of value in the form of a standard commodity. Sraffa's attempt in this directions, as Moore has shown (*Scotish Journal of Political Economy*, 1966), has not been quite a success.

Criticisms

1. Richardo's handling of quality differences of labour is unsatisfactory. He said that wage adjustment in the market will even out the quality differences among labour through the market system. But he was seeking a measure of market value, in the first place. This appears to be a circular type of reasoning.

2. Role of demand is not properly taken into account, excepting in the case of scarce goods.

3. Ricardo has not taken into account depreciation on capital and rate of interest in the matter of commodity values.

4. He has not told as to how capital can be converted into labour.

5. How to convert different types of labour into standard units? Ricardo has not cleared it.

6. According to Ricardo, rent does not enter into price. It is not a cost factor. This is, however, true if land does not have any alternative use. However, as is well-known, land has many alternative uses.

RICARDO EFFECT

Ricardo effect says that if wages rise, the relative prices of goods in the production of which fixed capital or high durability capital enters, will lar-

---

2. S. Kaushil, "The Case of David Ricardo's Value Analysis", *Indian Economic Journal*, October-December, 1972, p. 320.

3. S. Kaushil, *op.cit.*, p. 320.

4. *Ibid.*, p. 321.

gely fall and the relative prices of goods which are produced mainly by labour with less fixed capital or with fixed capital of less durable character, will rise. This proposition is known as *Ricardo Effect*. Simply speaking, if wage level goes up, the cost of labour-intensive goods rises relative to capital-intensive goods. This is *Ricardo Effect*.

In the Ricardian system, it is possible to convert circulating capital into fixed capital. This is evident in his chapter on *Machinery*. But Ricardo brushed aside the manifold relations of substitutions that exist within the universe of production technology. Ricardo was too much given to accepting the sequences on technological data and to neglecting the effect that durabilities have no economic variables.

The Ricardo Effect was used by Hayek in his explanation of business cycle. Hayek says that depression starts by a fall in the inducement to invest. A fall in the inducement to invest is explained by a fall in the rate of profit in the consumer goods industries. It is compatible with the Ricardian proposition that a rise in the real wage will encourage the capitalist to substitute machinery for labour. Conversely, when the real wage goes down, more labour is used instead of machinery. In other words, when the wage level rises, more capital-intensive method of production is used, and when the wage level goes down more labour-intensive method of production is used. Capital-intensive method of production is more round-about than labour-intensive method of production. Thus, the Ricardo Effect ultimately affects the technique of production in a capitalist economy.

According to Hayek, in the later stages of expansion, the real wage rate goes down. This brings about a shift to the less capital intensive method of production and reduces the demand for loanable funds, and initiates a depression. Similarly, at the last stage of depression, the real wage rate begins to rise. This eventually leads to a substitution of capital-intensive method of production; demand for loanable fund increases and it brings about a general revival. Thus, Hayek's theory of trade cycle is based on what is called *Ricardo Effect*. This shows that any change in wage-profit rate necessarily changes the structure of prices and, therefore of value.[5]

Comparison Between Smithian and Ricardian Value Theories

	Smith		Ricardo
1.	Labour is emphasised as the main source of value.	:	Labour is emphaised as the main source of value.
2.	Labour can be converted into capital.	:	Labour can be converted into capital.
3.	Labour is the invariable measure of value (disutility is the standard measure of labour).	:	Money made of gold is an invariable measure (*corn* was used as an invariable measure in Ricardo's *Essays on Profit*). Ricardo ultimately adopted labour-content as the invariable measure

5. M. Blaug, *op.cit.*, pp. 99-100.

	Smith		Ricardo
4	Labour commanded is the invariable measure in advanced economies.	:	Labour-embodied is the invariable measure in the advanced economies.
5.	Relative value is not emphasised.	;	Relative value is emphasised.
6.	Rent enters into price.	:	Rent does not enter into price.

THEORY OF DISTRIBUTION[6]

Ricardo was interested in finding out the principle by which the income of different factors of production can be determined. Ricardo had a macro theory of distribution. According to him, distribution is the principal problem in political economy. His concern with the problem of income distribution arose from his interest in the question of relative share. Ricardo was of the view that as the economy develops, the relative shares of wages, profits and rent will vary.

According to Kaldor, Ricardian theory of distribution is based on two principles: (i) Marginal principle, and (ii) Surplus principle. The marginal principle discusses the share of rent and the surplus principle is applied to the explanation of the division of surplus between wages and profits. In Ricardo's analysis, output of the economy is distributed among three major shares: rent, wages and profits. Rent is the reward for the use of the services of land. It arises due to the law of diminishing returns. Rent is the difference between the product of labour on marginal land and that on the given average land. Wage is a return to labour. Wage is equal to subsistence. Profit is the residual. It is the income which is left after the payment of wages and rent. Ricardo says that the agricultural sector, in a sense, is more fundamental than the industrial sector. The pattern of distribution in the economy must arise from the agricultural sector, first. Rate of profit in the agricultural sector determines the rate of profit in the industrial sector. In the Ricardian system, the employment of labour depends on wage rates. In industry, the money rate of profit depends on the corn rate of profit in the agricultural sector.

Rent is the difference between the average product and the marginal product of labour for any given volume of employment. This is shown with the following diagram:

In the diagram, rent is the difference between AP and MP, that is, the area BDLS. Rent depends on the elasticity of these curves and on the extent of diminishing returns. Marginal

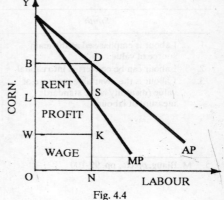

Fig. 4.4

6.   N. Kaldor, *Essays on Value and Distribution*.

productivity of labour is equal to wages and profit. Thus, there is exploitation. The wage level is at the level of subsistence, and is shown by the area ONKW. The wage is determined by the supply price of labour which is constant in terms of corn. At the prevailing wage rate OW, there is an infinitely elastic supply curve of labour. And profit is WKSL area which is a residual. Thus, Ricardo has been successful in finding out the shares of labour, land and capital. Ricardo took the following assumptions: *(i)* Law of diminishing returns; *(ii)* Malthusian theory of population; *(iii)* Perfect competition; and *(iv)* Full employment.

It is pointed out by Ricardo that there is a continuous tendency towards a fall in the rate of profit in the system. Ricardo says that wages and profit are inversely related. This is, in fact, his fundamental theory of distribution. However, it is not necessary that wage has to fall in order to have an increase in profit. Empirically, both may increase at the same time. With economic progress, the money rate of wage goes up, because the subsistence level goes up and, after some time, the profit level will fall, and at the level of stationary state, the profit will be zero, and the rent will be rising.

According to Ricardo, technical progress cannot be so rapid as to suspend the operation of diminishing returns. He had assumed the Malthusian law of population which has been falsified in the western countries. In the advanced countries, the share of wage was constant for a very long period of time. Similar is the case with the share of profit. Ricardo did not take into account the rate of interest and the different capital compositions of different industries. His theory of distribution is based on his theory of value. The Ricardian theory of wages and profit contains a mixture of confusion and achievement. He was not able to show that the fall in profit could not be due to an increase in wage. However, Ricardo's declining rate of profit theory is analytical. Diminishing return was never applied by Ricardo beyond the agricultural sector. His distribution theory, that if wage increases, profit falls, depends on his measure of value. If the value of labour increases, the value on his measure of value. If the value of labour increases, the value of capital falls. But this is not equivalent to saying that an increase in wage will lead to a decrease in profit.

Thus, it is clear that although logically the Ricardian mode of distribution was internally consistent, still the assumptions and the foundation of his analysis were not satisfactory. Ricardo, more often than not, was consistently wrong regarding his theory of distribution.

Criticisms

1. Ricardo has accepted the law of diminishing returns to be valid. But the operation of this law can be halted by technical progress, which Ricardo did not consider.

2. The Malthusian theory of population is also not found to be empirically correct.

3. Ricardo says that rent does not enter into price. This is true only when land has no alternative use. However, Ricardo should have included rent as a cost of production, as Smith did.

4. It is not empirically valid to say that wage and profit go in the opposite direction. Both these can go in the same direction.

5. His theory is a macro theory of distribution. It does not tell us anything as to how individual wage, profit and rent are determined.

Barkai's Criticisms

H. Barkai, in an article published in *Ecnomica,* August 1959, has pointed out that Ricardian theory of distribution is indeterminate.[7] In his theory of distribution, Ricardo has assumed linear productivity function and generalised it for the economy as a whole. The share of rent will rise if the value of elasticity of the average product curve goes on falling as more and more of variable inputs are applied. i.e., if the gap between the AP and MP curves increases. However, the elasticity of the average product curve does not necessarily fall along a production function showing diminishing returns. "Diminishing returns is a necessary but not a sufficient condition of an increase in the rental share."[8] The Ricardian proposition is true if the proportionate rate of change of MP is always greater than that of AP, that is, if the value of elasticity of AP curve falls. However, it can be shown the over a certain range of output, the elasticity of AP curve rises. This is shown in the following diagram:

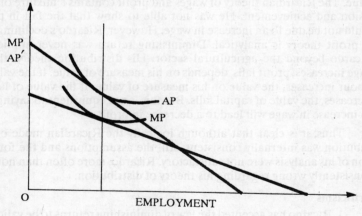

Fig. 4.5

In the diagram the value of elasticity of the AP curve is rising because the proportionate rate of change of MP is less than that of AP. In such a case, the Ricardian prediction that the share of rent rises in the long run is reversed. The fact is the the productivity function is not necessarily linear.

---

7. See, H. Barkai's article in *Economica,* August, 1959.

8. M. Blaug, *op.cit.,* pp. 108-110.

Unless one is going to accept a particular quadratic production function, it must be noted that the rental share is indeterminate. If it is so, then the shares of wages plus profits in the income also become indeterminate.[9] This implies that diminishing return is insufficient as the basis on which Ricardo drew his general theory of distribution.

RICARDIAN THEORY OF RENT

According to Ricardo, rent is a surplus of product on superior quality land. Rent is a payment arising out of the original and indestructible powers of the soil. The differential surplus which is called rent, arises whenever inferior lands are brought into cultivation. Rent arises because good quality land is scarce in supply. Thus, rent is not due to the bounty of nature but due to her niggardliness. According to Ricardo, rent does not enter into price. The market price of any agricultural commodity is equal to the cost of producing it on the marginal land (price is equal to marginal cost). Rent is really a surplus over cost. Rent does not determine the price, but it is determined by the price. When the price is high, the rent is high. Similarly, when the price is low, the rent is low. Rent is a form of unearned income. It does not represent any labour or efforts on the part of the land-owner. Rent arises whenever the market price is higher than the average cost of production. The rent of a plot of land tends to be equal to the difference between its yield and the yield of marginal plot. This is shown in the following diagram:

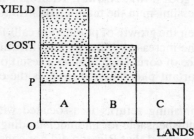

Fig. 4.6

As the diagram shows, the cost of production of 'C' grade land (marginal land) is equal to the yield on that land. OP being the cost of production, the 'C' grade land does not yield any surplus. The cost of production of this land is exactly equal to the value of its output. Therefore, it is a no-rent land. However, 'B' grade land and 'A' grade land generate some surplus over the cost of production, which can be called rent (as shown by the dotted portions). The 'A' grade land is the most fertile land. Therefore, it has the highest surplus or rent. The second best land is 'B'grade land which generates surplus little less than the surplus of 'A' grade land.

---

9. M. Blaug, p. 109.

Ricardo's theory of rent was developed as a protest against the landed aristocracy in England when the *Corn Laws* created a great sensation. Through his rent theory, Ricardo wanted to point out the manner as to how a tenant is exploited by the landlords. It also indicates the impact of technical change, population change and economic progress on landlord-tenant relationship. Ricardo wanted to disprove the physiocratic misconception that bounty of Nature was the cause of rent. He believed that technical improvement in the short run will lower the rent. Therefore, the landlords are not interested in applying technical improvement on land.

Ricardo recognised the conflict of interests of landlords and other classes. It is shown that, by the improvement of land, the landlords are benefited and not the labourers. Rent theory is the reverse of Ricardian theory of value. Rent does not influence value. It is not a cause of value but is its effect.

Ricardo was of the opinion that in the long run, the rent share goes up and the money rate of wage also increases and the share of profit declines. Ricardo has not only shown the possibility of increase of accumulation of unearned income in the hands of the landlords but he has also shown concern over the unproductive nature of the landlord class. Ricardo was much upset by the increasing price and rent during his time in England. However, Ricardo was not correct when he said that the share of rent increases in the long run. History has shown sufficiently clearly that as the society progresses, the share of rent goes down. Anyway, Ricardian framework of the theory of rent shows pessimism in the matter of distribution of income.

Rent appears when the growth of population calls for the cultivation of less fertile lands. The increased difficulty of cultivating the less fertile lands increases the price of corn. High rent, as a result of high price, constituted the most important phenomenon towards the end of eighteenth century in the U.K.

The law of diminishing returns is associated with the Ricardian theory of rent and is indispensable for an understanding of the Ricardian framework. It should be noted that Ricardo did not consider the absolute rent, but he was interested in the differential rent. The exclusion of absolute rent was essential if the theory of value was to remain coherent. Ricardo explained the possibility of rent under certain conditions and also explained its absence under certain other conditions.

Criticisms

The following points of criticism may be levelled against the Ricardian theory of rent:

(i) Ricardo has not defined fertility of land.

(ii) It is not true that people first cultivate the best quality land, and then the second quality land and so on.

(iii) The power of soil may not be indestructible as Ricardo thought.

(iv)   Ricardo's non-rent land is not to be found in actual practice.
(v)   It is not true that rent does not enter into price. Rent as a cost of production does enter into price.
(vi)   According to modern theory, rent is due to the inelasticity of supply, i.e., to the scarcity of superior factors of production.

RICARDO ON MACHINERY AND EMPLOYMENT[10]

Ricardo's views on machinery followed the traditional analysis of Smith, supplemented by Say's Law of Market, to prove the impossibility of technological unemployment. In the first and second editions of his *Principles of Political Economy and Taxation* Ricardo pointed out the price-reducing effect of machinery. He observed that machinery benefits all classes of people, including producers and consumers. Machinery increases per capita output by promoting more and more division of labour. It also moderates the effects of diminishing returns on land. Machinery can led to a number of advantages such as increased profit, increased size of the wage fund and a higher wage level for the workers.

When Ricardo's *Principles* was published in the same year, John Barton wrote a pamphlet: "Conditions of the Labouring Classes of the Society." In this pamphlet, Barton showed that machinery may displace labour and may also increase unemployment of workers. In this way, Barton questioned the favourable effects of machinery. The logic of Barton was accepted by Ricardo, and he accordingly changed his ideas in the Third Edition of his *Principles*. Ricardo admitted that machinery may be injurious to the working class. Subsequently, the whole idea and attitude of Ricardo on machinery underwent a drastic reorientation. Ricardo observed that his mistake arose from the supposition that whenever the net income of the society (profit and rent) increased, its gross income would also increase. He believed that machinery may lower output for a period of time, and thereby it can make more people unemployed. Moreover, if the introduction of machinery is accompanied by the direct conversion of circulating capital into fixed capital, the wage fund may be reduced. Therefore, the means of employing labour is reduced. Ricardo is of the opinion that if machinery is purchased from the wage fund, it will lead to a reduced demand for labour and increase in unemployment. However, if machinery is purchased from out of capitalist saving, employment will not be affected and at the same time, productivity and economic growth would be stimulated.

Knut Wicksell has raised an interesting point in connection with the discussion on Ricardo's machinery question. Wicksell observes that Ricardo's thesis is not theoretically tenable. If machinery increases unemployment, then the wage rate will come down relative to capital expenditure. Therefore, labour-intensive method of production would be profitable. Thus, production would he divided into labour-intensive and

---

10. Lekachman, *History of Economic Ideas.* pp. 170-172.

capital-intensive methods, and the net profit in both methods would be great.[11]

The use of machinery reduces current output below the previous level, while the rate of profit remains the same. As the quantity of wage goods utilised declines, the demand for manufactured articles falls accordingly, and some labour is permanently displaced.

Machinery and labour are in constant and permanent competition with each other. In this competition, the former cannot frequently be employed unless the labour cost rises. If real wages go down, firms try to substitute labour for machinery. *Ricardo effect* under British conditions, where food demand was very high, and cost much labour for its production, implied a constantly rising ratio of capital (machinery) to labour. The demand for labour may continue to increase with an increase in capital, but it may not be in the same proportion as the increase in capital: the ratio would necessarily be a diminishing one.

The introduction of machinery may not always be so bad. If the introduction of machinery leads to technical improvement, capital accumulation and saving may be higher, and the demand for labour may be as high as before. In fact, technical improvement may lead to an improvement in the standard of living of the labourers.

As McCulloch observes, the short-run effects of machinery on output have nothing to do with the benefits of machinery. Ricardo also believed that under certain circumstance, the use of machinery may reduce the gross output. In such case, the price is likely to rise and the demand for labour is likely to go down.

Ricardo never integrated his revised views on machinery with the rest of his analytical framework. The distinction between sudden and gradual change in technology clouds the issue in Ricardian economics. The sudden change in technology may involve an absolute decline in employment, but a gradual change in technology may not involve any technological unemployment. An analysis of *Ricardo Effect* demonstrates that technical progress takes the form of rising capital requirements per unit of labour and of output leading to secular lag in employment behind growth. This process is also known as *capital deepening*. If we want to reabsorb labour, it is necessary to have *capital-widening*, i.e., increase in capital proportionate to output.

Ricardo's discussion in the chapter on machinery opens up the whole series of many unanswered questions about Ricardian economics. His chapter on machinery gives up the assumptions of fixed technical coefficient of production. Ricardo did broach the distinction between innovation due to technical knowledge and innovation due to increased factor price. Ricardo's seminal views on machinery, unfortunately, were not taken

---

11. Knut, Wicksell, *Lectures on Political Economy*, Vol.I, pp. 137-38.

seriously by his followers. The chapter on machinery shows the flexible attitude and flinching mind of Ricardo.

RICARDO-MALTHUS GLUT CONTROVERSY

(For discussion on this topic, see Section on *Malthus. infra*).

RICARDO ON TAXATION

Ricardo defines taxation as a portion of the produce of the land and labour of a country placed at the disposal of the government. Taxation is really a burden. Taxes should be so levied as to fall on every person equally, so that it will interfere as little as possible with the natural equilibrium of the system. Taxes should avoid penalising capital. The additional taxes are to be paid out of increased consumption or by diminishing consumption. The burden of the tax should fall on the revenue (income). However, if unproductive consumption is not diminished or production does not increase, the burden of tax will fall on capital, which is not desirable.

A large portion of his book, *Principles of Political Economy and Taxation*, is concerned with the problems of taxation. Ricardo was more concerned with the analysis of the incidence and effects of taxation. He analysed taxation with reference to political economy. Ricardo was in favour of bringing equity in taxation. In such a case, the economy would be free from disturbances. Ricardo's views can be summed up in the following sentences: When wages are at subsistence, direct taxation either on wages or on the products of labour have to be shifted. These taxes can be shifted to profit. But there is a danger. When profits reduce, the motive for capital accumulation goes down. This will also reduce the size of the wage fund. Thus, taxation on profit may be injurious indirectly to the working class. Sometimes, taxation reduces the rate of capital accumulation and may also possibly reduce the means of the country to employ labour.

Taxation imposed on the transfer of property increases the revenue of the state. This will help the state to maintain unproductive workers at the cost of capital of the people. The capital is helpful for maintaining the productivity of the workers. Taxation on property transfer prevents the national capital from being used most profitably. Let us now discuss some individual taxes and their effects and incidence.

Tax on Wages : This tax will increase the wage level, and will decrease correspondingly the level of profit. This tax is not favoured by Ricardo because it may lead to many undesirable consequences.

Tax on Rent : A tax on rent is shifted by the landlord on to the consumers. Such a tax will discourage the cultivation of land, as a portion of this tax will be on the profits of the landlord.

Tax on Profit : Tax on profit will be shifted to the consumers. The prices of commodities will increase. The landlord will get more rent, but he will have to pay more for purchasing the manufactured articles. If the profit of the farmer is taxed, the price of his raw produce will go up. Ricardo observed that if there is proper regulation, the prices of the produce will come back to their original level.

Tax on Commodities : Tax on commodities will increase the prices of the commodities. The tax imposed on manufactured articles will produce the same effect on wages as tax on food. Such a tax will also affect the foreign trade of a country.

Tax on Luxury : A tax on luxury articles will be shifted to the consumers. This tax will neither increase the wage level nor reduce the profit level. It will only raise the prices of luxury articles.

Tax on Houses : The incidence of this tax will fall on the occupier of the house. This is a type of rent which the tenant has to pay. In the case of this type of tax, the demand for houses will decline, and rent will decline. Thus, ultimately this tax may be paid by the owner of the house.

Tax on Gold : There may be a tax on the total amount of gold in circulation, or a tax on the annual production of gold. The effect of gold tax is to reduce the quantity of gold. Therefore, there would be a rise in the value of gold.

Tax on Raw Materials : Such a tax will increase the cost of production. Thus, prices of the produce will rise. The incidence of this tax will be shifted onto the consumers. This tax will increase the wages of the workers. If the price does not rise as a consequence of this tax, the cultivator on whom this tax is imposed will stop cultivation. Thus, production would be curtailed.

Land Tax : It is applicable to a type of land which yields rent or surplus. It does not apply to the marginal land. If this tax is imposed on all cultivated lands, it will be a tax on the produce, and it will increase the price level of the produce.

One-third of the *Principles of Political Economy and Taxation* is devoted to the discussion on taxation. Ricardo has given a great deal of attention to the discussion on different types of taxes. Ricardo is inclined to treat all taxes as special cases. He, therefore, does not develop a general principle of taxation. He has not given any theoretical formulation for discussing the effects and incidence of taxes. He discussed the temporary effects of taxes (impact) and not the ultimate effects. His discussion on taxation is devoid of any theoretical foundation.

RICARDO'S MONETARY THEORY

Ricardo has also contributed to the understanding of monetary economics. He was concerned with the monetary problems of his time. His idea on currency can be appreciated from his two writings: *(i) Proposal for an Economical and Secure Currency*, and *(ii) High Price of Bullion*. Gustav Cassel drew inspiration for his purchasing power parity from the writings of Ricardo.

Ricardo in his book, *High Price of Bullion*, explained clearly the theory of exchange rate under two conditions. The first condition was with respect to the gold bullion standard and the second was regarding inconvertible paper currency standard. Ricardo said that in the case of gold standard, the exchange rate can be determined by the *Mint Par*, i.e., the gold content of domestic and foreign currency, subject to some upper and lower species points. In the case of incovertible paper currency, exchange rate can be determined by the purchasing power of the two currencies. He pointed out in this connection that "while the circulating medium consists, therefore, of coins undebased or of paper money immediately exchanged for undebased coins, the exchange can never be more above or below the par than the expenses attaining the transportation of precious metals. But when it consists of depreciated paper money, it necessarily will fall according to the degree of depreciation."

Ricardo also had the understanding about the value theory of money. According to him, the value or purchasing power of money depends on velocity, confidence, quantity of money supply and credit policy of the bank. Although Ricardo did not explain the pure quantity theory of money, still he had the understanding of the relation between money supply and price level. Ricardo was writing at a time when the price level went up so much in England. Ricardo anticipated Wicksell in finding out certain suitable remedies for controlling the fluctuations in the price level. Ricardo, like Wicksell, conceived of the effect of the divergence between money rate of interest and natural rate of interest. He observed that such a divergence leads to fluctuating price level. However, Ricardo could not explain how the divergence between the natural rate of interest and the money rate of interest could be the cause of economic fluctuations. But, nonetheless, Ricardo could suggest some very practical measures.

Ricardo's *High Price of Bullion* was concerned with the contemporary inflationary problem of England. During the Napoleonic Wars, there was a hot controversy known as the *Bullionist Controversy*. Ricardo contributed notably to the understanding of this controversy and to its solution. During the period of Napoleonic Wars, the U.K.'s price level went up very high. The paper currency was also not convertible into good at a fixed price on demand. The gold reserve of the Bank of England fell down considerably and the Bank notes depreciated in value. Ricardo blamed the Bank of England for over-issuing currency notes, which was the cause of hyper-inflation. He observed that the price level in England went up because of an increase in the quantity of money in circulation. Ricardo advised that the remedy proposed for all the evils in the currency is that banks should gradually decrease the amount of their notes in circulation until they shall have rendered the remainder of equal value with coins which they represent. In other words, this should be done till the prices of silver and gold bullion are brought to their Mint Par point. In this way, Ricardo contributed to the understanding of the genesis of inflation and to anti-inflationary measures. He was of the opinion that it was the drastic depreciation in the value of currency which was necessarily responsible for the outflow of gold from England.

In his book, *Proposal of Economical and Secure Currency*, Ricardo analysed the factors which were responsible for the determination of value of money. He observed that under competitive conditions of money supply, the value of money will depend on its cost of production. He was of the opinion that a proper control over money supply can maintain the value of money at a level which will neither cause inflation nor cause depression. He was in favour of a paper currency standard but he suggested for the proper regulation and control of the paper money. In this connection, Ricardo suggested the nationalisation of banks. He was in favour of a gold bullion standard in which there would be no gold coins, but the bank notes will be convertible at a fixed rate into gold bars. Ricardo was fully convinced of the superiority of bank notes (paper currency). But he suggested that the circulation of bank notes must be based on 100 per cent gold reserves. Ricardo prescribed state regulation over banking policy. Ricardo strongly recommended the introduction of paper currency because he thought that such a system could lead to convenience., stability and automaticity. Ricardo's plan to nationalise the bank was a clear recognition of the necessity for a well-defined monetary policy by the central bank.

RICARDO ON FOREIGN TRADE

Ricardo's major contribution to the theory of international trade was the introduction of the principle of comparative advantage. Ricardo made a distinction between inter-regional trade and international trade. Like Adam Smith, Ricardo was initially interested in the application of the principle of absolute advantage in the case of international trade. However, later on, he realised that absolute advantage could not properly explain the special situation of international trade between two different countries. Adam Smith, in fact, could not understand the situation where a single country had absolute advantage of producing two commodities in a two-country, two-commodity and one factor (labour) model of trade. Smith did not go into such a complicated special case. Ricardo explored such a situation with minute interest, and the result was the theory of comparative cost.

Ricardo observed that the same theory which could explain inter-regional trade in a country with reference to absolute cost of advantage, could not explain the situation of international trade. Thus, Ricardo explicitly recognised the need for a separate theory of international trade. This separate theory of Ricardo was the theory of comparative cost advantage. According to some people, the theory of comparative advantage was first found out not by Ricardo but by Torrens from whom Ricardo might have borrowed the term. Be that as it may, it was Ricardo who clearly and elaborately explained the theory of comparative advantage as it was made applicable to international trade. Ricardo said that the theory of absolute cost advantage was applicable to the case of inter-regional trade, but for international trade, we had to apply the theory of comparative advantage. The theory of comparative advantage says that a country may need to enter into international trade even if it can produce commodities at the lowest cost. This situation was not realised by Adam smith. Within a nation, trade between two regions requires an absolute cost difference, but a comparative cost difference is a sufficient condition for the existence of international trade.[12] What is to be compared is not really costs but cost ratios of commodities.[13]

Ricardo explained that international trade could be beneficial for both the countries entering into international trade. Foreign trade raised the living standard of the population of the involved countries. Ricardo had a two-commodity, two-country and one factor (labour) model of international trade. Ricardo observed that other things remaining the same, a country would specialise in the production of those commodities and would export those in which it had the maximum comparative cost advantage or minimum comparative disadvantage. Ricardo made the following assumptions for explaining his theory of comparative cost advantage:

(1) There is constant returns to scale.
(2) There is free trade.
(3) Labour is homogeneous.
(4) Labour is perfectly mobile within a country but immobile internationally.
(5) There is perfect competition.
(6) Cost of production is measured in terms of labour only.
(7) Labour is the only one productive factor.

In order to properly understand the theory of comparative cost advantage, it is essential to consider the three types of cost differences: (i) Equal cost advantage; (ii) Absolute cost advantage; and (iii) Comparative cost advantage. They are explained in the following table:

Labour Hours Required to Produce One Unit of Cotton and One Unit of Jute

Country	Equal cost difference (I)			Absolute cost difference (II)			Comparitive cost difference (III)		
	Cotton (C)	Jute (J)	Domestic rate of exchange	Cotton (C)	Jute (J)	Domestic rate of exchange	Cotton (C)	Jute (J)	Domestic rate of exchange
India (I)	10	20	$I_C = 0.5$	20	10	$I_C = 2J$	10	20	$I_C = 0.5J$
Bangladesh (B)	15	30	$I_C = 0.5J$	10	20	$I_C = 0.5J$	15	25	$I_C = 0.6J$

---

12. M. Blaug, *op.cit.*, p. 128.
13. *Ibid*, p. 127.

Country	Equal cost difference (I)	Absolute cost difference (II)	Comparative cost difference (III)
Necessary Conditions :	$\left(\dfrac{C_1}{C_B} = \dfrac{J_I}{J_B}\right)$ $\left(\dfrac{10}{15} = \dfrac{20}{30}\right)$	$\left(\dfrac{C_1}{C_B} > 1 > \dfrac{J_I}{J_B}\right)$ $\left(\dfrac{20}{10} > 1 > \dfrac{10}{20}\right)$	$\left(\dfrac{C_1}{C_B} < \dfrac{J_I}{J_B} < 1\right)$ $\left(\dfrac{10}{15} < \dfrac{20}{25} < 1\right)$

(C and J denote the number of labour hours required to produce one unit of cotton and one unit of jute and subscripts I and B indicate India and Bangladesh.)

Trade Positions : No trade	India will export jute to Bangladesh and Bangladesh will export cotton to India	India will export cotton to Bangladesh and Bangladesh will export jute to India

In the above table, Case I shows equal cost difference between India and Bangladesh ($I_c = 0.5J$). Therefore, the comparative cost ratio is the same for both the countries. Therefore, there is no scope for international trade. The domestic cost ratios are equal.

Case II of the table shows absolute cost difference which will be favourable for both the countries to enter into international trade. In this case, India will have absolute advantage in the production of jute and Bangladesh will have absolute advantage in the production of cotton. Therefore, India will export jute to Bangladesh and Bangladesh will export cotton to India. This is evident if we compare the domestic exchange ratios of the two countries.

Case III of the table shows the comparative cost difference. It will be seen that India has absolute advantage in the production of both cotton and jute. So, apparently, India will not enter into trade with Bangladesh. But Ricardo's comparative cost principle points out that even in this case of comparative advangate of both the commodities, there would be international trade between India and Bangladesh, because of the domestic exchange rate differences in both these countries. It would be more advantageous for India to export cotton to Bangladesh, and it would be more advantageous for Bangladesh to export jute to India. By exporting one unit of cotton to Bangladesh, India can get 0.6 unit of jute, but in the absence of trade, India would have exchanged one unit of cotton with 0.5 unit of jute inside the country. Similarly, by exporting jute (0.6 unit), Bangladesh will get more than one unit of cotton from India which is an advantage for Bangladesh because in Bangladesh, 0.6 unit of jute can fetch only one unit of cotton.

The necessary conditions of equal cost difference, absolute cost difference and comparative cost difference are also given in the table in the form of ratios.

The table shows that comparative cost differences are very crucial for the existence of international trade. It can explain satisfactorily the presence of international trade even in the case of absolute advantage of a single country in the production of both the commodities. Case III clearly shows that India has a comparative advantage in the production of cotton (the domestic exchange rate is $I_c = 0.5j$), and Bangladesh has a comparative advantage of producing nuts (the domestic exchange rate is $I_c = 0.6j$). This is a distinct case and cause of international trade which was revealed by the Ricardian theory of comparative cost advantage, and which was overlooked by Adam Smith. However, in the Ricardian theory of trade, many questions remained un-answered. These questions are:

(i) How could the theory be extended to take into account several countries and several commodities?

(ii) How are the gains of international trade divided among the participating countries?

(iii) What should be the role of money in international trade?

Ricardo could not satisfactorily answer these questions, excepting the last one. Ricardo pointed out that money is not so important in international trade.

Ricardo observed that in the case of free trade, the interests of the country and of the individuals are never inconsistent. They are always compatible. Ricardian theory of trade considers the labour cost theory of value. He did not modify the analysis of international trade on the basis of qualifications that he introduced in the case of labour theory of value. Ricardo presumed that in the case of international trade, commodities produced by unequal quantities of labour are exchanged between the countries. Capital is regarded as an immobile factor of production in the international market.

Ricardo was a perfect free trader. He is well-known for his theory of comparative cost. He demonstrated that balance of trade would be automatically adjusted through the mechanism of rate of exchange. In this connection, his *Mint Par theory* is an important contribution. Ricardo's advocacy for free trade was supported by the following reasons:

(i) Free trade can lead to maximum benefits from territorial division of labour.

(ii) The automatic adjustment mechanism operating through free trade can give guarantee for equilibrium in the balance of trade through changes in the rate of exchange between the two countries.

(ii) Free trade will check the high prices of corn, high rent and lower profit which were existing in England during the time of Ricardo. Ricardo was interested in the import of cheaper food grains from other countries to England. Ricardo was a more staunch supporter of free trade than Adam Smith. Ricardo's confidence in self-adjusting specie flow mechanism strengthened his faith in free trade.

RICARDO ON ECONOMIC GROWTH: IDEAS ON STATIONARY STATE

Ricardo was concerned less with growth and more with income distribution and foreign trade. Ricardo pointed out that unless more land could be brought under cultivation, or unless food could be imported cheaply from abroad, the limits to growth in income will be quickly

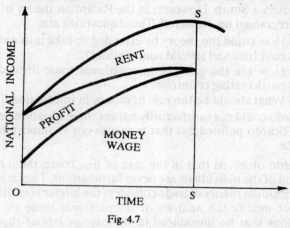

Fig. 4.7

reached. Ricardo believed that growth resulted from capital accumulation. But capital accumulation was a function of profit which depends on wage. Wage level depends on the prices of food grains (wage goods). Food prices depend on the availability of either land or food imports. In a growing economy, as output (income) increases, rent rises for the relatively scarce factors and profits fall for the relatively abundant factors. At the point of stationary state (S point in the diagram), the profit rate becomes zero, rent becomes very high and money wages rise considerbly. The stationary state is shown in the diagram on previous page.

Growth is possible only up to a point but cannot continue because of diminishing return to labour and capital. Land at the margin of cultivation cannot produce enough for feeding the labour at the level of subsistence, even after the profit rate had fallen to zero. All expansion stops. At the level of stationary state, since profit rate is zero, no new investment (new capital accumulation) can take place. According to Ricardo, the logical result of all economic progress is stagnation. The stationary state arises in the following manner.

The average rate of wage is determined by the proportion of fixed and circulating capital (wage fund) to the population. So long as profit is positive, capital stock goes on increasing and the increased demand for labour will also increase, at least, temporarily, the average wage rate. But as the wage rate goes beyond the level of subsistence, family size of the labourers expands and population increases. This necessitates either the import of food or the cultivation of inferior land. This leads to an increase in rent and a fall in profit and ultimately, the stationary state is reached where the rate of profit becomes zero. (See, for a detailed discussion, the section on J.S. Mill in *Chapter 5 infra*).

Evaluation

Ricardo was a pioneering classical economist. He succeeded even more than Smith in isolating the chief categories of the economic system. He was out-and-out an analytical economist. His main purpose was to build up an engine of analysis. The analytical prowess of Ricardo was better than that of Adam Smith. Ricardo was more consistent and logical in his approach. He was the first economist to have used a theoretical, abstract method in the analysis of economic problems. He modified in some important ways some crucial elements of Smithian theories, e.g., value theory, distribution theory, theory of trade and so on. The disintegration of labour theory of value started with Ricardo's immediate followers. Ricardo's emphasis on the distribution of product raised the question of class relation and directed attention to social, political and historical factors in the realm of economic analysis. Ricardo can perhaps be regarded as the first of the socialist economists. He provided the building block for socialist economics, and brought on the surface the question of class conflict in capitalism. Ricardo did not cover many aspects of economic analysis, but his treatment was more rigorous and more scientific.[14]

However, Ricardo had the bad habit of applying very simple abstractions to the solution of practical problems. This habit is regarded by Schumpeter as *Ricardian Vice*. Ricardo dominated the economic thinking for many years in Britain. He was responsible for many social and economic reforms. Marx had a warm praise for Ricardo. In fact, in our times, Russia is re-discovering Ricardo through Marx. It is sometimes said that Marx is Ricardo minus diminishing returns. Ricardo was partly responsible for the invention of marginal analysis.[15] As a matter of fact, Ricardo applied marginal principle in his theory of distribution, as Nicholas Kaldor has observed. Ricardo made positive contributions to the analysis of rent, taxation, monetary economics and foreign trade analysis. Ricardo's analysis connecting the changes in the relative shares of land, labour and capital with the rate of capital accumulation still remains important in modern economic analysis. In this sense, Ricardian economics seems to be alive till today.[16] In the words of Lord Keynes: "Ricardo conquered England as completely as the Holy Inquisition conquered Spain. The completeness of the Ricardian victory is something of a curiosity and mystery"

14. J. Schumpeter, *Economic Doctrine and Method,* p.80.
15. M. Blaug, *op.cit.,* p. 141.
16. *Ibid.,* p. 142.

THOMAS ROBERT MALTHUS (1766-1835)

Malthusian Theory of Population

The pre-Malthusian theory of population was not systematic. Malthus was the first economist to propound a systematic theory of population. Thomas Robert Malthus enunciated his views regarding population in his famous book, *Essay on the Principle of Population as it Affects the Future Improvement of the Society.* This book was the outcome of the discussion between him and his father who agreed with the Utopian vision of his friend, named Godwin. Godwin believed that humanity was on its way to form a society in which disease, melancholy and war could be abolished. Godwin pointed out that a perfect state could be attained if human restraints could be removed. Malthus revolted against the prevailing optimism shared by his father and Godwin.

Malthus retained the Ricardian pre-occupation of land-using bias of economic development. His thesis was, for the first time, an analytical work on population. Here lies the greatness of Malthus. He refuted the optimism of Godwin. He laid the foundation of subsistence theory of wage. His essay on population was published in 1798. However, in the second edition of his *Principle*, he made the following changes:

1. In the second edition of his *Principle*, Malthus took notice of the census of 1801. But he did not examine the situation in England which had been experiencing a population explosion.
2. In the second edition, he emphasised birth and marriage rates and even in the later editions of his *Essay*, he seriously underestimated the fall in the death rate that had taken place.
3. In the second edition, he also took into account the preventive measures for population control, and in later editions, he introduced moral restraint from marriage.
4. The law of diminishing returns was mentioned by Malthus in the second edition of his *Principle.*

Malthus pointed out that population increased at a much more rapid rate than the production of food did, and as such, it was useless to think of human prosperity. The gap between the population growth and the increase in food supply barred the realisation of the vision of prosperity of mankind. He said that the pressure of increasing population on food supply will destroy perfection, and there would be human misery. Malthus was severely criticised as a pessimist. He collected empirical data to support his thesis. Malthus got published the second edition of his book in 1803 when he modified some of his views expressed earlier. But essentially, his original thesis stands.

Influences on Malthus

William Godwin's book which says that the government was to blame for the unhappiness and misfortunes of human beings, impelled Malthus to write his *Essay.*

Malthus was distressed at the prevailing conditions in the U.K., and this led him to propound his theory. In the first half of the 18th century, England was a prosperous agricultural country, but at the end of that century, there were unemployment, famine, misery and distress. There was excessive pressure of population on land. The price levels of essential commodities had more than doubled. Malthus as a thinker wanted to find out the cause of and the solution to this problem. Ireland was then overpopulated and poverty increased with the rapid growth of population till famine turned the country into a hell. Malthus was deeply influenced by the economic conditions of his time and his reaction found expression in his *Essay.*

The Industrial Revolution brought simultaneously both prosperity and poverty. The society was divided into two classes— the haves and have-nots. The workers were exploited by the capitalists' class. Many people were reduced to paupers which moved the sentiment of Malthus. Malthus became necessarily a pessimist.

Godwin in his book, *Enquiry Concerning Political Justice and its Influence on Morals and Happiness,* which was published in 1793, pointed out that human beings themselves were responsible for their sorrows and happiness. He was contemplating a golden age for mankind. Malthus was not prepared to accept the ideas of Godwin, because the ideas went against historical evidence and the personal observation of Malthus.

The ideas of Malthus were much influenced by the writings of Botero, Petty, Sir Walter Raleigh, Sir Mathew Haley, Green, Robert Wallace, Joseph Townsend, Rogers and Smith who showed that a rapidly growing population was the cause of famine and poverty.

Thus, the ideas of Malthus were the product of the circumstances of the time in which Malthus *wrote.*

Assumptions of Malthusian Theory

1. The sexual desire of human beings remains stable. Therefore, the desire to reproduce also remains stable. The development of science and progress of civilization cannot change this desire.

2. There is a direct positive correlation between population growth and standard of living. As the standard of living goes up, the desire to reproduce also increases. Conversely, as the standard of living goes down, the birth rate also goes down.

3. The law of diminishing returns operates in agriculture.

Salient Features of Malthusiann Theory

1. There is a natural sex instinct in human beings which can increase at a very fast rate. Population increases in geometrical progression (1, 2, 4, 8, 16, 32...) and if unchecked, doubles itself every 25 years.

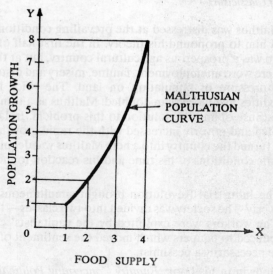

FOOD SUPPLY

Fig. 4.8

3. Population is necessarily limited by the means of subsistence. Human population increases when the means of subsistence increase, unless prevented by some powerful and obvious checks. Malthus also says that, in course of time, the growth of population will out-strip the increase in food output. When food supply runs short, people will starve and there would be misery. Thus, this imbalance can be corrected by checking the growth of population.

4. Since population increases in geometric progression and the food supply in arithmetical progression, population will outrun food supply. As a result of this imbalance, there would be over-population. In the race between population and food supply, the latter would be left much behind. "The power of population is indefinitely greater than the power on the earth to reproduce subsistence for men". The imbalance between the increase in food supply and population growth is shown by the diagram on the previous page.

A summary of Malthusian theory is given in the chart 4.3.

In the diagram, population in geometrical progression in measured on the vertical axis and food supply in arithmetical progression is measured on the horizontal axis. When the food supply is 4, the population growth is 8. Thus, this sort of imbalance raises the population curve upwards.

5. Malthus suggested two types of checks— preventive checks and positive checks. The preventive checks are applied by men to control the birth rate through late marriage, celibacy, moral restraint and foresight. If people fail to check the growth of population by preventive checks, positive checks operate in the form of misery, vice, famine, war, disease, pestilence,

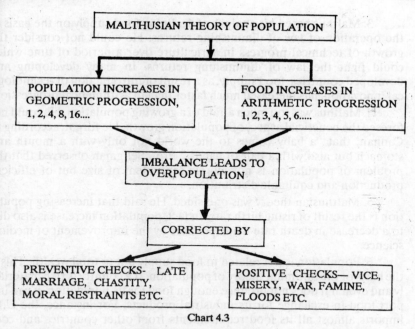

Chart 4.3

floods and other natural calamities which tend to reduce population, and thereby bring a balance between population growth and growth of food supply. According to Malthus, positive checks are crude, and in a civilised society, preventive checks are always in operation. "In proportion as mankind rises above the conditions of the beasts, population is restrained by the fear of want, rather than by want itself." Malthus appealed to his countrymen to adopt preventive checks in order to avoid vice or misery resulting from positive checks. Malthusian theory can be summarised in the form of a chart.

Criticisms

1. The mathematical form of the theory showing the relation between food supply and population growth is not empirically true. In many countries, food supply has increased more than in the arithmetical progression, while population growth has not been in geometrical progression so as to double in 25 years. However, Malthus deleted this mathematical form of relationship in the second edition of his *Essay*.

2. There is no direct positive correlation between the standard of living and population growth. Malthus says that when the standard of living goes up, population simultaneously increases, and when the standard of living goes down, the birth rate falls. This is , however, not empirically true. Biological laws show that when civilization grows, the level of fertility goes down. With a rise in the standard of living, people will desire for still better standard of living. At this stage, many will prefer a car to a baby.

3. Malthus based his analysis of declining food supply on the basis of the operation of law of diminishing returns. He could not consider the growth of technical progress in agriculture over a period of time which could fight the law of diminishing returns. In many developing and developed countries, food supply, as a result of introduction of technological innovation, has increased much faster than in arithmetical progression.

4. Malthus was too much afraid of a growing population. He could not foresee the beneficial aspect of population growth. He forgot, according to Cannan, that "a baby comes to the world not only with a mouth and stomach but also with a pair of hands." Prof. Seligman observed that the problem of population is not merely a problem of size but of efficient production and equitable distribution.

5. Malthusian theory was one-sided. He said that increasing population is the result of rising birth rate. In fact, population increase is also due to a decrease in death rate made possible by the improvement of medical science.

6. Population is not related to food supply but to total wealth. This is the basis of the optimum theory of population. If a country is rich materially and even if it does not produce enough food for its population, it can import food in exchange for its industrial products. For instance, the U.K. imports almost all its food requirements from other countries and concentrates more on the production of industrial output.

7. Empirically, the theory of Malthus is wrong. Population growth is a function of the level of the *per capita* income. When the *per capita* incomes increase rapidly beyond a critical minimum, the fertility rate declines. Dumont has shown in his Social Capillarity Thesis that with an increase in *per capita* income, the desire to have more children to supplement parental income declines. When people are habituated to a high standard of living, it becomes a costly affair to rear a large family.

8. Malthus assumes that the desire to reproduce is stable in human beings. This is not true. Sexual urge depends on age, health, psychological and mental make-up.

9. Malthus does not find any difference between the desire for sex and the desire for children. In actual practice, however, these desires are entirely different. Desire for sex is a natural instinct, whereas the desire for children is a function of religious, social and cultural circumstances. Prof. Huxley has rightly pointed out that "the fertility of human race should be assumed to decline with intellectual and moral development of the human race."

10. Malthus put more emphasis on the moral restraint to control population. Preventive checks do not pertain to moral restraint. He could not visualise the invention of contraceptives and other family planning devices for birth control. Moral restraint alone cannot help control the increase in population.

11. The positive checks, as Malthus said, are not really due to over-population. The natural calamities are not peculiar to overpopulated countries. The natural calamities are also found in underpopulated countries.

12. Malthus placed the law of population outside of man and not in man. Biologically, population cannot increase beyond a certain limit, say, 4 per cent.

13. Rapid population growth is very rare in history. There are many historical instances of stationary or declining population over a long period of time in Egypt, Ceylon, etc.

14. Malthus has been proved to be a false prophet. His theory of population is not applicable to countries for which it was propounded. In advanced western countries, his theory has been disproved. In such countries, the birth rate declined, food supply has increased, and production has outstrripped population growth.

Validity and Applicability of Malthusian Theory

Despite the weaknesses, the Malthusian theory of population cannot be said to be completely wrong. In all living animals, there is a natural instinct to multiply. Malthus was correct in holding the view that if the rapid growth of population is not checked, human prosperity would suffer. Overpopulation today is a fundamental obstacle to economic growth in many underdeveloped countries. In such countries, the Malthusian ghost has reappeared once again. European countries were made wiser by Malthus who had forewarned them of the evils of overpopulation. The use of preventive checks on an extensive scale proves the validity of the Malthusian law. According to Prof. Clark, "Malthusian law has been so frequently criticised as to prove its validity."

Many economists, *e.g.*, Marshall, Taussing, Pigou, Patten, etc., have incorporated the Malthusian law in their theories of production and distribution. Keynes asked, "Is it not the fear of Malthusianism which has created the problem of declining population in France?" Prof. Walker says that "Malthusianism has stood unshattered, impregnable amid all the controversy that has raged around it."

The danger of overpopulation in some countries is so great that the use of restraints and various birth control measures is very strongly recommended. Malthusian theory is important to understand the population behaviors of many countries where the balance of number and food supply is a vital factor. The population question has lost none of its importance today, although it has changed its aspect somewhat. Preventive checks are in full swing in every country, and the problem of effecting regular and universal decline in birth rate has attrracted the attention of responsible people. With the advancement of civilisation, preventive checks, as suggested by Malthus, have to very popular.

The influence of Malthusian doctrine spreads over two-thirds of the world. Almost all the parts of Asia, Africa and South America came under its purview. Positive checks operate, and birth and death rates are very high in these countries. The real aim of population policy is not to avoid starvation but to eradicate poverty so as to increase the *per capita* output in an accelerated way. Thus, the Malthusian theory remains largely valid even today, as it ever had been in the past.

MALTHUS'S THEORY OF GLUT : RICARDO-MALTHUS GLUT CONTROVERSY

Malthus propounded the theory of glut or overproduction as the basis of his analysis of the capitalist economy. He pointed out that in a capitalist economy effective demand can never be sufficient to clear the supply. Malthus wanted to demonstrate, not the possibility of temporary overproduction, but the permanent over production possibility of all commodities. Malthus's basic argument was that without exogenous spending by unproductive consumers, the process of capital accumulation would lead to secular stagnation. However, Malthus did not take into account purely monetary explanations of glut. He said that when saving was increased for the purpose of capital accumulation, effective demand would go down to that extent. Therefore, due to underconsumption, glut or overproduction would be the necessary outcome.

The concept of glut can be diagrammatically explained as below:

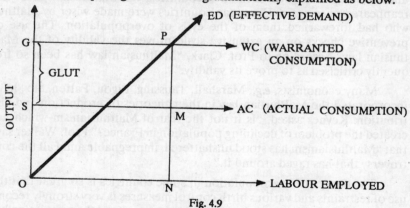

Fig. 4.9

In the diagram above, the varticle axis shows the output produced and the horizontal axis shows the amount of labour employed. Apparently, OG=PN. The demand in the economy is deficient to the extent of PM, because the actual consumption is lower than the warranted (justified) consumption. Hence, there arises the stock of unsold goods or what may be called glut. As the diagram shows, the extent of the glut is GS.

Malthus took the issue with Ricardo and the result is the famous controversy between these two stalwarts of economics on the problem of glut.

Ricardo and J.B.Say pointed out that general overproduction is impossible. Ricardo's conviction was based on Say's law of market which says that "supply creates its own demand." As soon as there is supply, it is demanded. Thus, Say's law of market assumes away general over production. Every demand has a corresponding supply. This law of market was developed by J.B. Say and later on Ricardo took it for granted The debate between Ricardo and Malthus on the possibility of glut would not have created confusion had the two writers made up their minds about the real meaning of Say's law of market. Ricardo took for granted the dogmatic assertion of Say's identity. Malthus, however, failed to challenge Say's law effectively. Ricardo said that in the long run, supply and demand are absolutely tied together and excess of supply over demand is impossible. However, Ricardo thought that there may be an overproduction of specific and single good. But the general overproduction is impossible in the long run.

Ricardo and J.B. Say observed that there should not be an accumulation of capital more than what is actually necessary for the country. A capital which cannot be productively employed is not accumulated: what is currently produced is also currently consumed. Just as there is a balance between demand and supply of ordinary goods, so also there is a balance between supply and demand of capital goods. When accumulation of capital takes place, wages go up. This has two consequences: *(i)* profit level goes down, so that accumulation cannot be sustained for a long time, *(ii)* an increase in the wage level leads to population growth, so that effective demand is increased and sustained. Thus, glut is an impossibility. Of course, during the process of capital accumulation, saving goes up but later on it comes back in the form of increased effective demand. This point of Ricardo is not accepted by Malthus. Ricardo can very well argue that due to accumulation, short-run profit may go up. This may also increase the effective demand. In any way, glut is not possible. Malthus's basic argument, however, stands that too high a propensity to save and invest leads to a reduction in consumption. Ricardo's basic argument is that capital accumulation cannot go on indefinitely unless the capital is productively employed. Thus, there cannot be a general overproduction of goods or of capital.

Ricardo and J.B. Say based their analyses on the following two main assumptions: *(i)* production is for use only and not for profit, *(ii)* money is a medium of exchange and it does not disturb the flow of real economic forces.

However, Malthus found that these assumptions were faulty. Malthus recognised the extreme importance of money in an exchange economy. He said that the store of value function of money disturbed the flow of real economic forces. Secondly, Malthus pointed out that in a capitalist economy, production is not for consumption but for profit. Wages and profit are regarded as the two components of value. Malthus said that all wages are spent and a fall in wages will reduce the volume of effective demand and will create underconsumption in the economy. Wage is an element of cost and an element of demand. If the capitalist pays low wages, the demand for his product will fall. Thus, Malthus says that it is very much possible to have overproduction of goods in a capitalist system due to underconsumption. Malthus said that unless a large class of unproductive consumers is maintained, there will be stagnation in the economy. Such a class of consumers will also reduce unemployment in the economy. Malthus has observed that, sometimes, effective demand may not increase even as a result of any increase in the wage rate, because the workers may prefer leisure to consumption. Thus, consumption remains the same and the glut becomes a possibility.

The power to produce, according to Malthus, may not generate an equal power to consume. Malthusian theory of glut is based on his theory of value. But, unlike Ricardo's invariable measure of value, Malthusian measure is a price deflator. Ricardo remarks that although the propensity to save and investment is very high of the capitalists, still general overproduction cannot become possible. Malthus says the if accumulation is very high, which is very likely in a capitalist economy, production will also be very high, which cannot be immediately consumed. Ricardo observes that the extra production can be consumed by the increased population made possible by a system of increased wage level. Malthus, however, retorts by saying that increased population cannot be brought into the market before some 16-18 years.

Malthus, like Ricardo and J.B. Say, rejected the monetary causes of business cycles. Malthus said that if there is a high rate of saving, it will lead to general overproduction. In such a case, the workers receive less, but rich people's consumption is not increased. However, Ricardo was of the opinion that saving will alleviate rather than aggravate the sufferings of the workers. Malthus's attack on Say's law failed due to his insistence that vanishing investment incentives can be explained mainly by the insufficient consumer's demand. Ricardo argued that saving and investment equality is ensured in the economy in the long run. If sufficient demand is not present in the economy, investment cannot be sustained and is not taken up.

Ricardo showed deficiency in the reasoning of Malthus. Malthus, like the physiocrates, argued that consumption will outstrip production, if proper emphasis is not given to agriculture. However, Ricardo fully emphasised the corrective effect of the classical atutomatic adjustment mechanism (market forces). If saving leads to more and more accumulation unaccompanied by increasing population, then Ricardo says that wages should be higher, but Malthus observes that under such circumstances, wages should be lower. Even if the wage level goes up, Malthus finds the possibility of the same amount of consumption, because of the leisure one of the important points of Ricardo-Malthus glut controversy. However, in the controversy, Ricardo wins over Malthus. It is said that good logic wins over bad logic. Ricardo's use of the Say's law of market was dogmatic and hardly impeccable. But, Ricardo had good logic, given the premises and assumptions of his system.[17]

---

17. M. Blaug, *Economic Theory in Retrospect.* p. 182.

5

Classical Tradition

JEAN BAPTISTE SAY (1767-1852)

J.B.Say has popularised the ideas of Adam Smith, although he has differed from Smith on many counts. He has defined political economy as a
study of the laws which govern wealth. According to Say, political economy
is concerned with production, distribution and consumption of wealth. Say
considers political economy to be a theoretical and descriptive science. Its
function is not to give advice but to analyse, observe and describe. Political
economy is not a pragmatic art. According to Say, political economy is
based on a few fundamental principles which can be helpful for drawing
certain valid conclusions.

Say's book, *Treatise on Political Economy,* contains his ideas on
economics. Say did not subscribe to the Smithian distinction between
productive and unproductive labour. He maintains that the services of
professional people can be regarded as productive because they do possess
exchange value. Say placed more importance on the idea of utility in the
determination of value. According to him, utility is the inherent capacity of
things to satisfy human wants, and value originates from utility. He
criticised Adam Smith for giving too much importance to the cost of
production aspect of value. He broke away from the classical labour theory
of value. However, Say could not find out an equilibrium theory of value.

Say contributed positively to the idea of production. He defined
production as the creation not of matter but of utility. He recognised the
importance of capital and land in production. He laid stress upon the
entrepreneur which was not emphasised by Adam Smith. According to
J.B.Say, value of factors of production was determined from the value of
their products. In fact, entrepreneurs provided an important link between
product market and factor market. Thus,Say introduced the fourth factor
of production, namely, *entrepreneur.* He regarded manufacturing as equally
important as agriculture. He also recognised both the advantages and disadvantages of the process of division of labour. It should be noted that
Smith emphasised only the advantages of division of labour. Say noted that
man does not create but merely transforms matters and that production is
merely the creation of utility. So production has been defined by Say as the
creation of utility.

Say also differed from Smith regarding government interference. Unlike Adam Smith, J.B.Say wanted the government to set up works of public utility in order to create more employment for the unemployed people.

According to J.B.Say, tax should be lighter because otherwise it will make people paupers. Extreme taxation will make the people economically worse-off without enriching the state. However, his view on taxation was not as general as that of Adam Smith.

Be that as it may, J.B.Say made the most notable contribution in developing his theory of market. Let us elaborate this.

SAY'S LAW OF MARKET[1]

The law of market given by J.B.Say states that *supply creates its own demand.* This implies that general overproduction or unemployment cannot take place. Production creates income to the factors of production. This income generates demand for the goods produced. In a barter economy, where goods are exchanged for goods, overproduction is an impossibility. However, for a money economy, it can be said that people make savings. But in the classical system, the rate of interest mechanism could ensure the conversion of saving into investment expenditure to ensure full utilisation of resources.

Say's law can be interpreted both as an *Identity* and as an *Equality.* While the identity cannot be refuted, the equality can be. If money is a veil and acts simply as a unit of account, and is regarded as *neutral,* Say's law can be applied in a money economy. Say's identity can be expressed in the form of *Walras's Law.* Even a money economy can be regarded as a barter economy, when money has no utility of its own, and it is not demanded *per se.* In that case the total value of goods demanded would be identical to the total value of all goods supplied, *i.e.,*

$$\sum_{i=1}^{n} P_i D_i \sum_{i=1}^{n} P_i S_i$$

Thus, excess supply is once again impossible. But when money acts also as a medium of exchange (positive demand for money holding), and when total demand for all goods (n-1) is equal to the total supply of all goods (n-1), Walras's law states that the demand for money (n^{th} commodity) will also be equal to the supply of money:

$$\sum_{i=1}^{n-1} P_i D_i = \sum_{i=1}^{n-1} P_i S_i, \text{ then } D_n = S_n$$

Thus, in the case of money, acting as medium of exchange, Say's identity implies that the money market is always in equilibrium, for supply of goods would mean **or** money for the purchase of other com-

---

1. See, M. Blaug, *op.cit.,* pp. 153-160.

modities, irrespective of the price level. A change in the price level does not disturb the relation between the goods sector and the money sector. Money is neutral.

Say's equality implies that a perfectly competitive economy has an inherent tendency towards full employment via wage-price flexibility (price mechanism). Say's equality assumed the possibility of temporary deficiency in demand. Excess supply in the commodity market implying excess demand for money will bring down general price level which will once again restore equilibrium between demand and supply of commodities, and between demand and supply of money. Thus, with the help of price flexibility, full employment equilibrium can be restored in the economy. The classical *Quantity Theory of Money* suggests, in fact, the same conclusion

Implicit Assumptions of Say's Law

(i) Expansion of market is possible. There is no deficiency of effective demand.

(ii) The govt. does not interfere with the automatic functioning of the economic system.

(iii) Automatic adjustment is possible in the economy.

(iv) Rate of interest is flexible and it can bring about necessary equilibrium between saving and investment.

(v) Labour and capital find their place in the market not by supplanting others, but by offering their own products in exchange.

(vi) Price mechanism is smoothly functioning in the economy.

(vii) All savings are automatically invested.

(viii) There is optimum allocation of resources.

(ix) Perfect competition prevails in the market.

(x) Commodity prices and factor prices are in perfect equilibrium.

(xi) There is free enterprise economy.

(xii) The equilibrium process in the economy is perceived from the long-term perspective.

It should be noted that these assumptions were not explicitly stated by J.B.Say; but these classical assumptions were implicit for the analytical validity of Say's law of market.

Implications of Say's Law

(a) The most important implication of Say's Law is that general overproduction and unemployment are impossible in an economy with price wage flexibility, *laissez faire,* automatic adjustment mechanism, and so on, as were assumed by the classical economists.

(b) Money has no important role to play in the process of development. It is simply a veil and does not disturb the real equilibrium of the system. But money is used simply as a medium of exchange.

(c) According to Pigou, wage rate is an important mechanism to bring about full employment and automatic adjustment in the market which is based on free and perfect competition.

(d) The flexibility of rate of interest is helpful for bringing about an equilibrium between saving and investment which ensures equilibrium in the goods market.

(e) There is no lack of purchasing power or of effective demand. Whenever any output is produced, it also brings an equivalent amount of income so that the output can be purchased. Thus, supply implies demand from the macroeconomic point of view.

(f) So long as there are unemployed resources, it is possible to increase employment and production.

(g) It is possible to pay remuneration to the factors of production from the growing national income which is made possible by the employment of new resources. Therefore, the community would be at an advantage by exploiting the idle resources.

(h) The economic system has a built-in-flexibility and it can work automatically without any external interference. Free economy automatically attains equilibrium at full employment level.

It is interesting to note that J.B.Say has never used the phrase, "Supply creates its own demand," to explain the law of market. The phrase was for the first time used by Keynes to explain Say's law of market. The classical economists never stated that aggregate demand is always equal to aggregate supply irrespective of variations in prices. They also did never say that there cannot be any deviation from full employment. They rather stated that a perfectly competitive economy always tends towards full employment.

What Say's law really conveys is that excess supply of goods or excess demand for money is self-corrected automatically through market forces. If the effective demand for goods is inadequate, prices must fall. This will increase the real value of cash balances (i.e. a positive *real balance effect*) which will increase the purchasing power and effective demand for goods in the economy, because the excess balance will be spent out. This additional demand for goods will eliminate the excess supply of goods in the commodity market. A zero excess supply of goods or a zero excess demand for money will mean the existence of an equilibrium condition in the market. Such an equilibrium condition can also be brought about by the situation of price rise (negative real balance effect) when there is deficient supply of goods or deficient demand for money in the economy. Thus, *supply creates its own demand* not despite price variation but because of price variation. This argument implies that same set of forces influences both absolute and relative price levels. In fact, for each set of relative prices, there is a corresponding set of absolute prices at which the money market would be in equilibrium.

Be that as it may, Keynes observed that a perfectly competitive mature capitalist economy does not automatically tend towards full employment. The attainment of full employment is prevented by many factors, such as, *liquidity trap,* wage-price rigidity, low interest, elasticity of investment and so forth. During the *Depression of Thirties,* Keynes showed that supply automatically could not generate corresponding demand. Keynes postulated that current income is not automatically spent on consumption goods and investment. Income is not spent at a rate at which all the factors of production could be employed. The gap between income and expenditure leads to the deficiency of current effective demands. Thus, market is not automatically cleared and supply cannot fully create its own demand. Thus, Keynes denied the validity of Say's law of market in a capitalist economy. In this regard, the views of Keynes and Marx were similar.

VON THUNEN (1783-1850)

Von Thunen was a German agriculturist. However, he contributed to the development of many aspects of economic science. Thunen was a practical man but he was interested in the development of theoretical economics. His most famous book is *The Isolated State.* He is credited with a number of original contributions and insights. He has developed the concepts of rent, theory of distribution, diminishing returns and so on. His contribution to the theory of location is a pioneering one. He has also developed marginal analysis in a very systematic way.

Method of Analysis

He understood the proper relationship between theory and facts. This is very important for any scientific investigation. Thunen used the classical abstract method of analysis. The method of analysis is deductive in nature. However, he also experimented with the empirical method of study which is evident in his study of location problem. Thunen also utilised what is called the marginal analysis in the development of price and distribution theories. He has used the method of imputation in order to find out the contribution of a factor of production.

Value Analysis

Thunen may be placed under the category of utility theorists. This is because *(i)* he took for granted the existence of a market price and tried to develop his theory of distribution on the basis of this market price; *(ii)* his work on the theory of distribution is more or less in line with the similar work of the utility theorists.[2] In the determination of price, Thunen has emphasised demand and supply. He has tried to explain in this way the equilibrium price. Thunen has distinguished between two types of prices - market price and average price. According to him, the market price seldom equates with the average price. The market price hovers around the average price. He explained the determination of the average price from

---

2. Eric Roll, *History of Economic Thought,* p. 331.

the long-run point of view. His concept of average price seems to be the same as the classical natural price. Thunen observes that the price must cover the cost of production. Price, according to Thunen, should be equal to the marginal cost of the amount required by the society. In his analysis, there is an adjustment process through which the market price becomes equated with the marginal cost.

Theory of Location

Von Thunen considered an imaginary state, circular in geographical form, with a city at the centre. In such a state, all lands are of equal fertility and all labourers are equally productive. Under this situation, it is possible to find out the area of cultivation of each crop and commodity. According to Thunen, locational factor is very important for the analysis of rent and price. He considered the best system of land use. Von Thunen is regarded as the father of location theory of economics.[3] The pattern of land use has been described by him with reference to a series of concentric circles. The important factor in the analysis of land use pattern is the distance from the main city where all goods and services are sold. The land rents and transport costs are the main considerations in the locational decision. Thunen shows that it is better to produce the delicate, perishable and short-lived products near the city. These commodities are fresh vegetables, milk and so on. He has considered the entire problem in terms of transport cost. Since the rent is relatively high in the nearest area of the town, any crop which requires a large amount of labour cannot be produced there. As one goes further away from the city, the land rent goes on declining but the transport cost increases. According to Thunen, the successive regions of land are devoted first to forestry, then crop rotation, then grains, and stock farming respectively.

Thunen was more concerned with the unit of land rather than the unit of product. Suppose, that a given area is designated for wheat production. What should be the boundary beyond which production cannot be economically profitable? Thunen says that the boundary will be at a distance from the city where the net return to the farmer is zero. It should be noted that Thunen's model of location gives the least-cost location for each crop within the isolated state but the model can be generalised for more than two crops and for the industrial sector as well.[4] He was the first economist to study the influence of distance on the economies of agriculture.

Distribution Theory

Von Thunen is famous for his analysis of the theory of distribution on the basis of marginal principle. He says that the wage of the workers should be equal to the value of the marginal product of the workers. The same principle also holds good for other factors of production. Thunen has

---

3. Ekelund and Hebert, *op cit.*, p. 232.
4. Greenhut, *Plant Location in Theory and Practice*, pp. 254-255.

based his analysis on the law of diminishing returns and on the marginal analysis of distribution. He said that employment can be extended up to that point *(ON)* where the marginal productivity of labour becomes equal to the wage level, as shown in following diagram.

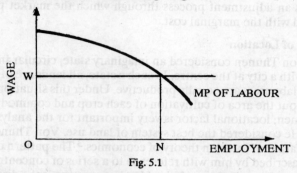

Fig. 5.1

Von Thunen was really worried about the bad economic conditions of the workers. He was in favour of giving more to the workers. His concept of natural wage includes the subsistence plus some amount which is required for maintaining and increasing the efficiency of workers. He was the first economist to view wages as something more than the mere subsistence.[5] He analysed the marginal productivity theory of distribution. He has calculated the natural wage (N_w) as $N_w = \sqrt{AP}$, where A is the subsistence cost, and P is the productivity of labour. He observes that wages of workers remain low because the capital gets more than what it should get from the total production. He considered two types of labourers, one producing capital goods and the other producing consumption goods. He concludes that through competition, wages in these two types of professions will get equalised.

According to von Thunen, rent is a sort of surplus. Rent is that portion of landlord's income which exists after the payment of interest. As is shown earlier, in the determination of rent, locational factors become very important in the analysis of Thunen. "The price of corn must be so high that the rent of that farm whose cost of production and delivery is highest, whose cultivation is at the same time necessary for the satisfaction of the demand for grain, shall not fall below zero."[6] A very crucial factor determining rent is the distance. Unlike Ricardo, Thunen has given more importance to the situation of land rather than to fertility. In his analysis, rent is not a fixed amount; it varies with the rate of interest and the price level.

Thunen applied the marginal principle in the determination of interest, *i.e.* interest would be equal to the value of the marginal productivity of capital. He, however, recognised the diminishing marginal productivity of capital in which case the rate of interest will go on diminishing. Thus, interest is determined by the marginal productivity of capital. He was in fact the

---

5.   A.Gray, *The Development of Economic Doctrine*, p. 246.
6.   *Ibid.*, p. 242.

first economist to have applied the law of diminishing returns to all factors of production.

State and Trade

Initially, Thunen was the supporter of free trade, but subsequently he changed his idea when he observed that free trade is not an absolute good. He said that under some circumstances, protection may be necessary for the growth of national industries. He suggested increasing role of state for introducing a number of necessary social reforms which are necessary for the economic progress of a nation. He said that regarding trade, both the national and the cosmopolitan views are valid in economics and that there is no contradiction between these two views.

Evaluation

Von Thunen can be regarded truly as one of the real founders of marginal analysis. He realised that the total product is maximised only when resources are allocated equimarginally. He was also the first economist to have worked out a scheme of natural wage and to have realised the importance of giving the workers a wage higher than the subsistence cost. He was also one of the first to introduce calculus in analysing economic problems. Mark Blaug has rightly called him the "first truly modern economist."[7]

HENRY C. CAREY (1793-1879)

Carey was an American political economist. He was initially a follower of Classicism. However, later on, he deviated from the Classical system, and became a critic of the Classical system. He witnessed the growth of American economy in the perspective of which he analysed his own views on economics. He was an optimist, and believed in the perfect harmony of nature and among different classes of society. His two most important publications are: *Principles of Political Economy* and *Principles of Social Science*.

His method of analysis is a mixture of deduction and induction. He also used mathematical technique of analysis. He believed in the efficacy of the universal law of nature which eliminated all conflicts between classes.

Value Analysis

Carey regarded value analysis as the centre of the system of harmony in a society. Value is determined by the amount of labour necessary for the production of a commodity at present and for the reproduction of the commodity in future. Value is caused by the obstacles to production. In a sense, it measures disutility in production. In fact, utility really implies man's power over nature. Value is determined by the labour cost of its replacement. When labour productivity increases, labour cost of production falls. This phenomenon of decreasing labour cost of production gives rise to the decreasing value of commodities. Carey used labour quantity theory of

7. M. Blaug, *Economic Theory in Retrospect,* pp. 321, 319.

value because he thought that labour is the basic cause of value. Thus, articles will be exchanged in proportion to the labour required for the production of these commodities. Since the cost of production goes on declining over time, commodities become cheaper in the long run.

Distribution

According to Carey, Ricardo's theory of rent is not correct. It is not true, as Ricardo thought, that the first-class lands are cultivated first and the second-class lands next. He, on the other hand, observes that bad land is cultivated first because these lands are light, sandy and easier to be cultivated. As the population increases, better quality lands are gradually brought under cultivation. Thus, with the progress of society, labour becomes more productive and wealth goes on increasing. In this way, people can experience the law of increasing returns in agriculture. With economic progress, agricultural rent will gradually disappear.[8] He argued that the Ricardian theory of rent is not applicable, at least, to the American economy.

Carey thought that land and capital are identical in nature. Land, in fact, is like a machinery, and a farmer is like a capitalist. In this scheme of distribution proposed by Carey, there is no clash of interest among the different classes of society. As the society progresses, the incomes of all the factors of production go on increasing. Wages increase both absolutely and relatively to rent and profit. The share of rent increases absolutely but it falls as a proportion of national income. The same is the case with the rate of interest. According to Carey, labour and capital are the two distinct factors of production. Combined together, these two factors can produce more than what one single factor is able to produce. Capital is nothing but dead labour. This is a classical notion. The interests of capital and labour are not necessarily contradictory. In fact, there is harmony of interest between labour and capital. He opposed the socialists by saying that over time, the share of wages goes on increasing.

Population

Carey considered the Malthusian theory of population as an incorrect statement of facts. According to him, as evident in America, food supply was increasing faster than the rate of growth of population. America was in need of a large number of people for the exploitation of its resources. Carey like Malthus was not a pessimist. He argued that the rate of growth of population will lead to a better division of labour, more urbanisation and higher output *per capita*.[9] According to Carey, as the human beings advance intellectually, the rate of growth of population is bound to slow down. The rate of reproduction tends to fall as we move from a lower to a higher level of life. "Each successive addition to the population brings a consumer and a producer." Food is abundant when the population increases. Carey does not consider the Malthusian statement that population

8.   Gide and Rist, *op.cit.,* p. 426.
9.   Haney, *History of Economic Thought,* p. 325.

increases in geometrical progression, and food supply increases in arithmetical progression to be true. Carey believes that increase in population necessarily implies increase in wealth. However, Carey foresaw the possibility of overpopulation in the very long run. But he said that this should not disturb us at the moment.

Protection

Initially, Carey, like Adam Smith, was a supporter of free trade ; but later on, he advocated protectionism for the American economy. According to him, protection will lead to a number of advantages, such as feeding the home market, encouraging competition for the purchase of labour, giving incentive for production, reduction in distance, and so on. Carey can be regarded as an exponent of protection. He was first of the nationalists and had a number of followers.

NASSAU WILLIAM SENIOR (1790-1864)

Nassau Senior is one of the important representatives of the Classical school of political economy. He not only supported some of the basic tenets of Classical economics but at times he also made some important modifications. He is important not only for his criticism against Ricardian economics, but also for his original contributions. His most important work is *An outline of the Science of Political Economy* which was published in 1836. Senior revised the book in 1850.

Scope and Method of Political Economy

According to Senior, political economy is the "Science which treats of the nature, the production, and the distribution of wealth." One can include government while broadly defining political economy, but that type of definition remains unscientific. Economics is a positive science, according to Senior. It must not include any normative value judgement. Economics is not concerned with happiness ; it is concerned with wealth. Economics has to be an exercise in reasoning. It must not be a fact-gathering science. Political economics is neither to advocate nor to recommend.[10] Senior's method of study of economics was deductive rather than inductive. Political economy should concern itself with the following four basic postulates:

(i) Each man desires to obtain additional wealth with little sacrifice.

(ii) Population is limited only by the fear of deficiency of food articles.

(iii) The powers of factors of production including labour may be indefinitely increased by using their products as the means for further production.

(iv) Skill remaining the same, addition of more and more labour on land will increase the production at a diminishing rate.

---

10. Nassau Senior, *An Outline of political Economy,* p. 2.

The basic principle of Senior's analysis is the economic rationality of human beings. He accepted the Malthusian law of population and the Ricardian law of diminishing returns. Senior made the law of decreasing returns more exact by adding that technology remains constant. Whereas he proposed the law of diminishing returns in agriculture, he visualised the law of increasing returns in industry.

Value and Cost

Senior modified Ricardian labour theory of value. He accepted the theory of utility in the value analysis. He also questioned the classical assumptions of free competition. Walras correctly credited Senior for the notion of marginal utility.[11] Senior recognised the importance of relative utility and also the interdependence between relative utility and relative scarcity in the determination of value. There are, according to Senior, three important determinants of value. These are: transferability, relative scarcity and utility. By utility he meant the want-satisfying power of a commodity. He came very close to the statement of the law of diminishing marginal utility. But he could not explicitly state the law formally. Senior recognised the pivotal importance of demand factors (utility) and the supply factor (scarcity) in the determination of value. According to him, value is that "quality in anything which fits it to be given and received in exchange, or in other words, to be lent or sold, hired or purchased." Senior unlocked the classical paradox of value. He maintained that of the three important determinants of value, the limitation in supply remains the most important factor. Senior introduced the cost of production theory of value and the demand and supply theory of value side by side. Thus, in a sense, he altered the Ricardian theory of value. He thought that value arises because the supply in the market is less than the demand. Cost production determines price only when there is free competition. Cost-determined price is in fact the long-run price which may deviate from the short-run market price.

Monopoly

There is always not the existence of free competition. There may be the existence of monopoly. This is very crucial for the analysis of supply in relation to demand for the determination of price. According to Senior, there are four types of monopoly in a market:

1. A monopoly in which the producer does not have exclusive producing power but in which he has exclusive facilities (as in the case of a patent).

2. A monopoly in which the monopolist is the only producer but because of the uniqueness of his product, he cannot increase the supply (as in the case of certain French vineyards).

3. A monopoly which can increase his product indefinitely (as in the case of book publishing).

4. A monopoly in which the monopolist is not only the producer but has peculiar facilities which ultimately will disappear as output increases.

---

11. Ekelund and Hebert, *A History of Economic Theory and Method*, p. 98.

The above types of monopolies affect the supply in some way or the other. In the first case, market price is very close to the cost of production. In the second case, supply is inelastic. There is no upper limit in pricing save the limit set by demand. The lower limit in price is the cost of production. The third case is the same as the first excepting that there is no upper limit to price other than the one imposed by demand. The fourth case is very general in nature. Senior regarded land rent as a monopoly rent. Before the analysis on monopoly by Cournot and Senior, the theory of monopoly was a very loose theory, particularly before 1938. An analysis of the above four cases of monopoly reveals, that in some cases, cost of production is the controlling factor, whereas in some other cases, demand is the controlling factor of price, but the two are always interdependent.[12]

Capital and Interest

Senior extended Ricardo's real-cost analysis by adding the cost of *abstinence* to the cost of labour. Senior, like the Austrian theory, believes that roundabout method of production is more productive than the direct method of production. However, for roundabout method, some sacrifice is necessary. Abstinence is a type of sacrifice. Abstinence meant to Senior, refraining from current consumption in order to accumulate capital, or intermediate goods. He says that technology and capital can indefinitely increase the products. Abstinence from consumption requires some reward. This reward is the interest or the cost of waiting, which is essential for capital accumulation. Senior considers interest as a return to abstinence. This is indeed the most original contribution of Senior to economics, which was soon absorbed in the mainstream of economics. His idea regarding the abstinence theory of rate of interest surpassed Smith, Malthus and Ricardo's. The idea stood as the most complete in British economics until the time of Jevons.[13]

In the calculation of cost of production, Senior included the cost of labour and cost of abstinence (interest). However, unfortunately, Senior did not give the details about the determinants of abstinence. Senior had the belief that capital is the result of abstinence. The income of the capitalist is regarded by Senior as a price necessary to pay in order to induce people to abstain from present consumption.

Distribution

Senior thought that wages depend on the wage fund. According to him, wages depend on "the extent of the fund for the maintenance of the labourers, compared with the number of labourers to be maintained." The rate of interest, according to Senior, is the reward for abstinence. Senior could not develop a cost of production theory of wages.

---

12. Ekelund and Hebert, *op.cit.*, p. 102.

13. *Ibid.*, p. 103.

Miscellaneous Contributions

Senior explained the concept of money. According to him, money is a substitute for credit. It is a medium of exchange. He regarded gold and silver as important metals for coinage. Money should have different qualities like portability, divisibility, durability and stability. He was in favour of a well-maintained paper currency system. The value of money depends on the cost of production and not so much on its quality or velocity of circulation. The demand for money depends on the factors that influence the money value of income.

Senior was not a strong advocate of *laissez-faire*. He was in favour of governmental action and help so long as they do not interfere with the free working of economic laws.[14]

Evaluation

Senior was a great economist of the Classical tradition. He was responsible for putting economics on a scientific track. He was one of the first to consider capital as the legitimate partner of value. He was one of the first again to give a systematic analysis on monopoly. All his contributions, though essentially modifications of Ricardo's, were extremely important modifications for the future development of economics.[15]

JOHN STUART MILL (1809-1873)

John Stuart Mill heralds the end of one epoch and the beginning of another in the development of Classical political economy. His work is transitional in nature. Mill's best known work is his *Principles of Political Economy*. He is recognised for his restatement of classicism. He defined political economy as a science dealing with the nature of wealth and the laws of its production and distribution. During his time, Classical economics rose to its apex and had also experienced its downfall.

Agreement and Disagreement with the Classical Writers

Mill both agreed and disagreed with the Classical writers on many important points. The following are the points of agreement:

(i)   Mill recognised the Classical theory of self-interest. It recognised the individual motive of having maximum pleasure and minimum pain.

(ii) Mill agreed broadly with Classical law of free competition and freedom of action.

(iii) Mill broadly agreed with the Classical theory of value-the demand and supply approach.

(iv) Mill was supporting the Classical theory of free trade with some modifications.

(v)   Mill accepted the validity of the Malthusian theory of population.

14. Eric Roll, *History of Economic Thought,* p. 353.
15. Ekelund and Hebert, *op.cit.,* p. 103.

(vi) Mill was a champion of liberty and liberalism.

(vii) Mill agreed with the Ricardian theory of rent.

(viii) Mill also accepted, up to a certain point, the validity of the Classical *wage fund* doctrine.

(ix) Mill also agreed to the ultimate end of economic progress in terms of stationary state.

However, the following are the points of disagreement between Mill and the Classical economists:

(1) Unlike the Classical economists, Mill thought that economic laws are neither permanent nor universal in character. The laws of distribution may be changed by human beings.

(2) Whereas the Classical economists considered political economy as a science of wealth, Mill considered it both as a science as well as an art. He also favoured inductive or empirical analyses.

(3) The Classical economists analysed economic phenomena in terms of static conditions, but Mill introduced dynamic analyses.

(4) Mill was not completely against the intervention of the government. He prescribed government intervention in certain cases.

(5) In the field of international trade, Mill suggested protection for domestic infant industries.

(6) Mill was also of the view that the wage fund doctrine is not fully correct. In fact, wages can be increased by the trade unions.

(7) Mill, unlike the Classicals, considered stationary state as a state of bliss and optimism.

Laws of Production and Distribution

Mill made a distinction between the laws of production and the laws of distribution. The laws of production partake of the character of physical truths. The laws of production are certain and sure laws. They cannot be changed by human volition. There is nothing optional or arbitrary about them. On the other hand, the laws of distribution can be changed by human beings through legislation or otherwise. The distribution of wealth and income depends, on the custom, tradition and laws of society.[16] Obviously, therefore, Mill advocated the plausibility of changes in the laws of distribution. But he said that the laws of production cannot be altered. The things once there, mankind cannot do away with them as they like. Mill pleaded for more and more competition in the spheres of production and exchange. He advocated many important types of reforms leading to the better distribution of income and wealth.

---

16. J.S.Mill, *Principles of Political Economy,* pp. 199-200.

By making this type of distinction between the laws of production and the laws of distribution, Mill observes that the functional distribution of income among the various classes of the society is influenced by the distribution of property, which itself is the outcome of historical change.[17] The distinction between the two kinds of laws is, however, not tenable. This is so because distinction implies independence of the forces of income generation and income distribution. Whereas, the laws of production are positive laws, the laws of distribution are normative laws. The former laws explain *what is* and the latter laws explain *what should be*. Needless to say, much depends on how such a distinction is actually applied in different cases. Mill's explanation suggests that distribution has nothing to do with the process of valuation.[18] This notion, however, is not correct. Production is not a matter of historical accident. In fact, it is very difficult to analyse the determination of relative prices in the product market on the basis of a given pattern of income distribution. Similarly, it is almost impossible to precisely determine the factor pricing like rent, wage, interest and so on in the factor market alone. Factor prices and product prices are simultaneously determined in both the markets.

The Classical people made a mistake by incorporating a dichotomy in the pricing process. According to the Classical economists, relative price is determined in the product market and the absolute price is determined in the money market. These two markets and these two prices, according to them, are independent of each other. This is precisely wrong. Patinkin showed that the Classical dichotomy was wrong. Patinkin demonstrated that markets are interdependent: they cannot be separated out. Everything in the economy depends on everything in the spirit of general equilibrium. Similarly, the factor prices and product prices are to be simultaneously determined through a process of general equilibrium which may use the technique of *Tatonnement* (trial and error method). Unfortunately, this important truth was not realised by J.S.Mill. Like many Classical economists, Mill could not distinguish the pricing problem with the given resources from feedback effect of the growth of these resources on prices.[19] He also could not explicitly explain the implications of short-run and long-run differences in the pricing problem. All this stood in the way of a meaningful presentation of value and distribution theories in a logical sequence. He never attempted a general equilibrium analysis.

Production

According to Mill, there are two important agents of production-labour and natural objects. Labour may be physical or mental. The natural objects are those which exist or grow spontaneously. Labour is always and solely employed in putting objects in motion. Goods are produced both by labour and nature. There are three kinds of utility produced by labour:

---

17. M.Blaug, *Economic Theory in Retrospect*, p. 188.
18. *Loc.cit.*
19. *Ibid.*, p. 189.

(i) Utilities fixed and embodied in outward objects. Labour is employed in creating external material things ; *(ii)* Labour may be employed for making human beings more useful and serviceable: and *(iii)* Labour may be used for producing direct utility. In this case, utility may not be fixed or embodied in any object.

Mill analysed the Classical theory of *productive and unproductive labour.* Unproductive labour is that labour which does not create any material wealth. Productive labour creates material wealth. However, Mill included more occupations and professions under productive labour as compared to Smith.

In addition to labour and natural agent, Mill also recognised the importance of capital as a factor of production. He advanced the following four fundamental features of capital:

(1) Capital is the result of saving.
(2) Industrial development is limited by capital.
(3) Capital is saved for the purpose of productive consumption.
(4) Capital is supported and employed by productive labour.

A circulating capital is only used once in the production process. Mill has recognised in the analysis of production, the role of the law of diminishing returns in agriculture. Under such a situation, the danger of overpopulation becomes serious. Mill also mentioned a number of advantages of division of labour. Like Smith, he also realised that division of labour is limited by the extent of market. He also observed that when, the market extends, labourers become more productive.

Distribution

Mill considered a threefold division of product among labour, land and capital. As has been pointed out earlier, the laws of distribution can be changed by human beings.

Wage : Mill observes that wages depend on demand and supply of labour, or are regulated by competition or custom. Wages also depend on the relative amount of capital and population. Wage is regulated by the *wage fund.* Wage level can be increased, either by decreasing the number of labourers or by increasing capital formation so that the size of the wage fund increases. Mill, however, later on abandoned the wage fund doctrine. He pointed out in an article in the *Fortnightly Review* that wages can very well be increased by the actions of the trade unions. It may be argued that Mill was never serious about the efficacy of the rigid wage fund theory.

Profit : Profit is the share of the capitalist. This is a remuneration for abstinence. Mill was not able to separate out profit and interest. He simply pointed out that profit is greater than interest. Profit arises from the fact that the labourers are given less than their products. The rate of profit as a return to capital must minimum. But the rate of profit, as Ricardo also realised, is also dependent on the wage rate. When the wage rate is very low, the profit rate is very high. Profit includes wages for superintendence and indemnity for risk. Mill thought that temporary wages are determined by the forces of demand and supply, but long-run natural wages are determined by the cost of maintaining the workers.

Rent : Mill accepted the Ricardian theory of rent. Rent is the excess of return over the worst land in cultivation enjoyed by the better lands. It is the result of monopoly on land. It is a payment for the superior power over that of the other areas for which no rent is paid. Rent does not enter into price.

From the above discussion, it becomes clear that Mill had been following the main Classical theory of distribution with very little modification. The modification is particularly noticeable in his *wage fund theory*.

Value Analysis

According to Mill, value is an important subject of political economy. Value can be used in the sense of value-in-exchange and also value-in-use. What is more important is the value-in-exchange. He emphasised the fact that there may be a fluctuation in the general price level but there cannot be any fluctuation in the value of a commodity. The changes in the values of commodities can only be with reference to the exchange value of another commodity. A commodity can have value only when it can satisfy human wants. There are three types of goods: *(i)* Goods having perfect inelasticity of supply or absolutely limited in supply; *(ii)* goods which are perfectly elastic in supply; and *(iii)* goods which are relatively elastic in supply or which can be increased only with the increase in cost. These types of goods and their valuation processes are shown below[20]:

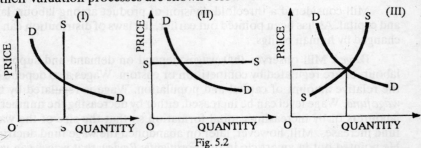

Fig. 5.2

The value of the goods of first category is determined mainly by the forces of demand and supply. In the second case of goods, the value is determined by the cost of production, and in the third case, value is determined by the cost of production in the most unfavourable circumstances. Mill is quite sure between the demand-determined price of category first type of goods, and supply-determined price of the second class of goods, but he fails to point out that the law of demand and supply is perfectly general and is applicable in both cases (Case Third).[21]

---

20. M.Blaug, *Economic Theory in Retrospect*, p. 205.
21. *Loc. cit.*

The law of demand has been explained by Mill in the sense that price varies directly with demand and inversely with supply. He also realised that it is not simply demand and supply which make a change in the price level, but it is equally true to say that price level also changes the volume of demand and supply. Mill asserts that price is fixed at a margin where the quantity offered is equal to the quantity demanded. In this way, he made the demand-equilibrium in this connection. This itself was a contribution to the price analysis. Mill observed that a change in the demand and supply can explain temporarily the value of commodities; but this type of explanation only refers to unstable value. On the other hand, cost production can explain normal, natural or permanent value of a commodity. This, then, can be regarded as a long-run normal price, which was explained by Adam Smith. Mill was very complacent with his explanation of commodity values. He joyfully declared: "Happily there is nothing in the law of value which remains for the present or for any future writer to clear up; the theory of the subject is complete." However, this complacency was his mistake. In fact, many things remained to be done towards the value analysis, which were attempted by the Marginalists and by Alfred Marshall.

Classical Stationary State : Mill's Views

In the Classical model, the end result of the capitalist development is stagnation. The Classical concept of stationary state is essentially a concept of mature economy in which, according to Adam Smith, wealth would be very great, yet there would be constant scarcity of employment. But unemployment does not play a decisive part in Mill and Ricardo's framework of analysis. According to Ricardo's concept, stagnation refers to "gross produce" or "gross national product at full employment," as we call today. Stationary state arises out of the falling rate of profit and consequent choking off of capital formation. Stationary state ultimately would lead to constant population but capital accumulation would stop earlier before population growth reaches its maximum. In Mill's stationary state, population and stock of capital would remain constant.[22] Ricardo thought that since there would not be any maladjustment, stationary state might be desirable.

Mill's Views

Mill, unlike other Classical economists, did not take the picture of stationary state as a gloomy one ; rather, he took a complacent and platonic attitude towards the stationary state, where, according to him, human improvement and technological progress were still possible. Mill stated that "when a country has long possessed a large production, and a large net income to make savings from, and when, therefore, the means have long existed of making a great annual addition to capital, it is one of the characteristics of such country, that the rate of profit is habitually within, as

---

22. Higgins, *Economic Development,* p. 98.

it were, a hand's breadth of the minimum, and the country, therefore, on the very verge of the stationary state."[23]

To Mill, the stationary state has become almost a kind of utopia, in which the state can try to achieve equality of wealth and opportunity. Mill was emphatic about the opportunity for personal development in a stationary state. The stationary state is a frictionless state. He considered such a state as a state of bliss rather than a state of human misery. Moral advancement will be at its height in the stationary state. There would also be real peace and harmony. There would be as much scope as ever for all kinds of menial culture and moral and social changes, as much room for improving the art of living. Mill has a strong optimism for the stationary state. In this state, distribution will be more even and the workers' lot would be improved. He said that "the stationary state would be on the whole a very considerable improvement on our present condition."

Magnificent Dynamics

William Baumol has presented a beautiful summary of the Classical "magnificent dynamics".[24] It mainly analyses the growth of population at different stages. At the state of maximum growth of population, the *per capita* income is just sufficient for population to reproduce itself at the physical minimum subsistence level. If the population is below its maximum, wage would be higher than the minimum subsistence, which will lead to further growth of population, and profit would be higher which will lead to more capital accumulation and investment to equip the workers with more working capital. When capital is nothing but wage funds, the accumulation from profits would be utilised in providing working capital to the larger amount of employed people.

But growth of capital and population will encounter diminishing returns in course of time due to the scarcity of natural resources. Ultimately, the gap between production and subsistence will be more and more narrowed and eventually, it would disappear. Therefore, profit would be eliminated and wage would no longer be above subsistence. When there is no profit, accumulation would stop. Stock of capital would be stationary. Similarly, when wage is at the subsistence level, population growth also will cease. Thus, the economy will be characterised by a stationary equilibrium.

Classical stationary state can be explained in the following diagram. The P curve is the aggregate production function which is associated with diminishing returns to labour and capital. Line OS stands for the volume of subsistence for labour proportionate to population growth. When population is less than OL, output can be higher than subsistence. At working population OA, total output minus rent is AC. In this case, AB is the wage and BC is the profit. As population and employment go on increasing, it can be shown that prfit level initially goes on increasing from BC to EF but

23. J.S.Mill, *Principles of Political Economy*.
24. W. Baumol, *Economic Dynamics*, pp. 11-19.

then it gradually comes down and ultimately at point *K* profit becomes zero. The level of wages remains at subsistence but the money wages go on increasing from *AB* to *DE* and then to *GH*. When the population is *OD*, the total produce minus rent is *DF* out of which *DE* goes to the labourers as wage and *EF* goes to the capitalist as profit. In the same way, when the total population is *OG*, the total output minus rent is *GI*, out of which *GH* part is paid as wage and *HI* goes to the capitalist as profit. In this way, employment may be extended up to the point *L* where the entire output minus rent would be eaten away in the form of wage by the labourers. So, there would be no profit. At this stage, the stationary state will come. Before the advent of stationary state, there would be more capital formation, more population and more employment. But the process is checked at point *OL* where profit ceases, growth of population ceases and wage becomes equal to minimum subsistence.

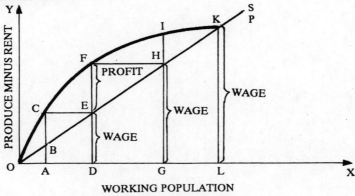

Fig. 5.3 Working Population

Criticisms

(1) Classical writers could not appreciate the great offsetting role of technology. Technological progress can lift upward the whole production function by raising capital per worker and thereby making each worker more productive. The race between technological improvement and diminishing returns has, in fact, been won by technology.[25]

(2) Some of the classical economists failed to foresee the potentiality of Asia and Africa which, in the subsequent period provided a vast scope for foreign investment for British capital and prevented the appearance of stagnation in the nineteenth century.[26]

(3) The classical concept of capital is deficient. It is nothing more than 'wage-fund'. Capital can provide more and better tools to workers with which they can increase productivity. If capital accumulation is faster than population growth, the limitations imposed by natural resources may

25. Ackley, *Macro-Economic Theory*, pp. 507-508.

26. Higgins, *op. cit.*, pp. 98.

be overcome, even with no technical progress. Thus, stationary state can be prevented.[27]

(4) In the analysis of population, the Classical economists concentrated only on two relationships : (i) Wages to population growth, and (ii) diminishing returns to labour and capital. Although mainly economic factors are important in the explanation of population dynamics, there can be other more important factors. Thus, the restricted base on which these two relationships were formulated does not appear to be relevant in our times.[28]

Though logically valid, the Classical stationary state has not been encountered in any country.

Fig. 5.3 Working Population

27. Ackley, op.cit., pp. 507-508.
28. Ibid., pp. 508-509.

6
Critics of Classicism

JEAN CHARLES SISMONDI (1773-1842)

Sismondi was more and less than a classical writer. He was the first systematic writer to write against the classical economic system, although he was basically a classical economist. He wrote two important books. His *Commercial Wealth* was published in 1803. It contained an exposition of classical ideas. His *New Principles of Political Economy* was published in 1819.

Sismondi and the Classicals

Sismondi was initially a classical economist. He was a faithful follower of Adam Smith. He supported the classical principles of economic liberalism, free trade, and *laissez faire*. He also subscribed to the natural philosophy of Adam Smith. Thus, both theoretically and practically, Sismondi was by heart a classical economist in the early years of his career. However, later on, he completely turned away from the classical system of values and belief. But, unfortunately or fortunately, he could not completely break away with the classical system. He thus, agreed with the classical method of analysis and the classical conclusions and policy prescriptions. He brought out the evil effects of machinery, exploitation of labour under the classical system, low wages and unsatisfactory working conditions of the labourers.

Nature and Method of Political Economy

Sismondi considered political economy "as a moral science where all facts are interwoven and where a false step is taken whenever one single fact is isolated and attention is concentrated upon it alone." According to him, political economy is essentially a moral science which should look after the well-being of mankind. Ethical consideration dominated the ideas of sismondi. He regarded political economy as an art. Classical political economy was the science of wealth or *chrematistics* as called by Aristotle. Sismondi did not like this definition of political economy. He said that real purpose of a science should be man and his well-being. Sismondi considered man more important than wealth in political economy.

A science is to be based on experience, observation and history. Thus, it is found that political economy is not concerned with wealth as such, but with man. Political economy is a study of economic activity in relation to human welfare. This definition of political economy as given by sismondi is more or less like the definition given by Alfred Marshall. Sismondi gave more emphasis on distribution rather than production, because he was concerned basically with the problem of social justice.

He criticised the abstract deductive method of analysis of the classical economists. He was in favour of an inductive, historical method of analysis. He thus, anticipated the historical school of analysis.

Distribution

Sismondi was essentially interested in the well-being of the masses of society. In this regard, Sismondi considered the problems of distribution as more important than any other economic problem. He said that the largest possible aggregate production does not necessarily mean the greatest amount of happiness for the people. On the other hand, he believed that a smaller aggregate of wealth, distributed properly, can bring about more happiness and well-being to the people. Sismondi, thus, insisted that distribution should not be left to the blind market forces, but should be regulated by a proper state-sponsored machinery of distribution. He also advocated the distribution of property and means of production among the people who can really use them. He said that benefits accruing from farming should go to the peasants alone. In his analysis of distribution, Sismonndi was pro-labour. He advocated the intervention by the state in the matter of distribution of the national product.

Machinery, Overproduction and Crisis

Sismonndi found class conflict in society. He was one of the earliest economists to observe the existence of opposing classes in a society. Marx was greatly indebted to Sismondi for his analysis of class conflict. Sismondi observed that machinery was against the interest of the working class. It reduced employment, increased competition, reduced wages and reduced the demand for the products. Machinery always displaces labour from employment. Machinery can be advantageous provided society can provide alternative jobs to the unemployed people. Sismondi found contradiction in the capitalist system. Whereas production increases under capitalism, purchasing power goes down. Like Malthus, Sismondi also observed that it is impossible for the workers to absorb the whole lot of output of the industries. Overproduction arises from a competitive zeal to produce even if the demand remains the same or goes down. This leads to a glut or excess production from time to time. With the introduction of machinery, unemployment is created and this, once again, decreases the purchasing power of the workers. Sismondi was not in favour of competition. He said that competition increased exploitation and it also increases overproduction.

Sismondi did not believe in the truth-value of Say's law of market. According to him, under the factory system of production, labourers are paid only the subsistence wages. These are inadequate to cope with the growing production of output and services. This results in underconsumption and crisis. According to Sismondi, crisis is caused by mainly three factors: *(i)* unplanned production and excess competition. *(ii)* Production is not based on demand consideration but is based on the growth of capital. *(iii)* Separation of labour and ownership of production. This increases the profit of the capitalists, but it keeps intact the wage of the labourers.

The capitalists cannot increase the demand for the product, excepting increasing temporarily the demand for some luxury goods for them. The progressive concentration of capital deepens the crisis of overproduction. In fact, in a capitalist economy, as Sismondi observed, there is an inherent tendency to widen the chasm between production and consumption.

Suggested Reforms

Sismondi suggested the following methods of reforming the economic system: *(i)* More and more intervention by the state in the matter of distribution. *(ii)* He rejected communism and feudalism as correct systems. *(iii)* Need for the equilibrium between production and consumption. *(iv)* Revival of the independent producers-small farmers, artisans and so on. *(v)* Slackening of industrial progress and invention in such a way that the necessary adjustment can be made without overproduction. *(vi)* Increase in the welfare of the masses. *(vii)* There should be unions of property-owners and labourers. *(viii)* Limitation of child labour, shortening of hours of work and abolition of Sunday working.

Criticisms

(i)   Sismondi was against the classical deductive method. But he himself adopted the deductive method while propounding his theory of overproduction as the cause of crisis.

(ii) Most of the fundamental economic concepts and categories used by Sismondi were vague or confused.

(iii) Sismondi is regarded as a pessimist.

(iv) Sismondi's reform proposals contain some degree of hesitation due to the perpetual conflict between the head and the heart. Sometimes, he could not suggest the proper remedy.

(v)   Sismondi was neither a full-fledged Adamite, nor a hard-boiled liberal. He was not a full-fledged socialist.

(vi) According to J.S. Mill, Sismondi's analysis of overproduction is not correct because while there may be overproduction for some particular commodities, a uniform and general overproduction of all commodities is simultaneously impossible.[1]

---

1.   J.S. Mill, *Principles of Political Economy*, ch. 14.

(vii) Sismondi had a very uncertain type of position because he, on the one hand, was not anti-capitalist but he was a strong supporter of workers.

However, in spite of the above points of criticism, it can be said that he rendered a distinct service by systematically exposing the weak points of classical political economy. His method of analysis is an anticipation of that of the Historical school. His emphasis on the importance of state ushered in an epoch of state socialism. Although he was not himself a socialist, still his studies have always provided a lively source for the socialist writers. In fact, he was the source of inspiration for Rodbertus and Marx. He will be regarded as a champion fighting against depression and overproduction. It is indeed difficult to ignore Sismondi's influence on the later socialists.

SAINT SIMON (1760-1825)

St. Simon is regarded as a utopian socialist. He wrote many books including *Industry, The Organiser, The Industrial System* and so on. Simon analysed the social problems in terms of economics.

Social Order

Simon wanted to establish a system of social order in which equality will prevail. There will be no class distinction and there would be only two categories of people: workers and idlers. However, in course of time, the idler class will disappear from the new society. The working class will include manual workers, agriculturists, artisans, bankers, manufacturers and servants. Simon was in favour of improving the economic conditions of the backward classes. But he was against the system of forced equality. In the new regime, the industrialist will get due honour in the society. The main feature of the social order will be the exploitation of economic resources to the maximum possible extent. In the new social order, the noblemen, clergy and the politicians will have no place. In such an order, everybody will get his due share according to his potential capacity to produce. He is not hostile to the capitalists because they invest for the growth of the economy. Simon is against the landed aristocrats. Simon had a plan for social reform and for the re-construction of society along appropriate lines in which one can reap all the advantages of industrial and technical improvements.

Industrial State

Simon wanted to have a new industrial order of society. He conceived the society as a huge workshop without any coercision or exploitation. In his industrial state, the capable people who are very productive will lead the society. Distribution in the society is to be based on the productive contributions of its members. In such a society, there would be no exploitation and people will remain equal, peaceful and organised. He strongly advocated the need of increasing industrial productivity. He was in favour of organising the industry on modern lines. He wanted to create a modern industrial society. In such a society, the interests of all classes like workers, consumers and entrepreneurs would be well looked after.

Simon is not regarded sometimes as a socialist because he did not explicitly advocate the abolition of private property. However, he was not in favour of the abuse of private property. He stood for the equality of opportunity and abolition of privilege. St. Simon was a collectivist. According to St. Simon the institution of private property is a changeable institution and it is an important plank for the socialist criticism against the classical system which took for granted the institution of private property.

Role of Government

According to Simon, government interference is not essential in the new industrial society. The interference should be minimum. The role of government will be like an association which will look after the security, freedom and welfare of the workers. In the new regime, the power of government will be curtailed. It will give simply new direction for the betterment of the society. The new regime will have the executive power vested in the chamber of deputies recruited from the representatives of industry, agriculture, commerce and manufacture. The executive so constituted will either reject or accept the legislative proposals of the two other chambers. These chambers will be *(i)* Chamber of scientists and industrialists and *(ii)* the second one will consist of engineers and artists. The main function of government will be the development of the potential wealth of the country by the maximum exploitation of all types of resources. The government will prepare the public works programme for providing employment to the workers and providing defence of the industrialists. Simon's industrial government has to perform economic duties rather than political duties. The basic purpose of the government will be to properly administer things instead of governing its people. Through the help of the government, the entire nation is to be transformed into a highly productive association. His idea of government is different from the earlier ideas of political government. Simon thought that the aim of the new government will be to combine all the forces of society in such a way as to ensure the successful execution of all those works which will improve the lot of the workers, both morally and physically.

Critical Estimate

St. Simon was an ardent liberalist and a social reformer. Although he did not directly advocate the abolition of private property, his followers undertook a scheme of social reconstruction to include the abolition of private property. Simon, however, believed that beyond a point, property and inheritance are unjust because they lead to exploitation of the class of have-nots. St. Simon wanted the government to be the sole inheritor of all forms of property. Simon is regarded as a socialist only because of his sympathy for the workers. According to some, he is a collectivist and not a socialist in the strict sense of the term. On the one hand, he advocated private property and on the other, collectivism. This is indeed a contradiction in his thought.

ROBERT OWEN (1771-1858)

Robert Owen is considered as the father of British socialism. He was a practical socialist who practically examined the theoretical underpinnings of socialism in many countries. For experimenting with the practicability of the idea of socialism, he opened a workshop in New Lanark, where he introduced many reforms regarding the working conditions of the workers. These reforms included: *(i)* abolition of child labour system under the age of ten; *(ii)* reduce the number of working hours to ten hours per day from seventeen hours; *(iii)* eliminated the practice of imposing fines for damage done by the workers; *(iv)* provided model dwelling houses, encouraged saving habit and hygienic living conditions among the workers. The above steps did not reduce the profitability of his industry. During his time, Lanark became a model factory for the labourers.

He also experimented with the idea of establishment of model communities, each having members between three hundred and two thousand. But the ideal number, according to Owen, should be between eight hundred and twelve hundred. This community will reside in a big building and will work jointly and the total output would be shared by them all. He established such communities in the U.S.A., the U.K. and Scotland. This experiment, however, could not be a success due to many reasons. However, what he wanted to do was the abolition of profit and of the interference by the middlemen.

Owen thought that profit is the root of all evils. It is a forbidden fruit and it implies injustice because it is the amount over and above the *just price* (cost of production). The labourers are given by the employers only the subsistence wage. Under this situation, increase in production leads to oversupply and crisis, owing to the deficiency of effective demand. According to Owen, crisis is the result of a disparity between the productive power of a society and the purchasing power of it. The introduction of machinery leads to sufficiency in production, but unless the purchasing power of the workers is increased, there is bound to be overproduction or what is called a *glut*. This type of glut was evident after the Napoleonic wars. There must be a parity between the cost of production and the price. Profits are realised in the form of money. Therefore, Owen advocated the abolition of money. He was in favour of the introduction of *labour notes* instead of money. The labour notes will specify the number of hours of labour. Whenever a labour produces a commodity, he works for a number of hours, according to which he is paid. Now, this payment would be in terms of labour notes specifying the number of hours. These labour notes can be exchanged between the consumers and the producers for the purchase and sale of any commodity. Since labour is the cause and the substance of value, labour can be used also as the measure of value. The producer who wishes to dispose of his products will be given labour notes in proportion to the number of hours worked for the commodity. Thus, the labour notes will eliminate the use of money and also profit which is a dirty concept with Owen. Owen established the National Equitable Labour Exchange. The members of this exchange were allowed to value their products in terms of the number of hours worked. On this basis, the exchange will issue them the labour notes of equivalent value, which could be exchanged for the purchase of goods and services in the market. However, this idea of Owen failed due to the following factors: *(i)* the members dishonestly exaggerated the value of their products in terms of number of hours worked. Thus, the value as not properly estimated. The labour notes could not become the universal medium of exchange; *(ii)* the valuation process was entirely subjective; *(iii)* the goods which were very useful, could be sold out from the exchange, but the goods which were not of immediate use, were lying idle in the Exchange; *(iv)* the labour notes were not registered in the name of the members. The non-members made huge amount of profit by speculating in the labour notes market. Thus, the system was a failure.

Owen thought that environment is very important for moulding and shaping the character of men. He believed that man by nature in neither good nor bad. It is the environment which makes him either good or bad. A capitalist is not necessarily a bad person. But due to the institution of private property, there is concentration of wealth in the hands of a few persons. This leads to inequality and poverty. Owen was against the institution of private property. Private property must be eliminated. He wanted to establish a harmonious society based on *cooperation*. Owen's name is linked with the growth of cooperative movement in England. He was always in favour of cooperation and against competition. He wanted that labour and capital must work in cooperation with each other and must live in harmony.

Owen was against the principle of payment according to capacity. He advocated that payment should be according to the needs. He was in favour of higher wages because they are helpful for maintaining the health of the workers and improving their efficiency. He was deeply involved in the labour legislation which could improve the lot of the workers.

Critical Estimate

Owen's ideas were not fulfilled into action. But he is always remembered as a practical socialist who translated his ideas into practice. He was out and out a reformer. He is still remembered as the pioneer of cooperative movement.

CHARLES FOURIER (1772-1837)

Charles Fourier was, strictly speaking, not a socialist but he was an associationist. He was in favour of rural life. His *New Industrial and Social World* was his important work which was published in 1829. He was in favour of establishing harmony and peace. He was against the abolition of private property. He is sometimes regarded as a bourgeois socialist.[2] Fourier's slogan was *Back to Land*. He was against the growth of big cities. He had great contempt for industrialism. He was in favour of the growth of agriculture. By agricultural growth, he meant the growth of horticulture, poultry farming, agriculture and so on. He wanted dispersion of big cities and the growth and development of the rural areas which will have all the amenities of life.

Fourier recognised twelve major passions in human beings such as feeling, love, ambition, desire for union and so on. For fulfilling these passions, men required a suitable environment. Therefore, Fourier wanted to establish such organisation which will guarantee the fulfillment of these passions. These organisations are known as Phalanges/Phalansteres.

Phalanges/Phalansteres

The phalanges are communal organisations. Fourier wanted to establish a phalanstere of nearly sixteen hundred members (four hundred families). These phalanges would be organised throughout the country. These are voluntary organisations. Every phalange will have a common kitchen, library, dining halls and so on. Every phalange will have a big building to accommodate its own members. It would be a community living centre. The members will live separately in their rooms. Works and services would be jointly performed by the members. Through these phalanges, it would be possible to achieve harmony and happiness of making, as was the belief of Fourier. The phalanges would be self-sufficient organisations regarding production and consumption. However, in case of need, phalanges can exchange their products with each other. The phalanges would be based on economies of scale, so that the cost of services including food, clothing, shelter and so on would be the minimum. This type of organisation, according to Fourier, will be very essential for promoting the feeling of happiness and brotherhood. The organisation will undertake the production of the things required by its members. Then every phalange will have an area of four hundred acres of land which can be utilised for the production of food. The members will work on the basis of division of labour. Every phalange will be established as a joint stock company which will pay dividend on a fixed basis: labour is to get 5/12, capital 4/12 and management 3/12.

The management of the phalanges would be in the hands of competent persons elected by members. The members will have complete freedom of action regarding the choice of work. Every phalange will be a combination of industrial and agricultural activities. In such phalanges, women may be held in common and the children would be given the duties to attend to animals, repair roads and work in the slaughter houses. Fourier wanted to give enough freedom to women. He was not in favour of marriage, because married people become selfish to their own families.

---

2.   Gide and Rist, *A History of Economic Doctrines*, p. 255.

The phalanges would be situated in beautiful surroundings such as near beautiful rivers. The phalanges would be self-sufficient and would be run on democratic lines. The capital of all the phalanges would be at Constantinople. The phalanges will have short working sessions, minute division of labour, guarantee of minimum subsistence to everybody, development of the spirit of emulation and co-partnership among the members.[3] Phalanges would be able to reap a number of advantages: *(i)* Increase in productivity. *(ii)* Possibility of full freedom. *(iii)* Enjoyment of leisure. *(iv)* Each member will have the pride of being a cooperative owner rather than mere wage earner. *(v)* There would be harmony between individuals. *(vi)* Labour will be able to exercise his own faculty and judgement. There would be no compulsion or coercion. *(vii)* Mobility of labour would be present. *(viii)* The worker will have an effective say in the management of the phalanges.

This type of phalange will have no class conflict between labour and capital, between debtor and creditor and between consumer and producer.[4] Fourier became very famous for his ideas on phalanges. Of course, his ideas would not gain momentum during his life-time, but after his death, his ideas were appreciated, particularly in the U.S.A., France and England. The idea of phalange is really the idea of the formation of cooperative societies. If it is interpreted this way, then one has to admit the success of his ideas.

Fourier's ideas were in many respects different from those of Simon. Fourier advocated decentralisation and ruralisation but Simon was in favour of centralisation and industrialism. Fourier believed in the self-assertions of individuals but Simon laid much emphasis on production and work. According to some, the whole idea of Simon was utopian.

LOUIS BLANC (1813-1882)

Louis Blanc held a position in between socialists and associationists. He represents a transition between associationism and socialism on the one hand, and between utopian socialism and scientific socialism, on the other. Blanc deviated from utopian socialism to proletarian socialism. He was in favour of the working class. According to him, utopian socialism was by itself unrealistic. Therefore, he wanted to introduce a realistic type of socialism. In such a socialism, the capitalist class would be gradually abolished, and the workers will manage the whole show. He also found the necessity of state. This is why, sometimes he is regarded as a socialist. His main work was *The Organisation of Labour* which was published in 1841. In this book, he depicted an outline of French socialism.

According to him, competition is the source of all economic evils such as industrial crises, disputes, poverty, crime and moral degradation. However, competition can be eliminated by forming new associations among

---

3. Alexander Gray, *Socialist Tradition*, pp. 185-186.
4. Gide and Rist, *op.cit.,* p. 260.

the workers. These new associations will be based on the principle of cooperation. Therefore, it is through cooperation that Blanc wanted to eliminate the evil effects of competition.

Social Workshop

Blanc was in favour of organising workers of the same trade in a social workshop. In such a workshop, the resources would be pooled together and there would be large-scale production. There would be no intervention by the entrepreneur. In the social workshop, the government will provide the initial capital and will also help in the management of the workshop initially. Management of the workshop will be in the hands of the elected representatives. The workers will elect their own leaders. The cost of production of the product will consist of wages and interest. All the workers will be paid equal wages. The products will be sold in the market and the profits will be divided into three components: one part of the profit will be meant for social insurance and social security of the workers, one part would be distributed among the workers as bonus, and other part will be used for capital formation and internal financing. This part would be responsible for depreciation, expansion and the change of equipments. However, one-fifth of the profit would be kept apart for reserves before the distribution of profit among the above three heads. There would be free competition among the workshops. The state will provide the necessary finance through taxation. However, the state will be paid interest for its capital investment.

As a result of free competition among the workshops and the private enterprises, the workshop would get stronger and more efficient day by day. This will gradually abolish the private capitalist system from the economy. The scheme of social workshop is to be managed entirely by the workers and for the workers. Thus, there would be no question of exploitation of workers. This type of social workshop will bring about a new social order which was the idea of Blanc. The workshop will help reduce the cost of production of goods being produced.

Evaluation

The social workshop was a means to achieve worker's control and management. It is a means of eliminating competition through cooperation among workers. It was a new way of achieving socialism. The idea was realistic. Blanc formulated the principle: "From each according to his ability, to each according to his needs." Louis Blanc occupies indeed a unique position in the history of French socialism. He is really a unique combination of state socialism, associationism and proletarian socialism.

PIERRE JOSEPH PROUDHON (1809-1865)

Proudhon was neither a socialist nor a communalist nor an associationist. He was not a socialist because he did not advocate socialism as such. Socialism is utopian in nature. Proudhon was against communism, because even in communism, the property institution exists and it leads to inequality. Under communism, according to Proudhon, the weak people exploit the strong people. Communism is merely an inverted form of private property. According to him, socialism is really nothing. Communism cannot grant full freedom of thought, mind and action to the individual. He also opposed associations and organisations as being detrimental. Proudhon's famous book is: *What is Property?* which was published in 1840. He also wrote another book: *Philosophy of Poverty* (1846). In this book, he condemned private property but did not advocate its abolition. This point was criticised by Marx in his book: *Poverty of Philosophy*, which was a reply to Proudhon's book; *Philosophy of Poverty*. Marx called him 'petit-bourgeois', mainly because Proudhon defended the institution of private property.

Property

What is property? Proudhon observed that *all property is theft*. According to him, property is a kind of robbery. He rejected the arguments in favour of private property. All abuses in the society arise out of private property. Property leads to inequalities among the people. It gives the owner the power of exploitation of other people. Property is attacked because it gives to the owner of property a right to an income which is not properly and honestly earned, but it is inherited. Proudhon, in fact, was against inherited property. It is not property as such but the right to exert an unearned tribute which is the point of attack. A property-owner lives on the labour of other people. Proudhon opposed this system of living of the property-owners. Proudhon, in fact, attacked not the use of property but the exploitation through it in the form of rent, interest and lower wages. It is, however, surprising that Proudhon did not advocate the abolition of private property. Proudhon supported private property on the following two grounds: *(i)* private property is an expression of liberty, and liberty is a very valuable necessity for human beings, *(ii)* if the element of exploitation can be removed from the private property, the system can work in the society. He was in favour of property which is acquired by human beings through their honest and genuine labour. Any property out of honest income can be supported on moral and economic grounds. "He believed in private property, in income and in the most complete and thorough going enjoyment by an individual of what he himself produces or acquires."[5]

He felt that property was the root of all evils and injustice in society. Proudhon supported the demand for equality of property and the rights to labour in land. Property created despotism in the society. Gray observes that "Proudhon perhaps believed that if property could be purified by the inclusion of justice with the result that the elements of hostility to sociability were eliminated, it (property) would then not be a bad thing." His theory of property was, in fact, a theory of position. According to him, every person should have the right to utilise the fruits of his own labour in a way he likes but he should not be allowed to exploit others in the society.

---

5. W.A. Scott, *The Development of Economics*, p. 274.

Surplus Value

Proudhon believed that the productivity of a group of labour is higher than the sum total of their individual productivities. Thus, the indifference between these two types of productivities will lead to a surplus. The surplus is pocketed by the capitalist. The capitalist gives the impression that every labour is paid according to his productivity, which is not true. In other words, in a capitalist system, workers are exploited because wages are much less than the productivity of the workers. His idea of surplus value influenced Marx in the formulation of his surplus value analysis. Of course, Marxian analysis of surplus value has altogether a different meaning. Proudhon believed in the efficacy of the classical labour theory of value. But he was against the exploitation of labour in a capitalist society. He considered that labour alone was productive. Without labour, land and capital become useless. In fact, a capitalist receives payment for doing nothing. His payment is really a kind of theft. Between the capitalist and the worker, there is a continuous misunderstanding and miscalculation. The surplus value of Proudhon represents capitalist's profit.

Equality, Liberty and Government

Proudhon was out and out a supporter of equality and liberty. He wanted to harmonise property and community through liberty. He had enough love for liberty. According to him, liberty and equality are inseparable. The society must make all attempts to give encouragement to liberty and equality. The political organisation of his society was *social mutualism* which meant the abolition of state.

There will be no inequality in the social order suggested by him. Such a social order will be established but it will take some time. In this society, there would be no state intervention. There would also be no rate of interest. Proudhon advocated a system of zero rate of interest. According to Proudhon, law is not necessary for a society. It can be replaced by a system of contract. He also suggested system of decentralisation. He wanted a system in which all the people will absolutely be free and there would be absolute liberty for all. He said: "Liberty is the sum total of my system". He wanted to remove the fundamental character of property which leads to exploitation of labour. For the abolition of exploitation, he advocated the establishment of an exchange bank.

Exchange Bank

He was in favour of the establishment of a national exchange bank. Such a bank will have no capital of its own. The bank will issue notes to the borrowers (generally workers) against the deposit of goods or promissory notes. These notes can be used in the market by the borrowers for the purchase of tools and instruments. The notes would be advanced by the bank without taking any rate of interest. The notes of the bank will be returned to the bank at the end of the production period. The borrowers then get back their promissory notes. The loans from the bank would be helpful for the purpose of production of goods and services by the borrowers. Thus, there would be no instrument of exploitation and the society will get rid of inequality. In this way, true liberty and equality will be established in the society. The quantity of notes to be issued will depend on the volume of trade. Therefore, there would be no inflation or depression in the economy. This was translated into practice during Proudhon's time. But it was a failure due to some organic defects in the implementation of the scheme.

Evaluation

Proudhon will ever be remembered for his analysis of private property, and for his theory of *Anarchy* in the history of economic thought.

FRIEDRICH LIST (1789-1846)

List is considered as the father of American Protectionism. The ideas of List were influenced by the backward economic conditions of Germany, when List was writing. List had, at the beginning, a liberal view about foreign trade. But this view was subsequently changed. List wrote a very fascinating book, *The National System of Political Economy*. List's economic ideas are the best examples of relativist analysis. His ideas on theories were the product of circumstances prevailing in the then Germany. By 1830, the German states were asking for economic unity and uniform tariffs. In fact, Germany was passing through a stagnant industrial period. This situation compelled List to take interest in the study of the relevance of free trade.

List was strongly opposed to the cosmopolitan and absolutist notions of classical political economy. List argued that the principles of classical political economy are not applicable to all countries under all circumstances. By contrast, the principles introduced by List were strongly nationalistic and historical. He examined the classical principle with reference to the German economy, and came to the conclusion that classical economics was not applicable to Germany.

Theory of Nationality

List gave importance to the necessity of study of every nation very carefully. He said that every nation is a different world with its own problems, possibilities and prospects. Every man forms a part of some nation and his prosperity as a human being depends to a large extent on the political power of the nation.[6] Nations are of unequal strength. Every nation must pass through several stages of growth.

Ultimately, it will come to a stage when it will get independence and become a strong power. List favoured economic nationalism for every nation. Thus, the political economy of every nation is different from that of every other. The national economy of every state shows the path along which its economy can grow, attain its economic culture and can freely mix up with the other independent nations of the world. In finding out this path

---

6.   F. List, *Nationalist System of Political Economy*, p. 87.

of development, a nation cannot segregate economics from politics. He did not approve of *laissez faire* or non-intervention by the government. He supported the view that the government must come in the forefront of action for the economic development of the country. The government must know how the productive power of a nation can be increased, protected and maintained. List subordinated economics to politics in general. The government must know the economic effects of every political change in the country. List argued that in a country like Germany of that time, free trade which displaced population and domestic industry was undesirable. List was in favour of sacrificing the present for the future. According to List, the ultimate objective of economic activity is the national development and development of economic power. In this process, industry becomes a very potent force. He said that industry is a social force which can itself create and improve labour and capital. In addition to improving the present, industry can also give a direction for the future development of a nation. Thus, List recommended the introduction of industrialisation even at the cost of temporary loss.[7]

Theory of Productive Power

List advocated the creation of potential productive power. He said that the potential productive power is more important than the present productive power. He said that the nation's growth depends on the potential productive power. List did not accept the labour theory of valuation. He said it is simply a shopkeeper's theory. He is of the opinion that every change in the government action influences the productive power of the nation. In this connection, as already pointed out, List observed that the present temporary gain may be sacrificed for the greater future gain. The crucial economic magnitude in the process of development is not wealth but the productive power. In the words of List: "The power of producing wealth is... infinitely more important than the wealth itself." List speaks of properly utilising the economic resources for the future development of a nation. In this connection, List justifies protection to the developing or infant industries. He criticises the classical notion of capital accumulation by saying that the accumulation of exchange value is not at all important. In this connection, List says that it is necessary to properly maintain the economic, political and moral institutions of a nation. However, the best productive power of a nation is its manufacturing industries. Therefore, it must be noted that a nation should develop, first of all, its manufacturing sector. Manufactures permit a better utilisation of the product of a country as compared to agriculture. He is of the opinion that tariff can be utilised as an instrument of industrial development.

Stages of Economic Development

According to List, an economy must pass through the following five stages of development before it attains *maturity*. These stages are: (1) bar-

---

7.   Ekelund and Hebert, *op.cit.,* p. 156.

baric, (2) pastoral, (3) agricultural, (4) agricultural-manufacturing, and (5) agricultural-manufacturing-commercial.

List found that in the case of first three stages, free trade between the nations will be very helpful, but economies in transition between the last two stages require protection by the government until the final stage of development is attained. Similarly, at the final stage of development, free trade can be helpful. In fact, in such a situation, free trade will guard against retrogression and indolence of the manufacturing industries. List observed that until all nations reached the final stage of development, international competition is not justified, because the nations will be on an unequal footing. Therefore, any exchange before the attainment of the final mature stage, will be an unequal exchange. In this connection, he favoured the imposition of protection on the underdeveloped German industries because at the same time the German economy could not attain the final stage of economic development.

List was in favour of free trade in the first stage for the promotion of agriculture. In the second stage, the nation should develop manufacturing industries. Foreign trade should be developed in the third stage and protective measures may be adopted in the fourth stage. Unrestricted competition can be allowed between nations only in the fifth stage of development.

Protectionism

It must be noted that List was not out and out a protectionist. He felt that protection was justified only at some critical stages in the history of development of a nation. He, however, supported the view that for the growth of infant industries, it is necessary to protect these industries. List was neither a protectionist nor a free trader. He was a supporter of both. He observed that each policy must be considered against the economic situation of a nation. The following are the important features of List's theory of protection: *(i)* Protection can be granted for giving industrial education and for attaining industrial independence. *(ii)* No protection should be given to agriculture because it will lead to higher food prices and higher cost of living. *(iii)* Equal protection should not be granted to all types of industries. *(iv)* Protection should be granted to the infant industries. *(v)* Protection is desirable for those industries which are facing foreign competition. *(vi)* Protection should not be granted to the developed industries.

Evaluation

List adopted in his analysis the method of historical comparison. He has shown the importance of the relativist economic analysis. He has also given a number of valid points against the economic orthodoxy of classical liberalism.[8] He has provided the necessary spring-board for the German Historical School. In an important sense, List may be considered as the real forerunner of this school.[9]

---

8. Ekelund and Hebert, *op.cit.,* p. 156.
9. *Loc. Cit.*

7

Historical Critics of Classicism

HISTORICAL SCHOOL (1843-1883)

The *Historical School* was first started in Germany in the forties of the nineteenth century. It was the outcome of realistic research in the social sciences. The Historical School developed the historical method of study. The school had two branches: the older and the young. The older group of writers is represented by William Roscher, Karl Knies and B. Hildebrand. The younger group is dominated by a Gustav Schmoller. The British historicism is represented by Bagehot, Spencer, Darwin, Ingram, among others. Institutional school is a part of historical school.

Rise of Historical School

Historical School is a reaction against the classical school of economic thought. Historicism grew in Germany at a time when the German economy was backward, and it was undergoing a process of economic development. There was an air of change in every walk of life in Germany in the mid-nineteenth century. Germany, during this period, witnessed the existence of the classical system of economic philosophy and also a wave of economic liberalism. There was the growth of criticism against the classical philosophy. There were several reasons for the growth of historicism in Germany:

(1) The German economic thought was not till then strong enough to have any independent philosophy of its own, and there was no strongly entrenched economic doctrine prevailing in Germany. Theoretical economics had never become firmly established in Germany.[1] Schumpeter observed that theory was an alien plant in Germany. It was therefore, a virgin soil for the growth of indigenous theory.

(2) German philosophy was based on an organic approach against the classical individualistic approach. The German approach to life and things was considerably influenced by the philosophy of Hegel and by the organic jurisprudence of Savigny. Hegelian philosophy which was so influential was based on the concept of *change and relativity* which gave a new direction and a new thinking like historicism. Hegelian philosophy did not tolerate individualism of the classical system. Savigny had a profound influence on

---

1. Ekelund and Herbert, *op. cit.,* p. 193.

the growth of historical school. He showed that the formulation of laws required a historical study of socio-economic phenomena. Hegel laid much stress on the evolution of ideas as the motive force for social change. This idea had a positive effect on the growth of historical school in Germany.

(3) Freidrich List and Adam Muller had also the formative influence on the growth of historical movement. These writers emphasised the need for a national economy and a benevolent state for the growth of German economy. The studies made by List were based on historical evidence and data.

(4) William Dilthey advocated historical studies for realistic results and conclusions. He also spoke on the need for understanding historical events. He said that, on the basis of the understanding of history, the real foundation of a social science like economics can be built up.

(5) L.V. Stein, a distinguished contemporary thinker in Germany, combined Hegelian idealism with French philosophy to explore the possibility of a new approach to the study of economics.

(6) Sismondi, another contemporary thinker, criticised the classical approach to economic analysis, particularly of Ricardo. He emphasised the need for historical study of facts and environments for the proper growth of economic science.

(7) The contemporary economic problems in Germany could not be solved by the classical line of approach. New labour and industrial problems arose in Germany which could be tackled only by a new type of approach which found expression in the growth of historicism.

The Historical School had its origin, on the one hand, in German *Romanticism* and, on the other, in the opposition to classicism. The former gives the school an anti-individualistic trend. The Historical School was very influential for nearly forty years. The school started its career with the publication of Roscher's *Grundriss*. The Historical School did not oppose the growth of capitalism, but it simply wanted to reform capitalism. The Historical School was not very opposed to classical political economy, but the younger generation of the historical school, particularly Schmoller, was vehemently opposed to the classical philosophy.

Historical School's Criticism Against Classicism

The Historical School levelled the following charges against the classical economists:

(i) The classical system of economy is too much individualistic. It is based on free individual choice, liberty, free trade and so on. It is not nationalistic. Nation is not given supreme importance in the classical system of analysis. Nation is subordinated to the individual will and freedom.

(ii) The classical system of political economy is based on materialism. It is based on the concept of monetary gain, optimum return and national wealth. It is, essentially, a system of the wealth of nations.

(iii) The classical system is based on the system of *laissez faire*. The system does not allow for the beneficial role of the government. The role of government is reduced to the least intervention in economic, social and political matters. This is not justified according to the historical school. The government should come to the forefront of all activities particularly in the matter of economic development.

(iv) The classical school also neglected the role of environment and institutions. Needless to say, they have important influences on the life of nations and individuals. The classical economists have made a serious mistake by neglecting the role of these very crucial factors.

(v) According to the historical school, the classical law or theory is supposed to be universal or absolute in character. This is great sin of the classical economists like Adam Smith, Ricardo and Malthus. The classicists believed that economic laws were operative everywhere and always. The historical school stressed the idea that no law is absolute or universal in character. Every law is subject to change in theory and practice. The character of law is only relative. The laws are provisional in the sense, that the economy is dynamic in character, and every time the progress of history gives rise to new facts, on the basis of which laws are to be modified. For example, free trade may be very good for some countries, but it is not good for all the countries for all the times. For the developing countries, protection may be a more desirable rule. Therefore, the laws are only conditional, based on certain assumptions and circumstances. The exact laws of physical sciences cannot be applied to a social science like economics. Moreover, the laws of physical sciences are also not absolute. They are also provisional and conditional. Alfred Marshall also pointed out that economic laws are only statements of tendencies. Knies clearly stated that economic laws are necessarily conditional.

However, it must be noted that the classical writers never strongly denied the relativity of their own generalisations and conclusions. J.S.Mill particularly stated that laws of distribution are man-made laws. Therefore, these can be changed by human beings in times of necessity.

(vi) The classical economists treated human beings as self-interested entities. They were guided by the concept of *homo-economicus* or economic man. The classical concept of man was simply a man always after gain. The historians observe that a man is not simply a profit-maximiser. He has many other interests and motives, such as desire for glory, pleasure, sense of duty, love, pity, benevolence and so on. The historical school did not approve of the classical self-centred man. This crude psychological assumption about man was not accepted by the historical school. Schmoller raised objection against the classical self-interested man. According to Hildebrand, if the classical concept of man (Homo-economicus) is taken as the basis, the political economy could be a mere natural history of egoism.[2]

---

2. Gide and Rist, *A History of Economic Doctrines,* p. 397.

However, it must be noted that J.S. Mill realised that self-interestedness is not the only motive of human beings. A man is governed, according to him, by other motives as well. Therefore, this criticism of the historical school is not wholly correct.

(vii) According to the historical school, the classical school has wrongly used abstractions and deductions. The deductive or *a priori* method used by the classical school is wholly unjustifiable. Instead of deduction, the historical school suggested the use of induction based on observations. Inductive method of reasoning is the essential feature of the historical school. The historians pointed out that the premises for the deductive reasoning, as used by the classical school, were based on empirically wrong facts. Therefore, the use of such method is capable of doing more harm than good. Schmoller observed that "only by patient observation and careful induction can we hope to build up an economic theory that shall take full account of the complexity of economic phenomena."[3] It is pointed out by the historical school that the classical analysis is incomplete, wrong and hasty.

However, it has been pointed out by some authors that even the deductive method is useful. In this connection, Schmoller remarked that induction and deduction are both necessary for the growth of science. However, Pareto is of the opinion that discussion on method is purely a wastage of time. The aim of any science is to discover uniformities which can be done by following an suitable method of enquiry. It must also be noted that J.S. Mill spoke about the necessity of inductive or empirical studies in a science like economics. His principles on experimental verifications are well-known to students of logic and scientific method.

Positive Ideas of Historical School

The following are the major positive ideas of the historical school:

(i) The classical economists analysed economic phenomena mechanically with the help of certain simplifying tools and assumptions. In this way, they reduced the complex phenomena into some simple generalisations. In other words, the classical economists used a simplifying procedure known as *reductionism*. The historical school, on the other hand, gave importance to environment. The historians pointed out that a mechanical view of life is inadequate for analysing the complex socio-economic phenomena.[4] An individual as a social being must be studied with reference to environment and society which was entirely neglected by the classical school.

(ii) The historical school observed that without the study of social organisations and institutions, it is not possible to get a fruitful result. The historians considered the *organic view of society*. They laid emphasis on the study of economic phenomena with reference to the social facts. Such a line of approach was advised by A. Comte.

---

3. Gide and Rist, *op. cit.,* p. 398.
4. *Ibid.,* p. 403.

(iii) The historians took a dynamic view of life and considered the economic system as dynamic in nature, which means a constant need to write and re-write the political economy with reference to new facts and materials.

(iv) The historical school clearly recognised the importance of the application of historical or inductive method in the analysis of economic phenomena. The school was of the opinion that without studying the facts of life, we cannot get any realistic picture. Abstract reasoning is useless. Only historical study can lead to important policy prescription.

(v) The historical school gave importance to the study of the past which can provide an important insight into present events. Hildebrand observed that human beings are the children of civilization and are products of history. The historians emphasised on the importance of the study of the different stages of historical development of a nation so that every phenomenon can be explained with reference to the stage of the history. History should be regarded as the organon of social science. Comte wanted to found sociology of which political economy was to be a single branch. The historical school regarded economics in the same spirit.[5]

(vi) The historians advocated the importance of state in the economic activity of a nation. They did not favour the classical idea of *laissez faire*. The historians were of the opinion that without the help of the state, national development is not possible.

(vii) The historians favoured a national system of development and the growth of nationalist economic system, and not a simple general economic system. This idea found its best expression in the writings of F.List. In a sense, the historians were nationalists of the first order.

(viii) It was one of the essential features of *historismus* to advocate for a complete knowledge of history and historical sequences. According to the historians, without the knowledge of history, it is impossible to appreciate the socio-economic events; and it is also impossible to find out the solution required. Knowledge of history is a thing of primary importance.

(ix) All social aspects, including the geography, the social structure, the natural resources, the character of the people and so on are essential for a proper study of economic life of a nation in the context of the whole milieu. A complete understanding of a single aspect of life requires a careful study of the whole society.[6]

Critical Appraisal

The following points of criticism can be levelled against the historical school:

(1) Historical study is not always very helpful. Historical study provides some descriptive facts. However, a science is necessarily explanatory rather than descriptive. Aristotle observed that there can be no

---

5. *Ibid.,* p. 407.
6. *Ibid.,* p. 403.

science without generalisation. Historical studies cannot provide any explanation. Therefore, it is not a scientific method.

(2) Historical method recommends the introduction of induction or empiricism. But successful empiricism must be based on some theory. Therefore, sometimes, it is pointed out that a correct method of analysis must take into account both deduction and induction, or what is known as *logical positivism*. Even Schmoller laid stress on the importance of deduction.

(3) In fact, the historical explanations of many historical events may not be correctly known. History itself requires explication. It is a mistake to observe that history alone can provide explanation for every event.

(4) Historical method is a partial method. There is a counterpart of it known as the deductive method. Just as the deductive method is not a complete method, so is the historical method.

(5) The historical method put emphasis on the question of relativism. It said that everything is relative in character. But still it did not question the existence of the capitalist system. It did not say that capitalist system is a relative system and a passing phase.

(6) The historical school's criticism against the classical system was too much exaggerated. In fact, some of the classical economists advocated government intervention, for the need of empirical study and also for the dynamic analysis of economic events. In this connection, the name of J.S. Mill is noteworthy.

(7) The historical school could not find out any historical law of development.

Decline

Because of the above defects and criticisms of the historical school, many people did not take *historismus* as a complete substitute for the classical system. Nor was it taken as a superior school of analysis. Menger, an Austrian economist, vehemently criticised the historical school. This caused a severe damage to the reputation of the historical school. The school did not find any favour with French political economists. So, there was, in course of time, a decline of the historical school. In America, the historical school led to the development of *Institutionalism* under the leadership of Thorstein Veblen. The publication of Marshall's *Principles*, which provided a synthesis, brought about the complete eclipse of the *Historical School.*

Merits (Impact)

In spite of the above points of criticism, the merits of historical school can hardly be neglected. *Historismus* was clear enough in emphasising the importance of the study of historical facts or empiricism. It provided a realistic and dynamic approach to the study of economic problems. It also realised the importance of historical facts and institutions. The school was responsible for the refinement of many of the classical economic ideas. The historical school has shown the limitations of economic science by pointing out that its analysis is relevant with reference to only particular time and place. The school brought to the forefront the importance of relativism in the study of economic phenomena. Jevons clearly noted the importance of statistical verification for economic analysis. Marshall lauded the work of the historians. Keynes observed that the study of economic history plays a distinct part in perfecting political economy. The historians encouraged high-level historical studies in economics. According to Gide and Rist, the historical school has been instrumental in broadening the scope of economics.

Some Authors of the Historical School

The renowned authors of the old historical school are William Roscher, Bruno Hildebrand and Karl Gustav Knies. The most important representative of the young historical school is Gustav Schmoller. Let us discuss their contributions very briefly.

WILLIAM ROSCHER (1817-1894)

Roscher is famous for his *Principles of Political Economy*. He is really the founder of the German historical school. He also published his book, *Outline of Lectures on Political Science According to the Historical Method*. Roscher regarded historical study as the foundation of any analytical study. In his *Outline*, he has stated the principles of historical method and has recommended the introduction of historical method in economic investigation. According to him, the classical method was abstract and hence useless. He wanted to investigate into the laws and the characters of various economic institutions. He referred to his method as the Physiological or Historical Method. According to him, the historical method was more scientific and practical. He suggested the importance of both historical data for the analysis of the economy and of the institutions.

Roscher introduced the importance of acknowledging the relative nature of economic theories and laws. Political economy is really a relative science. He also observed that institutions are partly good and partly bad. Economic relations between individuals reflect a social and cultural evolution. In fact, the state is not just the sum total of its members. It is more than that. Roscher was of the opinion that for establishing an economic truth, more and more historical data should be studied. The historical method attempts to combine organic, statistical and biological analyses to discover certain laws. These laws are relative in character. It should be noted that Roscher was not an extreme historicist. He did not totally reject Ricardian economics.

Roscher was not willing to consider economics as simply a set of normative principles. He did not favour normative analysis of economics. He considered economics with various social configurations. He was in search of laws of socio-economic development. He argued that "Once the natural laws of Political Economy are sufficiently known and recognised, all that is needed, in any given instance, is more exact and reliable statistics of the facts involved to reconcile all party controversies on questions of the politics of public economy."

Roscher thought that economics cannot be meaningfully separated from other disciplines and phenomena. Roscher used in his study many historical and statistical data. However, in spite of all this, he was not able to establish any law of historical development. He was unable to re-orient the method of economic analysis.[7]

BRUNO HILDEBRAND (1812-1878)

In 1848, Hildebrand published his book, *National Economy of the Present and Future*. In this book, Hildebrand challenged the claim of classical economists that they had found out the natural economic laws which are valid for all times and for all countries. He separated theoretical analysis from practical economic questions. He laid more emphasis on theoretical analysis. Hildebrand did not believe in the existence of natural laws of any type which could be made universally applicable. He did not also believe in the harmony of class interests, which the classical economists had postulated. He did not accept many of the classical propositions. He criticised the classical proposition that man is the end object of political economy. Hildebrand did not believe in the cosmopolitan nature of economic laws. He was of the opinion that knowledge of history will not only be helpful for the growth of economic science but it also helps to recreate it along more scientific and realistic lines.

Hildebrand proposed a stage theory of development based on historical evolution. According to him, the evolution of the economy would be through different stages of history, such as, means of exchange, money stage, credit stage, and so on. The credit stage would be the final stage of economic evolution. He was interested in finding out the basis of economic civilization of different nations. He was primarily interested in finding out the *historical law of development*. But unfortunately, he could not find out any such law till the end of his life.

Hildebrand observed that the aim of political economy is to open a way for a historical standpoint, and to transform the science of political economy into a body of doctrines which will be mainly concerned with the development of national economy. Hildebrand rejected the classical notion of atomistic society. He also could not agree with the classical materialistic view of life and society. According to him, political economy has to be based on the welfare of the people and of the state. He clearly indicated the use of historical method. Hildebrand was interested in the application of statistics for economic analysis and research. This itself was a distinct contribution.

---

7.   Ekelund and Herbert, *op. cit.,* p. 196.

KARL GUSTAV KNIES (1821-1898)

Knies was the third member of the German historical school. His book was on the *Political Economy from the Standpoint of the Historical Method(1853)*. He also wrote a book on *Gold and Credit*. His work on *Gold and Credit* is an outstanding contribution to the theory of money, banking and currency. Knies was a vehement but systematic critic of the classical school. According to him, Roscher was not a systematic and clear critic of the classical school. He chided Roscher for approving the classical method of analysis. He observed that Hildebrand also could not perfectly realise the mission of *Historismus*. According to Knies, Hildebrand's law of development was a concession towards a pure theory. Knies believes that historical studies are the basis of economic analysis, and that the economic system passes through a number of different phases which are dependent on the stage of civilization. No economic system can be regarded as the final and as the last one.

According to Knies, there is nothing like economic laws. Every economic aspect must be examined with reference to history. Economic generalisations are never universally valid. They are simply relative in character. He rejected the cosmopolitan view of economic laws. Knies criticised Hildebrand and Roscher for their failures. But all these writers agree to the fact that historical studies are the only legitimate basis for economic analysis. He paid a good deal of attention to the development of analytical method in economics. He never advocated the use of a partial method of analysis. He was well aware of the difference between economic history and political economy.[8]

GUSTAV SCHMOLLER (1830-1917)

Gustav Schmollor was the founder of the younger historical school of Germany. His book *Outline of General Economic Theory* (1900-1904) contained the most outstanding contribution of Schmoller towards the development of the young historical school.He presented a dynamic view of economic life. He was also interested in the theoretical analysis of economic problems, and offered solutions to these problems. He analysed the historical evolution of various economic institutions. In his analysis of economic problems, he profusely used statistical analysis.

The most important contribution of Schmoller was his ideas on the use of methodology. Unlike the members of the German historical school, Schmoller was in favour of using both deductive and inductive methods of analysis. He said: "Induction and deduction are both necessary for the science just as the right and left foot are both needed for walking". The same view was also later on accepted by Marshall. The new historical school concentrated more on the practical problems.

---

8.   W.A. Scott, *The Development of Economics,* p. 228.

Schmoller had the ambition to develop economic science through historical and descriptive facts. He was a very liberal member of the historical school. Schmoller believed in the existence of economic laws. He was very critical of the *laws of development* propounded by Hildebrand. According to him, it is very necessary to make economics more pragmatic for national policy and development. In his *Grundriss* (Outline...), he dealt with a number of topics on economic problems.

Schmoller observed that all received economic theories, like Ricardian theories, are not only useless but also pernicious. Schumpter noted that Schmollerian economics was essentially a historical sociology. Schmoller made an attempt to study economics in its organic perspective. But Schmoller's search for the laws regulating the economic organism failed. Since the time of Schmoller, the German historical school began to slowly disintegrate, partly due to the induction of inferior members and partly due to its bias in favour of an incomplete methodology, namely, deduction. As pointed out earlier, the German historical school was eclipsed by the rise of the Neo-Classical school.

Part Three
Reconstruction of Economic Science

8

Austrian (Subjective) School

CARL MENGER (1840-1921)

Carl Menger's *Principles of Economics* was published in 1871. According to some, Menger's claim to the invention of marginal principle was as good as Jevons's. Menger is sometimes regarded as a marginal economist. In what follows, we will examine some of the contributions of Menger in the different areas of economics.

Methodology of Economics

Menger considered individual as the centre of economic analysis. But his approach is quite different from that of others. Menger observes that the atomistic approach is a methodological necessity and that it has no ethical foundation. Menger was the first economists to invent subjective theory of value which is free from hedonist philosophy. When Menger was writing, the Historical School was at the apex of glory. However, Menger castigated the historical method of study of economic phenomena. He was not in favour of exclusive emphasis on the historical method of studying economic problems. He also criticised the German Historical School for neglecting altogether the deductive method of study. Menger reverted to the classical deductive method of analysis, with some modifications.

The Menger-Schmoller controversy, known as *Methodenstreit,* was a significant step forward in the realm of economic methodology. The historical school was against economic laws and economic theory. The school preferred the term 'economic regularities' and also substituted the term 'doctrine' in place of economic theory. According to the German historical school, economic theory was not really necessary for scientific research. Menger was in favour of the deductive method and the theoretical analysis of economics. This does not mean that he was against the historical method. He simply pointed out that historical method alone was insufficient. Menger emphasised on subjective factors and defended self-interest, utility maximisation and complete knowledge as the grounds upon which economics must be built.

Goods

Menger made a systematic discussion on different types of goods prevalent in an economy. Menger classified goods according to the directness with which they satisfied human wants. *Goods of the first order* satisfied human wants immediately. *Goods of the second and higher order* satisfied human wants only indirectly. Goods of the first order are mostly consumption goods, whereas goods of the second and higher orders are capital and production goods. In order that a thing may be a good, it must satisfy the following four conditions:

1. There must be a human need.
2. The good must be able to satisfy the need.
3. The consumer must recognise the want satisfying capability of the good.
4. The individual has the power and ability to apply the good to the satisfaction of the one.

There are some goods which are scarce in supply in relation to demand. There goods are called *economic goods.* However, when the goods are plentiful in supply in relation to demand, they are called 'non-economic goods' or 'free goods'. There are some goods known as complementary goods which can be used only combination with other goods.

In the transformation of higher order goods into lower order goods, time is very essential. According to Menger, economic progress requires the increasing use of goods of a higher order.[1] Menger also emphasises the basic complementarity and interdependence among all the goods we consume. In this way, he forms the basis for constrained utility maximisation.[2]

Value

As has been pointed out earlier, the economic character of goods is the consequence of a single cause—scarcity. Menger observes that the value of goods arises from their relationship to our needs, and it is not inherent in the goods themselves. Needless to say, value will differ as the relationship differs. Goods which are very essential for life would be consumed first and goods of lesser necessities would be consumed later. We must satisfy the more important needs first and the less important needs subsequently. According to Menger, value is not dependent on the total utility, but on the lowest utility one derives from the good. Although Menger did not clearly state the law of diminishing marginal utility, still it was implicit in his analysis. Value is, according to Menger, basically an individual phenomenon and it is independent of the laws and the state. However, to discover the value of a good we have to measure the satisfaction which will have to be sacrificed, if that portion were deducted from the total quantity. In other words, the value of any portion of the available quantity of goods is equal to the significance attached to the least satisfaction made possible by a single portion of the total quantity available. This means that value depends on the marginal utility of a good. This is the same Jevons's

---

1.   Robert Lekachman, *A History of Economics Ideas,* p. 251.
2.   Robert Ekelund *et.al., A History of Economic Theory and Method,* p. 277.

final degree of utility. According to Menger, subjective value is the basis of price determination.

When two persons are actually exchanging two goods, the relation between the subjective values of the two goods will alter until the relation is the same for both the persons. In other words, in equilibrium, the ratio of the marginal utilities of the two goods will be the same for both the parties exchanging the goods.

Menger explained in his own remarkable way the law of equimarginal utility which can be explained from the following chart :

I	II	III	IV	V	VI	VII	VIII	IX	X
10	9	8	7	6	5	4	3	2	1
9	8	7	6	5	4	3	2	1	0
8	7	6	5	4	3	2	1	0	
7	6	5	4	3	2	1	0		
6	5	4	3	2	1	0			
5	4	3	2	1	0				
4	3	2	1	0					
3	2	1	0						
2	1	0							
1	0								
0									

In the above chart, ten goods are arranged in a descending order of importance to the consumer such that good one (I) is having the highest utility and goods (X) is having the lowest. Good I may be regarded as food. Every column of the chart shows the units of satisfaction which the consumer can get by consuming the successive units of the commodity. For example, if one unit of commodity (I) is consumed, the consumer will get ten units of satisfaction, and then nine units, then eight and so on. It is assumed that the satisfaction from the consumption of a good is independent. The price of one unit of any good is assumed to be rupee one. The consumer with the given income will start purchasing the first good which is a sheer necessity (food). The consumer spends his money in such a way that the marginal utilities derived from the purchase of different goods will be equal. Thus, if the consumer has three rupees to spend, he will purchase two units of good (I) and one unit of good (II). In this case, the marginal utility will be nine from both the goods. In the same way, if the consumer has ten rupees to spend, he will purchase four units of good (I), three units of good (II), two units of good (III) and one unit of good (IV), so that the marginal utility in every case becomes seven units. This equalisation of marginal utilities is a way of attaining consumers' equilibrium as has been explained by Carl Menger. This law reveals that given the scarce means, the individual will arrange his various consumptions in such a way that at the margin, satisfactions are all equal.

In Menger's analysis, it is the least urgent satisfaction obtainable from a given stock of goods which gives value to that good. Menger also considered the impact of the differences in the quality of goods on their value. He also analysed the effects of competition and monopoly on the value analysis. He, however, did not relate satisfaction to the demand curve. He, like Jevons, ignored consumer's surplus. Menger observed that the values of the higher order goods depended on the expected value of goods of the lower order they serve to produce. In the Austrian theory, it is possible to get the value of the producers' goods from the value of the consumers' oods. Value, after all, is a judgement of the mind.

mputation

Mengers' theory of distribution is based on his theory of imputation. mputation is a term which makes the value of the productive agents rest the value of their products. It must be noted that the value of the goods a higher order (including the value of the factor of production) is conditioned by the value of the goods of the lower order which these goods produced. Thus, the value of flour depends on the value of the bread it produces. In the same way, the value of labour depends on the goods it produces. From this observation, Menger develops the marginal productivity theory of distribution. The share of a factor of production is to be determined by the loss in value which the product would suffer if that the factor was withdrawn from the production process. In other words, value of a factor of production depends on the marginal value of productivity of that factor. Thus, it can be shown that Menger was developing and supporting marginal analysis. An outstanding merit of Menger's distribution theory was that a single analytical treatment was given to all the productive services.

Menger also wrote on the origin of money. He considered that the inconveniences of barter were responsible for the development of money. Money also fecilitated the quantification of subjective value. Money acted as a price index and as a medium of exchange. However, Menger's contribution to economics was not free from criticism. The following points of criticism can be levelled against Menger:

Criticisms

1. Menger did not give us a satisfactory theory of price.

2. He neglected the role of diminishing returns in the explanation of supply.

3. His theory of imputation has many difficulties regarding the method of valuation.

4. The classification of goods of different orders is not scientific and precise.

Despite the criticisms, his masterly explanation of utility, value and imputation cannot be minimised in any way. It is to be noted, that he is the father of the Austrian school of economic thought.

FREIDRICH VON WIESER (1851-1926)

Wieser wrote two important books: *Natural Value* and *Social Economics*. He was following the tradition set by Menger. His important contributions are discussed below:[3]

Value Theory

According to Wieser, value is determined by cost and utility. Menger did not give so much of importance to distribution as Wieser did. Wieser also gave much emphasis on *cost*. The Austrian theory of value had a gap of which Menger was aware. But he himself could not bridge the gap. It was Wieser who tried to fill the gap by introducing the cost element in the determination of value. Of course, Wieser did not use the concept of real cost. In the analysis of value, Wieser did not take into account disutility in the traditional sense. To him, utility was the cause of value. However, value is, after all, a circular process. According to Wieser, the value of goods of a higher order depends on the values of their product. This derived value can be regarded as the cost. He spoke about the *opportunity cost*. In the pricing process, cost and price become equal at the margin. His idea of cost is different from the classical and neo-classical concepts of cost. The cost element became the basis of his theory of value. Once found out, cost may be taken as given. His concept of opportunity cost may be regarded as: "Given the quantity of the factors of production, competition for the factors of production in the different lines of employment will distribute them in such a way that the values of the different products permit them to earn the same total amount in every alternative use."

According to Wieser, the value of producers' goods is determined by the value of their products. Thus, the value of the factor depends on its marginal productivity. In this sense, the classical cost of production is only a special case of the general marginal utility-based value analysis. Wieser observes that classical theory of cost of production is simply a utility concept. Wieser did not find any contradiction between utility and cost. He considered cost in terms of marginal utility. According to Wieser, classical labour theory of value is not conceptually correct. He sticks to the marginal utility approach of value and completely breaks away with the classical objective cost analysis of value. Wieser analyses value in terms of the subjective factor. Wieser clearly explained the law of diminishing marginal utility in connection with his value analysis. Thus, value necessitates scarcity.

According to Wieser, utility is the first principle in the undertaker's economy; but there may be conflict between exchanged value and social

---

3. The discussion is based on Robert B. Ekelund, *et.al., A History of Economic Theory and Method*, pp. 281-293.

utility. In such a case, it is the exchange value which emerges out victorious. He underlined the bad effects of monopoly on social utility which other wise is maximised under perfect competition. Wieser, in this context, advocated selected governmental interferences, particularly for the following four reasons:

1. Governmental interference is essential when the economy has a limited number of capitalists.
2. Government should eliminate the bad effects of monopoly and the concentration of economic power.
3. There are some areas such a education, police, defence, where governmental interference is essential.
4. Government should intervene in a situation where the product is to be supplied under uncertainty or where the profit is too low for the private enterprise to attract.

In a self-contained, idealised economy, value-in-use depends on utility, and goods are produced according to the rank of their value.[4] Exchange value, in this context, is the measure of personal acquisition. However, in a real economy, exchange value depends on both purchasing power as well as utility. The price of some commodities is determined by the valuation by the weakest (poorest) buyers. Thus, the prices in the real world do not reflect necessarily marginal utility.

Natural Value

Wieser's analysis of natural value is a distinct contribution to economics. Wieser defines natural value as "value as we should find it in a community at a high stage of development carrying on its economic life without price or exchange." This type of value exists in a communistic state. This value is relevant in an economy where goods are valued simply by the relation between the amount of the stock and the marginal utilities. It is not disturbed by anything like error, fraud, force and so on. In the real world, however, natural value is a single element in the formation of price. There may be many other factors responsible. Natural value, of course, is completely a neutral phenomenon.

The formulation of natural value requires, however, a market system of allocation. Natural value does not provide evidence either for or against a socialist system. Be that as it may, it must be noted that Wieser was the first economist to point out the generality of the theory of utility valuation and also the usefulness of the market system of allocation

Theory of Imputation

According to Wieser, Menger's method of imputation was defective in the sense that it could lead to overvaluation of inputs. Wieser assumes that all production goods are actually employed in an optimum manner and those resources are combined in fixed proportions. In his theory of im-

---

'.   *Ibid.,* p. 285.

putation, Wieser showed with the help of simultaneous equations that every input has a definite share in the total product and that the total product is exhausted if the factors are paid their shares. Wieser replaced the negative imputation method by a positive method of imputation. He said that the contribution of a factor can be measured by the productive contribution that is made by the addition of a factor to the total value. Wieser observes that the withdrawal of a factor affects the productivity of other factors, too. This was not realised by Menger.

Wieser explained that when a factor is used in the production of a number of goods, its value will be determined by the least valuable good it produces. Input value is imputed, and the value of the input establishes the opportunity cost of utilising it in other directions. Through the opportunity cost, values of inputs and outputs are determined in a system.

The value of an extra unit of input applied to production is determined by the marginal utility of the additional units produced rather than by a marginal value of productivity. In this sense, the Austrians have a *marginal utility product theory* of input valuation. It must be admitted that value analysis of the Austrians reached its peak with Wieser's *natural value* which can be regarded as the highest theoretical achievement of Wieser.

Social Economics

Theory of Social Economics is a seminal work of Wieser. It has four parts covering the theory of simple economy, the theory of social economy, the theory of state economy and the theory of world economy. Economics is concerned with social process. Therefore, it has to be based on social economy. Wieser came to the conclusion that economic forces played a very dominant role in social revolution. He carefully analysed economic sociology. Wieser's theory of social economics is nothing but a theory of economic welfare. The evolution of economic society, according Wieser, is determined by certain characteristics of human nature, and mostly, by the elements of power and leadership. These developments led to a stratification of social structure which leads to the fragmentation of utilities and prices. On the basis of his theory of social Development, Wieser was able to make normative evaluation and to place labour and business power block at the centre. He argued for the establishment of labour unions as a countervailing force in the labour market, particularly against the exploitation by the monopolist and oligopolist. Wieser wanted the labourers to unite and use *strike* as a defensive weapon. He was also in favour of the expanded role of state for protecting properties, for national progress, for economic welfare, and for the regulation of social economy. State's role was essential for the establishment of certain types of industries like public utilities. The state is helpful for the social equalisation of use-value.

His social economics is a normative programme for economic policy. His view of economic process was Darwinian but he did not advocate stationary state. His was a theory of power-oriented evolution with a framework of static utility analysis. He deduced conclusions regarding the effects of power on welfare. Wieser favoured private property. His contribution lies in combining utility theory with an evolutionary theory of institution. The importance of his contribution lies in the solution he suggested to solve the paradox that exists between private property and maximisation of utility.

EUGEN VON BOHM BAWERK (1851-1914)

Bohm-Bawerk's Theory of Capital[5]

Bohm-Bawerk's contribution lies in the theory of capital and interest. His contribution to capital theory can be known from his book, *Positive Theory of Capital.* A number of influences contributed towards his theory of capital. Firstly, there was the desire to apply more consistently the theory of marginal utility to the Problem of interest. Secondly, he wanted to make some original contribution to the theory of capital.

Bohm-Bawerk defines capital "as a group of products which serve as a means to the acquisition of goods". According to him, *capital is a produced means of production.* The aim of production is the making of goods for consumption. Goods may be produced either directly or indirectly. The indirect method is the round-about process which takes time. The round-about process calls for the production of producers' goods (capital) before the production of consumption goods. Bohm-Bawerk treats capital as a factor of production because it is the source of income in the form of interest. Capital is the result rather than the cause of profitable method of production. According to him, capital is an intermediate product of nature and labour. He says that there is a close relation between saving and capital formation. Capital goods can be regarded as future goods. Capital is not a third and independent factor of production.

Capital is an intermediate factor whose supply is dependent on land and labour expended for the production of capital in the past. The distinction between the original factor of production (like land and labour) and the produced factors of production is very crucial to Bohm-Bawerk.

The importance of capital in production is to permit the introduction of more productive and at the same time more time-consuming round-about, method of production. The round-about method of production is a check against the production of capital in abundance. It is complemented by the situation of *time preference.* The ultimate limitation to investment is imposed by time one is willing to wait for return.

The round-about method of production gives a better result than the direct method of production. This is one of the most fundamental propositions of production theory. However, Bohm-Bawerk observes that round-about methods are necessarily and always more time-consuming than direct methods. It has to be noticed that with every increase in time re-

---

5.   See, M. Blaug, *Economic Theory in Retrospect* (3rd Edition).

quired for the production, the total product increases at a diminishing rate. The round-about method of production has been found to be more productive than ordinary direct method of production.

According to Bohm-Bawerk, since capital is stored-up labour, the more the capital, the older is the average age of the capital stock. However, his theory of capital makes much better sense when it is realised that his concept of capital incudes only circulating capital (*i.e.*, funds tied up in the form of goods in process).[6] The function of the working capital is to support labour during the gestation period of production. On the assumption that labour remains fixed, longer production time requires more capital per worker when it is found that period of production can be extended.

Bohm-Bawerk also made a distinction between the produced means of production and other forms of capital because he was trying to solve the problems connected with interest and rent. He also make a distinction between national capital and individual capital. He made it clear that he was concerned with the problems of national capital.

Productivity, on account of round-about process of production, increases due to technical improvement. He observes: "This is the true importance which attaches to our entering on round-about ways of production, and this is the reason of the result associated with them: every round-about way means the enlisting in our service of a power which is stronger or more cunning than the human hand; every extension of the round-about way means an addition to the powers which enter into the service of man, and the shifting of some portion of the burden of production from the scarce and costly labor of human beings to the prodigal powers of nature."

When the round-about method of production increases productivity of capital, every capital increases the demand for capital. Bohm-Bawerk observes that every lengthening of the round-about process is accompanied by a further increase in the technical result, and as the process is lengthened, the amount of product increases in a smaller proportion. The demand for capital is mainly because of its necessity in production and because of its higher productivity as compared to the direct method of production of consumer goods. The demand for capital cannot be infinite because of the decreasing marginal productivity of capital in a round-about method of production.

In Bohm-Bawerks's theory, it is very important to find out the length of the period of production. What determines the average period of production?[7] If the flow of input is equal to the flow of output in an economy, the average period of production can be regarded as equal to the value of capital invested in the plant divided by the value of the flow of input or output per year. The quotient or average period of production is

---

6. M. Blaug, *Economic Theory in Retrospect* (Third Edition), p. 527.
7. The discussion is based on M. Blaug, *Ibid.*, pp. 535-542.

lengthened either when more capital is invested during a period of time or when the same capital is frozen in production for a longer period of time. The average period of production in a one-sector economy is equal to $\theta = \dfrac{K}{I}$ (where K is the amount of real capital and I is the flow of inputs or investment). In a stationary state, the net investment being zero, the application of inputs corresponds to capital consumption. The workers' consumption is fully replenished.

When capital consists of consumer goods in process, "the average period of production is simply the sum of investment periods of all the labour inputs weighted by the number of inputs. The average period of production remains a weighted arithmetic mean of labour-days per year weighted by the duration of labour services up to the moment of final sale, divided by the total number of labour-days applied." The basic objective of calculation of average period of production is to get an index of capital intensity for the purpose of comparison in a production process which is characterised by varying capital structure.

Bohm-Bawerk's Theory of Interest

The most important contribution of Bohm-Bawerk to the theory of interest can be found in his book *Capital and Interest : A Critical History of Economic Theory*. His first volume entitled *History and Criticism of Interest Theories* contains a criticism of earlier theories of interest. His book entitled *Positive Theory of Capital* contains his own theory of capital and interest. Before giving his own theory of interest, Bohm Bawerk critically examined all the existing theories of interest, including the Marginal Productivity Theory, the Abstinence Theory and so on. He found that all the existing theories of interest were unsatisfactory. In his theory of interest, Bohm-Bawerk introduced the importance of *time element* in the determination of the rate of interest. According to him, interest is a social as well as a political problem. In fact, the problem of interest is a problem of distribution because out of the total flow of national income, a portion goes to the capitalist as interest income. Bohm-Bawerk thinks that since capital is not an original source of wealth, the problem of interest is not a problem of production theory. Why is interest paid?

Bohm-Bawerk explains the existence of interest and its size on three grounds (the famous *dire grunde*). The two of the grounds are psychological and the third ground is technical in nature. Bohm-Bawerk observes that an individual faced with a choice between present and future goods will normally overestimate future resources and underestimate future wants. Hope is the cause of the former and lack of imagination the cause of the latter. These two causes help to increase the marginal utility of goods in the present as compared to the marginal utility of goods in the future. Therefore, they create an *Agio* or a premium on the present goods. To call forth a supply of present in return for future goods, an *Agio* or premium has to be paid. Another reason for preferring present to future is the uncertainty of life and things in future. Bohm-Bawerk asserts that present goods are preferable instruments for the satisfaction of human wants and desire. Therefore, they have a higher marginal utility than the future goods. Another reason for the emergence of interest is the superiority of round-about method of capitalistic technology which is used for production. More can be produced by a wisely-chosen round-about method of production than can be produced by the direct method. The round-about method of production uses capital which is more productive. Therefore, some interest has to be paid for its use. This method of production requires present investment which will command a premium because of the promise of future increased output at a reduced cost and also because of the sacrifice on the part of the saver to part with his capital. From all this, the payment of interest appears to be justified. *Interest* is a natural phenomenon which cannot be dispensed with even in a socialist economy.

What determines the rate of interest? The rate of interest is determined by the demand for capital and the supply of capital. The demand for capital depends on the marginal productivity of capital. The demand for capital can never be unlimited. The supply of capital or saving is dependent directly on the rate of interest. The higher the rate of interest, the higher is the supply of capital, and the lower the rate of interest, the lower is the supply of capital. It has to be noted that capital mainly consists of means of subsistence advanced to the labourers. Therefore, the determination of the rate of interest is a matter of exchange of labour for consumer goods. With a given supply of subsistence fund, the rate of interest is determined by the marginal productivity of lengthening the average period of production. At a lower rate of interest, the profitable period of production becomes longer. In Bohm-Bawerk's analysis, the equilibrium rate of interest is determined by "the productiveness of the last extension of production economically permissible." In other words, the marginal productivity of extending the period of production actually determines the rate of interest. Interest arises from the productivity of capitalistic method of production. Many factors such as the size of the subsistence fund, number of workers and technological conditions are responsible for a change in the rate of interest.

Bohm-Bawerk's *Agio Theory* of interest was the first systematic theory of interest which is still regarded as the foundation of the classical and the neo-classical theory of interest. Bohm-Bawerk's theory of interest is original in nature. However, it has been criticised by many on different grounds. His theory has been attacked at least on three grounds:

1. He had either misunderstood or misinterpreted all the earlier theories of interest.
2. His own theory of interest is nothing but a new interpretation of the earlier theories.

3. His own assumptions and reasoning are inadequate and in-
    complete.

Despite Bohm-Bawerk's criticism against productivity theories of interest, his own theory of interest has remained essentially the same as the
marginal productivity theory of interest.

9

Marginalist School (1870-1914)

SALIENT FEATURES OF MARGINALISM

Economics became a science since 1870 with the rise of marginal economics. Marginal economists introduced a new technique in the analysis of economic phenomena. The new technique, known as marginal analysis, is the heart of marginal economics. According to some economists, the real story of the growth of economics as a science is the improvement of its technique. Marginal revolution was a revolt which was in favour of a genuine liberation, a shift from compiled literary generalisations to precise logical formulation. Marginal revolution of 1870 started with the discovery of the principle of diminishing marginal utility which became the fundamental building block of a new kind of micro-economics popularised by Jevons, Mengers and Walras.

The basic objective of Marginal economics was to search for the conditions under which optimum results could be obtained by the allocation of scarce resources. For the first time, economics became a science that sought to study the relationship between given ends and given scarce means that have alternative uses. The dominant role of the concept of substitution at the margin accounted for the sudden appearance of mathematical reasoning. Economic functions were assumed to be differentiable continuous functions. The marginal economists wanted to attain the maximisation of certain objective functions such as profit, utility and so on. The maximisation principle was applied both in the case of households as well as in the case of firms. In the consumer's equilibrium, the marginal economics introduced equimarginal principle.

The marginal principle was applied in the case of value, production and distribution. The classical theory of value based on the concept of labour-embodied stood changed as a result of the introduction of the marginal utility theory. The marginalists paid little attention to the cost of production and laid more emphasis on utility. However, it was Marshall who combined the classical notion of cost of production and marginalist notion of utility demand. Marshall, in fact, was adhering to the new marginal analysis. The entire neo-classical school adopted most of the major doctrines of the marginal school, so much so that some people think that neo-classical and marginal schools are one school. This is, however, not the fact. These two schools are in fact separate. But, marginalism found its comprehensive application in the writings of Marshall who used the marginal principle extensively in the explanation of demand, supply, production and their interaction.

Marginal economists put emphasis on the attainment of equilibrium. Economic discussion shifted from *total quantity* to small changes in these totals. The contribution of the marginal economists to the development of macro-economics was almost nil. The marginalists argued for the welfare-maximising effects of perfect competition. They borrowed from the earlier English economists some subjective principles like human rationality, equilibrium technique, importance of competition and so on. They added an emphasis on demand. The market pricing of factors was explained by them on the basis of their marginal productivity.

Marginalism is a new paradigm in economic science. However, this is not a new principle. Even Ricardo and others were aware of the *Margin*. The concept of margin was brought from the earlier economists. Be that as it may, some economists consider marginalism as the economics of the rentier class, as Bukharin did. Marginal utility analysis is regarded as nothing but the bourgeois answer to Marxism.

Marginalism (or Marginal Analysis) is generally thought to be an analysis of economic behaviour. This theory of economic behavior is based on the assumption that the individual maximises something which is a function of a set of variables which are relevant to the economic position of the individual and which are under his control.[1] Marginal analysis is nothing but a detailed spelling out of the theory of maximisation. In the case of households, utility is maximised and in the case of firms, profit or sale or output is maximised. Marginal analysis is still retained because it yields as conclusion the assumptions about behaviour function which are the postulates of economic analysis.[2]

The whole structure of micro-economic analysis has been developed through marginalism. On the basis on marginal analysis, the old puzzle about the pricing of diamond and water is easily solved, and the tail wagging dog demonstrated. The importance of the marginal lies in the fact that proper attention to the margin will enable consumers and producers to get the best out of their limited resources. On the part of the consumer, the price would be equal to the marginal utility of the commodity concerned; and as for the produces, the value under perfect competition in the long run must be equal to the marginal cost from the standpoint of supply. The profit of the firm is maximised when marginal revenue equals marginal cost. This equality is a necessary condition for the firm be in equilibrium. Marginal analysis is applicable to all types of markets — perfect competition, monopoly and monopolistic competition. Marginal analysis has also been employed in macro-economic theory. Keynesian concepts of mar-

---

1. K.E. Boulding, *The Skills of the Economist,* p. 28.
2. *Ibid*, p. 29.

ginal efficiency of capital and marginal propensity to consume are based on marginal analysis.

The concept of margin has also been used in the modern theory of distribution, which is called marginal productivity theory. The Austrian school of thought has used Ricardian marginal analysis. A distinction is made between pricing of output and of the factors of production.Here again, marginalism is the technique which facilitates the achievement of the result. The classical economists emphasised the problem of sharing of the national product between the factors of production more than the problem of determination of the prices of factors of production. But between the two approaches there is an obvious similarity in that, the former can be said to be a mere aggregation, at the level of the economy, of the picture at the micro level. Moreover, if the total product of a firm is exhausted by the factors of production, as Euler's theorem shows, the sharing of national product is a direct consequence of the sharing at the micro level. The modern as well as the classical treatment is known as the theory of distribution. The classical economists, particularly of the Ricardian tradition, looked upon distribution of the national product as an important element in the explanation of the behaviour of national product itself.

Ricardian theory of distribution is partly based on marginal principle which seeks to explain the share of rent. Rent is nothing but the difference between average and marginal products. The marginal productivity theory of distribution which is essentially a neo-classical theory developed by Marshall is partially derived from the marginal principle of the Ricardian theory. In the simplest form, the marginal productivity theory states that the price of a factor is equal to its marginal productivity. An important corollary from the marginal productivity theory is the Exhaustion theorem or Euler's theorem which demonstrates that if the production function is of the Cobb-Douglas type, total product is exhausted, if every factor is paid a reward equal to its marginal product.

A familiarity with the marginal principle prepares our mind to note the difference between transformation or opportunity relations, on the one hand, and preference functions, on the other. The marginal analysis draws our attention towards the problem of optimum, although there is no simple rule of finding it. At least, the principle points out the illusion based on average behaviour.

Marginal anlaysis is sometimes criticised as an analysis of behaviour. But in its generalised form, it is not an actual analysis of behaviour, but an analysis of advantage. It, however, becomes an analysis of behaviour if we further assume that men always act according to their best advantage, which is only rarely true.[3]

But marginal analysis does not depict a true equilibrium system. In order to have a true equilibrium, the second order condition, over and

---

3. *Ibid.*, p. 60.

above the first, has to be satisfied for a firm, which implies that the marginal revenue curve must be intersected by the marginal cost curve of the firm from below. The great defect of the marginal analysis is the absence of any information system.[4] If we do not know where the optimum point is located, we cannot move towards it. If the marginal cost curve or marginal revenue is of way character, there is the possibility of occurrence of multiple equilibria, and the unique equilibrium may not be available for study.

Marginal analysis has been empirically challenged by studying the actual behaviour of the firms. Thus, Hall and Hitch have shown that producers determine their selling prices on the basis of full average cost, rather than marginal cost and marginal revenue. Pricing is generally based on average cost plus some profit margin. But the study of Hall and Hitch has been criticised by Haley and Machlup. Hall and Hitch did not put forward a full alternative theory to marginal analysis. They studied the oligopolistic concerns, whereas the marginal analysis is applicable to perfect competition. Recently, Earley's empirical study of 110 companies supports marginalism — not marginalism on the sitting but marginalism on the wing.[5] It appears that for its simplicity, the generalised marginal analysis will hold sway until a better alternative is found out.

To sum up : Marginalism can be said to have the following characteristics : (1) emphasis on resource allocation, (2) application of a distinct technique of analysis, (3) introduction of static method, (4) emphasis on relative prices and not on absolute prices as the classicals did, (5) consumption is emphasised, (6) distribution is based on imputed values (marginal productivity of a factor), (7) emphasis on micro analysis, (8) absence of class conflict, and (9) possibility of factor substitutability in production.

HERMANN HEINRICH GOSSEN (1810-1858)

Gossen's Contribution to Economics

Gossen will remain ever important in the history of economic thought for his contribution to the development of marginal utility doctrine. He developed the marginalist doctrine in his book, *Development of the Laws of Exchange among Men* (1854). It is said that his contribution is well-comparable with the contribution of Copernicus. According to Gossen, there exists some confusion in economic theory owing to the lack of mathematical treatment. If mathematics is not introduced in economics, the analysis cannot be complete and precise. Therefore, he suggested the mathematical interpretation of economic analysis. He even pointed out that while it is not possible to measure absolute quantities of satisfaction, comparisons can always be made on the basis of geometrical principles. His book is an attempt to interpret economics on the basis of mathematics. Gossen's book is the result of twenty years of research and meditation.

4.   *Ibid.*, p. 62.
5.   See Earley's study in *American Economic Review*, March 1956.

Gossen is a utilitarian philosopher. He asserts that every man should try to raise his enjoyment of life to a maximum. On the basis of satisfaction and utility, Gossen has formulated the following three principles or laws :

1. The marginal utility derived from the consumption of any particular commodity goes on decreasing as the consumer increases the consumption of that commodity. This process goes on till the relevant want is completely satisfied and the point of satiety is reached. This is the first law of Gossen, which can be regarded as the law of diminishing marginal utility.

2. Gossen states that when a consumer is to consume different goods, then he equates their marginal utilities in order to derive maximum satisfaction from the total consumption.

Thus, if he consumes three goods (x, y and z), he will equate the marginal utilities of these goods divided by their respective prices

$(P_x, P_y$ and $P_z)$ or $$\frac{MU_x}{P_x} = \frac{MU_y}{P_y} = \frac{MU_z}{P_z}$$

This is the second law of Gossen. In modern times, this law is known as the *Law of Equimarginal Utility*. Obviously, this law applies to a situation where the consumer is not able to satisfy all his wants at a time completely.

3. Gossen's third law follows from the above two laws. Since the marginal utility of a good diminishes with its stock, the good will have positive marginal utility only so long as its supply falls short of its demand. If the supply is in a position to satisfy the wants fully, the marginal utility of the commodity will come down to zero.

These laws are based on assumption of rationality on the part of consumers. It is also based on the assumption that every consumer wants to maximise his pleasure and minimise his disutility (or pain).

According to Gossen, things have value in proportion to their ability to satisfy the wants. On the basis of this, Gossen has divided commodities into the following three types :

(i) There are goods which have all the properties of satisfying wants. These commodities are called 'consumer goods'.

(ii) There are some commodities which cannot alone satisfy completely the needs of the consumers. These commodities are called 'complementary goods'.

(iii) There are goods like land, machinery and so on which have an indirect value due to their ability to produce goods of the other two classes. These goods are called 'producers' goods'.

Gossen has also, in this connection, developed his *Theory of Imputation.*

According to Gossen, goods which can satisfy only one type of want have limited consumption and use. Regarding the contribution of cost, Gossen states that the different goods require different degrees of exertion (disutility) for their production. He says that the value of a commodity reaches its maximum when the quantity *AB* is produced, *i.e.,* when production is continued up to the point which equalises disutility (difficulty) and the utility (value). This is shown in the following diagram.[6]

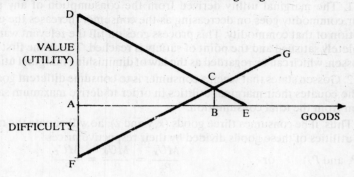

Fig. 9.1

In order to to achieve maximum satisfaction, men have to spend their time and energy in such a way that the last unit of any one satisfaction is equal to the amount of disutility which will be caused if that unit is produced in the last moment of exertion (*i.e.,* at the margin of disutility).

Gossen has always distinguished *needs* from *luxury* or *pleasure*. The meanings of these concepts are self-explanatory.

However, Gossen has emphasised the subjective aspects of value. His classification of goods into different types is suggestive of Menger's analysis. Gossen's theory of value remained, in a sense, incomplete. Gossen gave more importance to utility rather than to the cost of production. Cost of production was looked upon as a form of disutility. He equated marginal utility (value of the good) with the marginal disutility of its production. However, Gossen's analysis of marginal utility is very precise and complete. But the chief criticism levelled against Gossen is that his analysis lacks elegance and clarity in exposition. Gossen anticipated much of the recent developments in the theory of economics. He developed the subjective side of value and formulated the idea of marginal utility of value. Jevons drew most of his inspiration from the writings of Hermann Heinrich Gossen. In fact, Jevons' theory of value is based on Gossen's ideas on utility.

WILLIAN STANLEY JEVONS (1835-1882)

Jevons's Contribution to Economic Analysis

Jevons attempted a comprehensive theory of value on the basis of the earlier utility analysis. His main work, *The Theory of Political Economy,* was published in 1871. According to him, economic laws can be reduced to certain basic mathematical principles and these principles can be derived from human actions. Jevons maintained that value depends entirely on utility.

6.   L.H. Haney, *History of Economic Thought,* Surjeet Publications, Delhi, p. 592.

Utility can be defined as the quality possessed by an object of producing pleasure and preventing pain. He has distinguished between total utility and final degree of utility. His final degree of utility can be regarded as *marginal utility*. According to him, the final degree of utility decreases as the quantity of commodity increases. According to Jevons, value is equal to the final degree of utility. Total utility never interested Jevons. To Jevons, final degree of utility was more important than total utility. He also did not entertain the idea of inter-personal comparison of utility. In Chapter 3 he defined utility as "the abstract quality whereby an object serves our own purpose, and becomes entitled to rank as a commodity. Whatever can produce pleasure or prevent pain may possess utility." The utility, however, is not proportional to the quantity of the commodity, but quantity does influence its amount.

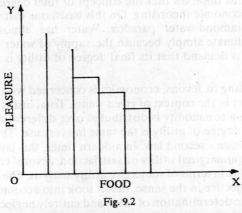

Fig. 9.2

The relationship between the amount of commodity and the utility has been explained by Jevons in terms of a figure, as given above.[7]

In the above diagram, each rectangle measures the utility of an increment of food. As the first two increments were vital to life, according to Jevons, they can be left as undefined. In fact, they had no limit. In case, we assume that the increments of foods are infinitely small, we can draw a continuous line as in the diagram 9.3.[8]

The figure 9.3 shows total utility as an area and the degree of utility as a line, such as *CD*. If *u* means the whole utility of consuming *x* then *u* is a function of *x*. In the above figure, *DF* is an increment of *x*, *DCEF* is an increment of *u* and *CD* is an increment of *u* increment of *x* or the degree of utility. Since the limit of increment of *u* increment of *x* is du/dx, the degree of utility can be regarded as the differential coefficient of *u* as a function *x*.

7. Robert Lekchaman, *History of Economic Ideas*, p. 244.
8. *Ibid.*, p. 245.

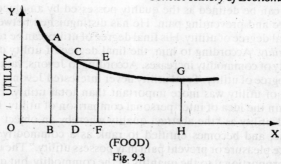

(FOOD)
Fig. 9.3

The final degree of utility is the utility from the last unit of the commodity. Jevons observes that the concept of final degree of utility is very crucial for economic theorising. On this basis, one can very easily explain away the diamond-water paradox. Water has almost no value in a temperate climate simply because the supply of water is so abundant in relation to its demand that its final degree of utility is reduced to nearly zero.

According to Jevons, economics is concerned with the maximisation of total utility in the context of given wants. Total utility, however, is maximised when a commodity is distributed over different uses in such a way that its final degree of utility is the same in every use. This law is the adaptation of Gossen's second law. In modern times, this law is interpreted as the law of equimarginal utility or satisfaction. Jevons' contribution lies in analysing value in terms of subjective utility analysis. The classical theory of value was objective in the sense, that it took into account the whole social process in the determination of value and entirely neglected the subjective factors. Jevons was not satisfied with the classical objective theory of value. He, therefore, introduced his subjective theory of value based on utility.

Jevons also introduced the theory of exchange which explained prices in actual markets. His concept of market included at least two persons trading in commodities. Each trader was aware of the supply and the price response of the commodities. Every trader wanted to maximise his own interest (profit) and exchange in the market takes place on the basis of that slightest possibility of profit. According to Jevons, competitive market requires complete knowledge for its smooth functioning.

Jevons introduced the concept of *trading body* for the management of demand and supply in the market. Trading body was designed to solve the problems of price determination in the market. However, his concept of trading body is not different from the concept of individuals in the market. Jevons explained the problems and difficulties involved in the process of market exchange. He also realised the importance of bargaining capacities of buyers and sellers in the market. Jevons also recognised the possibility of market distortion through differing marginal utilities of money of different persons operating in the market. He observed that exchange produced equality of final degrees utility for every individual. Exchange maximises utility only for a given income distribution.

According to Jevons, labour changes the supply of a commodity and thereby changes the final degree of utility (marginal utility). In this way, labour can have some effects on prices. But he remarks that labour is never the cause of value because value depends on the final degree of utility. In his explanation, cost of production determines supply, and supply determines the final degree of utility which determines the value of a commodity.

Jevons did not give any complete theory of distribution. His analysis of distribution depended mainly on Ricardo's theory of distribution. He, of course, anticipated Austrian capital theory. He explained the possibility of

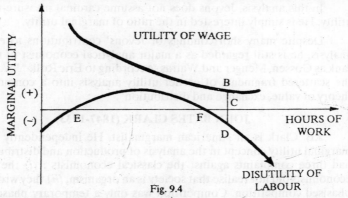

Fig. 9.4

a backward-sloping supply curve of labour. His rent theory was purely Ricardian in nature. In the analysis of wage, Jevons explained the importance of the balance between pleasure and pain. This can be explained in the above figure.[9]

In the figure, hours of work are shown on the horizontal axis and marginal utility on the vertical axis. The top curve which measures the utility of the wage to the labourer declines gradually according to the law of diminishing satisfaction. The bottom curve measures the disutility or pain of the labour to the worker. Every work involves some disutility. Since initially every work involves some inertia, the bottom curve has a negative portion to the left of *E*. Some moderate amount of labour gives pleasure and therefore, it can be depicted by the segment between *E* and *F*. Larger and larger amount of work will cause pains and drudgery and can be explained by the negative segment to the right of *F*. The point at which *BC* and *CD* become equal is the amount of labour which will equate the pain of the work with the utility of the wage, and labour will stop there.

---

9. *Ibid.*, p. 246.

It should be noted that Jevons theory of exchange is till now considered as very relevant. For the analysis of exchange problems in economics concerning individual, he gave us the law that the ratio of exchange of any two commodities will be the reciprocal of the ratio of the final degree of utility of the commodity available after the exchange is completed. To convert Jevons' expression into the modern consumer's allocation formula, we can say that an equilibrium allocation of expenditures implies the satisfaction of the following situation :

$$\frac{MU_x}{MU_y} = \frac{y}{x} = \frac{p_x}{p_y} = \frac{MU_x}{p_x} = \frac{MU_y}{p_y} = \frac{y}{x}$$

(Where, MU_x is the marginal utility of commodity x, MU_y is the marginal utility of commodity y, P_x is the price of x and p_y is the price of y.)

In this analysis, Jevons does not assume cardinal measure-ability of utility. He is simply interested in the ratio of marginal utility.

Despite many shortcomings of Jevons' contributions to economic analysis, he is still regarded as a major analytical economist of the same rank as Gossen, Menger and Walras. According to Eric Roll, "Jevons made the scattered fragments of earlier utility analysis into a comprehensive theory of value, exchange and distribution".

JOHN BATES CLARK (1847-1933)

J.B. Clark is an American marginalist. He independently used the marginal utility concept in the analysis of production and distribution. He had three complaints against the classical economists : *(i)* the classical economists did not realise that society is an organism, *(ii)* they wrongly emphasised competition. Competition was only a temporary phase, *(iii)* by postulating economic man, the classical economists neglected the real motive of human behaviour. Clark wanted to remove the classical defects from his analysis.[10]

Clark's Contribution to Economics

Clark wanted to confine himself to deductive analysis. He used a unified philosophy for the analysis of economics which was absent in the American economic thought. Marshall in England and Clark in the United States adjusted the situation in the fine spirit of scientific continuity.

Methodology

Clark based his analysis on marginal principle. The exposition of marginal productivity principle is the most important contribution of J.B.Clark. In analysing so, he postulated individual freedom, private property, mobility of labour and capital and the desire of the individual to satisfy certain basic ones. Clark pointed out that society is like an organism and the economic laws are valid only if the moral sense of the society ap-

---

10. Eric Roll, *History of Economic Thought,* pp. 424 ff.

proves of those laws. He also used static and dynamic analysis. Clark divides the economic universe into three parts. The first explains the universal laws which are related to isolated human beings. The second and the third are related to static and dynamic socio-economic phenomena.

Clark abandoned the limitation of the economic man by removing the distinction between productive labour and unproductive labour. He made a distinction between marginal utility and effective utility. Effective utility is measured by the alteration in the subjective conditions. Clark also introduced the concept of social value in explaining economic phenomena.

Clark's Marginalism[11]

Clark's economic analysis was essentially static in character. He enunciated five principles according to Paul Homan for the explanation of economic phenomena. These are : *(i)* capital and labour are freely mobile, *(ii)* economic activity is motivated by man's attempt to satisfy wants, *(iii)* private property is the basic social institution, *(iv)* governmental interference should be selective, *(v)* individual freedom operates through competition.

Marginal Utility Theory of Value

Clark's theory of value is essentially the same as Jevons' theory. He, however, worked on this theory independently. Clark expanded the marginalist theory of value by considering both qualitative and quantitative increments. He thought that most economic goods are not simple utilities but bundles of utilities. Value, according to Clark, is a measure of utility. Clark focussed on the fact that the last increment of a good does not alone determine price every time, but an increment of quality in that incremental good generally does. Value is determined by final utility which is a combination of many utilities like necessity, luxury and so on.

Marginal Productivity Theory of Distribution

In his book, *The Distribution of Wealth*, Clark specifically mentioned that final productivity is the regulator of value for every factor of production. Clark recognised that the returns to labour and capital can be expressed as a differential surplus. This can be shown in the following figure. In the figure, *BC* is the marginal product of labour (*CD* is the wage rate), the wage bill for *AD* workers will remain *AECD* and *EBC* will be the differential surplus which goes to the capital in the form of interest. In this way, he showed that the return to every factor can be calculated on the basis of marginal productivity of the factor.

It has to be noted that Clark was successful in integrating the theory of distribution and the theory of value with the help of the same marginal principle. The marginal productivity theory used by Clark is an extension of the Ricardian rent principle.

---

11. Ekelund and Hebert, *A History of Economic Theory and Method,* p. 379.

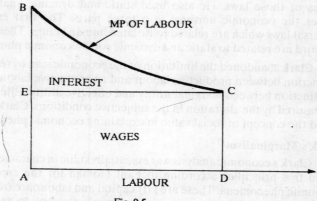

Fig. 9.5

Clark limited his analysis to two factors : labour and capital. He realised that when all factors are paid according to their marginal productivity, the total product would be exhausted. This is known as the *adding-up* theorem. Thus, *A, B, C* can be regarded as the three factors of production, each discrete and homogeneous, and *P* is the product. The production function then defined as $P = f(A, B, C)$. It is assumed that the production function is of the form, such that if $P = f(A, B, C)$ then, $mP = f(mA, mB, mC)$, for all positive values of m Thus, it follows from the rules of partial differentiation :

$$\frac{\delta P}{\delta A} \cdot A + \frac{\delta P}{\delta B} \cdot B + \frac{\delta P}{\delta C} \cdot C = P.$$

The above expression means that the total product equals the quantities of various factors multiplied by their respective marginal productivities. This theorem is valid if there is a constant return to scale. From here, Clark observed that when every factor is being paid according to its marginal productivity, there is no question of exploitation of any factor of production as pointed out by the classical economists. Clark also does not find any disharmony of interest among the different classes of people in a society.

Critical Estimates

1. Clark's theory is not a supply-and demand theory of price. He did not take into account the demand and supply factors. This is regarded as a weakness of his theory.

2. Clark has used purely static and competitive conditions where uncertainty and risk are absent.

3. Clark considered marginal productivity theory on the basis of the normative principle. He used this theory to justify income distribution under competition.

However, despite the above points of criticism, Clark's contribution can be regarded as substantial. He also provided inspiration and leadership to a large number of leading economists of his time. He is also one of the founders of marginal analysis.

10

Mathematical School

AUGUSTINE COURNOT (1801-1877)

Cournot was a mathematical economist. He interpreted economics in his own original way. He wrote a number of books including *Researches into the Mathematical Principles of the Theory of Wealth* (1838), *Principles of the Theory of Wealth* (1863), *Review Summary of Economic Doctrines* (1876). He also wrote extensively on the theory of political economy.

Economic Theory

Cournot explained the importance of mathematics in the analysis of economics. He examines meticulously the theory of price. According to him, demand for an article varies with its price, but demand, supply and price are all inter-related variables. He analysed the theory of demand. He was responsible for the introduction of demand curve in economic analysis. He stated that demand is a function of price $D=f(P)$. The quantity demanded is a function of a number of variables such as income, wealth and so on. But these are assumed as constant at the time of drawing the individual demand curve for a commodity. Cournot, however, noted that if any one of the above variables changes, the demand for the commodity ultimately changes. Cournot understood the importance of the assumption of *other things remaining the same (ceteris paribus)*. His law of demand is similar to the modern conceptions of the demand function.

Cournot gave much importance to empirical analysis based on observations of facts. Cournot rejected utility as the foundation of the demand analysis presented by him.[1] He observed that sales or demands increase when price decreases. He was concerned with the average annual price. Cournot explained the theoretical foundation of negatively-sloped demand function.

Monopoly

Cournot explained the profit maximising behaviour of monopolists with reference to his classic example of the proprietor of a mineral spring. Cournot demonstrated that a monopolist does not necessarily charge the highest price, although he can get it. A monopolist generally adjusts his

---

1. Ekelund and Herbert, *op.cit.*, p. 211.

price so as to maximise his net income. In the case of zero cost, the monopolist will maximise his gross income. This occurs when the marginal cost equals the marginal revenue In the case of zero cost, a maximum occurs when marginal revenue equals zero. Cournot's analysis of monopoly can be explained with the help of the following figure. As shown in the figure, the owner of the mineral water having zero cost will adjust the sale of mineral

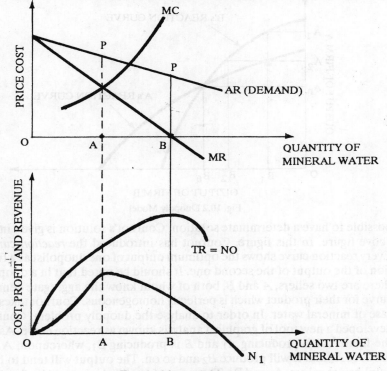

Fig. 10.1 Monopoly Model

water in such a way that he is able to sell *OB* amount at *BP* price. At this quantity, the marginal revenue is equal to marginal cost, *i.e.*, *MR=MC=zero*. As shown in the figure in the case of zero cost, the total revenue curve *(TR)* becomes the profit function N_0. Cournot established that profit will be maximum at a point where *MR=MC*, and this point of output is *OA* and price will be *AP*. It is to be noted that in this case of positive cost, the output would be lower and the price will be higher than those in the case of zero cost. The mineral spring is not operated to maximise gross returns at *OB* but to maximise the net returns at *OA*. Needless to say, Cournot's work on monopoly is well-comparable with any one of the modern works in the same subject.[2]

2. *Ibid.*, p. 213.

Duopoly Model

Cournot is very famous for his duopoly analysis. His theory of duopoly is based on the assumptions that buyers quote prices and sellers merely adjust their output to those prices. Every duopolist calculates the demand function for the product and then sets the quantity sold.[3] In this process, he assumes that his rival's output remains unchanged. In this situation, it is

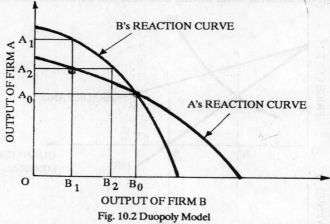

Fig. 10.2 Duopoly Model

possible to have a determinate solution. Cournot's solution is given in the above figure. In this figure, Cournot has introduced the *reaction curves*. Every reaction curve shows the optimum output of one duopolist as a function of the output of the second one. It should be noted that in a duopoly, there are two sellers, A and B, both of whom know the aggregate demand curve for their product which is perfectly homogeneous. Cournot takes the case of mineral water. In order to analyse the duopoly problem, Cournot developed a new tool of graphical analysis known as reaction curve. As per the figure[4], A is producing A_1 and B is producing B_1, whereupon, A will produce A_2 and B will produce B_2 and so on. The output will tend to have equilibrium values, A_0 and B_0. The point of equilibrium would be P. At this point, the duopolists will share the profits and charge a common price which is lower than the simple monopolist's price but higher than the price in a perfectly competitive market. According to Cournot, the output under duopoly will be two-thirds of the output produced under perfect competition. In fact, output can be determined by the formula : $n/n + 1$(where n is the number of producers). Thus, if the number of producers is 2, the output would be 2/3 times of the competitive output. If there are five producers, the quantity of output to be produced would be 5/6 times the competitive output. Cournot pointed out that if there is collusion between the two duopolists, the result would be a monopoly. This will have its effect on output and price.

---

3. M. Blaug, *Economic Theory in Retrospect*, p. 333.
4. *Ibid.*, p. 334.

Evaluation

Cournot was an original writer. He provided many theoretical innovations in his analysis of economic problems. He analysed many important problems in economics such as a discussion on stability conditions of various economic equilibria, composite and derived demand and also a clear statement of the simple competitive model. However, of all these, Cournot's reputation lies in his analysis of monopoly and duopoly. But, subsequently many of the assumptions of Cournot were changed by later theorists like Edgeworth and Bertrand. Bertrand criticised Cournot's solution of duopoly, and suggested that it can be assumed that the sellers set prices and that every seller determines his price on the assumption of his rival's price. He found that this is more realistic than the output setting behaviour of the duopolist. Similarly, Edgeworth modified Cournot's analysis of monopoly and introduced uncertainty of mutual reactions.

Be that as it may, many of the important developments in the areas of monopoly and duopoly in our times are explained with reference to the solution already attempted by Cournot. His simple model till now stimulates many ideas on similar problems in economics. He had a grand insight into economic theories. He was, moreover, equipped with the necessary tool kit of analysis of explaining the economic problems on empirical foundation. However, unfortunately, economic historians could not properly appreciate the contributions of Cournot.

GUSTAV CASSEL (1866-1945)

Cassel was a Swedish economist. He can also be categorised as a mathematical economist. He is renowned for his work on monetary economics. He was the author of many publications, including *The Nature and Necessity of Interest, The Theory of Social Economy, World's Monetary Problems* and so on.

Price and Value

Cassel in his *Social Economy* explained price and value systems. Cassel thinks that human wants are unlimited but the means to satisfy these wants are limited. Therefore, there must be a proper adjustment between the limited resources and the unlimited wants. According to him, the system of price can be an instrument for checking the human wants. He took note of the scarcity problem in the economy. He rejected the theory of value and the theory of marginal utility. According to him, economic theory is not able to deal with reality. It is indeed very difficult to know value in the proper sense of the term. The subjective value has no scientific basis. Therefore, it can be relegated to the background. He wanted to make the science of economics objective and abstract. Although he took for granted the existence of utility, still he discarded the concept of utility at the margin. He wanted economics to be a science dealing with empirical things. To him, scarcity was the fundamental basis of price. In this connection, he explained the equilibrium price which was determined at a point of intersection between total demand and total supply. However, Cassel observed that it is very difficult to measure the emotional intensity of demand by any means excepting the measuring rod of money. This is one of the ways in which one can get an idea about the subjective valuation of a commodity. When value is expressed in this way by money, we get the price. Thus, it is more meaningful to speak about price than about value. An exchange economy which deals with money must use the expression 'price' and not 'value'. The concept of value must be excluded from the science of economy.

General Equilibrium

Being a mathematical economist, Cassel has discussed the pricing process through a system of analysis known as general equilibrium. In this analysis of general equilibrium, he has taken into account a set of demand functions, such that every demand function for every good is dependent on the price of the good and also on the prices of other relative goods. Cassel assumed a trendless economy with perfect competition. In his analysis, the demand for every good must be equal to its supply in equilibrium. In his analysis, supply depends on the factors of production available. The prices of the factors of production are regarded equal to the prices of the goods and services they produce. The prices of factors of production are related to the money income of those factors. In this way, Cassel shows inter-relationship and interdependence in the economic system, and through a set of simultaneous equations, he presents the demand, supply and prices of all goods and services available in the economy. He then arrives at a determinate solution to the problem of general equilibrium much like the same way as the Walrasian general equilibrium analysis. Such a solution can give us a set of relative prices. In this system, if one price is specified, all the other prices can also be specified. We can have different sets of equilibria. Every equilibrium value would be different from every other equilibrium value. When the variables are changed, a new equilibrium would be created. In his system, there are a number of equations for finding out a number of prices. If the prices are known, demand for every commodity can be estimated. In his subsequent analysis, Cassel relaxed many of the assumptions and got more realistic results. He also analysed the problem of price determination in a dynamic economy. However, Cassel was more concerned with the determination of relative prices and not so much with absolute prices.

Monetary Theory

He discussed the problem of monetary economics and the effects of gold and other standards on the price level. Cassel was not happy with the marginal productivity theory of distribution. Cassel pointed out that a trade cycle occurs because of the fluctuations in the production of durable capital and its use. Rate of interest is the outcome of *waiting* for a period of time for the durable good. It is the waiting, that is, the time factor involving a sum of money, which generates the rate of interest. Cassel observed that the rate of interest cannot fall below a critical minimum rate.

Purchasing Power Parity Theory

According to this theory of Cassel, the external value of a currency depends upon its internal purchasing power. The equilibrium rate of exchange between two currencies must stand essentially as the quotient of the internal purchasing power of these currencies. Thus, if £15 has the same purchasing power as Rs. 10, the rate of exchange should be £1.50 = Re.1. In other words,

$$\frac{£1}{\text{Re.1}} = \frac{\text{Purchasing power of } £}{\text{Purchasing power of Re.}} = \frac{\text{Price level in India}}{\text{Price level in U.K.}}$$

The rate of exchange between £ and Re. will be equal to the ratio between the purchasing power of each currency. The purchasing power parity theory of Cassel is, however, only true under special conditions.

11
Lausanne School

LEON WALRAS (1834-1910)

Leon Walras's General Equilibrium

General equilibrium is a type of equilibrium in which a number of economic variables are studied to see the interrelations and interdependence among the variables for the proper understanding of the economy as a whole.[1] Whereas in the partial equilibrium analysis, only two variables are taken into account, in the general equilibrium analysis, all the relevant variables are brought to play their part.

Leon Walras is the most famous exponent of general equilibrium. But recently, prof. Leontief has also developed another variant of general equilibrium through his input-output analysis.

Assumptions
1. Constant returns to scale
2. Full employment
3. Perfect competition
4. Homogeneous units of a productive service
5. Tastes and income of the consumers are given
6. Constant production technique
7. Mobility of factors of production.

Walras makes a distinction between the product market and the factor market. According to him, the consumers are buyers in the product market and sellers in the factor market, and the producers are buyers in the factor market and sellers in the product market. In the Walrasian system,[2] if there are m products, n factors, m product prices and n factor prices, and mn technical coefficients, the total number of unknowns adds up to $2m+2n+mn$. This was reduced by Walras by 1. Therefore, the total number of unknowns become $2m+2n+mn-1$. He reduced the number by one, because one of the products serves as *numeraire* (measure of value) in which all other prices are expressed and which itself has the price of 1.

---

1. M. Blaug, *Economic Theory in Retrospect,* pp. 523-24.
2. L. Walras, *Elements of Pure Economics,* 1954.

In his system, the number of unknowns is matched by m-1 demand equations for products, m cost equations, n quantity equations for factors of production, n price of productive services, mn technical coefficient equations, i.e., $2m+2n+mn$-1 equations. Thus, the number of unknowns exactly matches the number of equations, and general equilibrium is established.

In the demand equations, the quantity demanded of a product is related to the price of the product and the prices of all other products and factors of production. The prices of factors of production influence the income of the consumers and, therefore, their demand for products and the prices of other products. The demand equations are based on utility functions which are maximised when consumer prices are equal to marginal utilities. The demand equation for one product must be discarded because it is not an independent equation but is obtained from the informations contained in all other equations. If the demand for all but one of the products can be ascertained, so is the demand for the one, provided the consumers' income is equal to their expenditure for products.From this equality through budget equation, it becomes clear that what is spent on one product is the difference between income and expenditure for all other products. Walras' law means that, under certain conditions, equilibrium or the absence of excess demand in m-I markets implies equilibrium or the absence of excess demand also in the remaining markets. This law points out the structure of the involved quantitative relationship.[3]

In his cost equations, the product price equated to the quantities of the factors embodied in it, each multiplied by the factor prices. Prices are equal to the average cost of production—neither profit nor loss.

An example of Walrasian procedure can be gathered from his cost equations, a_t, a_p, a_k, b_t, b_p, b_k, c_t, c_p, c_k, d_t, d_p, d_k, which indicate the quantities of each of the productive services: land (T), labour(P) and capital (K) and which are used for the production of one unit of each of the products $(A),(B),(C),(D)$. The prices of services and products are denoted by P_t, P_p, P_k and P_b, P_c, P_d respectively. Then

$$a_tP_t + a_pP_p + a_kP_k + \ldots\ldots = 1, \qquad (P_a = 1)$$
$$b_tP_t + b_pP_p + b_kP_k + \ldots\ldots = P_b$$
$$c_tP_t + c_pP_p + c_kP_k + \ldots\ldots = P_c$$
$$d_tP_t + d_pP_p + d_kP_k + \ldots\ldots = P_d$$

The quantities of productive services demanded are equated to the quantities supplied in equilibrium and the market for productive services is cleared. This is true of the quantity equations for the productive services.

The supply equations for productive services relate the quantity supplied of a service to the prices of all services and products.

3. Friedman, "Leon Walras and His Economic System", *American Economic Review*, 1955.
4. Spiegel, *The Growth of Economic Thought*, p. 553.

For the purpose of simplification, Walras first adhered to the assumptions of fixed coefficient of production.[4] His technical substitution equations indicate the quantities of each of the productive services that will be combined for the production of a product. The combination will reflect the lowest cost, where marginal productivities will be proportional to the prices of the productive services.

Later, Walras expanded his system and introduced additional unknowns and equations to account for capital formation, saving and money-holding. But in doing so, he maintained throughout the formal symmetry of his system.

Walras, with the help of his mathematical technique, demonstrated that a perfectly competitive economy will tend to approximate equilibrium positions, and with this in mind, he developed his theory of *tatonnement*— gropings or approximations— which can explain the movement of market towards equilibrium. *Tatonnement* works through the taking up of arbitrary price to begin with, until equilibrium is set up finally.

Importance

1. In the Walrasian system, it is pointed out that a private enterprise can attain equilibrium where waste of resources can be prevented, and economic welfare maximised.

2. With the help of his analysis, the actual working of the economic system in the real world can be understood.

3. It helps to appreciate the actions and reactions of a change in the variables on the other variables, and thereby the actual functioning of the economy.

4. General equilibrium analysis is helpful in integrating the various individual decisions which are affected by price changes. A change in the relative price level changes the decisions of the consumers and the producers. The type, amount and method of production also undergo a thorough change.

5. Lastly, this analysis has been mainly responsible for the recent development of input-output analysis which is increasingly being used as a planning technique in backward countries.

Criticisms

1. It is a static model. No time-lag is taken into account

2. It is based on unrealistic assumptions, *e.g.,* perfect competition, constant returns, etc.

3. The set of simultaneous equations will break down, if these assumptions are discarded.

4. Its application is practically limited. It is based on a complicated and difficult set of equations. The technique cannot be used by those who are not trained in mathematics.

5. Equality in the number of equations and unknowns is neither a necessary nor a sufficient condition for the existence of a solution. In fact, it is possible to find a system of two equations in two unknowns which has no solution in the domain of real numbers, the domain which is economically meaningful. The unique general equilibrium solution may involve zero prices (free goods) or negative prices (nuisance goods). Walras considered only normal goods. Hence, Walrasian demonstration of the existence of a general equilibrium remains unsatisfactory.[5] However, it was A. Wald who demonstrated in 1933, that given certain assumptions, Walrasian general equilibrium system can provide a unique non-negative solution.

VILFREDO PARETO (1848-1923)

Pareto's Contributions to Economics

Pareto belonged to the Lausanne School. He was a follower of Walras. He extended Walras' general equilibrium economics and developed a more elegant version of equilibrium.

He wanted to develop formal and positive theory of economics which will be free from ethical considerations. However, his book, *Cours d'-Economic Politique* contained many normative postulates. He supplemented the neutral and formal analysis of equilibrium with socio-psychological theorems. But like Marx, he could not integrate his sociology with his economics. To him, economics remained strictly a pure science.

Pareto was a mathematical economist. He followed mathematics in the analysis of his economic ideas. From the simple, mathematical rules regarding the determinacy of a system of equations with N variables, Pareto was able to show the general interdependence of the entire economic system. He hoped that a time will come when the unknowns in his algebraic equations will be filled up with quantitative values drawn from the real world.

Pareto made a distinct analysis of income distribution. On the basis of some statistical study, Pareto came to the conclusion that income distribution shows a high degree of constancy in different countries and at different times. If this type of distribution is plotted on a logarithmic graph, it will give a straight line sloping down to the right, and its inclination will be extremely stable. Thus, this can be regarded as the numerical expression of Pareto's income distribution. But his statistical data were not sufficient for the study of income distribution. Criticism has also been made against Pareto's special definition of income inequality. According to Pareto, constancy of inequality in the pattern of income distribution suggests inequality of human ability. However, for this to be valid, Pareto will have to show that there is every where and at all times a definite distribution of

---

5. M. Blaug, *op.cit.,* p. 608.

human beings according to their ability to earn income and that income distribution is mainly based on the distribution of ability. But his book, Cours, did not provide any such evidence. Pareto pointed out that a reduction in inequality can be achieved by a rise in average income so that production grows faster than population. This conclusion of Pareto was also challenged by his critics.

However many of the views of Pareto underwent drastic changes in course of time. This is true both regarding his idea about economic theory and also about politics.

Pareto was not very clear about the *ordinal* character of utility. He became more conscious of the necessity of the empirical fact of choice regarding the study of consumer's equilibrium. According to him, the concept of utility was confusing. Therefore, he introduced some less confusing terms like *ophelimity*. However, this was not sufficiently different from the concept of utility. Therefore, his new concept could not replace the concept of utility.

In his book, *The Manual of Political Economy,* Pareto discarded the theory of value and introduced the theory of price which was unrelated to the subjective factors. Since utility was not measurable, he introduced the ordinal concept of utility for formulating the theory of choice. This notion was based on the scale of preference as revealed by the consumers. The scale of preference can accommodate any number of utility functions. However, Pareto could not give a complete theoretical underpinning for the analysis of choice. However, an important beginning was made by Pareto. Pareto used the concept of *indifference curves* originally introduced by F.Y. Edgeworth in his *Mathematical Psychics* in 1881. On this basis, it was possible to construct a theory of consumer's equilibrium. In this analysis of indifference curve, many combinations of two goods can be made out of which the consumer has to choose one. The combinations on a particular indifference curve will mean the same level of satisfaction to a consumer. A higher indifference curve will mean a higher level of satisfaction and a lower indifference curve will mean a lower level of satisfaction. A number of indifference curves can be represented by an indifference map which will show different levels of satisfaction. It will then be possible to represent an equilibrium system in terms of indifference through a number of differential equations. In this analysis, the concept of utility does not have any role to play.

Welfare Economics

Pareto contributed substantially to the development of new welfare economics. It must be noted that all writers before Pareto ignored the question of comparing different optima associated with different levels of income distribution. In his *Manual of Political Economy* (1906), Pareto rejected the traditional concept of cardinal utility and restricted himself to the welfare conclusions which did not depend on any interpersonal comparison of utility. Pareto defined optimum position as a situation when nobody could be shifted to a higher indifference curve without causing a downward shift for someone else. In other words, it is a situation in which it is not possible to make any one person better off without making another person worse off. The Pareto optimality can be achieved by satisfying the following conditions :

(i) For the optimum allocation of goods, the marginal rate of substitution (MRS) between any two goods must be equal for any pair of individuals who own these same two goods.

(ii) For the optimum degree of specialization, the marginal rate of transformation (MRT) between any two products must be equal for any pair of firms which produce them.

(iii) The optimum utilisation of factor can be achieved if the MRT between any factor and any good is the same for any pair of firms using the factor and producing the goods.

(iv) For optimum allocation of factors, all the factors should be used to the maximum capacity. The optimum allocation of resources will be attained only when the MRS between any two factors is the same for the firms.

(v) For the optimum direction of production, the goods produced must be distributed in the best possible manner. This implies that the MRS between any two goods for any consumer should be the same as the MRT between the two goods for the society.

(vi) For the optimum allocation of a factor unit's time, the MRS between leisure and income must be the same as the MRT between work and the product for the society.

(vii) For the intertemporal optimum allocation of assets, the MRS between assets at any two points of time must be the same for any two individuals.

(viii) The above *Marginal Conditions* (first order conditions) do not necessarily establish Pareto optimality. Apart from these, we require some stability conditions which may be called the *second order conditions*. The fulfillment of the second order conditions means that in the neighbourhood of maximum welfare, all indifference curves must be convex to the origin and all transformation curves must be concave. The convexity of indifference curves implies diminishing marginal rate of substitution between two products for a consumer, and the concavity of transformation curves implies diminishing returns of increasing cost conditions in production. Hicks observes that to attain the largest maximum welfare, *total conditions* should be satisfied. These conditions are *true sufficient conditions*, according Mishan. These conditions are fulfilled when "it must be impossible to increase welfare by producing a product not otherwise produced; or by using a factor not otherwise used."[6]

---

6. Reder, *Studies in the Theory of Welfare Economics,* p. 37.

Pareto's optimum can be easily attained if there is perfect competition. Pareto's analysis of welfare in terms of Paretian optimum leaves a considerable amount of indeterminacy in the solution. There can be an infinite number of points on the contract curve in Edgeworth-box diagram, which can be Pareto optimum. "The indeterminacy is the consequence of considering an increase in welfare to be unambiguously defined only if an improvement in one individual's position is not accompanied by a deterioration of the position of another. This indeterminacy can only be removed by further value judgments."[7]

Pareto's marginal conditions may be summed up thus : Between any two goods (production factors), the subjective and objective marginal rates of substitution must be equal for all households and all production units respectively, and these ratios must be equal to each other. However, as Blaug observes, even if both first order and second order conditions are satisfied, we cannot be sure about the reaching of maximum maximorum point.[8]

7. Henderson and Quandt, *Micro economic Theory,* p. 208.
8. M. Blaug, *Economic Theory in Retrospect,* p. 628.

12

Swedish (Stockholm) School

KNUT WICKSELL (1851-1926)

Wicksell is a very renowned representative of the Swedish school. He has made important contributions to the development of the theory of value, theory of distribution, theory of capital and monetary theory. He developed the marginal productivity theory of value and distribution. His most famous contribution is towards the monetary theory. He has also contributed to the theory of business cycle. The most important expression of his ideas can be found in his book, *Lecture of Political Economy*. His another famous book is, *Interest and Price*.

CAPITAL AND INTEREST

Wicksell used the Austrian definition of capital. However, he made sufficient improvement over the Austrian theory of capital. Wicksell considered interest as the return on capital. "Interest is an organic growth out of capital, a certain percentage." According to him, capital is saved-up labour and saved-up land. Interest is the difference between the marginal productivity of saved-up labour and land, and of current labour and land. In the current period, there is abundance of labour and land relative to the stored-up land and stored-up labour. The stored-up land and labour are separated from the current land and labour through a time element. Wicksell argues that if the productivities of stored-up land and labour and those of current land and labour are equal, there would be no rate of interest. When the rate of interest is low, there would be increased demand for long-term capital investment. This will gradually relate to a rise in the rate of interest. However, ultimately there would be a tendency of the rate of interest to be equal for different maturity periods of capital investment. In other words, the short period and the long period rate of interest will be equal.

The equality of interest rates assures a constant amount of saving of both land and labour. This type of relationship should be maintained over the years, otherwise, interest might disappear. When the short rates and long rates are equal, an equilibrium will be established between the amount of capital and the rate of interest on the basis of marginal productivity. For Wicksell, interest is the marginal productivity for waiting. Wicksell thinks that whereas a high rate of interest stimulates saving, a low rate of interest discourages it.

Capital Structure[1]

Wicksell gives a broad definition of capital which includes all sources of income. In the narrow sense, capital is the intermediate product. Wicksell observes that from a micro point of view, where the price or value of capital is taken as given, one can fully apply the marginal productivity theory. But micro-economically, every increment of capital leads to a change in wages and interest rates. According to Wicksell, capital structure has both vertical and horizontal aspects. The horizontal aspect or width means the proportion of primary factors invested every year for replacement of capital goods. The vertical dimension or height implies length of time for capital investment. The horizontal and vertical expansion of capital can be shown in the following diagram.[2] The width refers to the *capital*

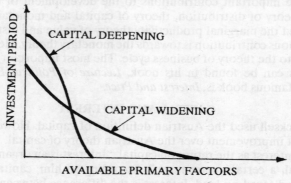

Fig. 12.1

widening and the height refers to *capital deepening*. Wicksell thinks that, in the initial stage, there may be capital widening. This, however, reduces the rate of interest and tends to raise the real wage and rent. This situation will disturb the composition of equilibrium capital stock and will encourage capital deepening, which will counteract the declining tendency of the rate of interest and rise in wages and rent. Labour-saving innovation will make deepening more attractive and may also lead to a reduction in the wage level. However, deepening of capital increases the marginal productivities of capital and labour. Thus, capital deepening and capital widening may go hand in hand. According to Wicksell, a capitalist saver is basically a friend of the workers.

Wicksell Effect

An increment of capital changes wages and interest, and hence the purchasing power of the capital. This is called precisely the *Wicksell Effect*. The Wicksell effect is the key to the whole theory of capital accumulation, according to Joan Robinson. When capital is defined as goods in process, the value of capital in terms of the product rises when wages rise and the

---

1. See, Mark Blaug, *Economic Theory in Retrospect*, pp. 583-585.
2. *Loc. Cit.*

rate of interest falls. But when capital includes durable assets, then an increase in wages is accompanied by a downward revaluation of capital through a reduction in the rate of interest. Wicksell effects says that a fall in the rate of interest tends to increase the value of capital by more than the increase in its physical stock. In fact, the real Wicksell effect involves a change in the technique of production induced by a change in the rate of interest. A negative Wicksell effect is a situation where capital-intensive technique of production is chosen at a low rate of interest. After all, Wicksell believed that the demand for capital is inversely related to the rate of interest.

MONETARY THEORY

Wicksell is more famous for his contribution to monetary economics. He recognises the existence of two rates of interest : *Natural rate of interest* and *Market rate of interest*. The relationship between these two rates of interest is an important determinant of price level. The natural rate of interest is that rate which tends to equate saving and investment in the economy, and tends to equal the expected yield on capital. This is almost the same concept as that of marginal efficiency of capital of Keynes. The natural rate of interest is also the rate of interest which equates the demand for capital and the supply of saving. The market rate of interest (bank rate) is charged by the institutions. As shown in the figure below, the market rate of interest may be lower or higher than the natural rate of interest. When the market rate of interest is below the natural rate, saving will decrease and expenditure will go up on capital outlay and on consumption. This will tend to increase the level of prices.

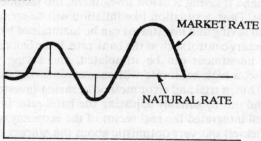

Fig. 12.2

With the market rate of interest exceeding the natural rate of interest, the reverse situation will follow. The monetary equilibrium will be maintained, according to Wicksell, if the following three conditions are fulfilled : *(i)* The demand for capital is equal to the supply of saving. *(ii)* The commodity prices are stable. *(iii)* The natural rate of interest is equal to the market rate of interest. Under a situation of monetary equilibrium, money will be neutral. These three criteria must be satisfied simultaneously. When there is monetary equilibrium, there is obviously equilibrium in the money market. However, Wicksell observed that money is not always neutral.

Wicksell understood the full implication of *real balance effect,* i.e., the effect produced by change in the price level on consumption and saving. He demonstrated the *real balance effect* as an equilibrating mechanism which ensures stability in the money market. He did not accept the rate of interest as a purely monetary phenomenon.[3] Wicksell's dynamic analysis took the form of a cumulative process. His analysis of cumulative process is based on an inter-relationship between money market and product market. He gave an important role to the rate of interest and aggregate demand in explaining aggregate adjustment to changes in money supply. His monetary theory has done an important job by filling up the missing chapter in the neo-classical monetary theory. His theory of interest is really a synthesis of Austrian marginal productivity theory and the general equilibrium theory of Walras. He was one of the first economists to formulate ideas explaining price movements. He was an independent discoverer of the marginal productivity theory.

Once the price level is changed, Wicksell observes that it becomes cumulative. However, ultimately,the cumulative process comes to a halt. Wicksell's cumulative process is concerned with the determinants of money supply under various situations. It shows that it is not proper to describe the quantity theory of money as merely a theory of demand for money, as regarded by Milton Friedman.

SAVING AND INVESTMENT

Wicksell considered saving and investment in an *ex-ante* sense. In this sense, saving and investment are equal but if saving exceeds investment, income is reduced, consumption goes down and the price level falls. On the other hand if saving is below investment, the income level and price level will rise. Thus, a situation like inflation will be created. The relationship between saving and investment can be maintained by the use of technique of monetary control such as the bank rate. If the bank rate is kept sufficiently low investment can be stimulated, and saving will be discouraged. Likewise, a high bank rate will encourage saving and discourage investment. Thus, a trial and error method of saving-investment equilibrium can be found out by suitably adjusting the bank rate. In an important sense, Wicksell integrated the real sector of the economy with its monetary sector. Wicksell was very optimistic about the efficacy of monetary policy in bringing about monetary equilibrium.

TRADE CYCLE

Wicksell's analysis of trade cycle springs from his analysis of cumulative process. Trade cycle essentially arises out of disequilibrium in the monetary sector. Another reason for the growth of trade cycle is the disequilibrium between technical progress and population growth. He introduced *period analysis* into the explanation of capital formation and capital

3. Ekelund and Hebert, *A History of Economic Theory and Method*, p. 399.

productivity. He was one of the earliest economists to explain the price movement inter-temporally. He explained the inflation between 1895 and 1910 as due to the over production of gold in the Transvaal. He explained the decrease in the price level during the 1930s as due to a fall in the production of goods and services. Wicksell ultimately gave up his own perception on economic crises, and adopted the Spiethoff theory and to some extent, Aflation's theory.

EVALUATION

Wicksell will remain an important monetary economist for all times to come for his path-breaking analysis of the nexus between natural and market rate of interest and his analysis of monetary equilibrium. He has been a source of inspiration to many Swedish economists like Ohlin, Lindhal and Myrdal.

13

Socialist School

KARL RODBERTUS (1805-1875)

Rodbertus was a German socialist. He is known for his works on *Our Economic Condition* and the *Normal Working Day*. He also wrote a book called *Social letters*. Rodbertus was an original writer. He was called the *Ricardo of Socialism* by Wagner. Rodbertus was similar to Marx in many respects, but in many others, his idea were different from Marx's ideas. Whereas Marx was a revolutionary, Rodbertus was an evolutionary. Rodbertus explained socialism in terms of morality and ethics, but Marx analysed socialism in terms of economics. But like Marx, he analysed the exploitative nature of capitalist society. For both Marx and Rodbertus, socialism was essential for the betterment of the economic lot of workers.

State Socialism

Rodbertus was in favour of state socialism. He simply believed that poverty and crises can be removed and distributive justice can be attained by the socialisation of property. All this can be done by the state which should be a neutral agent. Rodbertus explained the evolution of society at three stages : *(i)* In the earliest stage, human beings were used as slaves and the slaves were exploited by landowners, *(ii)* In the Christian Germanic stage, land and capital became private property for the use of which rent was demanded by the owners. Thus, owners lived on unearned increment. *(iii)* In the third stage, capital and land, as Rodbertus believed, would be nationalised and this will make an end to the clash of interest between the different classes of society, particularly between land and capital. But such a state of affairs may take nearly five hundred years. Rodbertus pointed out that such a stage will come only through evolution.

Ideas on Production

Rodbertus observed that society is based on the idea of division of labour. If society were to progress smoothly, then production, distribution and exchange must go on smoothly and according to needs of society. He lamented that production is not organised on the basis of the needs of society but rather it is guided by the market forces of demand and supply. When production is based on market forces, the guiding principle becomes profit maximisation and not the fulfillment of needs. According to him production should be sufficient to satisfy demand, and it should utilise the economic resources of the country, and thirdly, the products should be distributed on the basis of some just principle. Production of social needs cannot be fulfilled in a capitalist economy but it is only possible under socialism.

Ideas on Distribution

Rodbertus pointed out that the wage level in a society is based on the subsistence law of wage. This is also regarded as the *Iron Law of Wages*. When the wealth of the country goes on increasing, the share of wages goes down and, therefore, the relative purchasing power of the workers also goes down simultaneously. This important law of diminishing wage share was analysed by Rodbertus very clearly. He observed that when the national income goes up, the share of profit and rent goes up. As a result, the labouring class becomes poorer but the other classes become richer. This leads to increasing injustice towards the labourers. The labourers cannot also purchase the increasing amount of goods and services being produced in a growing economy. Thus, the wage share does not keep pace with the increasing industrial productivity. Owing to the lower purchasing power of the workers, underconsumption takes place and overproduction or glut becomes the ultimate outcome of a capitalist society. This line of argument has also been given by Karl Marx in his theory of crisis.

Rodbertus believes that all products are made by labourers, either directly or indirectly, through the use of tools and equipments. Thus, the labourers are entitled to the whole produce by way of remuneration. But the capitalists are giving them a wage which is merely equal to the level of subsistence. The crisis that follows leads to unemployment and underemployment of various types. According to him, the crisis is the result of the private ownership of the means of production and also the consequent exploitation. The same line of argument is also put forward by Karl Marx. Capital is also a kind of labour—the dead labour or the stored-up labour. Rodbertus never explicitly stated that labour alone creates value nor did he deny it.

Rodbertus distinguished between two types of rent: land rent and capital rent. Rent was the outcome of surplus labour productivity over and above the subsistence wage. This provides the economic explanation of rent in the analysis of Rodbertus. Rent also arose in a system of private property and capital. In such a case, the surplus created by the labourers is taken away by the property-owners. Rodbertus opposed the subsistence theory of wages. Rodbertus put forward a number of suggestions for the improvement of society: *(i)* social ownership of the means of production, including property, *(ii)* nationalisation of property, *(iii)* price fixation of commodities on the basis of labour embodiment, *(iv)* fixation of working hours and increase in the share of wages in national income, *(v)* protection of workers against trade cycles, *(vi)* evolution of a proper distribution system, and *(vii)* increasing the role of state. He looked upon state as a historical organism which alone can eliminate the inherent defects of capitalism.

FARDINAND LASSALLE (1825-1864)

Lassalle was a German socialist. He was another founder of state socialism. His ideas were influenced by the ideas of Rodbertus, Karl Marx and others. His book,*The System of Acquired Rights,* is considered the best exposition of the legal philosophy of Lassale.

Lassalle and Marx

Lassalle in many ways was influenced by the writings of Marx. Like Marx, he also pointed out the exploitative nature of capitalistic economy through the subsistence wage of the workers. Lassalle called this as the *brazen or the iron law of wage.* However, Lassalle differed with Marx in the following respects: *(i)* Lassalle argued that the workers' fate can be improved only by capturing the state machinery and utilising it for the purpose of workers' welfare. Marx, on the other hand, opined that nothing short of a revolution organised by workers will help the workers in getting their objectives achieved. *(ii)* Whereas Lassalle regarded the state as an important organisation that can be used for the benefit of the workers, Marx never regarded the state as basically a legislative machine in favour of the workers. Rather, Marx looked upon the state as essentially an instrument of a particular class. The state is coercive in nature and it is an instrument of the class of people which is ruling the state.[1] *(iii)* Lassalle advocated universal suffrage for the workers for getting hold of the state machinery, but Marx said that the class nature of state cannot be changed by merely extending universal suffrage to workers. *(iv)* According to Lassalle, Malthusian law of population is primarily responsible for the low wages of workers, but Marx did not accept the Malthusian law of population.

According to Marx, workers' wage is lowered down primarily because of the capitalist monopoly over the means of production which enabled the owners to pocket the surplus value created by the workers. In fact, low wages under capitalism, according to Marx, is mainly due to the inherent contradictions in capitalism. Regarding policy recommendations for the improvement of the lot of workers, Lassalle differed from Marx on many important points.

Production Management

Lassalle argued that the position of labour in a capitalist economy ruled by the brazen law of wage is simply hopeless. He observed that the sooner capitalism is abolished, the better it is for workers. He said that it would be better if producers' associations are established. These associations will be granted credit and help by the state, and the state will be the instrument for maximising the welfare of the entire people, including the labourers. For capturing state machinery, the workers must unite and have

---

1.   G.D.H. Cole, *Marxism and Anarchism : The Socialist Tradition,* p. 82.

their own votes. If the workers can have control over the state, they can get anything done in their favour through the help of the state. This arrangement will do away with the necessity of capitalist employers. The labourers would be their own employers. Thus, there would be no exploitation, and the workers will enjoy the whole product produced by them collectively. Whereas Marx was in favour of trade unions for the improvement of the conditions of workers, Lassalle was doubtful about its efficacy.

Lassalle was in favour of the development of cooperative workshops by the workers. In such a system, the state will provide the necessary help for the benefit of workers' cooperatives. He was thinking of a system where industrial management would be gradually regularised by the producers' associations to be owned and controlled by the workers.

Ideas on Capitalism and Classical Economics

Lassalle observed certain inherent defects under capitalism. He said that a capitalist economy has a built-in bias against the workers. Ricardo, in fact, carried the bourgeois economy to its apex where the only possible further development was to transform the capitalist economy into a socialist economy.[2] The classical theory of division of labour meant that the individual worker who was producing only a part of a unit of product was not free to sell it out in the market or use it for its own consumption. Thus, under capitalism, workers do not have individual freedom. In fact, workers were separated from their products. This was Marx's theory of *alienation*. Lassalle observed that social and economic evils like crisis, famine, war, etc., are the result of maladjustments in a capitalist order of society. Capitalist economy depends too much on the market. But the market cannot always give a proper signal. It is imperfect and it is based on an incomplete information system. Thus, under capitalism, there are many examples of market failures.

Lassalle observes that capital is the outcome of some type of historical development. It is stored-up labour. But it is an active agent of production. The introduction of capital, however, minimises the importance of labour. In order to eliminate this defect of capitalism, Lassalle suggested social control. He hoped that in future the state will gradually suppress private property and eliminate capitalism. He was in favour of full-scale state intervention and management. He advocated strong organisations for workers, by workers and of workers.

KARL HEINRICH MARX (1818-1883)

Karl Marx is one of the greatest thinkers of all ages and of all schools. Marx was essentially a classical economist. It was he who also coined the term *Classical Economics*. Marx's writing has a philosophical flavour. It is also based on some amount of abstraction. Marx's thought ranged over philosophy, history, economics and sociology. In terms of paradigm, Marxian economics introduces a new epoch in economic thought. His writing

---

2. Alexander Gray, *Socialist Tradition*, p. 337.

was mainly directed to the critical analysis of capitalist development and to its ultimate transition to the desideratum of socialism. Marx considered capitalism as a passing phase. He considered economic life in terms of conflicts of interest between the owners of capital and of labour. Marx's most famous works are *The Communist Manifesto* and *Das Kapital*. The first volume of *Kapital* appeared in 1867, but the second and the third volumes appeared only after his death, and the fourth volume was published only in the twentieth century. In what follows we will make some topical discussions on the various aspects of Marxian economic thought.

Materialistic/Economic Interpretation of History (Historical Materialism)

Marx's basic purpose was to uncover the general process of historical change. There are mainly, according to Lenin, three components of Marxism which culminated into 19th century intellectual development: (a) German philosophy(mainly of Hegel), (b) French socialism and (c) British political economy. For Hegel, the society is always dynamic and the change from one situation to another is based on conflict. The process of change in which new ideas did not so much eliminate the old as resolve conflicts within them, Hegel called that *Dialectic*. In this process, the new stage is an advance over the old.

Marx was more profoundly influenced by Feuerbach who was a *materialist*. He asserted that far from man's consciousness dominating his life and existence, it was man himself who dominated his consciousness. Marx extended Feuerbach's materialism to the explanation of all dominant ideas prevalent in the society. Secondly he extended Feuerbach's idea to history. Feuerbach's analysis was entirely historical and non-dialectical. To Marx, what matters most is the way production is organised. This was the abstraction he made.

In contrast to the Hegelian dialectical progress of ideas, Marx took the contradiction between the forces of production and the relations of production as the motive force of historical change. Man's consciousness was crucial in Marx's thought, but it could only be understood in relation to man's historical, social and material situation. Marx was also influenced by the ideas of French Revolution (Liberty, Equality and Fraternity). He believed that a socialist society, in which classes would eventually disappear, would be based on the productive power developed by capitalism, organised according to a plan formed by full decision-making participation of working people. Marx explained all history as the reflection of class struggle: "The history of all the hitherto existing society is the history of class struggle." *(The Communist Manifesto).*

Marx has elaborately explained the materialistic conception in his *Preface to a Contribution to a Critique of Political Economy*. In organising production, men enter into relations with each other as slaves or masters. These relations are specific to modes of production and are studied as class relations. These relations are the base for other political, legal and intellectual life which can be regarded as the *super structure*. A society's production relations correspond to, however, a definite stage of development of society's material productive forces. Production relations can influence the momentum and qualitative direction of the development of the productive forces. Historical materialism contends that class conflict and the basic trajectory of human history are accounted for by the advance of the productive forces.

In entering into production relations, man inevitably finds in his social existence, in his practical day-to-day life, the unconscious rationale for the system. It has to be noted that production exists independently of the choice of men even though they have been historically made by men in their own development. The serf feels bound by loyalty to master and king. The wage-earner has freedom to sell his labour. He can strive for higher wages, but does not question the wage system.

All this demonstrates the stability existing in a given mode of production. Instability can be caused in the system historically when the forces of production, crudely the technological ability to produce, are held back by the relations of production. The forces of production tend to be dynamic, changing frequently and placing great strains on production relations which are sluggish and somewhat inflexible. Attempts to accommodate the new forces of production within the existing relations bring a breakdown in those relations and with this also falls down the old superstructure of ideology, and so on.

However, these changes do not come about overnight but are contained in a century of progress and stumbling. The development of production relations depends on the outcome of class struggle. The ruling class of any mode of production always resists the advance of the conditions favourable to the class that is to be dominant in the new society. Working people will be torn between two competing systems of oppression, until under capitalism, they constitute the emerging ruling class.

Any change becomes essentially historical in nature, when one wants to, as Marx did, lay bare the economic law of motion of modern society. Marx said that the course of history can be explained because it is governed by certain laws that can be discovered. Hegel emphasised the role of ideas in shaping history. Marx rejected this and substituted in its place the concepts of *mode of production and class struggle*. Marx has assigned the highest place to economic structure of society (base). All other structures depend essentially on the economic structure. In the course of time, the mode of production undergoes a change and this necessitates suitable changes in social relationships. The existing relationships become incompatible with the alterations in the mode of production, and it is the conflict between these two that generates a social change.

Laws of Motion (Laws of Development) of Capitalism

According to Karl Marx, there are certain laws or general tendencies in a capitalist economy. These tendencies arise out of the capitalist mode of production. The laws of motion of capitalism, as discussed by Marx, are given below:

1. Every capitalist economy is concerned with accumulation of capital. Every capitalist wants to become supreme in competition with other capitalists. There is, therefore, competition such that the big enterprises engulf the small ones. Because of this tendency, the average size of the big firm grows continuously. At the same time, many companies destroyed by competition are absorbed by the large companies. In capitalism, *industry will become more and more centralised* and economic power will be concentrated in the hands of a few capitalists.

2. *Larger and larger accumulation of capital* is the law of capitalism. This is done for survival and for gaining supremacy.

3. In a capitalist economy, the ratio of constant capital to variable capital (labour), goes on increasing. This is known as *increasing organic composition of capital.*

4. Due to increasing organic composition of capital, the rate of profit goes on falling. When the rate of surplus value is constant, a higher organic composition of capital will mean a *falling tendency in the rate of profit.*

5. The introduction of machinery and the substitution of more capital for labour lead to unemployment. Thus, there arises a *growing industrial reserve army.*

6. Capitalism will lead to the *increasing proletarianisation of the working population,* as a result of unemployment and exploitation.

7. Capitalism ultimately faces crisis.

8. Capitalistic production develops circumstances for the *objective socialisation of production,* as a result of growing interdependence.

Contradictions in the Capitalist Mode of Production

A series of fundamental contradictions in the capitalist mode of production can be traced from the laws of motion of capitalism.[3] Ernest Mandel has specified the following points of contradictions, as found out by Marx:

1. There is a contradiction between the objective socialisation of production and the private exploitation, appropriation of profit and the ownership of the means of production by the private sectors.

2. There is a contradiction between expanding production of the capitalist system and the limited consumption of the working class.

3. A contradiction is revealed in a capitalist system between the planned production in each firm and organisation and anarchy in the whole

---

3. Earnest Mandel, *From Class Society to Communism,* pp. 46-47.

of the capitalist productive system. This results from the existence of private property and a generalised system of commodity production.

4. There is a contradiction between the expansion of science and technology to emancipate the humanity and the tendency of the capitalist to exploit the masses, particularly, those who are workers. These expansionary forces also lead to the destruction of humanity through war, aggression and so on. Thus, the humanity is confronted with two contradictory situations like socialism and barbarism.

5. There is, in capitalism, an inherent tendency towards a class struggle existing between labour and capital.

6. Capital accumulation is done with a view to earning higher profit. But in actual practice, capital accumulation leads to a falling rate of profit.

The contradictions under capitalism arise out of the conflict rooted in the *forces of production* which are dynamic and the *relations of production* which are static.

Marxian Theory of Surplus Value

The theory of *surplus value* as given by Marx is based on his theory of value. If the exchange value of a commodity is equal to the labour time contained in it, then the exchange value of a given amount of labour time must be equal to its product. Really speaking, the wage of labour must be equal to the productivity of labour. But this does happen under capitalism. In such a system, the exchange value of labour is less than its product. The explanation for this can be provided by examining Marx's theory of surplus value.

If we take into account a system of simple commodity production, we find that the producers sell out their products in the market in order to purchase some other necessary products. Thus, the producers start with commodities, convert them into money and the same money is converted into some other commodities. This relation that obtains in simple commodity production can be written as C-M-C. But under capitalism, the process is changed. The capitalists here start with money for the purchase of commodities, then those commodities are again sold out for money. Thus, money comes at the beginning and also at the end. This can be written as M-C-M. Here, money acquires the character of capital. It must be noted with interest that in capitalism, money is the beginning and money is the end. In this process of conversion, the money that is obtained at the end, *i.e.*, M' is greater than the money at the beginning, *i.e.* M. This is a very important feature of capitalism. The qualitative transformation of use-value here is replaced by a quantitative explanation of exchange value as the objective of production. The difference between M' and M is the surplus value which is the income of the capitalists.

In a capitalistic economy, labour power is a commodity. Therefore, it must have a value. The value of labour power is determined by the labour necessary for the production of an article. The production of labour power requires subsistence and maintenance. The value of labour power is the subsistence necessary for the maintenance of the labour.

Marx observes that labour is paid only a subsistence wage in capitalism which can only purchase subsistence goods (wage goods) necessary for the maintenance of the labour. A labour suppose, requires four hours of labour to earn his subsistence, then, assuming twelve hours' manday, the value of the product created by the labourer for the remaining eight hours can be regarded as surplus value, i.e., labour over and above the subsistence requirement. Marx says that under capitalism, labour power is the source of surplus value which is pocketed by the capitalist. Thus, a man-day can be divided into two portions: one portion is devoted by the labourer for earning his subsistence and the rest is devoted by the labourer for the creation of surplus value for the capitalist for whom he is working. Thus, it can be said that a labourer is paid less than his productivity, which means that there is exploitation under capitalism. The working day of the labourer which can be divided into two may be called: necessary labour and surplus labour. Necessary labour produces subsistence and surplus labour produces surplus value. Under capitalism, the necessary labour is equal to the wage and the surplus labour is devoted to the production of surplus value.

Under capitalism, value of a commodity consists of three parts: *(i)* value of equipment, machinery and raw materials. All these come under constant capital (C). *(ii)* Another part of the value will consist of expenditure on labour power. This is called the variable capital (V). *(iii)* The third part is called surplus value (S). Therefore, the total value is equal to the value of the constant capital plus the value of variable capital plus surplus value. Or, total value = C + V + S. The rate of surplus value (S') can be regarded as a ratio of surplus value to variable capital, or, $S' = s/v$.

In a capitalist economy, the rate of surplus value is nothing but the rate of exploitation by the capitalists. The magnitude of the rate of surplus value or exploitation is determined by the following three factors: *(i)* the productivity of labour, *(ii)* the quantity of commodities entering into the real wage, and *(iii)* length of the working day. It is possible to increase the surplus value by extending the working hours, or by lowering the real wage rate or by increasing labour productivity. All the above three factors may also be used in combination. If the surplus value is increased by lengthening the working day (manday), it can be regarded as *absolute surplus value*. But if surplus value is increased by lowering the wage rate or by increasing productivity of labour, it is called *relative surplus value*. The creation of surplus value is a special feature of capitalism. This is inherent in the system and it cannot be helped, because the capitalist is a mere cog in the wheel of capitalist system. A capitalist worth the name of a capitalist can only progress by exploiting the labourers through the realisation of the surplus value. If the position of the workers and that of the labourers are swapped, the result will remain the same as before.

Marx made an important assumption that the rate of surplus value will remain the same in all the branches of industries and in all firms. Such an assumption is based on two propositions: *(i)* all firms and industries just use that amount of labour which is socially necessary—neither less nor more. This means that the production process everywhere is based on the same technique of production and the same labour-intensity; *(ii)* the existence of a labour force which is homogeneous, transferable and mobile. However, these assumptions are limiting.

MARX'S LABOUR THEORY OF VALUE

Marxian theory of value, commonly known as labour theory of value expresses a social relation in a capitalistic society.[4] A basic form of this relation is *commodity*. A commodity contains *use value* as well as *exchange value*. Exchange value is the quantitative proportion in which the use values of two commodities exchange.

It should be noted that Marx had in mind two types of value problems: Quantitative value and qualitative value. The qualitative value analysis seeks to find out the relation between producers under historical conditions. Quantitative value analysis is concerned with the determination of exchange value. In the process of exchange, something homogeneous is expressed. The only common property that every commodity has with every other commodity is that they are all produced by labour. The homogeneous(common and general) labour which produces commodities is called *abstract labour*[5] (muscle, nerves and brain powers). Value is then defined as the objectification or materialisation of abstract labour. Marx developed his value analysis in Vol. I of *Capital*.

Many bourgeois economists, such as Bohm-Bawerk, have criticised Marx for not taking into account two very important causal factors of value, *e.g.*, scarcity and demand and supply positions. Marx, in fact, was interested in finding out the existing production relation through his value analysis. Hence, his analysis had to be on a different philosophical plane.

What is the Measure of Value ?

Value is measured by measuring the abstract labour in units of time which is on an average necessary to produce the commodity in question, *i.e.*, socially-necessary (average) labour. When labour time is shortened, *i.e.*, less labour is required, the value of the commodity falls.

In Marxian analysis, exchange value is the necessary form of appearance of value. By neglecting the necessary form of value, Smith and

---

4. See, Tom Bottomore, *Dictionary of Marxist Thought and Science and Society*, Winter 1984-85.

5. In contrast, concrete labour is the qualitative counterpart of abstract labour. It is the tangible form of realisation of abstract human labour. It is the activity with useful effects (use values). Concrete labour produced material use-value and abstract labour social exchange value or value.

Ricardo divorced value from the specific relation of production, and their analysis was *formal* rather than *dialectical.*

As commodities, the products of labour have simultaneously a value form and a natural form. The social relation (nature) of value is expressed through the act of exchange. Value is not something intrinsic to a single commodity. It is the process of exchange which reduces all the different kinds of labour embodied in different kinds of commodities to their common quality of being labour in general.

While a commodity has both a use-value and a value, it only appears in its dual role when its value possesses a form of appearance, independent of and distinct from its use-value form. This independent form of expression is the exchange value. The value of a commodity has no expression except as exchange value, and exchange value is only expressed in terms of money.

Components and Creations of Value

What about plant, machinery and raw materials which are used along with labour for the creation of commodities? The value of the machinery and plant, according to Marx, is transferred to the product in stages, equal to their wear and tear at every stage (*i.e.,* depreciation). The means of production gives to the product that value alone which they themselves lose as a means of production. They do not create values. They are created by labour. They merely transfer the value already created by labour.

What about natural means of production, *e.g.,* land, air, water and so on? These means do not impart any value to the product.

The value of the raw materials is immediately transferred to the product produced by using them. They cannot create any new value. In the true sense, value is created by labour. The value of a commodity consists of the labour time required to produce it, including the labour time required by the subsidiary commodities which enter into its production.

A commodity is produced by labour-power. The value of labour-power is determined by the labour time necessary for the production and reproduction (subsistence) of this special article. Marx includes in the means of subsistence, cultural necessities (minimum), food, shelter, comfort (minimum) necessary for procreation and perpetuation of the labouring class. In other words, wages must be sufficient for the maintenance of the labourer and his family.

However, in capitalism, owing to the weak bargaining power of the worker, wage is reduced to subsistence (also due to the reserve army of labour). Labour market is buyer's market under capitalism. However, a worker produces for the capitalist much in excess of the wage paid to him. Thus, a worker's working time is divided into two parts : (*i*) In part one, he produces, the value for which he is paid his wage (necessary labour) and (*ii*) in part two, he produces the value which is pocketed by the capitalist (surplus labour). The value created by the surplus labour is called surplus value *(S)*. The rate of surplus value is :

$$S' = \frac{S}{V}$$

(S = surplus value, *V* = variable capital (labour), S' = the rate of surplus value). This indicates the rate of exploitation of labour. Thus, the value of a commodity consists of three elements :

$$C + V + S$$

(where, *C* = constant capital's value, *V* = variable capital (labour), and *S* = surplus value).

In the Marxian scheme, price which is equivalent to cost of production *(C+V)* plus profit may not always be equal to value. They are equal only under an ideal situation. They vary just as the natural price and market price vary from each other. The extent of such variations basically depends on the organic composition of capital *(C/V)* or capital per worker in the economy. The subject is analysed in detail by Marx in his *Transformation Problem*. Be that as it may, the divergence between value and price shows a clear departure from the labour theory of value.

MARXIAN TRANSFORMATION PROBLEM[6]

In Vol. I of *Capital*, Marx discusses the theory of value and in Vol. III, he analyses the theory of prices. Volume I ignores the problem of the effect of different capital compositions (constant and variable) on value. According to the labour theory of value's analysis of market prices, surplus value or profit should be higher (lower) in an industry having a larger (lower) variable capital (labour) proportion and a lower (higher) constant capital proportion. Thus, in this case, the profit rates would differ from industry to industry. This is shown in Table 1 :

Table 1
Capital Structure and Value

Capitals	Rate of Surplus Value(%)	Amount of Surplus Value	Value of Product	Rate of Profit (%)
I. 80c + 20v	100	20	120	20
II. 70c + 30v	100	30	130	30
III. 60c + 40v	100	40	140	40
IV. 85c + 15v	100	15	115	15
V. 95c + 05v	100	05	105	05

The above chart shows that the profit rate varies depending on the capital composition. Be that as it may, Marx observed in Vol. III of his *Capital*, that in a capitalistic economy, competition tends to equalise the

---

6. See, Lekachman, *History of Economic Ideas*, and M, Blaug, *Economic Theory in Retrospect.*

rate of profit. This proposition, needless to add, contradicts the two basic propositions of Marxian theory of value developed in Vol.I of *Capital.*

(i) Relative prices are determined by relative labour values.

(ii) Surplus value depends solely on variable capital.

Marx says that whereas the rate of surplus value is equal (constant) everywhere, the organic composition of capital (C/V) differs. Thus, the rate of profit must be different in different industries under such a situation. This follows from the equation :

$$r = \frac{\sigma}{q + 1}$$

where r is rate of profit, q is organic composition of capital, σ is the rate of surplus value.

The observation that rate of profit might be different is contrary to the law of uniform and equal rate of profit which Marx propounded. In other words, it is impossible to maintain the simultaneous equalities of (σ) and (r), excepting under a very special limiting situation. When the rate of profit is equal in all industries, prices cannot be satisfactorily explained by the simple labour theory of value. In fact, when capital composition differs, values of the commodities differ and labour theory of value miserably fails as an analytical tool.

Marx's first volume of *Capital* did not really explain market prices on the basis of different organic compositions of capital. The *Third Volume* propounded the theory of relative prices. Marx tried to solve the above problem of inconsistency by transforming values into prices at the macro level. This is the famous *Marxian Transformation Problem.* Let us analyse it with the help of Table 2.

Table 2
Capital Structure and Prices of Production

Capitals	Amount of Surplus Value	Value of Product (C + V + S)	Prices of Production (C + V + P)	Deviation from Value	Rate of Profit (P) (%)
I. 80c + 20v	20	120	122	+2	22
II. 80c + 30v	30	130	122	−8	22
III. 60c + 40v	40	140	122	−18	22
IV. 85c + 15v	15	115	122	+7	22
V. 95c + 05v	05	105	122	+17	22
Average 78c + 22v	22	122	122	0	22
Total		732	732		132

The transformation was made possible by setting total surplus value equal to total profit. Marx's solution consists of redistribution of surplus value such that we get an equalised rate of profit. In Table 2, there are five industries having different capital compositions but the total stock of capital (100) remains the same in every case. Price of production is the cost of production plus profit (P). Value of product is the sum of constant capital (C), variable capital (V) and surplus value (S). The average rate of profit (22%) is the total profit of industries divided by the number of industries (*i.e.*, 110/5 = 22). The table shows that the industries (I, IV and V) whose organic composition of capital is greater than the average organic composition of capital (*i.e.*, 390/110) will sell out their products at prices higher than their values. Prices would be lower than values for those industries (II and III) whose organic composition of capital is lower than the average organic composition of capital. Value and price will be exactly equal in an industry whose actual organic composition of capital would be equal to the average organic composition of capital.

Looked at in this way, there may be the possibility of an inequality between value and price at the micro level. But at the macro level, the total price (732) would be equal to total value (732), assuming total surplus value and total profit equal. Marx did not, thus, find the possibility of any inconsistency between value and price at the macro level where the theory of surplus value could be maintained along with the labour theory of value. Marx observed that as the total value of the commodities governs the total surplus value, and this again determines the amount of the average profit and consequently, the general rate of profit as a general law or a law governing fluctuations, the law of value regulates the prices of production.

Criticisms

1. Marx does not transform values on inputs as well as output into prices of production.

2. Marx assumed away joint products and variable techniques of production.

3. Marx defines average rate of profit in terms of direct prices (values). He shows that prices diverge from values. This implies that the rate of profit in terms of prices of production cannot equal the 'value' rate of profit.

4. This is purely an analytical construct. It does not describe a dynamic adjustment process.

5. Paul Sweezy and Bortkiewicz observe that Marxian theory of transformation involves logical inconsistency. According to Sweezy, the total quantities of constant capital used and produced are not the same in the Marxian scheme. Bortkiewicz notes that Marx made a mistake in carrying certain magnitudes without alteration from the table of values into that of prices. It is inadmissible to exclude from the recalculation the constant and variable capital in the various spheres of production.

The Solution by Bortkiewicz

This approach starts with the three equations of the following type :

Department I : $c_1 + v_1 + s_1 = c_1 + c_2 + c_3$
(Means of Production)
Department II : $c_2 + v_2 + s_2 = v_1 + v_2 + v_3$
(Consumption goods)
Department III : $c_3 + v_3 + s_3 = s_1 + s_2 + s_3$
(Luxury goods)

If x is the price-value ratio for means of production, y is the price-value ratio for the wage goods, z is the price-value ratio for the luxury goods and r is the average rate of profit, and further assuming that the transformation will not result in disturbing the conditions of simple reproduction, we get the following equations :

I. $c_1x + v_1y + (c_1x + v_1y) = (c_1 + c_2 + c_3)x$
II. $c_2x + v_2y + r (c_2x + v_2y) = (v_1 + v_2 + v_3)y$
III. $c_3x + v_3y + r (c_3x + v_3y) = (s_1 + s_2 + s_3)z$

In the above equations, there are three equations but four unknowns. Bortkiewicz reduces, therefore, the unknowns into three by making two assumptions: *(i)* value is expressed in terms of units of gold, and *(ii)* gold is produced in Department III. A unit of gold is the unit of value in the value scheme and it is also the unit of account in the prices scheme. In this situation, z, the price-value ratio of Department III, can be reasonably taken as one (1). In this case, the number of unknowns will match the number of equations. Therefore, the solution would be determinate. In such a system, it is possible to get the value of x, y and 4. The total profit comes out equal to total surplus value but the total prices many diverge from total values. Bortkiewicz notes that the total price exceeds the total value because Department III supplying gold which serves as a measure of value and price has a relatively low organic composition of capital.

Almost a similar solution to the transformation problems was provided by Winternitz. He does not agree with the view that the conditions of simple reproduction should necessarily form part of the conditions for any solution. When all is said and done, it must be noted that Marx's derivation of prices from values is simply a theoretical demonstration of the historical process. However, some defects remain in Marx's demonstration of the problem. But all this cannot disprove Marx's claim that the table of prices can be derived from the values.[7]

Marx's Theory of Capital Accumulation[8]

Accumulation is a necessary evil in a capitalist economy. Accumulation is the Moses and Prophets in capitalism. Without accumulation, a capitalist cannot stay in business. Accumulation is like a disease under capitalism. It is one of the laws of motion of capitalism which Marx has dis-

---

7.   S. Das Gupta, *Marxian Economics,* p. 81.
8.   See, P. N. Junankar, *Marx's Economics,* pp. 66-67.

covered. In the long run, accumulation is determined by many forces, including sociological forces.

Accumulation of capital is really the capitalisation of surplus value. The total profit of the capitalist is allocated between consumption and accumulation. Accumulation can also be for the purpose of expansion of constant capital or of variable capital. By accumulation, Marx means spending on constant and variable capital. Accumulation is done with a view to earning more and more profit. However, it is a contradiction that as accumulation progresses, profit goes on declining in the long run.

According to Marx, the accumulation of capital is limited by the realised profit of capitalist. The capitalist is confronted with a difficult choice of accumulation and of consumption. There is, in the language of Marx, a Faustian conflict between the passion for accumulation and the desire for enjoyment. In Marx's analysis, the marginal propensity of the capitalist to consume is regarded as constant. The main purpose of accumulation is to conquer the world of social wealth and to extend the area of exploitation, so that a more powerful supremacy may be established. In the short run, the capitalist does not automatically invest the entire amount of surplus which is left after his consumption. But in the long run, often, the capitalist invests all his surplus in accumulation after the satisfaction of his consumption.

Capitalists accumulate in order to compensate for the assumed downward trend in the rate of profit. It has been found that when the rate of profit goes down below some normal level of profit, then the capialists accumulate and introduce innovation through new technology. The relationship between capital accumulation and the rate of profit can be shown in the following diagram :

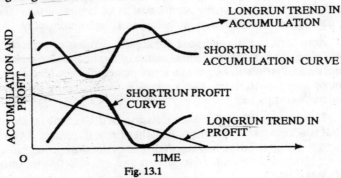

Fig. 13.1

The diagram shows that capital accumulation has a long-run trend to increase and profit has a long-run trend to go down. In the short run, when the rate of profit rises, accumulation falls and when the rate of profit falls, accumulation rises.

Accumulation, among other things, is determined by the prospect of sales of the commodities being produced. The expected future prospect of sales must grow at a constant rate for accumulation to continue. In Marxian economics, accumulation of capital is linked with technological change. Accumulation and innovation go hand in hand. In Marxian analysis technological change is of the embodied variety, *i.e.,* the latest technology is incorporated in the machine. The main justification for the accumulation of constant capital is the introduction of new technology to earn more profit at least temporarily, for in the long run, excess profit is competed away. The temporary benefits of innovation are reduced through competition.

The technological change will be either labour-saving or capital-saving. Marx gave a remarkable list of reasons for the introduction of capital-saving technology. However, Marx postulated that technological change will be of the nature of labour-saving type. Technological change, however, will lead to a contradiction in the capitalist society in the sense that the frequent the technological change, the greater is the chance of the existing machinery becoming obsolete. This lowers the economic life of the machine and increases the value of constant capital caused in the process of production.

During the process of accumulation, one notices an increasing division of labour in the production process. What happens is that a large firm can accumulate faster than the smaller ones. The larger firms can also take the advantage of the economies of scale and can also manage to lower the unit cost of production and thereby make a larger amount of profit as compared to the smaller firms. The larger firms also produce with technologically superior machines. As a result of all these factors, the small firms are driven into bankruptcy. The economic position of the small firms gets deteriorated. Increasing accumulation of capital ultimately leads to more and more *concentration of capital,* leading to monopoly.

Another force is generated during the process of capital accumulation. This can be called the *centralisation of capital.* As large capitalists accumulate and grow still larger and more powerful, they take over the small firms or merge with them. This process is facilitated by the formation of joint-stock companies.

The process of capital accumulation is dialectical in nature. When capital is accumulated by a firm, the other firms imitate it. As a result, the advantages of innovation are negated. The dialectical process also leads to the negation of the competitive system and gives birth to monopoly and concentration.

MARXIAN THEORY OF CRISIS (BUSINESS CYCLE)

Marx did not give any systematic theory of a business cycle. His discussion on crisis is scattered over his writings. According to Marx, crisis is inherent in capitalist economies. In Marxist language, the forces of production come into conflict with the relations of production, expressing themselves in a crisis. As a result of crisis, capitalism ultimately ends. There are several factors which are responsible for the generation of crisis in a capitalist economy. Breakdown of capitalism is, therefore, inevitable. We can now explain three main reasons for the crisis in a capitalis; economy.

1. Crisis Arising from Underconsumption

Underconsumption or lack of effective demand is regarded as one of the main factors responsible for crisis in a capitalistic economy. This can be called *realisation problem or realisation crisis.* Like Keynes, Marx believed that in a capitalist economy, consumption cannot cope with production. As the capitalist economy grows, there is tremendous growth of its productive power. However, the consumption power of the workers does not grow in the same proportion. The wage level remains static at subsistence. Therefore, the purchasing power does not increase at the same rate at which the productive capacity increases. Because of the limited consumption, it is difficult for the capitalist to sell out the goods and services produced by him. The capitalist is unable to realise the surplus value already created in the form of commodities. When the capitalist finds that his profit level is going down, which is inevitable in a capitalist economy, he reduces the wage level of the workers. This reduced wage level is mainly responsible for the reduced effective demand. Low wages narrow down the market and render crisis inevitable. In a capitalist society, the consumption of both the workers and the capitalists is limited by many factors. The consumption of the capitalist remains limited because of his desire to accumulate capital, and the consumption of the workers becomes limited by low wage, poverty and unemployment. Capitalism faces a crisis from the failure to realise surplus value when the capitalist market becomes limited. According to Marx, there is a contradiction between the forces of production and the forces of consumption. In fact, "the ultimate reason for all real crises always remains the poverty and restricted consumption of the masses as opposed to the drive of capitalist production to develop the productive forces as though only the absolute consumptive power of society constituted their limit."

2. Crisis Arising out of Disproportionality

Another cause of crisis is related to accumulation due to the disproportional growth of different departments. In Marx's analysis, the capital goods department expands more rapidly than other departments. This leads to a crisis because ultimately physical limits are reached and the capital goods sector is unable to buy inputs to satisfy its own needs. As soon as it is forced to slow down accumulation, via the circuits of capital, fluctuations in business get started. Production under capitalism is unplanned and anarchic. Production is based on market information which is imperfect. In such a situation, production cannot be expected to be equal to demand. Therefore, there is always the possibility of either overproduction or underproduction. In a capitalist economy, all the sectors of industries cannot grow in the same proportion. The demand and supply are not in balance. The classical theory of Say's Law of Market that supply creates its own demand does not apply in a capitalist economy, as Marx observes. This is mainly because investment decisions remain uncoordinated in a capitalist economy. Under these situations, disproportionality is the inevitable result. Thus, under capitalism, "crises originate because individual businessmen have, at best, only a partial knowledge of the market they are serving and tend to produce either too much or too little. These errors call forth adjustments, but only small errors can be corrected without general disturbance."

3. Crisis Arising out of Falling Rate of Profit

Marx devoted most attention to the falling tendency of the rate of profit as a cause of capitalist crisis. The endogenous fall in the rate of profit may be due to an increase in wage rate, in the short run. There is an inherent tendency of the rate of profit to fall in the long run in a capitalist economy. This can be shown from the following formulae.

Total value $= c+v+s$, ('c' stands for constant capital, 'v' stands for variable capital and 'a' stands for surplus value).

The rate of surplus value (s') can be indicated by (q)

$$q = \frac{c}{c+v}$$

The rate of surplus value (s') can be indicated by :

$$s' = \frac{s}{v}$$

The rate of profit (p) can be indicated by :

$$p = \frac{s}{c+v}$$

From the above ratios, it is possible to derive the formula for profit which is of great importance to Marxian theory of the falling tendency of the rate of profit. The formula can be derived with the help of the above ratios in the following way :

$$p = \frac{s}{c+v}$$
$$= \frac{sv}{v(c+v)} = \frac{sc+sv-sc}{v(c+v)} = \frac{s(c+v)-sc}{v(c+v)}$$
$$= \frac{s(c+v)}{v(c+v)} - \frac{sc}{v(c+v)} = \frac{s}{v} - \frac{s}{v} \times \frac{c}{c+v}$$
$$p = s' - s'(q)$$
$$p = s'(1-q)$$

The above equation shows that the rate of surplus value *(s')* remaining the same, a rise in the organic composition of capital will lead to a fall in the rate of profit. As industry grows larger, constant capital expands more rapidly than variable capital. Since surplus value is the product of labour power, the rate of profit necessarily declines. Marx's analysis assumes a constant rate of surplus value or exploitation. According to Prof. Dobb, falling tendency of the rate of profit is the main explanation for Marxian theory of crisis. With the accumulation of capital and rising organic composition of capital, profit rate declines which affects adversely the rate of investment and accumulation. Thus, Marx finds a contradiction here. The capitalists accumulate with a view to earning more profit but ultimately increased accumulation leads to declining rate of profit. When the profit rate falls, investment declines and this leads to business fluctuation caused by underinvestment. According to Marx, "the rate of profit, being the goal of capitalist production..., its fall checks the formation of new independent capitals and thus appears as a threat to the development of the capitalist production process. It breeds overproduction, speculation, crisis and surplus-capital alongside surplus-population."

As capitalism grows to maturity, the rate of profit tends to fall. However, it should be noted that even if there is a tendency of the rate of profit to fall, it does not imply a falling rate of *industrial profit*. It may imply a fall in the rate of rent or in the rate of interest or both. For Marx, profit includes rent, interest and industrial profit. Falling rate of profit does not mean that total profit falls. A falling rate of profit may very well show a rise in total profit. It should be noted that organic composition of capital is not the same in all industries. An industry with higher organic composition of capital will have lower rate of profit. Another factor behind the declining average rate of profit is slowdown in the turnover of social capital, which is due to an increase in the fixed capital and difficulties in marketing commodities. As a result, there is a decline in the annual mass of surplus value per unit of capital. The falling rate of profit (P) can be shown in the following diagram.

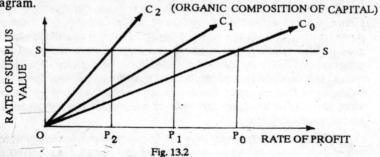

Fig. 13.2

In the above diagram, the rate of surplus value (S/V) is given (OS). Keeping this rate of surplus value (OS) as constant, a rise in organic composition of capital (C/(C + V)) will lead to a fall in the rate of profit

$\dfrac{S}{(C + V)}$, as evident from the diagram. In the diagram, $P_0 > P_1 > P_2$. Curves OC_0, OC_1 and OC_2 show organic compositions of capital such that $OC_2 > OC_1 > OC_0$. It is clear that highest organic composition of capital (OC_2 line) is associated with lowest profit (OP_2).

Determinants of Profit

There are many determinants of profit. *Firstly,* the rate of profit depends on the rate of surplus value. The higher the rate of surplus value, the higher is the rate of profit, other things remaining the same. *Secondly,* the rate of profit depends on the organic composition of capital i.e., the ratio between constant capital and variable capital (C/V). The higher the organic composition of capital, the lower is the rate of profit, for surplus value is created by variable capital. It is assumed that with the growth of capitalism, the organic composition of capital goes up. Therefore, there is a fall in the rate of profit. *Thirdly,* the rate of profit also depends on the rate of turnover of capital. The rate of profit is directly proportionate to the rate of capital turnover. The capital which has a faster turnover can exploit more labour in the course of a given period of time as compared to capital whose turnover period is longer. *Fourthly,* the rate of profit also depends on the amount of capital invested. The larger the investment of capital, the higher may be the rate of profit, other things remaining the same. *Lastly,* the rate of profit considerably depends on the economies in the use of constant capital. These economies may help to reduce the cost of production which may not only increase the rate of profit but also total mass of profit.

Factors Counteracting the Falling Rate of Profit

Firstly, by increasing the intensity of exploitation of labour, the rate of surplus value can be increased. Similarly, lengthening of the working day may also increase the rate of exploitation of labour or profit. *Secondly,* the falling tendency of rate of profit can be countered by decreasing the wage level below the value of labour power. *Thirdly,* the growth of relative over-population which makes possible the growth of reserve army of labour, can ensure industrial development with low organic composition of capital. Hence, it slows down the falling rate of profit. *Fourthly,* the same development which increases the mass of constant capital in relation to the variable capital reduces the value of its element as a result of increased productivity. Thus, cheapening of the element of constant capital can lower the organic composition of capital, and therefore, can slow down the falling tendency of rate of profit. *Lastly,* the super-profit earned by the capitalist from abroad has an important role to counteract the falling tendency of rate of profit at home.

The law of the falling rate of profit operates as a tendency which takes effect only under definite circumstances and over a long period of time. The law is indicative of the contradictions in capitalism, particularly between the aim of capitalist production and means used to attain this aim. The law aggravates the main contradictions of capitalism as the pursuit of profit accelerates the specialisation and concentration of production while the fruits are only privately appropriated. Capital accumulation is done with a view to earning higher profit. But in actual practice, capital accumulation leads to a falling rate of profit.

Criticism against the Theory of Crisis

(i) According to Paul Sweezy, there are some factors which may cancel out the effects of underconsumption. In the case of new industries having a large gestation period, factors of production can earn income much earlier than the production of goods and services. In such a situation, underconsumption does not necessarily follow.

(ii) Because of population growth, variable capital can grow without raising wages and the rate of profit may not be affected.

(iii) Marx himself has criticised the underconsumption theories put forward by other economists. But he himself has made this theory the basis of his explanation of economic crisis.

(iv) Marx observed that capitalist economy has developed tremendous productive capacity. But how can this happen if there is underconsumption? If underconsumption is that serious, the capitalist society should have faced realisation crisis much earlier.

(v) The falling rate of profit is correct if the rate of surplus value remains the same. However, the rate of surplus value does not remain the same. Given a constant rate of surplus value, a rise in labour productivity leads to higher real wages. Thus, under-consumption theory cannot be supported empirically.

MARX'S REPRODUCTION SCHEMA : SIMPLE & EXTENDED

Reproduction refers to the process of constant renewal and continual repetition of the production of goods and services for the maintenance of society. In reproduction, material goods, labour power and social production relations are all constantly renewed.[9]

Reproduction may be two types : *(i) simple* and *(ii) extended* or *expanded.* If the same quantity of products is produced in a society every time, year in and year out, we have *simple reproduction.* Simple reproduction is the basis of expanded reproduction. In the simple reproduction, renewal of production is on the same scale, and the amount of functioning capital remains the same. In such a process, the entire surplus value is consumed by the capitalist. And there is no new capital accumulation. It is the condition of a stationary or stagnant state or a static economy.

Simple reproduction is based on the following assumptions :

(a) The organic composition of capital (C/V) is constant over time, but it may differ from each other.
(b) There are only two classes : capitalist and labourers.

---

9. See, B.N. Ghosh, *Political Economy: A Marxist Approach*, Macmillan, 1990.

(c) Goods exchange at their values. So, there is no transformation problem.

(d) There is no technical change.

(e) There are constant returns to scale.

(f) There are two Departments in the economy. Department I produces capital goods and Department II produces consumption goods.

(g) Technology in each Department is productive.

(h) There is a unit turnover period of capital.

(i) Workers cannot save.

(j) Capitalists neither save nor invest. There is only replacement investment.

(k) The rate of exploitation is constant and equal in both the Departments.

(l) The economy is closed. There is no foreign trade.

Department I produces only the capital goods, a part of which is exchanged for consumption goods of Department II. Department II produces only consumption goods, a part of which is exchanged for capital goods of Department I. Needless to say, capital goods are necessary for producing consumption goods.

In simple reproduction schema, the equilibrium requires that : *(i)* the demand for capital goods must be equal to the supply of capital goods and *(ii)* the demand for consumption goods must be equal to the supply of consumption goods. In fact, the equilibrium condition simply says that the value of capital goods sold by Department I must be equal to the value of consumption goods sold by Department II.

In *extended reproduction*, new and additional production of material goods is the principal feature.[10] The scale of production is larger and wider, and the amount of functioning capital is greatly increased. In extended reproduction, the entire surplus value is not consumed by the capitalist, but a part of the surplus value is consumed by the capitalist and the other part is used for capital accumulation. Thus, new capital accumulation is the special feature of expanded reproduction. Extended reproduction represents the case of a growing economy or a developing state. With the help of additional accumulated capital, the capitalist can now expand both the stock of constant capital as well as the stock of variable capital. A capitalist under extended reproduction can hire more labour power (variable capital) and can generate more surplus value for further capital formation. Thus, extended reproduction implies expanded scale of exploitation of labour. Expanded reproduction can be effected in three ways : *(i)* by ensuring additional means of production *(ii)* by ensuring additional means of subsistence *(iii)* by ensuring the availability of the additional amount of free labourers required.

---

10. B.N. Ghosh, op. cit., Ch. 7.

In extended reproduction, production of material goods, labour power and relations of production is based on a progressively growing scale. In course of this process, competition among the capitalists also grows considerably and workers are much more *alienated* from the goods they produce.

Extended reproduction is an example of the model of balanced growth equilibrium. It is based on all the twelve assumptions which we have mentioned earlier in the case of simple reproduction, except the assumption relating to saving and investment i.e. assumption (j). This assumption is replaced by the following assumption:

(j) : *(i)* Capitalists in Department I consume half of their surplus value and invest the remaining half for capital accumulation in Department I.

(ii) Capitalists in Department II invest in Department II as much as is required to remain in equilibrium. They are simply the passive adjustment-makers.

(iii) The investment in each Department is such that ultimately the organic composition of capital (C/V) remains the same.

It should be noted that in pure capitalism, simple reproduction is not a relevant process of production. What is more relevant in such a process is the extended reproduction. Capitalism is characterised by the maintenance of capitalist form of human relationship. The definite relations among human beings in the production process are maintained and reproduced. However, reproduction of capitalist relations will imply that capitalist contradictions are also reproduced in the society, and under extended reproduction, the contradictions increase both in depth and in range, and the replacement of capitalism by socialism becomes imminent.

We can now explain the reproduction schema by taking some numerical examples and illustrations. As we have seen, constant repetition and renewal of production can be regarded as *social reproduction*. This involves the reproduction of social capital and all social products. The value of the product consists of constant capital (C), variable capital (V) and surplus value (S). "C" will indicate the amount of capital used in production, and V + S will be the new value produced. This new value produced can also be called *national income*.

There are two main Departments of production : Department I produces the means of production and Department II produces the consumption goods. However, needless to say, sale (realisation) of the finished products is a necessary condition for the renewal of production or reproduction. Therefore, reproduction is based on several conditions. Let us examine these conditions for both simple and extended reproductions.

Simple reproduction is not generally found under capitalism. Let us take a numerical case of simple reproduction where the aggregate social capital amounts to 750 units. Out of this amount of capital, 500 units are operating in Department I (400C + 100V) and 250 units are operating in Department II (200C + 50V). If the rate of surplus value is 100 per cent, the aggregate social product will be 900 units. Thus,

Department I : 400 C + 100 V + 100 S = 600 W

Department II : 200 C + 50 V + 50 S = 300 W

(W = the value of the aggregate social product = (600 + 300) = 900.

Out of 600 units of total output in Department I, 400 units must be spent in that Department to replace the constant capital used up in production. The remaining (100 V + 100 S) cannot be realised in Department I. As these 200 units consist of means of production, they cannot be used for personal consumption of capitalists and workers of this Department. Thus, these units (200) are to be exchanged with Department II for getting consumption goods.

Department II, 100 units (50 V + 50 S) of consumption goods are realised but the other 200 units cannot be realised. They have to be exchanged for means of production to replace the constant capital spent in Department II in the process of production. It is to be noted that in reproduction, Department I exchanges means of production for consumption goods of Department II, and that Department II exchanges consumption goods for means of production of Department I.

Thus, for simple reproduction, the *first condition* required for the aggregate social product to be realised is that (V + S) in Department I must be equal to (C) of Department II. Or,

$$I (V + S) = II (C)$$

The *second condition* for simple reproduction is that the total product of Department I (means of production) should be equal to the constant capital of the two Departments (I and II). Thus,

$$I (C + V + S) = I (C) + II (C)$$

The *third condition* required for simple reproduction is that the consumption demand of the capitalists and workers together must be equal to the total amount of consumption goods produced in Department II. Thus,

$$I (V + S) + II (V + S) = II (C + V + S)$$

Extended or expanded reproduction is typical of capitalism. Extended reproduction implies accumulation. Extended reproduction necessarily implies the generation of extra capital. Under extended reproduction a portion of surplus value becomes capital, and is added to constant and variable capital. The other portion of surplus value is consumed by the capitalist. Let us now take a case of extended reproduction for a system where there are two Departments.

INITIAL PERIOD

Department	Constant capital (C)	Variable capital (V)	Surplus value (S)	Value of the product (W)	Organic composition of capital (q)
I (Means of Production):	400	100	100	600	4(4/1)
II (Consumption goods):	150	75	75	300	2(2/1)

In the above chart, S (surplus value) equals 100 per cent. The total output produced in two Departments will amount to 900 units. In Department I, capitalists consume 50 (i.e.1/2 x 100S) and capital accumulation is 50 (i.e. 1/2 x 100S). Thus, in Department I, half the surplus value becomes additional capital. This additional capital is distributed between constant and variable capital in the same proportion of the existing constant and variable capital. Thus, out of total capital accumulation of 50, a share of 40 will be added to constant capital and 10 would be added to variable capital of Department I (because the existing ratio between C and V is 4:1). Thus, the consumption of means of production in Department I is now (400 + 40 = 440). So, the unrealised product in Department I would be (110 V + 50 S) which must be exchanged for consumption goods of Department II.

In Department II, capitalists accumulate just enough constant capital so that demand and supply of capital goods are equal. In Department II, the constant capital expended (150 C) must be replaced by new means of production. In addition, Department I has called for additional 10 units of consumption goods from Department II (variable capital has increased by 10 in Department I as a result of new capital accumulation). This gives scope for capital accumulation in Department II. Thus, 10 units of constant capital will be added to Department II.* So, constant capital in Department II will now be : (150 + 10 = 160 units).

This will necessitate the increase in variable capital in Department II. The ratio between constant capital and variable capital in Department II being 2:1, the increase in the variable capital would be 5 units (when increase in constant capital is 10 units). This increase in variable capital (5 units) has to take place through the conversion of surplus value of Department II. Consequently, in Department II, out of the total surplus value of 75 units, capitalists consume 60 units and new capital accumulation becomes 15 units (i.e. 10C + 5V).

We are now in a position to state the conditions required for realising the aggregate social products under extended reproduction.

Firstly, the sum of variable capital and surplus value in Department I must be greater than the amount of constant capital in Department II,

---

* The additional cosntant accumulated in Department II will be equal to : $W_1 - (C_1 + \Delta C_1) - C_2$, or $600 - 440 - 150 = 10$. In Department II, the accumulated constant capital should be just enough to equalise demand and supply of capital goods.

otherwise, it would be impossible to increase capital in Department I by adding surplus value. Thus,

$$I (V + S) > II (C)$$

This will lead to an excess of means of production necessary for extended reproduction.

Secondly, the total output of Department I must be greater than the sum of the constant capital expended in both Departments i.e.

$$I (C + V + S) > [I(C) + II(C)]$$

Thirdly, all the new value produced must be greater than the value of the product of Department II. Thus,

$$[I (V + S) + II (V + S)] > II (C + V + S)$$

The satisfaction of the aforesaid conditions will ensure balanced growth of departments and industries. But under capitalism, lack of planning, often gives rise to disproportionate development of individual industries. Owing to contradictions, the balance is upset and realisation (effective demand) crisis is very likely to make its appearance.

Critical Appraisal

1. The reproduction scheme of Marx is based on a number of limiting tacit assumptions, such as closed economy, normal prices, absence of technical change, constant real wage, constant real surplus per labour and the like.

2. Marx has divided industries neatly into two categories : capital goods industries and consumer goods industries. There are industries which produce both these goods (say, transport).

3. Marx has considered only a two-sector model.

4. Rosdolsky says that it is impossible to introduce into the scheme changes in productivity, organic composition of capital and rate of surplus value.

5. Luxemberg says that Marx has not taken into account the Third Department for the production of gold which serves as money.

Despite these points of criticism, Hilferding tried to employ the schema for an explanation of crisis. Some theorists hold that Marx's reproduction schema is somehow similar to Keynes's theory of effective demand. They have also been used as a basis for Harrod's growth analysis. Expanded reproduction model plays a definite role in the marxian system by suggesting the great improbability of smooth expansion.

MARXIAN THEORY OF ECONOMIC DEVELOPMENT

Marxian theory of economic development significantly differs from all other theories of growth that could be applied to explain the economic development of the capitalist countries of the West. His theory of economic development is difficult to isolate from the closely-knit theory of social dynamics which he had. All aspects of his theoretical framework show admirable blending of different elements—economics, sociology, politics, etc.

Marx was not a pure economic theorist. Most of the non-economic factors involved in the Marxian theory of development may be described as sociological. However, we are concerned here mainly with those factors that may be considered strictly as economic factors.

The theory of surplus value provides the framework on which Marx bases his analysis of capital accumulation and thus of economic development. As labour power, applied to means of production, can produce something more than its own value, the economy can have a surplus which is reaped by the capitalists who employ a part of it for further investment. Capital accumulation directly depends upon the ability of the capitalists to increase the surplus value. This can be done mainly in three ways : *(i)* by reducing the wages rates below the subsistence level, *(ii)* by extending hours of work, and *(iii)* through increasing labour productivity by means of technical improvements.

However, there are various difficulties with *(i)* and *(ii)* methods of increasing surplus value. If the wage rates are kept at a lower level than the subsistence requirements, there would be a secular decline in the supply of labour, which would tend to create difficulties with respect to the maintenance of the level of production and that of the economic surplus. Similarly, working hours cannot be extended too far. Thus, the best possibility of raising the volume of surplus value, at a certain stage of capitalist development, lies mainly in raising labour productivity,[11] which would, in turn, depend on technological improvement. Thus, capital accumulation, in the Marxian theory is mainly a function of technological improvement.

In the expanded reproduction scheme of Marx, capital accumulation takes place because the production of Department I (capitalist sector) is greater than the demand for constant capital in both Departments I and II. Thus,

$$(c_1 + v_1 + s_1) > (c_1 + cv_2)$$
$$(v_1 + s_1) > (c_2)$$

This shows that accumulation is taking place which is being invested in employment of more labour *(v₁)* and the means of production *(c₁)* in Department I than in Department II. All this, in turn, increases the surplus labour (See, the *Reproduction Schema of Marx*).

Marx not only had shown technological improvement to be the main lever of economic progress under capitalism, but also had shown this to be mainly responsible for the downfall of capitalism and the ultimate advert of socialist society. In this model, the compulsions of capitalist competition would induce the capitalists to introduce more capital-intensive technol-

---

11. Karl Marx, *Capital*, Vol. I, Moscow edition, p. 621.

ogy in order to raise the productivity of their workers over others. Thus, the organic composition of capital tends to rise. This would directly contribute to the falling rate of profit in the long run. Due to the unequal capacity of different capitalists to introduce technological improvement, the bigger capitalist would tend to kill the smaller ones, who would ultimately swell the rank of the proletariat.

In order to prevent the secular decline in the rate of profit, the capitalists would try to increase their rate of exploitation by all means, including wage-cuts and lengthening of the working hours, etc. But since every capitalist introduces new labour-saving and cost-reducing devices, the ratio of labour (hence, surplus value) to total output falls still further. The rate of profit declines all the more. Production does not become profitable. Consumption falls as machinery displaces men, and the industrial reserve army expands. The stage of capitalists crisis begins. Marx observes that the cause of economic crisis is the poverty and limited purchasing power of the people.

Overproduction in certain sectors of the economy is another cause of crisis in capitalist production. This arises out of imperfect knowledge of the manufacturers about productive activities, market conditions and consumers' behaviour in general. Therefore, overproduction is the rule rather than an exception under capitalist production. A crisis may overtake the capitalistic system also due to a state of underconsumption arising out of low purchasing power.

But this state of affairs does not continue permanently. A crisis always forms the starting point of large new investments. From the point of view of society as a whole, a crisis is, more or less, a new material basis for the next turnover cycle. Low price level, wage-cut, destruction of capital, etc., would tend to raise the profit rate which ultimately provides an incentive for new investments.

But, again, the same catastrophic situation would follow competition for labour, higher wages, labour-saving machinery, a reduction in surplus value and again a decline in the rate of profit. This development from crisis to depression followed by recovery and boom and then again crisis is an evidence of the "cyclical" character of the development of capitalist production. Marx's analysis of problems of cyclical fluctuations is decidedly a substantial contribution to development economics. He considered business cycle as an integral part of the capitalist system.

The labour class which is always increasing in numbers would protest against the exploitation and would combine in trade unions. The compulsions of capitalist development would increase, on the one hand, and the workers' resistance to it, on the other, would tend to generate greater centralisation and concentration of capital. The growing monopoly and centralisation of capital would be inconsistent with further technological progress. Thus, there would be a contradiction at the economic level which would make the main prop for capital accumulation weaker and would thus reduce the economic justification of capitalism as a system. Simultaneously, the growing resistance to capitalist exploitation bred by itself would ultimately sharpen the class struggle between the capitalists and the workers. Capitalism, therefore, would outlive its utility and ultimately be overthrown, as feudalism was overthrown earlier when it became an obstacle to economic development.

A Critical Appraisal

Marxian theory of economic development is based on Marx's theory of capital accumulation. However, Marx's approach was basically historical and descriptive rather than analytical.[12] Marx was proved to be a false prophet. For the working class, Marx predicted increasing misery. The rising level of real wages and improvement in the standard of living of the working class in the capitalist countries disprove Marxian analytical assertions.

Marx pointed out that capitalists will be able to maintain the industrial reserve army by introducing technological innovations. Technology has made strides and the productive efficiency of machinery has increased immensely in the wake of capitalist development; but the impact of this process on technological unemployment has not been so disastrous, as pointed by Marx. A 'permanent pool of unemployed' has hardly become a permanent feature of the developed countries. The middle class, contrary to marxian belief, has become a more dominant class.

The state has not withered away as pointed by Marx, but, on the other hand, has been playing an increasing role in the activities of the developed nations.

Marx did not see that innovations can be capital-saving as well as labour-saving. If capital-output ratio falls through improved technique, the rate of profit may rise along with the rise in wages.

Marx was trapped by the labour theory of value. By measuring everything in terms of man-hours, he attached wrong significance to a fall in the rate of profit in terms of man-hours. He could not realise that a rise in man-hour productivity and real wage rates can boost up money profit. Marx could not contemplate a process of economic development where technological progress by increasing output and productivity can also simultaneously increase wages and profit. According to Joan Robinson, Marxian "explanation of the falling tendency of profits explains nothing at all."

Marx's main ideas, such as, the importance of technological improvement in economic development and the role of entrepreneurs in innovation have been there ever since.

Marxian theory of trade cycle was an important step forward. His consideration for crisis in the analytical framework of capitalistic system led

---

12. S. Ghosh, "Economic Development of Underdeveloped Countries and Marxian Theory of Growth", Indian Economic Conference Papers (Madras, 1967, pp. 17-23).

him a little further than the classicists. He laid stress on the fact that capital accumulation led to a reduction in the demand for consumption goods and fall in profits. But he failed to foresee the fact that with economic development, the demand for consumer goods and the share of wages in national income need not fall. His theory overfocuses on the changes in labours' and capitalists' relative shares in national product and assumes the total output as unchanging. But a crisis implies a change in total output. Marxian theory, therefore, does not provide an adequate explanation of business cycle.

Despite its shortcomings, Marxian analysis, as pointed out by Schumpeter, is the only genuine evolutionary economic theory that the period produced. According to Schumpeter, "No social scientist has so deeply understood the impact of the capitalist machine, and shown in so grand a vision its immense power to transform human civilisation in the process of technological and social change."[13]

Some of the basic Marxian tenets can still be used for understanding the theory of economic development. These are : *(i)* technological progress, *(ii)* capital accumulation, *(iii)* business cycle, *(iv)* profit, *(v)* balance between investment and consumption, and saving-investment, *(vi)* reserve army of labour.

Keynes incorporated some of the Marxian assumptions into his economic analysis. Despite imperfections, the Marxian framework provides an important insight into the study of development. His analysis "still remains an appealing political religion challenging the future of poor and rich countries alike."

KARL MARX'S THEORY OF SURPLUS POPULATION

Karl Marx did not propound separately any theory of population. But his surplus population theory has been deduced from his theory of communism. Marx vehemently criticised the Malthusian theory of population. In his *Das Kapital,* Marx wrote thus :

"His work, in first form, was nothing more than schoolboyish, superficial and parsonic, declamatory plagiarism from Defoe, Sir James Stuart, Towsend, Franklin, Wallace, and others; and did not contain a single sentence throughout by Malthus himself."

According to Marx, increase in population in a country is not due to increase in fertility rate, but it is due to the capitalistic economic system. A capitalist gives to labour as wage a small share of labour's productivity, and the capitalist himself takes the lion's share. The capitalist introduces more and more machinery and thus increases the surplus value of labour's productivity, which is pocketed by the capitalist. The surplus value is the difference between labour's productivity and the wage level. A worker is paid less than the value of his productivity. When machinery is introduced,

---

13. Alfred Bonne quoting schumpeter in his *Studies in Economic Development,* pp. 244-45.

unemployment increases and, consequently, a reserve army of labour is created. Under these situations, the wage level goes down further, the poor parents cannot properly rear their children and a large part of the population becomes virtually surplus.

Increase in population, according to Marx, is not due to the ignorance of the poor people, but due to the evil impact of the capitalist economic system. Marx points out that landlordism, unfavorable and high man-land ratio, uncertainty regarding land tenure system and the like are responsible for low food production in a country. When the production of food is not adequate, population growth becomes a problem.

However, the workers work very hard to increase the capital accumulation by the capitalists, and ultimately the workers themselves become surplus. "It is the working population which, while effecting the accumulation of capital, also provides the means whereby it is itself rendered relatively superfluous, is turned into a relative surplus population; and it does so to an ever-increasing extent. This is a law of population peculiar to the capitalistic method of production."

According to Marx, poverty and misery are not natural consequences; they are the products of the capitalistic pattern of production. Poverty is the outcome of unemployment and under-employment created by the capitalistic system which cannot provide jobs at the same rate at which the population is growing. Marx held that man's tendency to press on the means of subsistence is due solely to the evils of capitalism, which can be abolished by socialistic reforms. Poverty can be abolished by increasing the productivity of labour through technological change. Marx believed that the appropriate method to deal with population-resource relationship is essentially holistic. The system should be internally dynamic to produce new operational methods, concepts and categories to properly deal with population-resource imbalance. In this way, Marx visualised the possibility of social transformation that could eliminate poverty and misery. Poverty and misery are not natural inevitabilities in the Marxian system. Thus, Marx looked at the population-resource problem from a very new angle of perception.

Marx points out that for every historical stage of production, there is a separate law of population. And since there are different stages of production, there are correspondingly different laws of population. In capitalism, the theory of relative surplus population becomes applicable.

V.I. LENIN (1870-1924)

Lenin's Theory of Imperialism

According to Lenin, imperialism is the highest stage of capitalism, and it will include the following five essential features:[14]

---

14. V.I. Lenin, *Imperialism—the Highest Stage of Capitalism*, Volkov (Ed.), *Dictionary of Political Economy*; Tom Bottomore, *A Dictonary of Marxist Thought.*

(i) Concentration of capital and production developed to such an extent that it has created monopolies. This condition is very decisive in economic life.

(ii) The merging of bank capital with industrial capital and the creation of finance capital. This leads to financial oligarchy.

(iii) Export of capital as distinguished from the export of commodities becomes a matter of great importance.

(iv) International monopoly combines of capitalists are formed which divide up the world.

(v) The territorial division of the world by the greatest capitalist powers is completed.

Imperialism is a stage of capitalist development when several developed capitalist countries (DCs) stand on a competitive footing with respect to the world market for industrial products. In this stage, monopoly capital is the dominant form of capital. One can easily witness during imperialism, a severe rivalry in the world market leading alternately to cutthroat competition and international monopoly combines.

In the period of imperialism, nationalism and militarism become weapons in the world struggle among rival groups of capitalists. The rise of militarism has far-reaching economic consequences : *(i)* it leads to the growth of specially-favoured monopolists in armament production. This group takes the lead in calling for an aggressive foreign policy. *(ii)* Militarism constitutes an increasingly important offsetting force to the tendency to underconsumption. *(iii)* It provides the capitalist class with increased opportunities for profitable investment of capital.

The net result of imperialism is to bind the middle classes closer to big capital and to widen the gulf between the middle classes and the working class. Lenin pointed out that when monopoly appears in some branches of industry, it increases and intensifies the state of chaos inherent in capitalist production as a whole. A state monopoly in capitalist society, Lenin observed, is nothing more than a means of increasing and guaranteeing the income of millionaires in one branch of industry or another who are on the verge of bankruptcy.

Lenin put forward the view that even a black capitalist nation may well become imperialist. Lenin's book, *Imperialism : the High Stage of Capitalism,* published in 1917 made a significant contribution to the understanding of imperialism in its various ramifications. His definition of the essence of imperialism has been well-confirmed by the subsequent history of imperialism. Free enterprise capitalism turned into imperialism at the turn of the century. Imperialism is not a new mode of production, but a stage in the development of capitalism. It exacerbates all the contradictions of capitalism. Imperialism, according to Lenin, is moribund capitalism which occurs on the eve of socialist revolution. In the epoch of imperialism, capitalist countries develop unevenly and spasmodically. During imperialism, all are exploited including colonies and dependent countries. Contradictions are aggravated between imperialist powers themselves in the struggle for the appropriation of monopoly profit. These struggle and contradictions lead to imperialism's ultimate downfall.

Export of Capital is a very distinguishing feature of Lenin's imperialism. It occurs in the context of a world divided by different ruling classes whose power is represented by states. Export of capital represents a mediating role of states and the potential conflicts of ruling class interests (which may be between a pre-capitalist and a capitalist state). Lenin placed particular stress on inter-capitalist rivalry. He observed that accumulation in the imperialist era generates a tendency towards inter-capitalist wars. Lenin's imperialism follows the Marxian theory of accumulation. As pointed out earlier, according to Lenin, two major factors—extension of accumulation and concentration on the international economy—contributed to the development of imperialism (which has been defined as the monopoly stage of capitalism).

The basic factor that contributes to the growth of imperialism is the investment of accumulated funds in the profitable channels in other countries. The glaring examples of the USA, England, France, Germany, etc., are before us. After the opening of the Suez Canal in 1869, the developed capitalist countries set up their colonies in Asia, Africa and South America. Imperialism and colonialism provided tremendous possibilities for the growth of foreign interests of accumulated funds, which, according to Lenin, led to the First World War.

Under imperialism, nationalism and militarism though bound together, cease to do the work of national unification, and become instruments, as pointed out earlier, to fight with one another. Militarism affords a profitable investment to the capitalist. Rosa Luxemburg has called militarism 'a capitalist disease'.

It must be noted that from imperialism has emerged *the theory of racial superiority,* according to which the dominant nation thinks that is has subordinated foreign nations on account of its racial qualities. However, because of the development of export industries, workers get more employment in an imperialist economy. But when several imperialist powers compete, the hours of work are increased and wages are depressed. Under such conditions, the interests of labour and capital clash.

As a result of imperialism, which reduces the power of the legislature as against the executive, the powers and function of state expand, and parliamentarianism declines. Imperialism leads to its own downfall and allows the development of socialism.

Limits to Imperialism

There are two main limits to the growth of imperialism :

(i) The growth of class conflict. The working class adopts an anti-capitalist attitude and tries to attain socialism. Socialism is opposed to international war and international/internal exploitation.

(ii) The second limit arises from the relations between the metropolis and the colony—the object of imperialist economic exploitation. When cheap commodities and capital are imported, the entire economy of the colony is disrupted. All this gives rise to the spirit of *nationalism* and the people struggle to throw away the shackles of imperialism.

Critical Appraisal of Lenin's Theory

1. According to Rosa Luxemberg, imperialism is not limited to monopoly stage. The explanation of imperialism in terms of monopoly was not first done by Lenin. The honour goes to Rudolf Hilferding. He did not treat it as a qualitatively new element in capitalist economy.

2. It is not rational to think that monopolies will have *super abundance of capital* to export out, particularly when, there is falling tendency of rate of profit. There is no theoretical reason to link secular falling rate of profit with growth of monopoly. However, it should be noted that Lenin himself never suggested in his book that there was a falling rate of profit.

3. Lenin treated the backward countries as essentially passive, waiting for the capital to arrive at from industrialised countries. This makes very little sense.

4. Lenin's view that export capital grows out of monopoly is not theoretically tenable. Lindsey has suggested that Lenin's definition of imperialism as monopoly stage of capitalism may not be the correct definition. In the late 19th century, there was considerable monopoly in Germany and U.S.A., and this was not the case in Britain and elsewhere, but Britain became imperialist power of the first order.

5. Does monopoly capitalism occur simultaneously with, after or before, the territorial division of the world? Lenin says that imperialism suggests a stage where territorial division is completed. However, in his book he showed that there is redivision of the territory. The acquisition of territory had nothing to do with monopoly or finance capital or with imperialism. Imperialism might remain important in Lenin's theory for the redivision of the world, but not its division (Kiernan).

6. Modern imperialism is, no doubt, rooted in the nature of capitalism. The process may be intensified under monopoly capitalism; but it is not qualitatively altered. The existence of monopoly and its internationalisation by the multinationals in the Third World are important issues to understand more the process of underdevelopment in backward countries than to explain imperialism.

7.Kautsky interpreted monopolism, literally, as the opposite of competition, signalling the end of inter-capitalist rivalry. However, Bukharin and Preobrazhensky took the middle position and said that there is no tion possible within capitalist countries during imperialism; but there may be competition between capitalist countries.

8. Though capital export is growing up in less developed countries (LDCs) from DCs, the share of LDCs is relatively declining.

9. Remittances from LDC's in the forms of profit, interest, royalty to DCs are exceeding capital export to LDCs.

10. Harry Magdoff rejects the fact of existence of surplus capital in DCs. Some amount of surplus is being invested by the capitalist countries for expansion and development of capital goods sector and R & D facilities.

11. *Decolonisation* policy of our times, seems to disprove the thesis of territorial division of the world.

12. The thesis about the absolute worsening of the conditions of labour has been more or less falsified in recent years in many countries.

13. Of late, the strategy of imperialism is being changed by the imperialist countries. They are using now more subtle and shrewd strategies rather than direct assault. These modern strategies have found expression in *Neocolonialism*. Thus, imperialism is not the last or highest stage of capitalism as Lenin described. The highest stage of imperialism is *Neocolonialism*.

Despite the above points of criticism, it cannot be gainsaid that Lenin was perhaps the first thinker to have supplied a systematic and composite picture of the genesis and growth of imperialism. There may be differences on minor points of detail but Lenin's theory provides a complete analytical framework for the explanation of imperialism as a necessary logical outcome of the capitalist form of development. Lenin's theory still remains the basic reference point for explaining the recent changes in the imperialist strategies of many capitalist countries of our times.

14

Neo-Classical School

ALFRED MARSHALL (1842-1924)

Economics started its career as a science since the year 1870. The year 1870 witnessed two important streams of thought: one was neo-classical school and the other was marginalist revolution. The classical period formally ended in 1870 but the dominating classical spirit still continued for quite some time. Marshall was also contributing profusely to economic thought since the seventies of the nineteenth century. He was the leader of the Cambridge school or what is popularly known as the Neo-classical school.

Marshall's Contribution to Economics

Marshall's *Principles of Economics* is divided into six books. Books I and II deal with *Preliminary Survey* and *Some Fundamental Notions*. Book III deals with *Wants and their Satisfaction*. Book IV deals with *The Agents of Production*. Book V deals with The *General Relations of Demand, Supply and Value*, and Book VI discusses *Distribution of the National Income*.

Nature, Scope and Method of Economics

For the first time, Marshall disintegrated economics from political economy. Economics was started as an independent science. In the introductory chapter, Marshall defined economics as follows: "Political Economy or Economics is a study of mankind in the ordinary business of life; it examines that part of individual and social action which is most closely connected with the attainment and with the use of the material requisites of well-being." He regarded economics as a science analysing wealth-earning and wealth-spending activities of human beings. To him, economics is a social science. It is not a Gospel of Mammon. Economics is a study of wealth, but more importantly, it is a study of man.

According to Marshall, "The function of the science is to collect, arrange, and analyse economic facts and to apply the knowledge gained by observation and experience, in determining what are likely to be immediate and ultimate effects of various groups of causes; and it is held that the laws of economics are statements of tendencies expressed in the indicative mood and not ethical percepts in the imperative. Economic laws and reasoning in fact are merely a part of the material which conscience and common sense have to turn to account in solving practical problems and in laying down rules which may be a guide in life."

The method of analysis that Marshall followed is called the partial *equilibrium analysis*. He concentrated on the demand for a single commodity in terms of the rest. In the partial equilibrium analysis, the interdependence in the economic system is not taken for granted. The analysis is based on a method where other things are assumed to remain constant (*ceteris paribus*). This takes into account one thing at a time by considering other things remaining the same.

He recognised the absence of a long chain of deductions in economics. According to him, no economist, not even Ricardo, attempted a simple deductive approach. He combined both deductive and inductive approaches.

Cardinal Utility

Marshall assumed that marginal utility is measurable in principle. Utility can be measured in terms of money. He also assumed the constancy of marginal utility of money. Marshall observed that marginal utility of a commodity is independent of the quantity of other commodities possessed. On the basis of these two assumptions, Marshall tried to analyse consumers' equilibrium.

Demand, Supply and Price

Marshall has reconciled the marginal utility principle of Jevons and the Austrian school with the classical cost of production theory by introducing time element into the analysis. He regarded as a great synthesiser. Marshall synthesised the earlier theories by introducing his theory of demand and supply as determinants of value. Behind demand is marginal utility and behind supply is the marginal cost of production. Marshall utilises the utilitarian approach of the Austrian school in the demand side and the cost of production approach of the classical school. Thus, Marshall brought about a harmony of two opposite trends of economic thought. As Marshall puts it: "We might as reasonably dispute whether it is the upper or the lower blade of a pair of scissors that cuts a piece of paper, as whether the value is governed by utility or cost of production. It is true that when one blade is held still and the cutting is effected by moving the other, we may say with careless bravity that the cutting is done by the second; but the statement is not strictly accurate.[1] Just as two blades of a pair of scissors are equally important for cutting a piece of paper, similarly both utility and cost (demand and supply) are equally important in the determination of value. The demand-supply construct is the most notable contribution of Marshall in the theory of value.

Marshall also introduced the *general law of demand* : the greater the amount to be sold, the smaller must be the price at which it is offered in

---

1. Alfred Marshall, *Principles of Economics*. p. 348.

order that is may find purchasers; or, in other words, the amount demanded increases with a fall in price and diminishes with a rise in price.

Marshall's analysis of price is based on time element. He distinguished between the market value and the normal value. Whereas the market value is a short-term phenomenon, the normal value is a long-term phenomenon. Marshall distinguishes four cases: Firstly, there are the market values equating supply and demand, supply being given. Secondly and thirdly, there are normal values which may relate to short periods or long periods. In the formal category, we conceive of supply as an amount which can be produced at a given price with a given supply of equipment and labour, and in the latter, supply means what can be produced by a plant which itself can be remuneratively produced and applied within a given period of time. Finally, in the very long run, we can take into account changes in the economic data like population, techniques, capital, organisation and so on. Thus, there would be slow and secular changes in normal values. It should be noted that demand is an active factor in the short period. Normal value is attainable only at a long period of time, which corresponds to the cost of production.

Agents of Production

The agents of production are land, labour, capital and organisation. The supply of land is fixed. It has no cost of production. Marshall observes that land is subject to the law of diminishing returns. This can be stated as follows: An increase in the capital and labour applied in the cultivation of land causes in general a less than proportionate increase in the amount of produce raised, unless it happens to coincide with an improvement in the arts of cultivation. Labour is defined as the economic work of man, either manual or intellectual. Capital is stored-up provision for the production of material goods and services. Capital is a derived agent. It is the combination of man's work and nature's assistance. In fact, wealth and knowledge can be had from the primary agents which are man and nature.

Law of Diminishing Utility

Marshall defines the law of diminishing utility as: the additional benefit which a person derives from a given increase of his stock of a thing, diminishes with every increase in the stock that he already has.

The demand price in Marshall's analysis is based on the marginal utility of a commodity. On this basis, it is possible to construct a demand schedule which relates quantities and amounts a person would be willing to pay for a commodity.

Elasticity of Demand

Marshall very precisely defined the elasticity of demand (E_d) as the percentage change in the amount demanded divided by the percentage change in price. Or,

$$E_d = -\frac{\delta Q}{\delta P} x \frac{P}{Q}$$

Where, δQ is the change in the quantity demanded, δP is the change in the price.

The elasticity of demand for a commodity in a market is great or small according as the amount demanded increases much or little for a given fall in price and diminishes much or little for a given rise in price. Marshall's analysis of elasticity proved useful in many practical economic applications. However, it must be noted that the concept of elasticity did not originate with Marshall. The concept was used by Cournot and others.

Consumer's Surplus

Marshall introduced the concept of consumer's surplus in connection with the price-utility relationship. Consumer's surplus is the surplus satisfaction that can be derived by a consumer when he buys a commodity at a lower price when he would be prepared to buy it at a higher price. It is the difference between the total utility *(OMPD)* and the marginal utility *(OMPK)*, as in our diagram. In the diagram, the consumer's surplus is *(DKP)*.

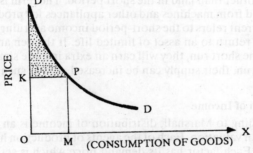

Fig. 14.1

The concept has been extensively used by the welfare economists. Marshall also used the concept of producer's surplus. This is measured by the difference between the market price and the supply price of labour and capital. The concept of consumer's surplus is based on the notion of interpersonal comparisons of utility. The concept of consumer's surplus has been borrowed by Marshall from Dupuit.

Internal and External Economies

The benefits of large-scale production are called *economies of scale*. There are two types of economies of scale: internal economies and external economies. Internal economies arise because of internal factors like specialisation, better management, efficiency and so on. External economies arise out of the external factors such as common transportation, common infrastructure, common information among a number of industries of the same type in a particular area of production.

Representative Firm

In discussing the factors governing the supply price of a commodity, Marshall introduced the concept of representative firm. A representative firm is one which has a fairly long life and fair success, which is managed with normal ability and which has normal access to economies—external and internal. Marshall introduced this concept to find a solution for the difficulties in determining the long-run normal value of a commodity whose production obeys the law of increasing returns. According to him, the long-run normal value should be equal to the cost of production of a representative firm. The representative firm remains about the same size, as does the representative tree in a virgin forest and that the economies resulting from its own resources are constant. This concept was developed by Marshall for analysing the supply price of a commodity.

Quasi-Rent

Quasi-rent is a kind of surplus income earned by the factors of production other than land in the short period. The term is used for the income derived from machines and other appliances for production made by man. Quasi-rent refers to the short-period income accruing to fixed capital. It is the net return to an asset of limited life. If the demand for machines goes up in the short run, they will earn an extra income similar to rent. But in the long run, their supply can be increased, and as such, quasi-rent will vanish away.

Distribution of Income

According to Marshall, distribution of income is an integral part of the process of valuation. Each of the agents of production has both demand and supply. Each factor has its demand price which is set by its marginal productivity, and its supply price which is set by its marginal cost. Marshall uses the demand and supply approach for determining the values of factors of production. His theory of rent is Ricardian in nature. Marshall, like Ricardo, emphasised the surplus aspect of rent. However, he has distinguished between pure rent and quasi-rent. The pure rent arises on land which has no supply price. Rate of interest is determined by the demand for and the supply of capital at least in the temporary period. The supply of capital is governed by the cost of saving and waiting, and the demand for capital is determined by the prospective gain and/or loss. According to Marshall, wage is determined by the joint influence of demand for and supply of labour. The supply price of labour is determined by the cost of rearing and training. Marshall calls profits as earnings of management and returns on capital. Profits fluctuate with price changes and depend on many factors. Profits are not certain income. In the short period, there may be or may not be any profit.

Marshall's distribution theory is but an extension of his general theory of value. According to Haney, "On the whole or at bottom, Marshall's theory of distribution is dominated by cost."[2]

Appraisal

Marshall is rightly considered as the father of modern economics. "Marshall for the first time revealed the unity of the economic system and presented it as a coherent whole of inter-related parts functioning in mutual dependence upon one another". He established the Cambridge school of economics which is still functioning with all the seriousness and originality. Marshall's remarkable work has guided the economic literature for more than a generation. He developed the new engine of analysis for unfolding the truth involved in economic phenomena. His *Principles of Economics* will remain a great book for all times to come. It has already earned its place as a classic. Marshall was one of the first economists to realise that economics is an evolutionary science. He was fully aware that he was building an essentially temporary structure. According to Lord Keynes, as a scientist he was, within his own field, Marshall was the greatest in the world in a hundred years. Marshall's tools of analysis have remained very useful particularly for the development of economic science. Though he had a static theory, he always looked beyond it and introduced dynamic elements whenever he could.

Marshall was the first economist to show that perfect competition will not always maximise output. Marshall anticipated the theory of imperfect competition. He had a definite theory of economic evolution which stood in the very centre of his thought process. His analysis was partial in nature. But, he made generalisations about the economic process and system.

Despite many limitations of his analysis, like incomplete distribution theory, partial equilibrium analysis, unrealistic representative firm and so on, Marshallian economics has stood the test of time. Marshall developed a system and analysed economic problems with his own tool kit to derive necessary conclusions. Schumpeter has rightly called him a great economist. Marshall "will stand in the history of economic thought as one who made more progress towards a united and consistent theory of value and distribution than any predecessor."[3]

2. L.H. Haney, *History of Economic Thought*, p. 646.
3. L.H. Haney *op.cit.,* p. 659.

APPENDIX

POST-MARSHALLIAN DEVELOPMENTS

Post-Marshallian developments have seen the emergence of many economists like Wicksteed, Piero Sraffa, Mrs. Joan Robinson,Edward Chamberlin, Sir John Hicks, Lord Robbins and so on. However, in this section, we will confine only to a few authors.

JOAN ROBINSON (1903-1983)[1]

Joan Robinson was brought up under the Marshallian tradition. She has written a number of books and articles. Some of her important publications are : *The Economics of Imperfect Competition* (1933), *Introduction to the Theory of Employment* (1937), *An Essay on Marxian Economics* (1942), *Essays in the Theory of Employment* (1942), *Collected Economic Papers* (1951), *The Rate of Interest* (1952), *The Accumulation of Capital* (1956) and *Economic Philosophy* (1962).

Her most important work is the *Economics of Imperfect Competition* which heralded the Cambridge revolt against the father of Cambridge economics (Marshall). Her book was published in 1933. She pointed out that perfect competition does not hold good in the real world. Therefore, she considered the situation of imperfect competition where the number of sellers is limited. The book consisted of examinations of pricing situations under monopoly with varying degrees of discrimination, and monopsony. She considered the fact that buyers show irrational preference for the products of some sellers. In the analysis of imperfect competition, she pointed out that the equilibrium price and output will follow the rule of equality between marginal revenue and marginal cost. But she did not take into account the cases of oligopoly, and selling cost. Her analysis shows that under imperfect competition, prices would be higher and output would be lower than under competitive conditions. Imperfect competition is marked by the presence of excess capacity. In her analysis, product differentiation and non-price competition do not play any important role. Joan Robinson has dealt with the cases of discriminating monopoly in a masterly way. She has shown that under imperfect competition, the demand curve for a firm is downward sloping from left to right.

Robinson's book had a number of chapters dealing with rents, supply curve, exploitation and so on. She showed that exploitation takes place on account of the absence of perfect elasticity in the supply of labour, which can be enforced effectively by trade unions.

Joan Robinson was also very much influenced by the Keynesian *General Theory*. Joan Robinson gave a popular account of Keynes's *General Theory* in her *Introduction to the Theory of Employment*. She was

---

1. The discussion is based on P.R. Brahmananda's article on Joan Robinson, *Indian Economic Journal*, July-Sept. 1983.

trying to graft the problem of long term accumulation to the short-period economics of the *General Theory*.

She was rather critical of Marx's neglect of the productivity improvement effect of the increase in capital-intensity of labour. However, she clearly expressed her ideological sympathies with Marxism. She was also a critique of Marx as she pointed out that some of the Marxian theories (for example, falling rate of profit) are simply truism and meaningless. She published her severe critique of dogmatic Marxists in her *On Rereading Marx*. But she agreed with Marx in his attempt to improve the lots of poor people.

Her book on *Accumulation of Capital* came out in 1956. This book brought her fame and name. In this book, she raised a number of issues regarding the meaning and measurement of capital, marginal productivity of capital and so on. She observed that the marginal productivity of capital could not be stated to determine the rate of interest, since without the rate of interest, capital could not be quantified as a value sum. In this book she made an attempt to integrate capital theory with growth theory. This book contains a great deal of analysis supporting the possibility of a sort of growth equilibrium. She adopted the approach of measuring capital through a process of dated labour years. Later, she referred to the measurement of capital by means of its deflation by the consumption goods' wage rate.

One fundamental view which Joan Robinson never deviated from was that money wage rates determine money prices. In other words, the level of money wage rates determines the level of money prices. Joan Robinson frequently used this approach in order to criticise the quantity theory of money. Her mind seems to have been almost continuously pre-occupied with a value theoretic basis for macro-economics. But in the area of macro-economics, she realised the importance of both Keynes and Kalecki. Ultimately, it was the empirical non-relevance of the theoretical economics that increasingly came to occupy the mind of Joan Robinson. She started liking empirical economics rather than theoretical economics. She observed that noe-classical economics could not capture reality because it did not study historical facts. She was a critique of neo-classical equilibrium economics.

She had a strong affinity with G. Myrdal in understanding the plight of the underprivileged persons in a society. Her sympathy with marxism was not on the score of her acceptance of Marxiam Economics which she rejected almost completely, but with the ideals that inspired some Marxists for a better order of society.

In the end, it must noted that her magnum opus, *The Economics of Imperfect Competition* is the first step in the rejection of Marshallian economics.[2]. It introduces non-competent markets as a normal analytical

---

2. See also the discussion on Edward Chamberlin in this book for studying the similarities and differences in their approaches.

phenomenon in the actual world. In her book, *The Accumulation of Capital*, she rejected any longrun tendency towards golden age path of growth. She found a contradiction between high potential profits and savings under a high degree of monopoly and the generation of required volume of effective demand for maintaining full employment in short period.

She has been praised by many great economists. Samuelson called her the greatest analytical economist of our times. Solow compared her to an irriated oyster producing pearls. However, she never took these complements seriously but went on knocking and knocking on the sensitive spots to unfold the truth. Joan Robinson lived and died for establishing a rationale for a cause which was nothing but the development of the science of economics.

EDWARD CHAMBERLIN (1899-)

As a contemporary of Joan Robinson, Edward Chamberlin published his doctoral dissertation on *The Theory of Monopolistic Competition* in 1933 in the form of a book. This was the same year in which Joan Robinson's *Theory of Imperfect Competition* was also published. Both books had many important similarities, but there were also decisive differences. Both Robinson and Chamberlin went away from the Marshallian tradition by emphasising the importance of imperfection in the market structure.

In the Marshallian tradition, it was customary to analyse price equilibrium from the point of view of perfect competition. Monopoly was regarded as an exceptional case. However, P. Sraffa suggested in 1926 that the actual conditions in the market are not either perfect competition or monopoly but are to be found scattered along the intermediate zone. This idea of Sraffa encouraged both Robinson and Chamberlin to have a new look at the problem of pricing and output conditions. Chamberlin attempted to blend the theories of monopoly and competition into a more general theory of value. The name of his theory is *monopolistic competition*. This is also a form of market imperfection. Chamberlin observes that sellers introduce imperfection in the market. Sellers are selling goods which are almost similar but they appear to be different. The products are in some way or the other differentiated. Every seller has a monopoly with respect to the supply and the price of his products. But since goods are similar, there is an element of competition among the sellers in the market. This is true in the case of consumer goods like tooth paste, soaps and so on. For selling these goods, selling and advertisement expenses are to be incurred by the sellers. The combination of monopoly element and competition is called monopolistic competition by Chamberlin.

In such a case, the seller has the choice of fixing the price of his product, and also deciding about the supply position of the goods. Chamberlin has taken a middle position between pure monopoly and pure competition. Monopolistic competition considers not only the problem of individual equilibrium but also the problem of group equilibrium. Under monopolistic competition, producers of similar products are always in competition regarding price and output. In fact, each is a monopolist but each has competition in the market. This type of analysis is more realistic than the analysis of pure monopoly or pure competition.

In Chamberlin's theory, there is no concept of industry. Every firm is a monopolist of its own product which is differentiated from the similar products of other firms. In his analysis of equilibrium, a group of firms and their products can be considered. Chamberlin has taken into account the cases of two producers (duopol) and also the cases of a few producers (oligopoly). Chamberlin calls his system monopolistic competition because in such a system, there is competition between monopolists of individual differentiated products. One of the most important elements of Chamberlin's theory of monopolistic competition is that most firms involve themselves not only in price competition but also in non-price competition. According to him, every monopolistic firm has a unique product or comparative advantage which gives it some control over price and output.

In Chamberlin's theory, equilibrium solution is attained when the marginal cost and marginal revenue are equal and also when the average cost and average revenue are equal. In such a situation, the demand curve is down-ward slopping from left to right. Under monopolistic competition, excess capacity exists in the market and output level goes down but price level goes up. Moreover, on account of selling expenses, the cost of supply increases. Thus, the purchasers have to pay higher price.

In Chamberlin's theory, product differentiation may convince the consumers that some differences exist among the products, although really there may not be any difference. The product differentiation may be due to brand names, trade marks, packings and economic space. Location may differentiate the products, and it may be indeed the overriding consideration. However, it must be noted that the differentiated products are highly substitutable. Chamberlin thought that under monopolistic competition, both price and products can be regarded as variables under the control of firms.

We can now attempt a comparison between Joan Robinson's imperfect competition and Chamberlin's monopolistic competition.

Robinson's Theory and Chamberlin's Theory Compared

There are many *similarities* between the theory of Robinson and the theory of Chamberlin:

1. Both Robinson and Chamberlin have gone away from the Marshallian tradition of perfect competition.
2. Both the writers have observed that market is not perfect.
3. Both considered the equilibrium position as one where marginal cost equals marginal revenue.

4. In both cases, the demand curve is down-ward sloping.
5. In both cases, excess capacity exists and supply is restricted but price is increased.
6. Both the writers have used the marginal apparatus.

The following are the major *differences* in the theories of Robinson and Chamberlin:

(i)   Whereas Robinson considers imperfect competition, Chamberlin considers monopolistic competition.

(ii) Robinson does not consider the cases of duopoly and oligopoly. Chamberlin does consider these cases.

(iii) Robinson does not take into account selling and advertisement expenses but Chamberlin takes into account these expenses.

(iv) Robinson does not consider product differentiation. Chamberlin considers product differentiation.

(v)   Non-price competition does not play any role in Robinson's theory. Non-price competition is important in Chamberlin's theory.

(vi) Robinson makes a dichotomy between competition and monopoly. Chamberlin makes a blending of competition and monopoly.

Chamberlin's theory of monopolistic competition is an important bench mark in the development of value theory in twentieth century economic analysis. Many economists like Fellner, Smithies, Machlup and others have followed Chamberlin's monumental work. His main contribution has been to strike a responsive chord in economic analysis by emphasising monopolistic element in the competitive proces. He has provided an alternative to the competitive model which is independent and in some respects goes ahead of Joan Robinsonian model of imperfect competition.

SIR JOHN HICKS (1904-1989)

Sir John Hicks occupied the Drummond Chair in political economy at the University of Oxford for many years. He has written a number of books and research articles. The following are his important books: *Theory of Wages* (1932), *Value and Capital* (1939), *A Contribution to the Theory of Trade Cycle* (1950), *A Revision of Demand Theory* ·(1956), *Capital and Growth* (1965), *Theory of Economic History*(1970, *Capital and Time* (1976) and *Causality in Economics* (1979).

J.R. Hicks was awarded the Nobel prize in Economics in 1972 in appreciation for his contribution to the general equilibrium theory and welfare theory. *Value and Capital* is his most outstanding publication. In this book he has popularised the concept of income effect and substitution effect and constructed a general theory of the working of inter-related markets based on the general equilibrium theories of Walras and Pareto.

His analysis of general equilibrium takes into account the conditions of perfect competition. He studied the problem from the point of view of individual firm. However, he observes that the concept of equilibrium has much wider application than that of the general equilibrium of exchanges. *Value and Capital* extends the concept of general equilibrium to those problems which arise from capital and interest. The importance of his book, *Value and Capital* has continued for a pretty long time.[3] The two books written by him in the 1970s, *Capital and Time* and *Causality in Economics* reflect a shift in view point from *Value and Capital*.

Hicks explained in his own way the concepts of *statics and dynamics*. He says that economic statics includes the study of those elements of economic theory, whose dating is not essential, but economic dynamics treats of those parts where every quantity must be dated. According to him, stationary state is but a special case of dynamic system. In such a state, tastes, techniques and resources remain more or less the same over the given period of time.

His *indifference curve technique* has provided a better alternative to the Marshallian theory of demand in the analysis of consumer demand theory. He has utilised the concept of preference in the analysis of consumers equilibrium. This concept does not require the Marshallian concept of measurability of utility which has been questioned by many economists. His theory also is not based on the limiting Marshallian assumption of the constancy of marginal utility of money. Hicks's theory has been able to show both income effect and substitution effect. Marshall ignored the income effect. Therefore, Hicks's theory is considered to be a better theory of consumer demand.

Hicks has also pointed out the weaknesses inherent in Marshallian analysis of consumer surplus. He pointed out that the gain accruing to the consumer can be better explained by the theory of *compensating variation in income*.

He was interested in applying the tools of value theory to issues of capital-theoretic nature. His early interest was to deploy Paretian theory of choice to illuminating the issues in the area of monetary theory. Hicks was interested in issues relating to endogenous movements of economic variables such as prices, interest and economic fluctuations on a capital-theoretic basis. He was profusely fond of the subject of capital as is borne out by his three outstanding books: *Value and Capital, Capital and Growth* and *Capital and Time*.

Hicks provided a widely used condensation of Keynes's theoretical schema, which became the working basis of much macroeconomic analysis of our times. This IS-LM paradigm hung around him as an albatross. In his *Contribution to the Theory of Trade Cycle,* he extended the Harrod-type

---

3. A good bit of the present discussion is based on S.Chakravorty, "Sir John Hicks: An Appreciation", *Economic Times*, June 26, 1989.

dynamic analysis to produce an elegant model of business cycle based on the concepts of multiplier and acceleration. According to Hicks, the limits of cyclical fluctuations are determined by the level of full employment and minimum investment.

In his *Capital and Time*, he adopted a neo-Austrian approach to explain the nature of *traverse* i.e. passage from one level of growth equilibrium to another. The main purpose of this theory was to study the economy in motion in real time. It was the study of the way in which a stationary economy moves into the growing phase. Hicks used insight to explain the growth problems in historical perspective. In his *Theory of Wages*, he argues that a rise in wages would lead to unemployment through a substitution effect against labour.

According to Hicks, growth theory is a part of that department of economic theory which deals with both trend and cycle. Growth theory is a branch of economic dynamics. In mechanics, statics is concerned with rest and dynamics is concerned with motion; but no economic system is ever at rest. In fact, production itself is a process.

Hicks's contribution to welfare economics lies in his rejection of the Paretian position that general welfare can be increased if the welfare level of some people goes up but no one is worse off at the same time. Hicks considered the over-compensation criterion which left room for cases in which some were better off and some worse off. Hicks emphasised on the total conditions rather than the marginal conditions.[4]

In his *Theory of Economic History*, he emphasised on the capital intensive and labour-displacing technical improvements in explaining the course of industrial revolution. Economic history had great fascination for Hicks. He felt that economics was at the edge of theory and history. This idea is implanted in his book, *A Theory of Economic History*. It analyses the historical processes from the vantage point of view of evolution of exchange. His book on *Causality in Economics* is a kind of self-examination to see whether economics has been able to find the appropriate method or not.

Hicks has also introduced the concepts of strong and weak orderings in the analysis of consumer behaviour in his book, *A Revision of Demand Theory*. Although all his publications are outstandingly original, his most famous book is *Value and Capital* which outlines his general equilibrium analysis. According to A.K. Dasgupta, judged by the totality of his achievements, Hicks must be ranked as one of the greatest economic theorists of all times.[5]

---

4. P.R. Brahmananda, "The Economics of John Hicks", *Indian Economic Journal*, Oct-Dec. 1972.

5. A.K. Dasgupta, "John Hicks: the Nobel Laureate in Economics", *Economic and Political Weekly*, November 25, 1972.

Part Four :
Modern Economic Thought

15

Institutional Economics

THORSTEIN VEBLEN (1857-1929)

Veblen's Economic Ideas

As an institutionalist, Veblen believed that economic institutions were the mainspring of economic changes. His analysis was purely in the light of economic motives and institutions. He criticised the classical school mainly on two grounds : *(i)* its concept of economic man and *(ii)* its belief in the harmony of interest. He found that the interest of the capitalist class was opposed to the interest of the community. In many respects, Veblen was like Marx. Both are institutionalists. However, Veblen was basically concerned with human motives and instincts. Velben's institutionalism was based on idealist philosophy.

According to Veblen, the striking feature of the leisure class is to maintain the superiority over their fellows. The rich people, Veblen finds, indulge in conspicuous consumption, conspicuous waste and conspicuous leisure. His analysis of *snob values* and *conspicuous consumption* earned him immense fame as a social economist.

In his famous work, *Theory of Business Enterprise*, Veblen distinguished between profit-making and goods-making. He observed that business people are interested not so much in making goods as in making money by hook or by crook. Thus, the ordinary people do not get the advantage of efficiency or technological improvement. The unjust profit through manipulations becomes later on a source of trouble to the capitalist : unsold stock-piling, deficiency in demand and business cycles.

Veblen's ideas on economic science are really interesting and original. According to him, the orthodox economics is at the taxonomic stage. It is simply classificatory in nature. In order to be progressive, economics has to be an evolutionary science. In such a situation, the role of institutions and their evolution cannot be denied in any way. However, because of the cultural lag, the clash of some institutions cannot be avoided at some stage. According to Veblen, society is not static but dynamic. The change that takes place is only evolutionary in nature. It cannot be regarded as revolutionary. Veblen's main concern was to show the evolution of institutions in a society. Veblen was a Darwinian evolutionist to whom the process of change was continuous and endless. However, the great force that makes this change possible is the technological process.

In his best-known work, *The Theory of Leisure Class*, Veblen made meticulous observations on the pecuniary culture of the rich people. Let us analyse his work in detail.

The Theory of Leisure Class

Thorstein Veblen's first and best-known work challenges man's standards of behaviour, and with devastating satire, exposes the hollowness of taste, education, dress and culture. According to Veblen, the leisure class (upper class) sets the standard followed by every level of society. The sign of membership of the leisure class is exemption from industrial toil and the mark of success is conspicuous consumption.

The institution of leisure class is found in its best development at higher stages of barbarian culture. This class takes up some employment, e.g.,army, which is honourable. They are exempted from low level industrial employment. These are noble and priestly classes. Evidence indicates that leisure class has arisen during the period of transition from primitive savagery to barbarism. It is the outgrowth of an early discrimination of employment (good/bad).

The beginning of a leisure class coincides with the beginning of ownership. These two generally stem from the same set of economic forces. However, the wealth and power must be in evidence for reputability. Hence, the rationale for conspicuous consumption. Conspicuous abstention does, of course, constitute a superior pecuniary achievement. The leisure class finds its most typical expression since the days of transition from predatory culture. In cultural pattern of this class, enjoyment of leisure is regarded as meritorious, honourable and decent, for, it is a conspicuous evidence of wealth, and is the conventional mark of social standing.

It is to be noted that leisure constitutes only the non-productive use of time. The leisure enjoyed by a servant is a vicarious leisure. The leisure class consumes goods which are very costly, for, such an act is an evidence of possession of wealth. High-bred manners and ways of living are items of conformity to the norms of conspicuous leisure and consumption. This class is employed in noble offices, *e.g.*, govt.jobs, fighting, hunting, ostensibly predatory employment, and not ignoble menial services. The wives are still considered as some form of a chattel by this class.

The consumption pattern of this class is emulated by the next higher stratum of the society. Leisure which is more valuable than consumption at the outset goes down in importance, and conspicuous consumption sequently gets the upper hand. Leisure is honourable because it is an evidence of exemption from ignoble labour. Since the expenditure pattern of leisure class is very high, they cannot afford to have many children (Malthusian prudential check).

The canon of conspicuous consumption also embraces the canon of waste and expensiveness. Even in modern cults, wastages are, in a sense, looked upon with some kind of veneration. The sensuous beauty of gems will not be so praised if they are cheap and not costly. They are adored because they are costly and to have these costly things is to have a punctilious mark of prestige (Veblen effect of prestige). To have prestige, an article of consumption must *be costly and also wasteful*. They should also be beautiful. A beautiful article which is not expensive is not *beautiful* to the leisure class.

The leisure class keeps some domestic animals for use. Doges are useful and have special gifts of temperaments. They can know well and moods of their masters. They are costly and serve no industrial purpose (conspicuous consumption). Horses are not so useful as dogs.

At a stage of economic development, when women are valued by the upper class for their services, the ideal of female beauty is a robust, large-limbed women (*e.g.*,the maidens of Homeric poems). Conformation of the face is secondary weight, physique is first. In subsequent development, the leisure class considered wife as the agent of vicarious leisure, and chivalric and romantic ideal of beauty takes cognizance of face, hand, feet, delicacy, and the slender figure (*Petite*), especially the slender waist (shift from woman to lady).

In the matter of choice and preferences, goods produced by hand-labour are preferred to machine-made goods, for, the former is a more costly and wasteful method of production. Machine-made goods are consumed by the common people. Therefore, the leisure class should not consume it.

The principle of conspicuous waste finds expression in dress also : dress is the evidence of our pecuniary standing. Greater part of expenditure incurred on apparel is for the sake of a respectable appearance rather than for the protection of the body. Expensive dress not only gives elegance but is also an insignia of leisure. Women's dress in particular (for the leisure class) must demonstrate expensiveness and inconvenience for ordinary work and employment, *e.g.*,French hill, skirt and corset. All these give reputability to the leisure class. Upto date style is very essential but it must conform to the requirement of reputable wastefulness and futility. Conspicuous waste and conspicuous leisure are reputable because they are evidence of pecuniary strength.

The leisure class is a stable and conservative class. And this is a mark of respectability. According to Veblen, this class exerts a retarding influence upon social development. This class retains much of the habits and ideals of the earlier barbarian period. Their martial spirit is of a very high order. Duel is a leisure class institution.

The leisure class believes in devout observances and luck. This class contains a disproportionately large number of believers in occult sciences of all kinds and shades.

Higher learning is a leisure class occupation. Their patronage also helps the spread of higher education. They help the spread and growth of formal and classical erudition, and not scientific and technological discoveries. It should be noted that to a considerable extent, the kindergarten education has been developed by the leisure class women. The leisure class, more often than not, uses obsolete idioms and king's/queen's English. Its orthography is archaic, cumbersome and ineffective. It makes punctilious use of ancient locutions so as to make the speech classic. These uses are reputable because they are cumbrous and out of date and involve waste of time.

These are most of the more important idiosyncrasies of the leisure class as depicted by Veblen in his *The Theory of the Leisure Class*.

Appraisal

The book is the most comprehensive book ever written on snobbery and social pretenses. Although it was primarily based on American life, it is still found to be relevant in modern societies even in the less developed countries. The book brilliantly and truthfully illuminates the effect of wealth on behaviour. The book is Veblen's revenge for the abuse to which he and his parents were subject to. It is a contempt extended to a class structure with class distinctions. What makes this book great is the passionless calm with which the author pursues his investigation without having any animus for and against the leisure class.

APPENDIX

AMERICAN ECONOMIC THOUGHT

American economic thought is developed by many writers like Henry George, J.B. Clark, Francis A. Waler, S.N. Patten, Frank A. Fetter, Thorstein Veblen and Frank H. Knight.

We have already discussed the contributions of some of the American writers elsewhere in this book. Thus,

J.B. Clark's contribution is discussed in Ch. 9, and Thorstein Veblen's contribution is discussed in ch. 15 of this book.

The contributions of a few more American economists are discussed in this section.

FRANCIS A. WALKER (1840-1897)

Francis Walker was one of the founder members of the American economic association. He was the president of this association for seven years. He was also associated with many economic organisations of America. He got his primary lesson on economics from his father, Amasa Walker, who was also himself an economist by profession.

Francis A. Walker wrote many books on economics, the renowned of which are: *The Wages Question,* (1876), *Money* (1878), *Political Economy* (1883), *Land and Its Rent* (1883), and *International Bimetallism* (1896).

Apart from all these books, he also collaborated with his father in writing the book on *Science of Wealth.* The most important publication of Francis Walker in terms of popularity was his book on *Political economy.* It can be seen from the list of above books that Francis Walker had interest in many areas of economics. In what follows, we can outline the main contributions of Walker to economic analysis.

Political Economy: In his book on Political Economy, Walker discussed the nature, meaning and method of Political Economy. According to him, "Political Economy or Economics is the name of that body of knowledge which relates to wealth: it has to do with no other subject, whatever, than wealth". His conceptualisation of Political Economy is almost the same as the Marshallian concept of economics. He (Walker) took into account three factors of production such as land, labour and capital. His book on political economy contained only six parts. Part one of the book discussed the meaning and method of political economy. Part Two discussed production, part three, exchange, part four distribution, part five consumption and the last part of the book discussed the application of economic principles.

Theory of Value: The question of value was discussed by Francis Walker in part three of his book on political economy (section on exchange). He considered utility as one of the basic attributes of value. According to him, an article possessed value not because it cost some labour, but because it could not be had without labour. That is to say, value depended not on the cost of production but on the cost of reproduction of the product. This shows, according to him, that some goods are reproducible and some goods are not. In the case of reproducible goods, value will be equal to the cost of reproduction.

Value is the power in exchange. Value gives in the hands of the possessor of article the command over other resources of the economy. This command is helpful for acquiring other commodities of equivalent value. He did not take into account the classical concept of cost of production either as the source of value or as the measure of value.

Francis Walker also developed another theory of value, which can be called the *demand and supply* theory. In this theory, he could combine the influences of both cost of production and utility, because demand side represents utility whereas cost of production is represented by the supply side. In other words, Francis Walker dealt with the modern theory of price determination which is based on demand-supply approach. In the case of non-reproducible commodities, the supply is limited by the stock of the commodities, even over a period of time. In the case of reproducible goods, the supply can be changed, and the cost of reproduction, of course, would be important for the determination of price. The supply may be changed, upward or downward, by adjusting the price level. Demand and supply are inter-related with the price level, which can considerably influence these forces. The price of a commodity, according to him is considerably affected by the substitutes it may have in the market.

Francis also considered the longrun normal price and the shortrun market price. The normal price is more or less equal to the cost of production and the market price fluctuates around the normal price. The market price may be a bit higher or lower than the normal price.

Theory of Distribution: Francis A. Walker is known for his theory of distribution. According to him, there are mainly four types of payments to be made to the factors of production. These payments are - rent, wages, interest and profit. His theory of rent is almost the same as the Ricardian theory of rent which is based in differential fertility of land. The lands having superior quality or fertility will earn rent, which can be called differential rent. Like Ricardo, Walker was of the opinion that rent does not enter into price. Rent is the first payment made by the cultivator to the landlord. The second payment is the payment of interest and the third payment is in the form of profit.

Interest is the reward made for the use of not money but capital. The supply of capital comes from abstinence but it is related to saving which depends on the rate of interest directly. The demand for capital is related to the productivity of capital. However, when the accumulation of capital goes beyond a level, the rate of interest comes down. But any artificial reduction in the rate of interest will adversely affect the supply of savings, and therefore, capital.

The third claimant of the national product is profit which goes to entrepreneurs. Profit arises out of differential abilities of entrepreneurs. An entrepreneur who is more able and capable can only earn profit. An ordinary entrepreneur who is just a marginal entrepreneur, cannot earn any profit, but he simply receives income equivalent to the wages of management. The payment of profit is just like the payment of rent because both arise out of differential superiority.

The last claimant of the national product is the wage. Wage is a payment made to labour. Francis criticised the classical *wage fund theory*. He observed that wages are paid not from capital but out of labour. His contribution to wage analysis is regarded as outstanding. Francis Walker discovered the *residual claimant theory of wages*. According to him, wages are paid after making all types of payments like interest, profit and rent. To him, after making all payments whatever is left out (residual) is paid as wages. Thus, wages are only residual payments made to the labourers. When the efficiency of labour goes up, the wages may also go up. His theory appeared at a time when the wage question dominated the discussion about the national issues. The residual claimant theory was Francis Walker's singular achievement in the analysis of distribution.

Walker also considered a separate class of non-profit entrepreneurs. But according to Cannan, Walker's theory of profit was one of the wildest creations of the 19th century economic thought. Some critics argue that his theory of wages is not a correct theory because wage is not a residual income. On the other hand, wage is always a contractual income which has to be paid to the labourers. It is not also sure that an improvement in labour efficiency will lead to higher wages, as Walker contemplates. This may be appropriated by the capitalist.

Theory of Money: Francis maintained that the value of money, like the value of any ordinary commodity depended on its demand and supply. The demand for money depends on its needs i.e. the work it performs. Generally, money is used for financing transactions in the market. The demand for money is not fixed in the market. The demand for money will depend directly on the production of goods and services in the economy. The demand for and supply of money will ultimately settle the value of money. According to him, the supply of money is nothing but the supply of money-force (supply of purchasing power). It is somewhat like the supply of total liquidity.

Walker wanted to have a proper control over the issue of paper currency. He observed that inconvertible paper money was useful but will be doing harm if its supply is not controlled.

At the end, it should be noted that Francis Walker is still remembered for his residual claimant theory of wages of which he has remained the original propounder.

FRANK H. KNIGHT (1885-1973)

Knight is famous for his theory of profit which is based on considerations of risk and uncertainty. Knight has written many books His main publications are :*Risk, Uncertainty and Profit,* (1921), *The Ethics of Competition and other Essays* (1935), *Freedom and Reform* (1947), *The Economic Organisation.* (1951), *On the History and Method of Economics* (1956).

Economics: Meaning, Nature and Method: Knight does not consider Economics to be an empirical science. It is also not a descriptive science. Technological consideration is not necessary in economics. However, as a science of price economics provides certain universal laws which are formally true but may not be materially so. Knight was very keen to bring into focus the institutional factors in economic analysis. This shows that he was interested in the analysis of political economy. He was not really discussing pure theory or even normative economics. He can be said to be also an institutionalist, like Veblen,

According to Knight, economic analysis depends on introspection and intuition. This is the reason why economics has remained basically a subjective study. Inferences are drawn in economics from certain abstract premises. Therefore, economics essentially remains an abstract science. Economics uses *a priori* statements; but these statements should not be taken too literally.

Knight has distinguished between statics and dynamics. The idea of statics has been taken from theoretical mechanics. Statics is found to exist in those forces that tend towards equilibrium. However, his concept of equilibrium is not one of the state of rest but it is simply a process. In the analysis of this process we start from a static economy, where resources have already been utilised and commodity supplies exhausted. Dynamic problem arises from the acts of saving and investments, which are very necessary for increasing the supply of goods and services. Knight has found that there may not always be a tendency of the economy to move towards equilibrium.

Demand - Supply Analysis: The basic purpose of economics is to analyse the want-satisfying activities. According to him, the law of diminishing marginal utility is not a satisfactory law, because it cannot help in the measurement of the additional units of satisfaction. However, the law is to some extent useful psychologically to interpret consumer's choice. Demand, as Knight observes, is related to the amount of commodity which can be taken out of the market at a particular price level. He says that demand is a function of price. There are mainly two elements in the analysis of demand, one must take into account various important factors such as money income, distribution pattern of income, prices of complementary and substitute goods, utility and so on. The demand for a commodity can be influenced by a number of factors, apart from price and supply. Demand can considerably be influenced by advertisement and publicity.

There may be a disequilibrium between the demand and supply. This is possible particularly in the short period. In the longrun, both demand and supply can be changed simultaneously. So, the possibility of disequilibrium becomes a distant possibility. According to him, price can easily adjust to the change in demand. But supply does not become a function of price.

Theory of Distribution: According to Knight, interest arises out of specialisation functions of the business people. Interest is a kind of income which arises out of abstinence. But time preference does not play any important role in the generation of rate of interest. The basis of rate of interest is the productivity of capital. If capital were not productive, there would not have been any rate of interest. Interest has been defined as anticipated specific productivity ratio. Interest estimation has to take into account *productivity* on the one hand, and the *cost* on the other. Borrowing will go up to that amount where cost of borrowing would be equal to the expected income from the new investment. The marginal productivity of capital will determine the yield as well as the rate of interest. Generally, the yield of capital borrowed should be equal to the rate of interest.

Knight is famous for his theory of profit in which he has made an original contribution. His analysis of profit is given in his book, *Risk, Uncertainty and profit* which was published in 1921. This book was his doctoral thesis. According to Knight, true profit arises out of uncertainty. He considered profit as residual income which was left out after making payment to all other factors of production. Profit is the reward for both risk and uncertainty. Business essentially involves risk. However, risk is something which can be insured against. Therefore, it is a part of the running cost (cost of insurance). But uncertainty in the market conditions cannot be insured. There is always an element of uncertainty in a dynamic economy. Under such a situation, an entrepreneur has to depend on probabilities in order to take business decisions. It is this uncertainty in the business world which needs entrepreneurial actions and decisions, which may be found to be wrong and damaging later on. Therefore, for inducing the entrepreneurs to take up decisions under uncertain conditions, there must be some temptation in the form of reward. This temptation for reward against uncertainty can be called profit. As a matter of fact, if there is no uncertainty in the world, an every-thing is sure and certain, there would be no *profit*. In that case, the entrepreneurs will simply get their remuneration for only managing the industry.

The most important contribution of Knight in the contemporary economic analysis was his theory of profit based on risk and uncertainty analysis. According to him, rent, wages, interest and profit are not really different categories; but essentially they are same in nature.

16
Welfare Economics

JOHN A. HOBSON (1858-1940)

Hobson's Contribution to Welfare Economics

Hobson studied the ins and outs of industrial civilization. He was much influenced by Toynbee, Ruskin and Veblen. According to Hobson, Economic Science does not appear to be correctly understood and interpreted. The main analysis of economics centres round the concept of money. However, economics should be concerned with *welfare*. Economics should not give undue stress on value, price and production. The object of economics is mainly to encourage human welfare. Hobson observes that there is no wealth but life which includes happiness, love, admiration, joy and so on. By welfare, Hobson meant good life. In his book, *Work and Wealth*, he pointed out that although economic science has become less material in its outlook and treatment, still the science has basically remained mechanical and unfitted for the performance of any human interpretation of industry. The most prominent defect of economics is the pecuniary motive utilised everywhere. He pointed out the three main defects of the science of economics.[1] Firstly, economics stresses more on production and neglects consumption. Secondly, the concept of economic system is too mechanical. Thirdly, there seems to be an inconsistency between the standard of value supported by economic science and human welfare. According to Hobson, wealth or money income should be estimated with reference to the vital cost of production and the vital utility of consumption.

Hobson realised that the classical analysis of economic phenomena is not really correct. Classical economics gives too much emphasis on free competition, market price and individualism. Classical economics is based on the notion of quantitative valuation of things. This is not proper in the context of of maximisation welfare. Market price cannot be a proper index of economic welfare. Moreover, classical economics is unduly production oriented. What is more important is, however, consumption, because production is after all meant for consumption.

Economic system unduly emphasises cost and underestimates human utility. According to Hobson, the human being is not given any special im-

---

1. J.A. Habson, *Work and Wealth* p. 9.

portance in the industrial system of production. This is evident from the fact that the workers lead a miserable life. Workers have to make a great sacrifice in the industrial civilization of our times. The sacrifice can be regarded as human cost. Since the workers are paid lower wages, their sacrifice becomes too high as compared to the persons who are paid high wages in industries. Thus, the highest-paid workers can consider their work as a pleasure but the lowest-paid workers have to undergo nervous disorders, physical fatigue and so on. Thus, to a low-paid worker, work is a drudgery. In this sense, the utility of work is greater than the human cost in the case of high-paid workers, whereas the utility of work is lower than the human cost in the case of a low-paid worker. Hobson also interestingly pointed out that since the people who are working on higher posts enjoy a feeling of power, position and joy, the disutility of work becomes much low. But in the case of low-paid workers, disutility from work become very high.

As against this, the incomes of upper and middle classes are higher than the money required by them for comfortable living. Therefore, these classes of people can save substantial income without making much sacrifice. However, saving by low-paid workers involves a lot of sacrifice. In fact, the sacrifice on the part of low-paid workers is much higher than the sacrifice on the part of high-paid workers for the same amount of saving. An analysis of welfare in this context of unequal sacrifice requires a thorough study. According to Hobson, welfare in this context can be achieved by working out a balance between human cost and utility.

However, there are different types of productive activity. And most of these activities involve cost and utility. There may, of course, be activities in which the human cost may be zero. But such activities are very rare. Economic welfare is related to an expanded and improved industrial occupation. Material welfare can be increased by improving the industrial system. But unfortunately, a large amount of goods and services produced by the industrial system becomes useless in course of time. Moreover, a large part of the production of the national wealth becomes an unproductive surplus. This is the direct result of wrong planning and defective management. A large quantity of goods and services produced in a country is wasted by conspicuous consumption like display, drink, sham culture and show. Hobson was in favour of reforming the socio-economic system. He advocated the following lines of reforms :

1. A better distribution system such that the low-paid workers can get compensation for their great sacrifice.

2. Labour should be paid according to its *labour power*. The higher the labour power of a worker, the higher should be his wage. In this context, Hobson brought in the concept of depreciation which is allowed for capital. A depreciation allowance should be paid to the workers for the wear and tear of his labour power. This depreciation charge would be helpful to the worker for the recoupment of the lost physical strength. A worker with

higher labour power will be given a higher depreciation allowance to keep himself fit as compared to the worker whose labour power is low.

3. Since the cost (sacrifice) in the case of low-paid labour is higher in the production process as compared to the high-paid workers, the low-paid workers should get a share in the surplus production. Their share should be higher than the share of the highly-paid workers. If the workers are not compensated, the purchasing power of the workers will remain low, and the goods and services produced by a growing industrial system cannot be sold out. This will result in overproduction owing to underconsumption.

4. Hobson suggested that there should be a human law of distribution through which the surplus product of the economy would be distributed equitably. The social reforms can bring about the desired pattern of distribution. Hobson believed that malproduction and malconsumption can be eliminated through a method of proper social control. The distribution strategy of Hobson has been discussed in his book, *The Industrial System*.

5. Hobson maintains that for a better distribution, intervention by the state is very essential.

6. The costs of production should be distributed among the individuals according to their abilities, and commodities should be allotted according to the capacity of the individual to derive utility from them. Thus, his method of reforms is to follow the principle : "from each in accordance with his ability and to each in accordance with his need as consumer."

7. He was in favour of social control, particularly with respect to public utility and over those organisations which are becoming monopolistic in nature. The monopolistic industries require socialisation.

8. Industries which are passing through the experimental stage and which are related to the production of artistic goods and services should be given freedom from control.

9. Industries should be subjected to a high profit tax and also minimum wage legislation.

10. He was in favour of not only the balancing between saving and investment but also between production and consumption so that economic welfare can be maximised.

Criticisms

The welfare analysis which Hobson has made has been subjected to several points of criticism. Some of the points are given below :

> (i) Hobson spoke about human cost and sacrifice involved in production. However, he has not given any methodology for the measurement of human cost and sacrifice. In the absence of such a technique of measurement, the talk of human welfare becomes an empty talk.

(ii) Hobson opines that a man who enjoys his work should be paid less than the main who does not enjoy his work. This does not appear to be a correct criterion of wage policy.

(iii) Hobson has also not spoken anything about the measurement of utility either from work or from consumption.

Despite the above points of criticism, Hobson's work on welfare economics was considered to be seminal for a long time, particularly in America, and it became an important source of Keynesian macro-economics.

ARTHUR CECIL PIGOU (1877-1959)

Pigou's Contribution to Welfare Economics

Pigou and Pareto have actually founded the modern welfare economics. Pigou's Economics of *Welfare is a magnum opus*. It represents the welfare tradition of neo-classical economics. Pigou was basically a neo-classical economist. In his work, the emphasis shifted from *happiness to welfare*. Most of the important theoretical terms applied by Pigou are obtained from Marshallian analysis. But there are many important ways in which Pigou has not followed the Marshallian traditions. Marshall was basically concerned with the *surplus analysis*. Pigou was fundamentally concerned with the *marginal analysis* which deals with balancing the advantages and disadvantages of very small changes in the output of different industries.

According to Pigou, economic welfare is a part of social welfare which can be brought directly or indirectly under the system of monetary measurement. Social welfare, according to Pigou, is the sum total of individual welfare. He also pointed out that individual welfare is nothing but the sum total of the satisfaction experienced by a person within a given period of time. To, him, economic welfare and national dividend are coordinates, because the former is affected by the latter in various ways.

Pigou, in his analysis, made many assumptions, such as :

1. Each individual tries to maximise his own satisfaction (or utility).
2. Interpersonal comparisons of utility are possible.
3. Welfare will increase if wealth is transferred from rich people to poor people.
4. Welfare analysis is normative in character.
5. Man's capacity for satisfaction is equal.
6. Persons having more real income will enjoy satisfaction than those having less real income.

Economic welfare has both a subjective as well as an objective or material counterpart. According to him, national income is the flow of goods and services produced annually after the maintenance of capital which is measurable in terms of money. For optimum output or ideal output, Pigou observes that society should maximise the increase in national dividends by equating marginal social products (MSP) in all the industries. In other words,

$$MSPx == MSPY ..... = MSPn$$

where x, y....n are all industries. The marginal unit of money must also yield the same amount of satisfaction to everyone. According to him, the national product will be maximum with the optimum application of economic resources when the value of marginal social net product (MSNP) is equal to the value of marginal private net product (MPNP). In Pigou's version, the social net product is the aggregate contribution made to the national dividend and the private net product is the contribution that is capable of being sold and the proceeds added to the earning of the person. However, there are several possible divergences between MSNP and MPNP. They are the following:

1. One possible divergence is connected with the separation between tenancy and ownership of certain durable instruments of production. It is possible that some part of the investment designed to improve durable instruments of production is made sometimes by persons other than the owners. If this happens, there would be divergence between MSNP and MPNP. This divergence will be normally associated with wasteful forms of tenancy laws.

2. The second type of divergence is associated with the external diseconomies in consumption, such as, the smoky chimney concept. In such a case, the production of commodity gives rise to incidental disservices or diseconomies to a party who is neither the producer nor the consumer of the product being produced but simply happens to be the resident of the locality where the production is being organised. Thus, the factory chimney only increases the laundery bills of the neighbours.

3. Another type of divergence between MSNP and MPNP is that in which the MSP of resources employed in an industry with decreasing supply price is greater than their MPP. In such a case, the output of that industry will be less than optimum.

It must be noted that the supply price of a commodity is different for the community and for the industry, and, secondly, the supply price of a commodity is also different for an industry and for an equilibrium firm. As in the case of an increasing returns industry, when the supply price from the industry is less than the supply price of the equilibrium firm, the MSP becomes greater than MPP. In such a situation, economic welfare can be raised by giving a subsidy to the increasing returns industries.

Pigou is concerned with an economic system which is fairly competitive and where MPNP = MSNP. This equality can be brought about by tax or subsidy. This is why, state intervention becomes essential.

Pigou measures economic welfare of society indirectly by measuring the physical national dividend valued at appropriate prices. For finding out whether any economic change has improved welfare or not, he applies the following double criterion :

(a) Economic welfare has increased if an increase in national dividend has taken place without any increase in factor supply.

(b) Economic welfare has increased if a transfer of wealth has taken place from the rich to the poor people.

Pigou observes that private interest and social interest are not in harmony. Modern analysis of *external effects* is to be found in a crude form in Pigou's distinction between social and private valuation of economic activities. In Pigou's analysis, the optimum output (ideal output) is reached when competition equalises the MPPs in all uses. It is an economic system where MPNP is equal to MSNP automatically. Pigou favours a policy of income equalisation.

Hla Myint observes a basic difference between Paretian optimum and Pigovian optimum. Whereas the Paretian optimum is not designed for practical application, Pigovian theory mainly deals with the practical application of welfare economics. Pigou's distinction between economic and general welfare, on the one hand, and that between marginal private product and marginal social product, on the other, are meant for solving some practical problems. Paretian optimum provides us with the methodological problems of the study of welfare economics, but Pigovian optimum has contributed to the growth of applied welfare economics. Pigou is concerned with the promising fruit and not with light alone.

Although Pigou represents the neo-classical school and has followed broadly the tradition of Marshall, still, one can find some differences between Pigou and Marshall. Pigou recognises all particular frictions which may develop under *laissez faire* and which were usually treated as special cases by most neo-classical writers. Pigou considered all conflicts that are likely to arise, under a generalised concept, known as a "marginal social product." Pigou's approach is more general with respect to the measurement of social economic welfare. Pigou's ideal output requires the following conditions to be satisfied:

(i) A given quantity of productive resources is being employed.

(ii) The movement between different occupations does not involve any cost.

(iii) Only one type of resources arrangements will make the national dividend optimum.

Critical Appraisal

Pigou's welfare economics is not an objective study. It is based on the assumption of man's equal capacity for satisfaction. Prof.Little has raised the following points of criticism against Pigou's welfare economics :

(1) Satisfaction cannot be added, as Pigou says. According to Little, it is impossible to make a sum total of satisfaction of the society.

(2) Satisfaction and happiness of different individuals cannot be compared without making value judgement.

(3) According to Little, Pigou's study is wholly based on a strict normative principle. Thus, welfare becomes ethical in nature.

Tapas Mazumdar and others have pointed out that Pigou's distinctions between economic welfare and general welfare are meaningless. Pigou has not considered the factors of immobility, indivisibility and imperfect knowledge. However, despite all this, "Pigou achieved what Marshall could not do in his written work —the integration of the normative problems with the positive ones the building-up of a rigorous theoretical analysis which would serve as a scientific theory of economic policy."[2]

2.   B. Datta, "Sir Arthur Cecil Pigou," *Arthaniti*, Nov. 1959.

17

New Economics

JOHN MAYNARD KEYNES (1883-1946)

Keynes is perhaps the greatest economist of the twentieth century and will remain one of the greatest in the history of economics. Keynes introduced a *new paradigm* in the analysis of economics. His new paradigm may be called a general macroeconomic analysis. He revolutionised economic thinking so much so that the Keynesin economics is called Keynesian revolution. Without going into the appropriateness of the term 'revolution' here, one can safely pen down the fact that Keynes introduced a school which can be called *New Economics*. Keynes was basically a classical economist. Keynes' contribution to the classical tradition is his famous *Treatise on Money*. Keynes is primarily a monetary economist. He analysed the monetary problems in macro prespective. Keynes found that the classical prescription of monetary policy could not eliminate unemployment and the great depression of the thirties. He then examined very closely the problems associated with unemployment and depression. This is treated in his *General Theory of Employment, Interest and Money*, which was published in 1936. Keynesian economics, therefore, is sometimes called the economics of depression. Anyway, Keynes pointed out the inefficacy of monetary policy and prescribed the use of fiscal policy for curing unemployment and depression. Keynes has written a number of books including *Indian Currency and Finance (1913), A Tract on Monetary Reform (1923)* and *How to Pay for the War (1940)*. However, the *General Theory* is his *magnum opus*.

Although Keynes was primarily a classical economist, still he differed on many important points from the classical economists. The main points of differences between Keynes and the classicists can be shown in the following chart :

	Classical Views		Keynesian Views
1.	There is a direct relationship between the money supply and the price level.	:	No such direct relationship exists. The relation is only indirect.
2.	Saving-investment equality is brought about by the rate of interest mechanism.	:	The equality between saving and investment is brought about by income level.

	Classical Views		Keynesian Views
3.	Rate of interest is a flow.	:	Rate of interest is a stock.
4.	Labour supply depends on real wage rate.	:	Supply of labour depends on money wage rate.
5.	There is no money illusion.	:	There is money illusion.
6.	The economy is at full employment equilibrium.	:	The economy is at under employment equilibrium.
7.	The automatic adjustment works.	:	There is no such thing.
8.	No speculative demand for money.	:	There is speculative demand for money.
9.	Wages are flexible.	:	Wages are rigid downward.
10.	Supply creates its own demand.	:	Supply is generally greater than demand (They are not equal).
11.	Money is a veil.	:	Money is important for dynamic activity.
12.	Rate of interest is a reward for saving.	:	Rate of interest is a reward for parting with liquidity.
13.	*Laissez faire.*	:	*No laissez faire.*
14.	When the wage level goes down, employment goes up.	:	When the wage level goes down, employment goes down.
15.	Saving is good.	:	Saving is bad.
16.	Balanced budget.	:	Unbalanced budget.
17.	Long-run.	:	Short-run.

KEYNESIAN MACRO MODEL

Keynes built up a short-run macroeconomic model with many variables. He divided the economy into the following three markets and analysed their economic variables and equilibrium conditions.

Goods Market

The equilibrium in the goods market is determined by the equality of aggregate demand and aggregate supply, or,

$Y = C_p + I_p$ (Income is equal to planned consumption and planned investment.)

$C_p = f(Y, r, A, \propto)$ (Planned consumption depends on income, rate of interest, real value of assets and income distribution.)

$I_p = f(Y, r)$ (Planned investment is a direct function of income and indirect function of rate of interest.)

$S_p = f(Y, r)$ (Planned saving depends on income and rate of interest.)

$I_p = S_p$ (Planned investment and planned saving are equal.)

Money Market

$M_d = M_s$ (Demand for money is equal to supply of money)

$M_d = L(PY) + L(r)$ (Total demand for money consists of transaction demand for money and speculative demand for money.)

$M_s = M_0$ (Money supply is fixed.)

Labour Market

$N_d = N_s$ (Demand for labour is equal to supply of labour)

$N_d = f(W/P)$ (Demand for labour is a function of real wage rate.

$N_s = f(W)$ (Supply of labour is a function of money wage rate.)

$Q = f(N, K, T)$ (Output depends on labour, capital and technology being given.)

Diagrammatically,

In the panels A and C : Given the equilibrium rate of interest (r_0) investment is I_0. Given the saving function S, at equilibrium, $I_0 = S_0$ and equilibrium income is Y_0.

In panel D : Y is the production function, corresponding to Y_0 and N_0.

In panel F : N_0 employment corresponds with W/P_0 (real wage rate), which is determined by real wage function W/P in panel (G).

In panels G and E: At P_0, the money wage rate is W_0, and money income is $P_0 Y_0$, then transaction demand for money (LPY) is MT_0.

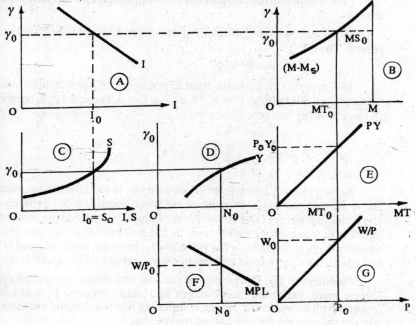

Fig. 17.1

In panel B : $(M - M_s)$ function divides total money OM between OMT_0 (active balance) and MS_0 (speculative balance) (at r_0 rate of interest). If the rate of interest is below r_0, income, investment, employment go up and the real wage rate goes down. The model clearly suggests that equilibrium may occur at any level of employment (N_0 is not necessarily full employment in the diagram) within the upper limit by the size of the labour force. It also denies the existence of any automatic adjustment mechanism because of the existence of rigidities caused by either endogenous or exogenous factors. This model prescribes government intervention for attaining higher employment and income.

Income Determination

Keynesian economics is basically concerned with the determination of income and employment. Keynes explained the income theory systematically through saving *(s)* and investment *(I)* equilibrium approach in his *General Theory*. The income theory upholds that aggregate demand is determined by aggregate expenditure *(E)* which consists of consumption expenditure *(c)* and investment expenditure *(I)*. Expenditure generates income in a macroeconomic sense, and income generates further expenditure. In this way, there is some circularity, where income *(Y)* and expenditure can be interchangeably used. Let us briefly explain his ideas :

$$E = C + I$$

(Total expenditure is equal to consumption and investment expenditures.)

However, one part of the income is saved and the other part is consumed. Thus,

$$Y = C + S$$

In Keynesian hypothesis, total expenditure *(E)* determines total income in such a way that : $E = Y$. Thus, $Y = C + I$. Income *(Y)* is composed of the following two sets of factors:

$$Y = C + I$$
$$Y = C + S$$
$$\text{or} \quad C + I = C + S$$
$$\text{or} \quad I = S$$

Saving *(S)* and Investment *(I)* equality is, thus, definitional. According to Keynes, saving-investment equality is a condition of equilibrium in the economy, irrespective of the level of employment. Saving-investment equality is, however, brought about by the mechanism of income and this equality leads to stability in the price level. However, when *(S)* and *(I)* are not equal, then price level and income level cannot be in equilibrium.

Needless to say, the process of income determination involves many forces, many variables, many stages and many sectors. In a simplistic analysis with a two-sector model, comprising households and business sector, the income generation can be regarded as :

$$Y = C_0 + bY + I$$ (where C_0 is autonomous consumption and b is marginal propensity to consume)

Given the values of $b(MPC)$, C_0 and investment (I), it is possible to find out the level of income. The equilibrium income is disturbed under the following two situations :

(i) If saving is not equal to investment.

(ii) If aggregate demand is not equal to aggregate supply.

If the level of investment changes, income will be changed. This can be explained with the help of the investment multiplier which says that if investment is changed, income will change by a multiple of investment. All this will give the short-run determination of income, as in the Keynesian theory. The income determination process can also be discussed with reference to the government sector and open economy.

KEYNESIAN THEORY OF EMPLOYMENT.

In his *General Theory,* Keynes attacks the classical theory of employment and systematically develops his own theory of employment, output and income. According to Keynes, total income of an economy is a function of total employment. The volume of employment depends on effective demand. The effective demand depends on aggregate demand price and aggregate supply price. The equilibrium point between aggregate demand function and aggregate supply function determines effective demand. In the Keynesian model, aggregate supply function is assumed as given, and the whole analysis centres round the factors that determine and influence aggregate demand function. Effective demand depends on consumption demand and investment demand. Consumption depends on the level of income and the propensity to consume. The propensity to consume does not increase in the same proportion as the increase in income. Keynes observes that in the short period, consumption function is more or less stable. Therefore, for increasing employment in the short period, the main emphasis is placed on investment. Investment bridges the gap between income and consumption. If the volume of investment is insufficient, the aggregate demand price will fall short of aggregate supply price, and employment and income would be reduced. Thus, variation in employment and income mainly depends on the variation in investment.

Investment depends on two factors : *(i)* marginal efficiency of capital, and *(ii)* rate of interest. Marginal efficiency of capital depends on the supply price of capital and the prospective yield from capital. The supply price of capital depends on the physical and technical conditions of production, which, in the short run, cannot be significantly altered. Therefore, in the short run, prospective yield becomes a more dominant factor in investment decision. When profit expectations are high and the entrepreneurs are guided by "animal spirits", the rate of investment generally becomes higher. On the other hand, when profit expectations are low, investment goes down.

The rate of interest (another determinant of investment) depends on the quantity of money and the liquidity preference. If the supply of money is given, the rate of interest will be determined by the liquidity preference. Liquidity preference depends on three human motives : (1) transaction motive, (2) precautionary motive, and (3) speculative motive. The first two motives for holding money are generally interest-inelastic, while the third one may be said to be interest-elastic. However, if liquidity preference is given, the rate of interest is determined by the monetary policy of the banking system. Investment can be stepped up either by raising the marginal efficiency of capital or by lowering the rate of interest, or by both.

Ordinarily, an increase in investment leads to increase in income and employment. But employment will not increase, if the propensity to consume of the people is reduced at the same time. In fact, consumption function is the "heart of Keynesian analysis" of employment and income. A rise in income and employment without a corresponding increase in investment, is sustained by increased consumption at least up to a point.

The importance of investment and consumption, for employment, income and output, in the Keynesian theory, can be best understood with reference to the operation of the multiplier effect. The multiplier refers to the numerical coefficient indicating the increase in income that results from a given increase in investment. The multiplier "establishes a precise relationship, given the propensity to consume, between aggregate employment and income and the rate of investment." A rise in investment leads to a rise in income, out of which there arises a higher demand for consumption goods which again leads to a further increase in income and employ-

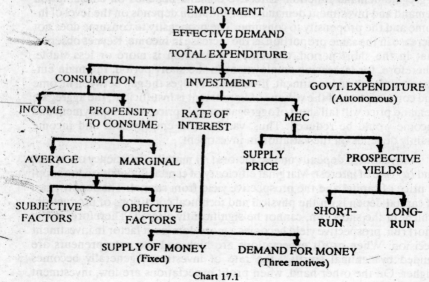

Chart 17.1

ment. When the process becomes cumulative, a given rise in investment causes a multiple increase in income, via the propensity to consume. The size of the multiplier depends on the marginal propensity to consume. If the marginal propensity to consume is high, the multiplier will be large and *vice versa*. Therefore, for increasing income and employment, both marginal propensity to consume as well as investment have to be increased. But since marginal propensity to consume is likely to fall with an increase in income, what is necessary is to step up the rate of investment in the economy. Investment demand along with consumption demand will determine the effective demand which, in turn, will determine the level of income and employment of an economy. This, in a sense, is the Keynesian theory of employment, income and output. Keynesian theory of employment is summarised in the chart 17.1.

KEYNES' VIEWS ON DEVELOPMENT

Keynes did not develop any systematic analysis on economic development in his *General Theory*. But his ideas on development can be gathered from the broad insight which he has given in his various writings. In an eassy,[1] Keynes suggested that the future rate of economic progress would depend on (1) our power to control population, (2) our determined effort to avoid civil wars and depressions, (3) our willingness to entrust to science the direction of those matters which are properly the concern of science, and (4) the rate of accumulation as fixed by the margin between output, production and consumption. These propositions outline the fundamental conditions of economic development.[2]

Keynes was a prophet of boom. He observed that if capitalism is modified through deliberate state action, if will not only be saved from the possible breakdown but also be a source of human progress.

Keynesian insights were used by Mrs. Joan Robinson, Harrod-Domar and others in constructing sophisticated models of economic growth. Without Keynes' theory of effective demand, Harrod's theory of growth might not have seen the light. Harrod gave long-run considerations to his theory and emphasised the capacity increasing aspect of saving in contradistinction to Keynes', demand decreasing aspect. Similarly, Domar synthesised Keynesian theory of multiplier with the classical theory of productivity. Keynes'*General Theory* was static in formulation. But it "opened the way for a great outburst of analysis of dynamic problems." Both Mrs. Robinson and Nurkse have used the tools of dynamic economics in analysing the problems of investment demand and capital formation in underdeveloped countries.

Kurihara observes that Keynes' national income analysis may be a useful basis for estimating consumption, saving, investment, employment

---

1. Keynes, "Economic Possibilities for Our Grand Children", in his *Essay in Persuasion*, p. 373.
2. Kurihara, *The Keynesian Theory of Economic Development*, p. 19.

and other operationally significant variables required under development programmes. Keynesian national income analysis unfolds the important fact that for guiding industrialization in under-developed countries, statistical data or techniques alone will be quite insufficient without some plausible hypothesis for interpreting the behaviour of various components of national product.

Keynes did not believe in the classical notion that the inherent tendency of an economy is to maintain full employment. He, on the other hand, demonstrated that the economy is always in underemployment equilibrium. Thus, Keynes, although in a different context, hints at the very basic characteristic feature of an underdeveloped economy.

Keynesian secular stagnation thesis reveals that if there are overproduction, underconsumption and very low marginal efficiency of capital, capitalism may face a breakdown. Keynes' advocacy of the increasing role of state in rejuvenating the economy might appeal to those underdeveloped countries which are trying to come out of the low-level stagnation trap mainly through state action. Keynes' analysis of 'Depression' is a pointer to the fact that economic progress cannot be attained without state help.

Economic progress requires increasing magnitude of investment. According to Keynes, if domestic resources are not sufficient for financing the required investment, deficit financing may be resorted to in the economy. This will not only make available the resources but also lead to all-round prosperity by creating a favourable climate for investment. A mild inflation will allocate resources in productive lines and will remove the bottlenecks in the way of production. Keynes believes that a mild inflation can augment investment, income, output and employment. In the context of limited economic resources, development plan can be based to some extent on this method of financing that Keynes prescribed.

Keynes thought that international economic homogeneity may serve as a useful path to universal prosperity and peace. With this aim in view, he advocated the establishment of a world bank for the purposes of reconstruction and development. He deemed that this bank would be able to make the savings' propensities of the rich nations compatible with the development requirements of the poor nations. The IBRD which has been guiding and helping the economic development of many poor nations of today owes its origin to the bold imagination and genuine internationalism of J.M.Keynes.

Criticisms

1. Some of the very crucial variables in the Keynesian system, for instance, consumption function, multiplier, etc., are insufficient and practically not very useful. His multiplier idea is tautological and instantaneous

2. His forecast that mature economies would experience secular stagnation has not been correct.

3. His model "is too aggregative."[3] Proper application of Keynesian model requires certain disaggregation. It should have contained more variables and relationships than it does.

4. Keynesian model, being static, fails to analyse short-run dynamics of income change.

5. His is a short-run model. He does not consider very long run economic problems. Keynes neglects long-run analysis by saying that "in the long run, everyone of us is dead."

6. It is alleged that Keynes has failed to take note of *Pigou Effect* or *Real Balance Effect*, and that it is not possible to attain equilibrium, as Keynes believes, at less than full employment level, if wages and prices are perfectly flexible.

7. There is hardly any significant difference between the classical and Keynesian models. Some economists are of the opinion that Keynesian model might better be considered as an extension and improvement of, rather than as a substitute for, the classical macroeconomic model.

In recent years, the outstanding macroeconomic problems appear to be associated with economic growth and inflation. While the Keynesian model cannot be made directly applicable to the problems of economic growth, it can be utilised for understanding the problems of inflation. Keynesian economics provides significant and new insights that were previously lacking. Despite limitations and deficiencies, the Keynesian analysis still provides the most useful points of departure in macroeconomic thinking. It has been a perennial source of encouragement to the great majority of significant works in the areas of both macroeconomics and growth economics in the contemporary world. As Prof. J.R.Hicks once observed, *"The General Theory* is neither the beginning nor the end of Dynamic Economics," but it remains the common starting point for a good many works on economics.

KEYNESIAN ECONOMICS AND UNDERDEVELOPED COUNTRIES

Controversy

Some writers are of the view that Keynesian economics does not command universal application. Its application, they say, is limited to advanced countries like the U.K. or the U.S.A. Keynesian economics is believed to be the economics of 'Depression'; and hence, according to some, it cannot be applied to the cases of under-developed countries, for such countries are in the midst of secular inflation. Schumpeter contends that "practical Keynesianism is a seedling which cannot be transplanted into foreign soil; it dies there and becomes poisonous before it dies." In the same sentiment, Harris writes that "those who seek universal truths applicable in all places and at all times, had not better waste their time on the *General Theory.*"[4]

---

3. Ackley, *Macroeconomic Theory,* pp. 412-418.
4. Harris, *The New Economics,* p. 40.

Some Indian economists also hold a similar view. A.K. Dasgupta remarks : "Whatever the generality of the *General Theory* may be in the sense in which the term 'general' was used by Keynes, applicability of the propositions of the *General Theory* to conditions of an underdeveloped economy is at best limited."[5] V. K. R. V. Rao observes that the "blind application of the Keynesian formulae to the problems of economic development has inflicted considerable injury on the economies of underdeveloped countries and added to the forces of inflation that are currently afflicting the whole world."

But there are others who hold quite opposite views. Some writers in this latter group maintain that "the Keynesian theory is a general theory of income determination; it is valid for a developed as well as underdeveloped economy." A few among these writers have challenged the views of the former group of writers who are opposed to the application of Keynesian economics to backward countries.[6] According to this latter camp, Keynesian tools and concepts are still applicable to cases of underdeveloped countries. Let us examine the views of both the groups of writers side by side with reference to Keynesian concepts, tools assumptions.

Nature of Unemployment

Keynes is mainly concerned with the problem of involuntary unemployment in the advanced countries and his whole thesis relates to the question of how to secure full employment in the case of these countries.[7] In Keynesian theory unemployment is caused by deficiency in effective demand. V. K. R. V. Rao maintains that in underdeveloped countries, there is no involuntary unemployment, but there is disguised unemployment. Again, unemployment here is caused not by lack of effective demand but by lack of complementary resources.

The above view, however, is not always correct for underdeveloped countries. In these countries, unemployment is rampant, both in the agricultural sector as well as in the industrial sector. Similarly, underemployment, be it visible or disguised, is partly involuntary in nature, and arises out of lack of alternative openings. It is also not right to say that in backward economies, there is always lack of resources. Underdeveloped countries are often rich in resources ; but the problem is that these resources are not yet properly utilised. These resources can be utilised with the help of higher monetary incentives and effective demand. In fact, effective demand in underdeveloped countries is not adequate.

Effective Demand

It is often contended that in underdeveloped countries, effective demand is quite sufficient, and the Keynesian analysis which mainly advo-

---

5. A.K. Dasgupta, *Planning and Economic Growth*, p. 34.
6. Among others, Ashok Mathur, Anthony Bottomley and C.T. Kurien hold this view.
7. V.K.R.V. Rao, *op. cit.*, p. 37.

cates the raising of effective demand for removing unemployment is not applicable in backward economies.

In underdeveloped countries, due to the low *per capita* income, effective demand (*i.e.,* purchasing power) is never adequate ; on the other hand, it is very low. The principle of aggregate demand has the same significance in the explanation of inflationary conditions in developing countries as in the case of the inflationary gap analysis in mature economies.[8] The principle provides a theoretical basis for policies aimed at controlling inflation in developing countries. But for the concept of aggregate demand and the related tool of analysis, the technique of national income accounting, which forms so important a basis for development planning, would not have been perhaps possible. Even in backward economies, the conditions of rising effective demand are essential for a favourable investment outlook, at least in the private sector. Rising aggregate demand is very important for breaking the vicious circle and for initiating a take-off.

Multiplier

Rao believes that Keynesian multiplier analysis does not work in underdeveloped economies.[9] The working of the multiplier requires the existence of the following conditions: (1) Involuntary unemployment, (2) Elastic supply of output, (3) Excess capacity, (4) Elastic supply of working capital.

According to Rao, absence of the above conditions in backward economies stands in the way of operation of the multiplier process.

We have already explained that involuntary unemployment exists in backward countries. Here, all the above mentioned conditions are very much present. Excess capacity in industries, particularly in the public sector, as in India, is a problem. Investment itself has capacity-creating effect in the long run.[10] Supply of output and working capital in developing countries is not completely inelastic. Monetary and credit-creating institutions have been expanding the supply of working capital in all such countries in recent years. Outputs of agricultural and consumption goods sector have also shown an upward movement in recent decades. There are enormous possibilities for increasing the output in these sectors still further. In the long run, forward and backward linkage effects may help to increase output. Rao views the multiplier process in a quite static setting. In a developing economy (and not in the traditional society of Rostownian type), in the long run, output cannot be inelastic. In the developing countries, interaction between the multiplier and the accelerator is likely to come about almost immediately after the initial injection of investment.[11] Multiplier in underdeveloped countries will increase output, and

---

8. Ashok Mathur, "On Throwing the Baby Away with the Bath Water," IEJ, 1965.
9. Rao, *op. cit.,* pp. 42-44.
10. E. Domar, *Essays in the Theory of Economic Growth,* 1957.
11. Ashok Mathur, *op. cit.,* p. 407.

bottlenecks and skill will not be stumbling blocks, if investment is taken up in moderate doses, and confined to quick-yielding type of consumer goods industries. In that case, Rao's fear of possible inflation may be eliminated.[12]

Rao asserts that the existence of disguised unemployment in backward countries hinders the working of the principle of multiplier.[13] To be operationally effective, multiplier requires, among other things, an elastic supply of labour force willing to accept employment at the current wage level. However, Rao's view is not a correct presentation of the real situation in backward countries. In such countries, labour is abundant and cheap. A high magnitude of unemployment in the industrial sector, not to speak of agricultural sector, makes the supply of labour elastic at current wages, as Prof. Lewis observes.[14] Disguised unemployment of the primary sector can also be mobilised, as shown by Nurkse, at the current industrial wage rate, which is higher than the agricultural wage.[15]

Deficit Financing

Prof. Rao maintains that the economic policy of deficit financing advocated by Keynes for securing full employment does not apply in backward countries.[16] He holds this view primarily on the ground that the supply curve of output is inelastic in an underdeveloped country, and deficit financing in such a context is bound to be inflationary.

Rao himself accepts that deficit financing need not always be inflationary.[17] It is rather self-liquidating in character. As we have already noted, supply curve of output in developing countries is not really inelastic. If deficit financing is used for increasing the capacity and for expanding the output in the quick-yielding type of consumer goods industries, it need not be inflationary. Deficit financing, on the other hand, creates forced saving in the economy and thereby can increase the rate of capital formation in poor countries. Prof. Rao accepts this to be true. Deficit financing should be properly planned and should be moderate in dose.

Saving and Investment

According to Prof. Rao, Keynesian policy of disregard for thrift is not helpful for economic progress in backward countries. He holds that the old-fashioned classical prescription of save more and work harder is relevant for poor countries.[18]

---

12. Rao, *op. cit.,* p. 41.
13. *Ibid.,* p. 43.
14. W.A. Lewis, "Economic Development with Unlimited Supplies of Labour," *Manchester School,* May 1954.
15. Ragnar Nurkse, *The Problems of Capital Formation in Underdeveloped Countries,* Ch. 2.
16. Rao, *op. cit.,* p. 49.
17. *Ibid.,* Ch. 5.
18. *Ibid.,* p. 49.

It is not right to believe that saving always determines investment. Saving and investment are independently taken up by different categories of people. Mere increase in saving cannot do anything favourable if it is hoarded or not productively utilised. It is investment and not saving that determines growth. The idea that low saving is bad arises implicitly from the connection that is believed to exist between saving and investment, more particularly from the connection that savings determines investment. In fact, more correctly, investment determines saving and not *vice versa*. Investment has its effects on prices, which in turn influence income distribution and shares of profit and wage; and given the marginal propensity to save, the magnitude of saving is determined. Low saving is sometimes beneficial. Low saving means higher consumption which means, other things being the same, higher profit, higher reinvestible surplus and higher investment. Thus, low saving need not hinder investment. The main bottleneck in underdeveloped countries is not low saving, but lack of utilisation of resources and of organisational ability. However, the bottlenecks can be reduced to a very great extent by increasing the tempo of investment, a large part of which can be financed by foreign capital. Thus, Keynes' analysis in which saving plays a passive role is still valid in backward countries.

Importance of Other Measures

Keynes lays great emphasis on the role of state in eradicating depression. In underdeveloped countries, state action is indispensable in guiding and in lifting the economy from the rut of low level stagnation trap. The state can increase investment in social overhead capital and can create a favourable climate for increasing private investment. In other words, without increasing state responsibility, no plan of economic development can be a success.

Keynesian policy of public investment to achieve a higher standard of living and to provide increasing employment opportunities is applicable to underdeveloped countries.[19]

Keynes emphasised the positive role of monetary and fiscal policies in advanced countries. In underdeveloped countries, monetary and fiscal policies are becoming more and more growth oriented. Keynesian monetary theory provides a logical framework for the discussion of the place of money in economic development.[20] His framework helps us to identify the points at which quantitative monetary expansion may fail to generate economic development.[21] Keynesian concepts of liquidity, national income accounting, inflationary gap and deficit financing, etc., are still being used with much popularity in developing economies.

---

19. A.K.Dasgupta, *op. cit.,* p. 37.
20. Anthony Bottomley, "Keynesian Monetary Theory and the Developing Countries." *Indian Economic Journal,* April-June, 1965, p. 345.
21. *Ibid.,* p. 346.

Conclusion

Keynesian analysis has been used in recent years by Joan Robinson, Harrod-Domar and others for analysing long-run dynamic growth problems. Though not in the stagnant traditional society, Keynesian economics is largely valid in the case of developing societies with a growing organised sector. Keynesian theory provides an apparatus of thought, and its essential contents can be used for analysing a wide range of problems under varying conditions. Keynesian concepts and tools may be more or less applicable in our context much the same way as Malthusian, Marxian or Marshallian concepts.[22] What is more important is not so much the written words of Keynes but the spirit of his analysis. Keynesian system as a whole may not be fully applicable, but taken with a grain of salt, the tool kits can be of great significance in the analysis and solution of economic problems in underdeveloped countries. To use Dr. K.N. Raj's words, "discarding the Keynesian thesis as altogether inoperative in underdeveloped countries, is really throwing the baby away with the bath water."[23]

22. C.T.Kurien, "Keynesian Economics and Underdeveloped Countries," *Indian Economic Journal,* July-September, 1966, p. 63.
23. K.N.Raj, "Dr.Rao on Investment, Income and the Multiplier in an Underdeveloped Economy—A Comment", *Indian Economic Review,* August 1952.

APPENDIX

POST-KEYNESIAN DEVELOPMENTS: A RESUME

Post-Keynesian developments in macroeconomics and monetary theory and policy have been made possible by the painstaking efforts of many economists, the prominent among which are Milton Friedman, James Tobin, William J. Baumol, J.F. Muth, Robert Lucas, Kreiger, H.Minsky, Arthur Laffer, N. Kaldor, Joan Robinson, Jan Kregel, Robert Clower,A.L. Leijonhufvud and Paul Davidson, to name only a few.

James Tobin has pointed out that keynesian revolution has produced three counter-revolutions since 1965. These three counter-revolutions are: (i) New Classical Macroeconomics based on the theory of rational expectation (ii) Supply-side Economics and (iii) Monetarism.

Apart from these, many minor and major modifications have also been introduced in various facets of monetary economics and macroeconomics. Let us briefly discuss some of these changes.

New Classical Economics : Rational Expectation Theory (Ratex)

The new classical economics (NCE) is a recent challenge to the structure of orthodox and contemporary macro-economic theory. NCE is based on two theories, namely, *theory of continuous market clearing* (CMC) and the theory of rational expectations (RE). CMC is based on the ideas of Walrasian general equilibrium and theory of efficient market. Efficient market hypothesis is basically concerned with prices and equilibrium in commodity market and financial market. Walrasian general equilibrium technique can determine equilibrium prices in all markets simultaneously. At these prices, there would be absence of excess demand or excess supply. The market would be completely clear.

The theory of efficient market utilises the concept of Walrasian general equilibrium and finds out a reltionship between prices and available informations. A market can be efficient if and only if it is able to quickly collect and utilise the available total information in the matter of price formation. Needless to say, market information affects prices considerably. Obviously, theory of CMC is a very crucial element in the development of the theory of new classical economics. In fact, if there is continuous market clearing, unemployment can hardly have any chance to exist, and no Phillips curve relationship is required to banish unemployment.

The theory of rational expectations (RE) is a serious challenge to orthodox Keynesianism.[1] According to RE, since human beings are rational, they rightly anticipate the results of actions and behave accordingly. All economic agents can form expectation pattern rationally on the basis of the available stock of information. RE theorists believe that an economy is es-

---

1. R.D. Gupta, "Rational Expectation: An Operational Illusion", MDU Research Journal, Oct. 1987.

sentially stable and any govt. can do no good but plenty of harm to the economy. Thus, govt. intervention must be avoided. In many countries, govt. has not been able to rectify the situation of *stagflation*.

RE is the application of the principle of rational behaviour to the collection and processing of information and to the formation of expectations. RE can be used for making predictions about many macroeconomic variables on the basis of given stock of information. RE is a new way of dealing with expectations, explaining mainly how they are formed. The latter aspect was neglected by Keynes.

Many economists have developed the theory of RE. Among others, they are, J.F. Muth, Robert Lucas, Sargent and Wallace. Muth observed that some expectations are rational in the sense that they are the same as given by predictions. But expected situation may of course differ from actual situation only by random forecasting error. In the theory of RE, the *stock of available information* can be thought of as some kind of resources which can be allocated in the best possible way.

However, a number of criticisms can be levelled against *Ratex*. *Firstly*, the market clearing assumption is not correct always. *Secondly*, it is very difficult to say as to how expectations are actually formed in the real world situation. *Thirdly*, the available stock of information may not all be correct. *Lastly*, it is not always correct to say that individual expectations are essentially the same as the predictions of the economic theory.

Thus, the rational expectation theory which has become a part of contemporary macroeconomics is not a very sound and developed theory.

Supply Side Economics (SSE)[2]

Supply side economics (SSE) is a reaction against the demand side economics of Keynes. Keynes evidently placed too much emphasis on effective demand creation and almost neglected the supply side. Many economists like Arthur Laffer, Evans, Craig and others, have developed the SSE. This theory believes that Say's law of market (supply creates its own demand) is still valid as a meaningful economic proposition. Secondly, SSE finds a negative correlation between tax rate and consumption and production. That is, a higher tax rate will lead to lower consumption and lower production. Thus, SSE advocates a regime of tax cut (*Reaganomics*, as it was advocated during Reagan's time in the United States).

SSE concentrates on increasing supply through efficiency and modernisation, so that cost is reduced. This will partly ensure increased demand for products. SSE mainly aims at increasing incentives and productivity by removing the constraints. It is pointed out by SSE that a high tax rate generates tax evasion, disincentives, misallocation of resources and harmful spite effect. In fact, a high tax rate discourages productive economic ac-

---

2. James Tobin "Supply Side Economics", Economic Outlook, Summer 1981, and R.D. Gupta, "Supply Side Economics", *Indian Journal of Economics*, April, 1982.

tivity. Therefore, SSE suggests that the rate of taxation should be minimal. SSE presumes that the higher the tax rate, the lower is the tax amount collected. This truth has been demonstrated by Arthur Laffer through Laffer Curve analysis. SSE assumes that since market is stable, optimum allocation of resources will require its free functioning without any obstacle or outside intervention. Govt. intervention may be allowed only to correct market distortions and market failures. Govt. is non-productive but is a necessary evil.

SSE wants to sustain the capitalistic system of production and exchange. It encourages private efforts and entreprises through various incentive schemes so that there can be promotion of wealth and welfare. It is in favour of a free market regime because it maximises the scheme of incentives. Production of wealth and economic growth remain the main focus of attention of the SSE. The emphasis is more on production and growth and less on income distribution.

The original root of the SSE is the classical Say's law of market. It is said that this law is valid in many less developed countries (LDCs) where whatever is produced is ultimately sold out. There is no overproduction or glut.SSE is, in a sense, the reincarnation of classical economics. The real problem in LDCs is sufficient quantitites. Under-development is a kind of supply side constraint, and the basic task of development constitutes the extension of production frontiers - right-ward shift of production possibility curve. SSE has a tremendous appeal to LDCs.

Be that as it may, a number of criticisms can be levelled against SSE. *Firstly*, it is at the most a partial truth, like the Keynesian demand side economics. *Secondly*, it cannot be regarded as a good theory of economic growth for it gives less role to the govt. *Thirdly*, it is not egalitarian in outlook: it favours the maintenance of inequality and skewed income distribution pattern. *Fourthly*, for its support of capitalistic order of society, it is likely to accentuate class conflict, poverty and unemployment. Market failures and crises are more likely in capitalist societies. Supply does not always create demand. *Lastly*, taxation is not a very dependable instrument for increasing saving or increasing production. In a developing country like India, tax-cut may produce more inequality but less revenue for development.

The dispute between SSE and Keynesian demand side economics is a sham dispute. As a matter of fact, both supply and demand are equally important for the proper management of the economy.

Monetarism[3]

Monetarism is a recent movement against Keynesianism or Fiscalism. The monetarist group represents, among others, Milton, Friedman, Karl Brunner, Allan Meltzer, Phillip Cagan, Don Patinkin, David Fand, Meisel-

---

3. See, B.N. Ghosh, "Monetarism Vs Fiscalism: A Reconciliatory Approach", *Indian Economic Journal*, July-Sept., 1982.

man, Anna Schwartz, L. Anderson, J. Jordan and K. Carlson. Milton Friedman is the leader of the Chicago school of Monetarism.

Monetarism is a form of counter-revolution against Keynesianism. The most important proposition of monetarism is that *money alone matters*. It observes that in the longrun, all economic activities and nominal income are determined and influenced by the stock of money (money supply). The flows themselves adjust to the stock. In fact, monetarists have the notion to regard money as the only important asset, and the real balance effect and wealth effect are assumed to be similar. Friedman observes that wealth effect is not important for explaining shortrun economic changes. This is the reason why he did not give any empirical weightage to inside-outside money.

In the longrun, proper growth rate of money stock is crucial for stable growth path of output and prices. In the shortrun, money supply will affect output within five to ten years, and in the longrun, it will change mainly prices within a time period of more than a decade. Changes in money supply modify relative prices and initiate a process of substitution.

Monetarists find a direct relation between money supply and price level, which is proportional in the longrun. They also believe that money and income are directly correlated. Monetary change affects longrun stock of real capital and hence output. Historically, changes in money and national income were largely caused by monetary policy. In many respects, monetary policy is better than fiscal policy. Fiscal policy could not control post-war inflation. Fiscal policy has a substantial *crowding-out effect*. Hence, it is more or less ineffective. Its effect on nominal income and price level is not very significant.

However, it is difficult for a flexible monetary policy to counter shortrun fluctuations. Thus, in the very shortrun, monetary policy is not very effective. This is mainly due to the fact that operational lags are much longer in the case of monetary policy. Given our ignorance, a discretionary monetary policy may increase the amplitude of business cycle. Hence, the monetary rule that, money supply should conform to the rate of growth of output, seems to be better than discretion.

The monetarists have a monetary theory of price level. Inflation is a purely monetary phenomenon and market mechanism or price system does operate as an efficient allocative mechanism in the economy. Monetary policy is effective in controlling inflation by restricting money supply. Money is basically neutral in the longrun in the sense that it does not disturb the real equilibrium of the system, and also maintains the real rate of interest. Monetarists assign a causal role to money, and since money is exogenous, it is possible to control disturbances by controlling the money supply, and thus, *money matters*.

Monetarists consider the quantity theory of money as basically a theory of demand for money. The interest elasticity of demand for money is found to be very low. The demand for money is essentially stable in the longrun and it can easily be predicted.

Monetary policy is distribution-neutral in the sense that it is less concerned with income distribution problems. But it is more concerned with the problem of allocation. The financing of govt. deficit by money creation is more effective than what is possible by the manipulation of fiscal instruments. Monetary policy is general in character and impersonal in effect. It permits the smooth operation of the market mechanism. Monetary policy is very flexible and affects the broad spectrum of economic units, as shown by Friedman's Study of the U.S. economy for the period 1867-1960.

Having outlined the three major counter-revolutions of the post-Keynesian era, we can now specify the various minute changes that have taken place in different facets of macroeconomics/monetary economics since the time of J.M. Keynes. These changes are discussed in the following pages.

Quantity Theory Reformulation

In this theory, the direction of change has been to rehabilitate the traditional quantity theory of money. Prof. Friedman has reformulated the classical quantity theory of money. Friedman has observed that quantity theory of money is basically a theory of demand for money. It is not a theory of price and output. The theory of demand for money is a special topic in the theory of capital: income is the yield on capital and capital is the present value of income. Money is an asset. Wealth is capitalised income $\left(W = \dfrac{Y}{r}\right)$. The demand for money has been related to various factors, *e.g.,* bond yield, equity yield, rate of change of price level, ratio of income from non-human to human wealth, *per capita* real income level and so on *i.e,*

$$\frac{Y}{M} = V\left[r_b, r_e, \frac{I}{P}, \frac{dp}{dt}\cdot w, \frac{Y}{P}, u\right]$$

where

Y = Nominal income (permanent income)

M = Nominal money stock

r_e = Equity yield

V = Velocity

r_b = Bond yield

w = The ratio of income from non-human to wealth.

$\dfrac{Y}{P}$ = Level of *per capita* real income

$\dfrac{I}{P}\cdot\dfrac{dp}{dt}$ = Rate of change of pricelevel.

u = Taste variable

Friedman has found a stable demand function for money. He made a conceptual integration of income and wealth. He gave particular emphasis to human wealth. He found interest-inelasticity of the demand for money, but also demonstrated that the income elasticity of the demand for money is greater than unity. His integration of capital theory with monetary theory is the most important significant development in the field of monetary theory after Keynes' *General Theory*.

The emphasis on money as an asset is in two directions. On the one hand, emphasis has been placed on the near-moneys (money substitutes) as a source of liquidity. In this connection, the work of Gurley and Shaw *(Money in the Theory of Finance)* is notable. In their analysis, NBFIs provide near-money assets. Side by side, with the work of Gurley and Shaw, there is the Radcliffe Committee Report which has widened the concept of money to make it co-extensive with the concept of liquidity.

Demand for Money

The other direction in which emphasis on money as an asset is placed is the development of the theory of demand for money. The demand for money is looked upon in the same fashion as the demand for assets, commodities and services. Friedman reformulated the classical quantity theory as a theory of demand for money. What is really important is the real stock of money and not the nominal stock (real money is more crucial for determining the command over goods and services). In the post-Keynesian period, the demand for money theory has been refined to a great extent.

Prof. Tobin has observed that the wealth variable is an important determinant of demand for money. Generally, the higher the amount of wealth possessed by an individual, the higher is the demand for money (Md). Total demand for money is a function of income, rate of interest, wealth uncertainty and expected change in the rate of interest, i.e.,

$$Md = f(y, r, w, u, r').$$

In the Keynesian approach, money demand is due to the passive balances and active balances. In order to remove this unsatisfactory dichotomy, two approaches have been suggested:

(a) The demand for money is one and single. It cannot be separated into two parts.

(b) Baumol and Tobin have explained transaction theory on the basis of capital theory. Money is a form of working capital or inventory. If it is so, transaction demand for money will have an inverse relation with the rate of interest (beyond a certain minimum rate of interest), and the same is the case with the precautionary demand for money. That is to say, the transaction demand will not be very different from asset demand. Diagrammatically,

However, there are not merely two types of assets-money and bond-as assumed by Keynes. There are many other types of assets. Again, it has been found that absolute liquidity preference (liquidity trap) is an unrealistic intellectual booby trap. In fact, there is some elasticity (less than ∞) in

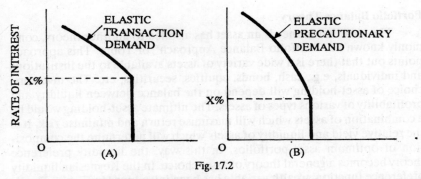

Fig. 17.2

the demand for cash balances and if money supply is increased, the interest rate will go down.

Gurley and Shaw demonstrated that with the introduction of NBFIs the demand for money in the society will change. This is shown in the following diagram:

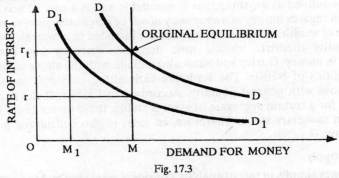

Fig. 17.3

When the NBFIs (non-bank financial intermediaries) are introduced the demand curve for money will shift from DD to D_1D_1 because NBFIs provide assets which are close substitutes for money. Therefore, money demand is reduced by MM_1 at r_t rate of interest. But since nominal stock of money and price level are unchanged, the rate of interest falls. The analysis has two implications:

(i) NBFIs create liquidity trap at a lower rate of interest than Keynesian liquidity trap.

(ii) NBFIs make money a smaller proportion of total assets. The velocity is increased and the relation between the rate of interest and velocity is weakened. Therefore, tight money policy is obstructed.

The choice as to how much money is to be held is a problem whose solution calls for the concept of capital theory.

Portfolio Balance Theory

The idea that money is an asset has also led to another theory, commonly known as "Portfolio Balance Approach" of Tobin. This approach points out that there is a wide variety of assets available to the institutions and individuals, e.g., cash, bonds, equities, securities, etc. The investors' choice of asset-holding will depend on the balance between liquidity and profitability of various types of assets. The ultimate asset-holding would be a combination of assets which will maximise return and minimise risk. It is the relative yield and liquidity of assets which will determine the composition of optimum asset-portfolios. In this way, the liquidity preference theory becomes a general theory of asset choice. In the Keynesian liquidity preference function, wealth variable has been introduced by Tobin. The liquidity preference theory of interest has been integrated with the noe-classical theory through the Hicksian and Hansenian IS and IM curves.

Concept of Money

In modern times, the concept of money has undergone changes. Money is defined as anything that is spendable and is a unit of accounts. Friedman regards money as a *temporary abode of purchasing power*. In fact, all forms of wealth and all stores of value are included in money stock. The neo-quantity theorists include time deposits, currency and demand deposits in money. Gurley and Shaw also include with the above variables, the liabilities of NBFIs. The Radcliffe Committee considers money as synonymous with general liquidity. According to Laidler, if the demand function for a certain aggregate of asset is stable, these assets could be included in monetary stock. Therefore, an asset is also considered money now-a-days.

Money Supply

Money supply, in recent analysis, considers asset choice. Money supply is no longer regarded as something exogenously given and institutionally fixed. If we discard the idea of the mechanical link existing among reserves, deposits and money, money supply assumes an independent and endogenous variable. The division of assets between currency and deposits is really a problem in capital theory. In the same way, the amount of reserves desired by the banks is also a problem in capital theory. The money supply analysis in recent years is an integration of monetary and value theories.

Say's Law and Quantity Theory

Patinkin has found that Say's Law and quantity theory are inconsistent. But Prof. Ackley has demonstrated that Patinkin failed to distinguish between the implications of money as a unit of account and as a medium of exchange. However, so long as the individual cash balance is zero, Say's Law and quantity theory can be shown to be perfectly consistent and complementary.

Real Balance Effect

The whole attitude towards the role of money was influenced by many factors, and one such factor was the role of real value of cash balance in affecting the flow of expenditure. It was emphasised by Haberler, Pigou (Pigou effect) and also by Patinkin (real balance effect). Real Balance effect is the relation between consumption, price level and the real value of cash balance. When the price level goes up, the real value of cash balance, held by individuals goes down, and as a result, consumption or effective demand will go down. The opposite would be the case when the price level goes down. It was proved by Pigou and Patinkin that if price-wage flexibility is permitted, full employment can be easily established, via the real balance effect, even in spite of the impossibility of negative rate of interest and the theoretical possibility of interest inelasticity of investment. Thus, Keynesian underemployment equilibrium thesis was smilingly discarded. Patinkin showed that Keynesian under-employment situation is really a disequilibrium situation. If there is underemployment, there is no equilibrium; and if there is equilibrium, there is no underemployment.

Integration of Value Theory and Money Theory

Patinkin has integrated classical value and money theories with the help of of real balance effect, and hence, he has removed the classical pricing dichotomy. The classical theory has been rehabilitated by making the demand and supply functions depend on the real value of cash balance and the relative prices. The real balance effect is the main equilibrating mechanism in the money market. If the price level is decreased the real value of cash balance will increase and both consumption and demand will increase. Therefore, price will ultimately increase. So, equilibrium will be established. Similarly, equilibrium will be established if the price rises and real balance effect operates. Thus, real balance effect disposes of the classical dichotomy. It makes it impossible to talk about relative prices without introducing money and the real value of cash balance.

Neutrality Debate

The real balance effect is also relevant to the neutrality/non-neutrality of money debate. If there is price-wage rigidity, real balance effect cannot operate. In that case, money will not be neutral. Patinkin observed that under certain assumptions, money will be neutral, e.g., price-wage flexibility, absence of money illusion, absence of distribution effect and so on. Metzler came to the conclusion that in a dynamic economy, money would not be neutral, because equilibrium rate of interest would change along with a change in money supply.

Gurley and Shaw introduced the concepts of inside money and outside money in the neutrality debate. They demonstrated that if one type of money (either inside money or outside money) was in circulation, money would be neutral, but if both the types of money were circulated, money would not be neutral. The debate is still alive.

Investment Function

Keynesian theory of investment has been modified in recent years as a process of capital accumulation (and not just a flow approach to investment). Keynes related rate of interest to investment. However, behind the propensity to investment, there is the consideration of real rate of return on investment. Marginal efficiency schedule is a function of such variables as capital stock, credit availability, income level, growth, profit, rate of interest and the value of cash balance. An important post-keynesian development is the apparent tendency of some parts of corporate earnings and cash flow to go into investment spending.On the side of inducement to invest, the most important development has been the introduction of the relation between capital stock and output as a determinant of investment choice. This has permitted the conversion of static equilibrium Keynesian system into cycle and growth models. Useful work has been done on inventory cycles. The modern approach is to look upon investment as a process of accumulating capital stock. It is a problem of adjusting the actual level of capital stock to the desired level of capital stock. The level of actual investment is a by-product of the relation between the actual stock and the desired stock. On this basis, acceleration or capital stock adjustment business cycle and growth models have been built up. Investment propensity can be treated as a topic in the theory of capital. Investment is not simply a flow comparable to consumption; it is a series of stages in the process of adjustment. It has also been found that investment is not completely insensitive to interest rates. When the borrowing cost is very high, investment is reduced. This shows that monetary policy is not effective completely.

Stock and Flow

Keynes' *General Theory* was concerned with income flows. The stock concept was implicit rather than explicit in Keynesian economics. In the post-Keynesian period, the stock concept became more explicit and important. Real balance or Pigou effect is the case in point. In his 1936 trade cycle model, Prof. Harrod made the accelerator relationship between capital stock and output flow more explicit. Kaldor proposed a model of trade cycle which made investment explicitly a function directly of the income level and inversely of the level of capital stock. Samuelson, Goodwin and Harrod have made a synthesis of accelerator and multiplier showing thereby how non-linearity could be established. The trade cycle of Hicks is based on non-linearity, which combines with it the exogenous exponential trends.

Income Distribution

Keynesian theory of income distribution has been improved by Kahn, Joan Robinson, Pasenetti and others. This is apparent in Joan Robinson's *The Accumulation of Capital.* Income distribution theory is becoming more and more a macro theory. This is evident in Boulding's *Reconstruction of Economics,* Hann's *Share of Wages in National Income* and in Weintraub.

Kaldor adheres to a theory of full employment brought about by equilibrating shifts in the distribution of income.

Consumption Function

Prof. Harry Johnson states that the consumption function and the propensity to invest beyond the domain of monetary theory. But still they are important because they fall within the general pattern of the application of capital theory to monetary theory.

The most interesting developments in macro theory have been those relating to the consumption function analysis, which were stimulated by the failure of a prediction of a major post-war slump and the apparent contradiction between the finding of Simon Kuznets that, in the long run, the proportion of income saved is constant, and the evidence of time series and budget studies that saving is a rising proportion of income in the short run. The efforts to reconcile short-run and long-run propensity to save have given rise to several reformulations of the theory of consumption function. Tobin has introduced the influence of asset as well as income on consumption. Duesenberry has implied the hypothesis that individual consumption behaviour depends on relative rather than absolute income. Friedman has observed that consumption is influenced by permanent (normal) rather than actual income. This is analysis refines the income concept. Permanent income is essentially a concept of wealth. We can regard wealth as a source of permanent income. Spiro's theory questions the Keynesian assumption of less than unitary marginal propensity to consume. Spiro's model is a real balance model of the Patinkin variety. Spiro has related saving to capital theory (accumulation of assets). Modigliani-Brumberg-Ando theory points out that consumption is governed by the maximisation of utility over the consumer's whole life. They have used the concept of income which is related to wealth. According to Johnson, Friedman's theory, MBA theory and Spiro's theory are particularly interesting for their attempt to relate consumption theory to the fundamentals of capital theory.

Economic Growth and Inflation

Since the 1950s, there grew up a new emphasis on the models of capital accumulation and technical change, particularly in the writings of Solow, Tobin, Samuelson, and others. Some of these models involved a departure from the depression version of the Keynesian system in which cheap money policy could have no substantial effect on investment spending.

At the end of the war, most people presumed that there would be a depression in the economy. So, money supply was kept at a high level in order to reduce the rate of interest to give stimulus to investment, income, output and employment. But contrary to the general expectation, in the post-war period, there came inflation. This once again changed the entire attitude towards money. Another development which stimulated interest in monetary policy was the disillusionment with the fiscal policy. In many countries, fiscal policy produced instability, and business fluctuations could not be controlled. So monetary policy revived. Keynes was thinking in terms of the possibility of demand-pull inflation in the event of increased money supply. It was found that even before full employment was achieved, cost-push type of inflation led to wage and price creep. Prof. Phillips found the co-existence and inverse relationship between inflation and unemployment. Structural mark-up and mixed inflations were also found to be in existence.

Monetary Policy

In the field of monetary policy, the direction of change has been away from what we may call "credit policy" to monetary policy (stock of money). From the situation of qualitative credit control the emphasis has shifted to quantitative control, although in many less developed countries, qualitative control is being given more importance. There has been a renewed attention towards attaining internal stability and external stability through monetary policy.

Monetary policy influences the composition of assets and also the rates of return on these assets. A change in monetary policy produces a chain of adjustments as there is a reshuffling of public portfolios of assets. This gives rise to a new set of rates of return on such assets. If investment is regarded as a flow of expenditure depending on the rate of interest and on the level of income, monetary policy does not face much of a difficulty. The question of different types of lags in monetary policy has become crucial in the context of the operational efficiency of the monetary policy. Monetary policy has to operate through the complicated process of rearrangement of assets via the lags.

NBFI (Non-Bank Financial Intermediaries)

Another difficulty for the monetary policy is the existence of NBFIs. Radcliffe-Sayers and Gurley and Shaw recognise the potential threat posed by NBFIs to the monetary policy. The NBFIs increase the interest elasticity of demand for money. They violate the monetary discipline of the economy. They create liquidity, change the composition of assets, create financial claims and compete with the banking system but they cannot be controlled by the central bank. Under these situations, the Radcliffe Committee gives a subordinate role to monetary policy. Gurley and Shaw maintain that if banking control is extended to NBFIs, the effectiveness of monetary policy can be strengthened.

There is no denying the fact that the whole area of monetary policy is in a state of complete flux. The role of monetary policy is only permissive. In order to make it more effective, an optimum monetary-fiscal mix is being worked out in most of the countries. In our times, monetary policy sets the tone of economic development, and it is becoming more and more growth-oriented, especially in less developed countries.

Importance of Institutions

Institutions, especially economic, social, and political institutions, are given special importance in the post-Keynesian economic analysis. The trend is noticeable since the time of Veblen who founded the Institutionalist school in the USA. This is a reaction against the neo-classical equilibrium economics which did not give any importance to institutional factors in economic analysis. The second reason for the importance of institutions is the belief of the post-Keynesian economists that institutions play a vital role in assimilating and propagating human behaviour. Economic development and institutions are inextricably related. Development is expressed through institutions and institutions are expressed through economic development. This great truth has been clearly brought out in the post-Keynesian period. Institutions are looked upon as the representatives of collective behaviour.

Rejection of Walrasian General Equilibrium Theory

The purpose of Walrasian general equilibrium theory was to find out through the process of tatonnement (Trial and error) the set of equilibrium price level which will clear all markets simultaneously. But this general equilibrium theory *fails* to take into account real and temporal historical order. Walrasian theory of general equilibrium as the micro foundation of macroeconomics has been rejected by the post-Keynesian economists. Walrasian system has been found to be inconsistent with the Keynesian economics.

Keynesian Macroeconomics vis-a-vis Kaleckian Macroeconomics[4]

Whereas Keyes laid more stress on the monetary factors in the development of macroeconomics, M. Kalecki has given more emphasis on the real factors. Many modern macro economists draw their inspiration from Kalecki. The works of Sawyer and Harcourt are cases in point. In a meaningful way, Post-Keynesian macroeconomics has become more and more Kaleckian rather than Keynesian. Kalecki's approach is supposed to be a more realistic alternative. Kalecki has developed an oligopolistic approach to the developed capitalist economy. To Kalecki, prices are determined mark-up which is in turn determined by the degree of monopoly power. Kalecki has given more importance to product market and less importance to labour market. The opposite is the view of Keynes. According to Kalecki, private investment is financed by retained earnings and bank money but Keynes holds that investment is financed by the issue of bonds.

Unlike Keynes, Kalecki does not give any importance to *equilibrium analysis*. Kalecki observes that the performance of economic policy ultimately depends on *interest groups* and institutional framework. These factors do not find any significance in Keynesian analysis. According to M. Sawyer, the most important point of distinction between the Keynesian

---

4.   See, P. Arestis and T. Kouras (Ed.), *Post-Keynesian Economic Theory*, Wheatsheaf Books, Sussex, 1985.

macroeconomics and Kaleckian macroeconomics lies in the fact whereas the former is based on the competitive framework, the latter is couched in terms of oligopolistic framework.

Conclusion

Post-Keynesian developments in the areas of macroeconomics/monetary economics seem to be more open and free from the clutches of dogmatic orthodoxy. It has now been possible to find many Keynesian macroeconomic myths (such as saving is a public vice and the like). Post-Keynesian developments have gone mainly in three directions, namely, development of monetarism, development of supply side economics and the development of New Classical Economics (Rational Expectation Theory). But none has been able to spread its intellectual sway over the others. Another remarkable development is the growth of Kaleckian approach to macroeconomics which is clearly distinct from Keynesian approach to macroeconomics. All these developments are running parallel in the post-Keynesian period where no single school or individual economist appears to have established the complete hegemony. The possibility of the emergence of a single unified approach does not seem to be in the offing in near future.

Part Five
Indian Economic Thought

18

Economic Thought in Ancient India

KAUTILYA'S ARTHASHASTRA (321-300 B.C.)

Economic Thought in Ancient India : Basic Features

Economic thought in ancient India can be gathered from a number of sources like the *Vedas, the Upanishads, Dharma Shastras, Neeti Shastras, Smrites,* Epics, and other religious books. Kautilya's *Arthashastra* is the first systematic treatise on economics which was written in the fourth century B.C. It has to be noted that in those days, the market economy and competition did not exist. Theoretical economics did not also make its debut in the realm of economic analysis. The ancient writers were concerned with the practical economic problems and their solutions. In ancient times, economic problems could not be separated from other problems. Economics did not spring up as a separate discipline. The study of economics was combined with the study of politics, philosophy and ethics. The ancient economic thought was welfare-oriented. It wanted to study the problems and prospects of the welfare state. Furthermore, economic life in ancient India was governed by religious ideals and moral sanctions.

Kautilya's *Arthashastra* was by far the most important treatise on economics which contained systematic ideas on a large number of practical economic problems, some of which are discussed below.

Kautilya's *Arthashastra* is a rare book of economics consisting of fifteen large sections (covering 430 pages) and 180 sub-sections. Kautilya (also known as Chanakya or Vishnu Gupta) was the Chief Minister of Chandra Gupta Maurya. The book was written for the streamlining of economic and financial administration of Chandra Gupta Maurya. It covers a very wide area of political economy. This book can be regarded as the first comprehensive book on economics dealing with various subjects like agriculture, land, wealth, taxation, finance, distribution, labour, population, trade and the like. It is regarded as the most authoritative of all treatises in economics. It is the representative of the ancient economic thought in India.

Economics

Kautilya regarded *Artha*(wealth) as the root of all disciplines. *Arthashastra* or economics is the basic discipline. *Artha* or material prosperity is the means for the achievement of salvation. For the country as a whole, it is the basis of all strength and power. The structure and organisation of the state entirely depends on the economic power and strength of the country. Kautilya has defined economics as a "collection of all the treatises promulgated by the early savants on the subject of acquiring and preserving or maintaining the earth."

Wealth and Population

The state power is based on wealth. In fact, wealth is the foundation of power and prestige of a state. Wealth includes the material resources and the human resources of a country. Manpower is an important source of wealth, apart from the natural wealth like land, mines, forests and so on.

A large population is regarded as a sign of prosperity of a nation. Population can be utilised for the exploitation of human resources. Kautilya recommended that the king should have separate colonies for the immigrated population. In ancient times, foreigners were tempted to immigrate into a country. According to the *Vedas,* ten sons were considered as the just number for a married couple.

Wealth is essential for the material prosperity of the nation. Wealth is correlated with welfare. Wealth included the necessary domestic animals like cows, horses and so on. Kautilya included in wealth, money and commodities, private property, precious metals and any other goods having a market value. Wealth must have transferability, reality, consumability and power of appropriation. Kautilya has pointed out that patience is required for the accumulation of wealth. Wealth is accumulated slowly and steadily. There are, generally, four purposes for which wealth is accumulated : for the sake of a good wife, a good son, a friend and charity. The accumulation of wealth has certain definite benefits. But wealth must be accumulated through the right and honest means. Wealth is a means; it is not an end in itself. Wealth is also accumulated for protecting and strengthening the country.

Land and Agriculture

Kautilya advised that those who perform sacrifices, spiritual masters, priests and other people well-versed in the *Vedas* shall be granted lands, yielding sufficient produce. They should also be exempted from taxation and fines. Lands may be confiscated from those who do not cultivate the land. Lands prepared for cultivation may be given to the tax-payers. Those cultivators would be supplied with the necessary inputs, who pay their taxes regularly. The king will do such favour and remission to the cultivators as will increase the wealth in the treasury. Anything which depletes the treasury should be avoided by the king. The king should also carry on mining, manufacturing, and exploiting timber and elephant forces, carrying on commerce, construction, road building, cattle breeding and so on. In other words, the king must supply the necessary infrastructure. The king should employ agricultural scientists for the development of agriculture. Slaves, labourers and prisoners may be employed to sow the seeds on the lands of the king. In Kautilya's *Arthashastra*, agriculture finds a prominent place. He said that even the Brahmins can take up the profession of agriculture provided they do not themselves hold the plough. Agriculture was given an important place because it provides products necessary for life, both of human beings and animals. According to Kautilya, Indian economy is basically agricultural in nature based on the system of peasant farming. The lands of the government were cultivated as state farms or by the tenants. The land, which was gifted by the king, was tax-free. However, the final ownership of land rested with the king.

Labour, Wage and Social Securities

According to Kautilya, wage of labour is to be determined with reference to the productivity of labour. He prescribed penalty for negligence of work, for non-payment of wages and also for not getting work done by the labourers. He also devised rules for dividing the total wages among workers, in the case of works which are done jointly by the labourers. The qualified persons are to be employed for works, and wages shall be fixed on the basis of the work done. The women should help the men by sharing the works. Kautilya prescribed penalty for those who refused to work after receiving the wages. He recommended leave for the workers. Kautilya did not recommend slave labour. He laid down a code of conduct for labour.[1] He accepted the dignity of labour.

During the time of Kautilya, the social security system was not a very elaborate one. However, he was in favour of granting social security. According to him, it was the basic duty of the king to provide employment to the workers and to provide charitable institutions and poor houses for the maintenance of the poor people of the state. The salary of a public servant, according to Kautilya, will be based on the following three criteria : *(i)* The salary will be consistent with the existing efficiency and effort, *(ii)* the salary of the public servant will be consistent with the status of the employee, and *(iii)* The salary will be in accordance with the loyalty of the employee to the king.

Public Finance and Taxation

Kautilya has very elaborately discussed the principles of income and expenditure of the government. Every tax involves a burden. The cost of collection of tax must be minimum. Tax should be collected on the basis of the paying capacity of the taxpayer. The tax amount must be spent in such a way that it gives benefit to the citizens by way of increased income and taxable capacity. The tax should be judiciously spent on the creation of infrastructure. The tax must not hamper the productive efficiency of the economy. Tax should be progressive in nature. Income should be regarded as the appropriate basis of taxation. Certain sections of the community should be exempted from taxation. The Brahmins are to be exempted from

---

1. Gairola, *Kautilya's Arthashastra*, pp. 387-391.

taxation. The government should try to have a surplus budget through economy in expenditure and increase in revenues. In the short run, the rate of taxation may be raised to meet an emergency situation, but in the long run, the state must not try to impose heavy taxation on the people. This will damage the creation of wealth and productive power. Heavy taxation is self-defeating in nature.

Kautilya attached great significance to the importance of public finance in the national economy. Kautilya suggested the method of forced loans in order to meet the situation of deficit budget. Tax may be imposed on three types of goods : (i) goods produced in the capital; (ii) goods produced in the country; and (iii) importable and exportable goods. He suggested a tax of twenty per cent of the cost of goods. But in the case of precious metals, the rate of taxation may be changed from time to time according to needs. There should be heavy taxation on the import of luxury goods, as these goods are not very necessary for the country.

Tax should be based on the following principles : (a) tax should be imposed yearly ; (b) tax should be based on the ability to pay; (c) tax should involve a minimum burden; (d) tax burden should be distributed properly without doing any harm to the state.

Kautilya suggested that those who increase the king's revenue and are loyally devoted to him, should be made permanent in service. The merchandise, which enters into the city gate, will have to pay a toll tax. The rate of toll will be fixed on commodities either old or new, and fines shall be fixed in proportion to the gravity of offences. The merchants shall pay the customary toll taxes.

The case of misappropriation of government funds will be severely dealt with.

According to Kautilya, land revenue forms an important part of the income of the state. The rate of land revenue varies between 8.5 per cent to 33 per cent of the produce of land. There are many other sources of revenue, such as, road tax, tax on trees, tax on commodities, tax on houses and so on. Kautilya was in favour of the generation of surplus from government controlled industries. Such industries can be a good source of employment to the people. Kautilya laid down the main principles for budget estimates.

He also discussed the main heads of public expenditure. These are : salaries and expenditure in the government departments, expenditure on public administration, defence expenditure, expenditure on store houses and stock, expenditure on new wealth and acquisitions and so on. After meeting the expenditure, whatever is left out of total income, is deposited in the government treasury as saving.

Pricing and Price Control

Kautilya discussed the market price system. He seems to have grasped the influence of demand and supply forces in the determination of market price. He also understood the effect of transport and communication on the pricing structure of commodities. Kautilya pointed out that when the price level goes up, there is the possibility of an increase in supply, which will, in turn, decrease the price level and profit level. But in the case of a market structure dominated by monopoly, price level may remain high and the level of profit may also be high. Artificial scarcity may be created by a monopolistic market. The concept of price, that Kautilya had in mind, was the medieval concept of just price or *justum pretium*. This price is nothing but the cost of production to which some mark-up is added. When the market price (actual price) is higher than the just price, the difference should go to the government treasury. This situation may be caused by a number of factors, such as a sudden spurt in demand, a sudden drop in supply and so on. Kautilya did not approve of profit beyond a reasonable limit. Supernormal profit was something to be penalised. During the time of Kautilya, a full-fledged market economy did not develop, but commodities were purchased and sold in specified markets on specified days of the week.

The superintendent of commerce had the duty to ascertain the demand position of a commodity, in order to set its price in a correct way. He will ascertain the time of distribution, purchase and sale of different commodities. The merchandise, which is widely distributed shall be centralised and its price will be determined properly. The imported merchandise shall be distributed in several markets for sale. Kautilya was against prices which will harm the people. Much emphasis was given to price control during the period of Kautilya. The basic objective of such a type of price control was to protect the interest of the consumers and to check the dishonest practices of the business people. Trading in essential commodities was in the hands of the state. The traders were allowed to make ten per cent profit on the imported commodities and eight per cent profit on the domestic commodities. Any profit beyond these levels was punishable by law.

Trade

A good deal of attention was paid to the regulation of trade during the period of Kautilya. Trade was a *vent for surplus*. For fixing the prices of traded commodities, the influences of demand and supply were taken into account. The infrastructure, which was necessary for trade, was the responsibility of the government. It was also the duty of the state to provide facilities to the traders by building rest houses, store houses, and the like. Different types of duties were imposed on trade. These duties were important sources of revenue to the state. Trade had no restrictions. But there were certain rules and regulations to be observed by the traders. Even, the state sometimes entered into trade for earning income and for distributing the commodities in a proper manner.

For the regulation of trade and commerce, the government used to have proper supervision on weights and measures. The superintendent used to charge four mashas for stamping weights or measures. Weights were made of iron or of stones or of such things as will neither contract when wetted nor expand under the influence of heat.

Distribution

Kautilya's discussion on distribution is not satisfactory. Interest was favoured; but interest was not charged beyond a reasonable limit. Interest was justified because of the productivity of capital. Interest was determined on the basis of the purpose for which the loan was taken. It also varied from class to class. Kautilya recommended fifteen per cent rate of interest, as a general rule. But he seems to have justified higher rate of interest, in case the money is lent out to the business people. No interest was recommended on the mortgages of property. He made a distinction between interest and profit. He suggested different rates of interest for different types of loans. Kautilya did not recommend any rate of interest on grain loans.

Regarding wages, Kautilya pointed out, that wages should be based on the productivity of labour. He recommended a reasonable normal profit for traders and capitalists. He made excessive profit punishable by law. The land tax was payable to the king. During Kautilya's time, India did not have any established class of landlords. The final ownership of all lands rested with the king. In Kautilya's analysis of distribution, *justice* was a guiding principle. Wages, for example, were determined on the basis of equity and justice. There was no exploitation of labour by capital. Profits were regarded as a reward for entrepreneurship and supervision.

Economic Functions of State

The state was given a number of important functions. It was the duty of the state to make available the necessary money in the form of coins.[2] Besides collecting from mines the ten kinds of revenue, the government shall keep both mining and commerce in minerals as a state monopoly.[3]

The state has to look after the social securities and the social welfare of the workers. Industrial development was an important function of the state. The state had the duty and responsibility of making the country self-sufficient and wealthy. The state also had to supervise farming, arts and crafts, spinning and weaving, livestock farming and so on. It was the duty of the state to ensure that activities like consumption, distribution and production are done efficiently and in accordance with the rules framed by the state. The state had overall control on the property of the individuals and the state. Kautilya's concept of state was a welfare state which looked after the maximum good of the maximum number of people. The state used to encourage and reward the good and honest people and punish the wrong-doers. The state used to frame rules and regulations for the citizens and ensured their proper implementation.

---

2. Kautilya, *Arthashastra,* Chapter XII.
3. *Ibid,* Chapter XII.

Evaluation

Kautilya's *Arthashastra* can be regarded as the first book on the Indian political economy. The treatise is not very scientific nor does it deal with pure economics; but it is systematic and comprehensive. It reflects the contemporary economic structure of society. The book reveals the areas of state direction and control. It is a book more on statecraft than on economics. Kautilya has described the socio-economic conditions of India vividly along with the attending complexities. He propounded certain general economic diplomacy and gave many new insights into the working of the state. *Arthashastra* is a thorough and exhaustive account of the ancient economy of India. This is a compendium of all the prevailing views on India's political economy.

19
Economic Thought in Modern India

DADABHAI NAOROJI (1825-1917)

The major economic ideas of Naoroji are contained in his book, *Poverty and Un-British Rule in India,* which was first published in 1901, and was revised in 1911. Naoroji has contributed to the understanding of the drain theory, national income analysis, poverty and public finance and public expenditure system in India. Let us discuss these one by one briefly.

Drain Theory

Dadabhai Naoroji was the first Indian economist to have discussed the draining away of Indian resources from India to England. The transfer of resources from India to England which started in the middle of the eighteenth century is regarded as the drain of Indian resources. Dadabhai Naoroji analysed the drain theory in 1871 in his book very elaborately. The drain took the form of unrequired export of goods from India. The drain arose out of the following items : (i) remittance of saving from India to England by the employees of the East India Company; (ii) remittances to England by European employees for the support of their families; (iii) remittances for the purchase of British goods; (iv) Government purchase of stores manufactured in Britain; (v) interest charges paid to England on public debt.

The remittances were responsible for creating a surplus of export in India's external trade. According to Naoroji, the extent of drain was to the tune of £350 million during 1814-1865. Roughly, the drain on the East India Company's account has been estimated to be £3 million per year. Later on, the drain went on increasing. There was also an internal drain in the form of transfer of purchasing power from the poor rural areas to the rich urban areas. Naoroji found that seventy-five per cent of India's tax revenue was collected from the poor people of India. Much of the public debt was also political in nature and the rate of interest on the public debt was also very high. The drain also consisted of the wastage of human skill and efficiency. When the Britishers destroyed villages, cottage and handicrafts, the artisans had to go back to the rural areas. In this process, a good deal of artistic efficiency and skill was lost. This is one form of drain of human resources. Agricultural export was the instrument through which the resources were drained out of India.

The drain of resources was responsible for the poverty and under-development of the Indian economy.

The drain included the profit of exports, freight and insurance. India had to bear the war expenditure of Britain. The expenditure on the maintenance of British army was also borne by India. There was also the draining away of professionally-skilled Indian people from India to England. This is what is regarded as the *brain drain* today. Dadabhai called it *a moral drain.*

National Income Estimate

Naoroji was not satisfied with the wrong estimation of national income in India by the British Government. The official estimate was not satisfactory, according to Naoroji. In the *Material and Moral Progress of India,* the British Government used to give some data regarding India's national income. Naoroji wanted that national income should be computed every year. For the year 1870-71, Naoroji's calculation showed that India's *per capita* income was only Rs. 20, whereas it was Rs. 420 in the United Kingdom. His calculation was based on the bare minimum needs of human beings to keep them in ordinary good health and decency. In this connection, Naoroji took into account the daily maintenance requirements of emigrant coolies, common agricultural labourers, lowest-paid government servants and prisoners in Indian jails. He found that the average daily requirement of these categories of people was to the extent of Rs. 34 for bare subsistence. Naoroji found that the *per capita* income was much less than the *per capita* requirement of average Indian people.

The main points of criticism against his method of calculation were that Dadabhai did not take into account many items like railway wealth, government stock, foreign trade and so on. Naoroji pointed that railways do not produce any wealth. It simply transfers wealth from one area to another area. Similar is the case of government stock. Stock does not increase the material wealth of any country. Similarly, house property and internal trade, etc., do not create any material wealth. Foreign trade, of course, does create wealth. But in the case of India, all profits from foreign trade go to England. These are the replies given by Dadabhai against the facts of non-inclusion of certain items in the calculation of India's national income, as pointed out by Danvers. V.K.R.V. Rao supported Naoroji's method of calculation of national income and pointed out that Naoroji's treatment of national income was based on "the physiocratic concept of the materiality of income."[1]

Poverty in India

The evidence of Indian poverty can be found from the data on *per capita* income, as calculated by Naoroji. The *per capita* income was Rs. 20 on an average, whereas the *per capita* subsistence cost in India was Rs.34. From here, one can gauge the extent of Indian poverty. Most of the Indian people were in the midst of adject poverty. They simply existed by drawing

---

1. V.K.R.V. Rao, *An Essay on India's National Income,* p. 22.

on the capital wealth, by incurring debt and by making dissaving disinvestment. A common man's economic position was much worse than that of criminals in jails. Dadabhai wrote : "Even for such food and clothing as a criminal obtains, there is hardly enough of production in a good season, leaving alone all little luxuries, all social sorrow and any provision for a bad season."[2] The economic position of the middle class and the rich class of people was certainly better. The pattern of income distribution was highly skewed against the poor people of India. The differences in income distribution were also accentuated by racial and regional disparities of income. The Indians used to get much less salaries than the English people in India. The people of India by and large were exploited by the British people. The exploitation led to poverty.

Another very important cause of Indian poverty was the economic drain from India. The drain which was on a regular basis reduced India to a land of paupers. Population of India was also increasing, but there was diminishing agricultural produce. The wages of the agricultural labourers were very low. The real wages still went down as the prices went up regularly. Poverty in India was due to the exploitation by British rulers of Indian agriculture, trade, manufacture and commerce. But overpopulation was not the real cause of Indian poverty. The real cause was the flight of Indian capital to England. J.S. Mill identified the scarcity of capital as the cause of industrial as well as agricultural backwardness of India. Along with poverty, there was a sense of alienation that haunted the people of India. Most of the good Indian jobs were taken up by the British people. Many Indians, though capable, had to remain unemployed and underemployed. The Indian people could not enjoy their legitimate rights, and they remained aloof from the drama of national development. There was a sense of frustration among the Indian people. In the opinion of Naoroji, the main reason for India's poverty was the exhaustion of the wealth of India and also the excessive expenditure on European service and public debt. Dadabhai tried to quantify the level of India's poverty and its deleterious effects. He showed the immiserisation of Indian people as caused by British rule.

Public Finance and Financial Administration

Naoroji showed the mismanagement created by the British rulers in the realm of income and expenditure. The bulk of the revenue was realised from the Indian people. The incidence of land revenue ultimately fell on the poor cultivators. The tax system was highly regressive in character. This was particularly true in the case of salt tax. The tax rate was very high. It was twenty-two per cent in India whereas it was merely eight per cent in England. But the British rulers maintained that the people of India were taxed lightly. There was another aspect of the Indian tax system. Whereas in the case of England, the tax-payers used to get some benefit in return from the government, in India, there was no such *quid pro quo* in return.

---

2.   Dadabhai Naoroji, *Poverty and Un-British Rule in India*, pp. 1-124.

There was also heavy expenditure on the army and defence. Gladstone admitted that the military expenditure in India in 1893 was indeed alarming. In India, the people did not enjoy benefits from the railways. Indian money was spent on the home establishment of the railway officials who were living in England. In the railways, the good jobs were meant for English people. The interest charges on the public debt in India were very high. Naoroji estimated the public debt in 1871 to be £100 million. The home charges were also very heavy. Dr. Ganguli points out that there are three areas of recurrent concern in the realm of public finance : *(i)* heavy burden of taxation in relation to limited taxable capacity in India; *(ii)* higher tax rate in India as compared to England; and *(iii)* a positive correlation between taxation and continuous flow of economic drain to Britain.

There was also tremendous export of spices from India to England and the consequence was the shortage of spices in India. The British people always kept the exchange rate against the Indian rupee as compared to British pound sterling. The Indian silver standard was at the disadvantage of India. The public debt of India was rapidly growing every year, and it became a matter of concern for every Indian leader. The debt servicing charge was also very high which was partly responsible for the poverty of Indian people. The financial administrative system was having a built-in bias in favour of wastages and unnecessary government expenditure. On every opportunity, the government was bleeding the Indian people.

Reforms

Naoroji suggested a few reformative measures for giving a better shape to things.[3] These measures are : *(i)* An equitable adjustment of financial relations between England and India. *(ii)* Permission to be given to India for the use of her own produce for consumption and investment. *(iii)* Increasing Indianisation of employment opportunities. *(iv)* Public loans for investment in India at a lower rate of interest. *(v)* Ceiling on government expenditure, pay, allowances, pension and so on. *(vi)* Interest rate on public debt to be reduced. *(vii)* The administrative expenditure to be reduced to the minimum. *(viii)* A comprehensive plan for national education. *(ix)* Attractive capital for cultivating wastelands, and supply of capital for public works programmes.

Naoroji assigned a positive role to be played by the state in the different areas of economic activities such as public finance, trade, employment, education and economic development. For accelerating the tempo of public works programmes, Naoroji advocated the import of foreign capital but not foreign capitalists. He was also in favour of mixed economy where the government sector and the private sector will work side by side. He rejected the classical *laissez faire* attitude. He urged the government to supply the necessary infrastructure and remove poverty from the country.

---

3. V.B. Singh, *From Naoroji to Nehru*, Macmillan. pp. 26-27.

He strongly advocated the stoppage of exploitation by manipulating the exchange rate. He observed that government should come forward to build up human capital in a backward country like India.

Evaluation

Naoroji can be regarded as the father of Indian political economy. His works on national income estimate and drain theory still remain the authentic works of reference for further research in these areas. His drain theory has been the starting point of the theory of imperialism. From his writings, we get the idea of the working of the economic process in British India, and the genesis of Indian poverty and underdevelopment. Dadabhai was in favour of a welfare state for India. Even in spite of the scarcity of statistical data, Naoroji was able to estimate India's national income more or less correctly. Naoroji occupies a place of pride among the nationalist economists of India.

MAHADEV GOVIND RANADE (1842-1901)

The economic ideas of Ranade can be found in his *Essays on Indian Economics* (1898). The main message of the work is given in the first chapter "Indian Political Economy". This chapter was discussed in the form of a lecture in 1892 in the Deccan College, Puna. The economic ideas of Ranade concentrate on mainly three subjects : *(i)* Methodology of study. *(ii)* Explanation of backwardness/poverty in India. *(iii)* Development and industrialisation of India and the role of state. Let us discuss these three aspects.

Historical Method of Study

Ranade was a great advocate of the historical method of study in economics. He said, "If the law of relativity and correspondence holds good in politics and social sciences generally, it ought to hold good equally in all kindred subjects, including among others, the science of National Wealth or it is more popularly described, Political Economy." He said that political economy is intimately connected with many other branches of social philosophy. He, like J.S. Mill, admits that the laws of distribution are partly human institutions. Therefore, these laws can be changed. He did not accept the classical notion of absolutism in economics. He was a practical economist. He did not like deductive method of analysis of the classical system. On the other hand, he thought that the historical method which takes the past into account in its forecast of the future is more appropriate than the deductive abstract classical method. It is relativity on which the practical science of economics stands. According to him, political economy is a hypothetical science where relative historical method seems to be more appropriate. However, he suggested the simultaneous study of theory and practice. "Theory is only enlarged practice and practice is theory in its relation to proximate causes." He criticised the classical economists for their unrealistic assumptions and absolutism. He said that the traditional assumptions of economic theory are not applicable anywhere except in

England. He rejected the assumptions of the British classical political economy in the light of facts in India. He castigated the classical writers for their historical approach to the study of economies. However, Ranade accepted the Malthusian theory of population for a country like India.

Backwardness/Poverty in India

He elaborated a number of reasons which are responsible for the poverty and backwardness in India. These factors are : Conservative attitude, uncertain conditions in agriculture, scarcity of capital, unskilled labour, unenterprising people, absence of desire for accumulation, drainage of resources and talents from the county and so on. In India, raw materials are produced only for export. Cooperation is almost unknown. Agriculture is carried on traditionally. There are petty farming, retail dealing and job working by poor people on borrowed capital.[4] In a country like India, there is complete absence of a landed gentry or wealthy middle class. According to Ranade, our laws and institutions favour a low standard of life, our religion condemns accumulation of wealth and power. Stagnation and dependence, depression and poverty-these are written in broad characters on the face of the Indian people.[5] Moreover, India has been losing every year sufficient amount of wealth and talent to Britain. This is a distinct cause of Indian poverty.

Poverty in India has increased quite considerably after the entry of Britishers. Indian industries are backward and lopsided. There is lack of proper credit facilities. The land policies are also defective. Lack of credit facilities stood in the way of industrial development. Ranade observes that the faulty British policy has made India a producer of raw materials for the British industries, and a ready market for the British goods. The basic cause of India's poverty is too much dependence on backward agriculture.

Development and Industrialisation in India

Ranade observed that Indian economy can be developed and poverty can be removed, provided certain steps are taken sincerely and appropriately. These are briefly discussed below :

In a country like India, industrialisation and urbanisation must be linked together. Agricultural growth should also be linked with urbanisation and industrialisation. India should concentrate more on the industrial development of the country. Indian industries require protection. Ranade wanted India to produce raw materials and process the same for export in the form of finished goods to other countries. He was in favour of import of skill and technique of production. He suggested the imposition of heavy tariff in the case of sugar import to India. He urged the Government of India to pursue a positive policy for the industrial development of India. In spite of the policy of free trade adopted by the British Government. Ranade thought that India should compete with foreigners. India has to or-

4. M.G. Ranade. *Essays on Indian Economics,* 1892, pp. 20-23.
5. *Loc. Cit.*

ganise labour and capital by cooperation and import freely foreign skill and machinery.

According to him, diversification of the Indian economy was the only remedy for making the country free from famines. He was in favour of development of certain strategic industries like the iron and steel industry in India.

Ranade's concept of wealth included not only physical capital but also education and technology. This idea is clearly stated in his essay on *Indian Political Economy.*[6]

Ranade suggested that land should belong to the actual tillers. He also suggested the fixation of the shares of farmers in the total produce. He advocated permanent Ryotwari land settlement for a period of at least thirty years. For facilitating credit in the agricultural sector, Ranade suggested institutional changes in the agricultural sector. In this regard, he suggested the promoting role of the state. He was advocating the removal of uncertainty in land assessment in India.

Ranade pointed out that economic development is a function of many factors : social, political, economic and institutional. He was also inclined to have a planned economy for India which would in fact be a welfare state.

Ranade suggested liberalisation of land policy and payment of tax according to the convenience of the cultivators. He wanted to have a proper reorganisation for streamlining the credit system in the country. The essential condition of rescuing the country from its helplessness, according to Ranade, is to effect a radical change in the relationship of soil with the persons who cultivate it. He stood for co-existence of different types of farming.

Ranade argued against the statement by the Britishers that torrid zones are meant for producing raw materials only. Ranade was against this motivated interpretation of the Ricardian comparative cost theory. He said that India can very well specialise in the production as well as in the processing of raw materials. He suggested remedies for boosting up domestic production.

He blamed Indians for hoarding of gold and silver. According to him, these precious metals can be used productively for the purpose of development. It is necessary to properly husband economic resources of the country. India has a distinct advantage in having large natural resources and abundant supply of labour. Thus, those industries can be started in India which require raw materials and labour.

Ranade was in favour of a balanced approach towards population policy for the country. He suggested that people should emigrate from thickly-populated areas to thinly-populated areas. He wanted a balance of population in the various regions of the country.

---

6. *Ibid.,* p. 19.

Ranade explained that agricultural development must be linked with the existence of the non-agricultural market. He accepted the existence of interdependence between agriculture and industry. The method of industrial development in India may be based on labour-intensive methods of production, as India possesses a large number of surplus labour. He suggested the development of the institutional lending system. India has capital but that capital has to be mobilised for the purpose of development. This requires institutions like banking and financial intermediaries. At the start of development, Ranade suggested protection to the developing industries.

Ranade was of the opinion that for the industrial development of the country, what is of utmost importance is the positive role of the state. Let us explain this point.

Role of State

Ranade urged the government to undertake a positive role for the industrial development of the country by protecting home industries and through various other ways. He said that the policy of the state in India has been harmful to both agriculture and industry. The British policy was mainly responsible for the economic backwardness and poverty in India. Ranade wanted the state to be a welfare state which has to undertake a number of reforms in various directions. Economic development in India was essentially dependent on political, social and economic institutions whose activities are to be channelised by the state. The state should come into the forefront of all actions, particularly because the private sector in India is almost conspicuous by its absence. "The state", said Ranade, "is now more and more recognised as the national organ for taking care of national needs in all matters in which individual and cooperative efforts are most likely to be so effective and economical as national effort. To relegate them to the simple duty of maintaining peace and order is really to deprive the community of many of the advantages of the social union.[7]

According to Ranade, for a poor country like India, the policy of *laissez faire* could be doing more harm than good. The state, in such a country, has to work like a friend, philosopher and guide. It has to give subsidies and bounties for industrial development. The state has to organise trade, finance and commerce. It has also to regulate cooperative efforts. Ranade praised the British government for providing capital to India at a low rate of interest. State has to look after education, communication, industrial development, agricultural development and so on. In this regard, Ranade supported the policy of Cultural System. The state has to take up a number of development-oriented measures and policies.

Evaluation

Ranade could not notice the plunder of Indian resources through the investment of British capital. However, Ranade was a practical economist.

---

7. *Ibid.*, pp. 31-32.

He suggested a number of important practical steps for the development of India. He is a nationalist economist and a relativist.

ROMESH CHANDRA DUTT (1848-1909)

Romesh Chandra Dutt was a civil servant and economic historian. He wrote two very famous books, *Economic History of India* (Two Volume), and *Famines in India.*

Dutt was moved by the poverty of Indian people. He took into account the various causes responsible for poverty in India. According to him, the Britishers were not interested in the development of Indian economy. However, he praised the Britishers for bringing into India modern civilisation, peace, modern education, modern science and technology and so on. They had built up a strong and efficient administrative machinery, and framed good laws. For all these, Dutt had high regards towards the British administration. But he was of the opinion that the British administration could not improve the material prosperity of Indian people, rather it had worsened gradually. Indian people became the victims of absolute and relative poverty. Famine was a contributory cause of poverty in India. But there were other causes responsible for Indian poverty.

Causes of Indian Poverty

1. Backwardness of Indian Agriculture. Because of the heavy taxation of land, the agriculturists in India could not generate any surplus for their own welfare and for the development of the agricultural economy. The land tax was very heavy and uncertain. It was even to the extent of eighty to ninety per cent in Bengal and Northern India of the rental. The realisation of the tax was done in a very crude manner by oppressing the people. Every time the tax was increased without giving any reason for such an increase. Some times, the land tax appropriated the whole of the surplus produce on land. All this implied that Indian agriculture was not in a position to generate any surplus, nor could it sufficiently maintain its dependent population. The result was heavy indebtedness and acute poverty. Agriculture lacked irrigation facilities and modern technology. The agrarian structure was highly traditional and unproductive. The technique of production was poor, equipment inadequate and soil condition poor. The prices of agricultural products were not favourable for the cultivators and the land tenure system was also very traditional. All these meant low productivity of Indian agriculture.

2. Downfall of Indian Industries. The Britishers were not interested in the industrial development of India. They wanted to make India only a market for the British goods and also the supplier of raw materials to the British industries. The Britishers arrested the development of Indian industries. Their commercial policy was selfish. It discouraged the growth of Indian manufacturing industries. Heavy tariff was imposed on the entry of Indian goods to Britain, particularly, the Indian silk and cotton goods. But British goods were admitted into India free of duty or on nominal duty.

Many skilled Indian artisans lost their jobs. The cottage and village industries were destroyed by the British Government. The artisans had to go back to agriculture where the pressure of population on land increased considerably, making the condition of poverty worse. The invention of powerloom brought about a complete decay of Indian industries. On the production of cotton fabrics, the Government of Britain imposed an excise duty. This resulted in the loss of competitive ability of Indian manufactures in the foreign market.

3. High Growth of Population. According to Dutt, Indian poverty was largely due to the high rate of growth of population. The high density of population was responsible for the low per capita productivity in Indian agriculture. The standard of living of the people went down considerably during the British regime.

4. Unsound Taxation. The land tax was very high, and it was based on uncertainty. Taxation was not based on a reciprocal advantage principle. The State was simply a taker, but it was not a giver of benefit to the people. The state did not develop new industries or revive old ones, but it always tried to squeeze the people for getting whatever maximum it can get out of them. According to Dutt, Indian tax-payer was taxed forty per cent more than the tax-payer in Ireland and Britain. Indian taxation was also not based on any sound principle. The heavy burden of tax was also due to the very costly financial administrative system. In many ways, the sources of national wealth in India had been narrowed under British rule.

5. Excessive Home Charges. A large amount of money every year was sent from India to England in the name of Home Charges. The earlier foreign rulers in India also exploited Indian people, but they spent the money here in India. Thus, indirectly, the Indian people were benefited. But during British rule, things were different. Indian money flowed into England on a regular basis. This impoverised India but enriched England. All the high posts were reserved for the English officers in India. The Home Charges rose gradually with excessive taxation. The Home Charges were a definite cause of draining away of Indian money and contributed heavily to the growth of Indian poverty.

Suggested Remedies to Remove Poverty

R.C. Dutt suggested a number of measures for the removal of poverty in India. The following are his main suggestions :

(i) The land revenue system should be rationalised. He suggested that land settlement should be made for a period of more than thirty years. The cess on land tax has to be used for the direct advantage of the cultivators. When the direct land revenue is collected by the state, the rate should not be more than twenty per cent in individual cases, and not more than ten per cent for the district as a whole.

(ii) The excise duties on mill industries should be abolished.

(iii). Rate of interest of public debt should be lowered.

(iv)   A sinking fund may be created for the repayment of public debt.

(v)   There should be the sharing of military and civil expenditure by the government of Great Britain.

(vi)   Civil charges may be reduced by employing more Indians in the civil services and in good jobs.

(vii) irrigation works should be extended to the rural areas, and the expenditure may be borne from the ordinary revenues.

(viii) Further construction of railways may be prohibited.

(ix)   Indian people should be given representation in the legislative bodies. In this connection, the Constitution of Indian may be changed.

(x)   He suggested the revival of cottage and small-scale industries.

(xi)   Economy in government expenditure.

(xii) Reduction in Home Charges.

(xiii) Extension of irrigation facilities to the agricultural sector.

Dutt observed that the expenses of Mutiny had increased the liability of India and had led to still heavier taxation. Most of this increased burden of taxation had to be borne by the agricultural sector. The construction of railways was a heavy burden on India's limited financial resources. This necessarily led to the growth of public debt in India. Under these circumstances, any country will be a victim of poverty. All this was due to the operation of certain economic laws which are constant and uniform in similar cases.

Famines in India

R.C. Dutt also studied the famines of India. His book on *Famines in India* came out in the year 1900. He has given a number of causes responsible for famines in India. He said that famine is mainly due to the very low purchasing power of the people. It is not necessarily due to low productivity or production. He has contested the misconceived ideas of the British people regarding the causes of Indian famines. The British people think that Indian famines are due to : *(i)* High rate of growth of population, *(ii)* Careless and excessive spending habit of the people, *(iii)* Exploitation by the moneylenders, and *(iv)* Crop failures.

According to Dutt, the rate of growth of population in India was much lower than that in England when Dutt was writing. He also did not accept the idea that Indian people were careless in spending. He says that Indian people are thrifty and frugal. The moneylenders, no doubt, exploited the Indian people but the cultivators of India are forced to go to the village moneylenders in order to pay taxes to the government. Dutt says that famines occur not because of crop failures but because of their inability to purchase the supplies from the neighbouring provinces which are rich in harvest. The root cause of famine is the lack of income. He observed that famines had desolated India in the last quarter of the nineteenth century very badly. The remedial measures against famines are common with the measures suggested for the removal of poverty.

Evaluation

Dutt's contribution to the analysis of famines and poverty is noteworthy. His insight into the economic history of India is remarkable. He rightly observed that the real cause of under-development of the Indian economy, during the British period, was the poverty of the Indian people. India's underdevelopment was due to the faulty British economic policy.

GOPAL KRISHNA GOKHALE (1866-1915)

Gopal Krishna Gokhale was more a political leader than an economist. He was the political *guru* of Mahatma Gandhi. Gokhale is known for his budget speeches and for his evidence before the Welby Commission on expenditure in India. Most of the views of Gokhale on economics can be known from a book entitled, *Gokhale and Economic Reforms,* by V.G. Kale. Some of the important economic ideas of Gokhale are discussed below.

Drain Theory

According to Gokhale, India's drain of resources has been created because of the economic and social conditions created by the Britishers. England imposed on India many undesirable policies such as free trade, destruction of industries and so on which are responsible for the creation of the drain. Gokhale thought that the poverty of India was because of the draining away of resources from India. He was in favour of industrial development for a country like India.

However, Gokhale was not blind to the intricacies of the theory of drain as propounded by Dadabhai Naoroji. Gokhale was very clear to point out that some of the payments made to England were against the benefits received by India from England, for example, borrowing of capital, maintenance of army and navy for the defence of the country. However, Gokhale observed that the amount of drain was very heavy and could be considerably reduced. He complained that the cost of Indian administration is very high. He was in favour of giving to Indians civil and military posts. Be that as it may, Gokhale warned that any sweeping generalisations regarding the effect of drain from India would be highly preposterous.

Public Finance and Public Administration

Gokhale raised four important issues before the Welby Commission. These important issues are : (1) There has been a high rate of growth of public expenditure in India without a corresponding prosperity of the country. (2) The charges between India and England are unevenly distributed. Therefore, Gokhale pleaded that these charges be equally distributed between India and England. (3) The provinces do not have sufficient financial power. Therefore, they should be given more and more financial power in the administration of the federal finance. (4) The Control of finances should be in the hands of the Viceregal Council which will consist of a reasonable number of Indian representatives.

Gokhale pointed out a number of unreasonable duties imposed by the British Government in India. These duties are salt duty, cotton duty and so on. The salt duty was most regressive in nature. Gokhale also wanted to abolish the cotton duty and the opium revenue. He was also against the duty on petroleum as it fell mainly on the poor people.

Gokhale found that for a few years, the British Government in India showed a surplus budget. The British Government claimed, it was a sign of prosperity of India. Gokhale refuted this point. He said that the surplus was merely a monetary surplus which did not indicate any prosperity in real terms. Secondly, Gokhale pointed out that the surplus budget implies that poor people have been more seriously taxed than what is justified. Thus, surplus budget means greater sufferings of the poor people. Thirdly, through the surplus budget, the government wanted to create a financial equilibrium at a time when the rupee had the lowest exchange value. Surplus budget creates a false notion of prosperity. It will also mean that the surplus money can be spent by the government in any way it likes. It gives more power in the hands of the government to play ducks and drakes with the lives of the people.[8] If there is really any surplus, the government should spend it for the welfare of the people, or should reduce the taxes of the people. It should be noted that Gokhale was immensely interested in the welfare of Indian people. The surpluses were created for the additional expenditures incurred by the British Government in India. But these expenditures were the sources of drain.

In his budget speech of 1902, Gokhale pointed out that there must be economy in government expenditure and taxes should be kept as low as possible. He wanted more funds to be spent on education, public health, agriculture, industry, sanitation and so on. He pleaded for the introduction of progressive taxation.

He was also concerned with the growing inflation of the Indian economy. He said that inflation caused acute sufferings to the poor people and an increase in the cost of developmental projects. Inflation also disturbed the currency. He pleaded for an enquiry into the high prices by an expert committee.

Gokhale analysed very competently the exchange rate manipulation by the British Government against the interest of India. He said that such a manipulation was done to increase the salary of the British people. Gokhale showed that because of the unjustified manipulation of exchange rate,

---

8.   V.G. Kale, *Gokhale and Economic Reforms,* p. 97.

the additional burden on the Indian tax-payer came to the extent of Rs. 30 lakhs a year.[9] He was in favour of exchange rate stability and reform.

Economic Conditions in India

Gokhale noticed the pauperism in India. He gave evidence in proving the growing poverty in India and refuted the British Government's statement that in India, there was a growing prosperity. He said that although there was a surplus budget, the tax burden of the people, which was an important cause of poverty, did not decrease. He said that the revenue under income-tax and salt tax did not even keep pace with the normal growth of population. This led to the conclusion that the material condition of the people of India was steadily deteriorating, and to him, the phenomenon was the saddest in the whole range of the economic history of the world.[10]

Suggested Reforms

Gokhale suggested a number of reforms for the better financial administration and management of the country and also for improving the welfare of the people. The following are the main suggestions of G.K. Gokhale :

(i) He was in favour of industrial development of India.

(ii) He recommended an enquiry for looking into the possibilities of the growth of sugar industry in India.

(iii) He pleaded for the introduction of permanent settlement in the matter of land revenue.

(iv) He urged the government to introduce land mortgage banks for reducing the exploitation by the moneylenders.

(v) He recommended the introduction of education, specially for child labour.

(vi) He moved a resolution for the prohibition of the recruitment of indentured labour for the colony of Natal. According to him, indentured labour was a *de-facto* slave system.

(vii) He pleaded more for protective irrigation than for famine relief from budgetary revenues.

(viii) He wanted to bring the railways under the management of the state.

(ix) Gokhale advocated the policy of protection (right kind of protection to the Indian industries.

(x) Training of selected Indians abroad and promotion of industrial and technical education.

(xi) Improvement of the living conditions of the workers.

(xii) Reduction in revenue.

(xiii) Creation of cooperative societies which will lend out money at a low rate of interest.

---

9. V.B. Singh, *From Naoroji to Nehru*, p. 82.
10. V.G. Kale, *op. cit.*, p. 109.

    (xiv)   Removal of agricultural indebtedness.

    (xv)   He advocated decentralisation of power.

Evaluation

    Gokhale is mainly known for his original views on Indian public finance and financial management. His view that where the private enterprise is weak, the public enterprise must fill up the gap, seems to be well-founded. He suggested a number of pragmatic reformative proposals for increasing the welfare of the Indian people. He well understood the implications of a change in the government expenditure on production, distribution and employment in the country. He was mainly concerned with the eradication of Indian poverty. Gokhale advocated provincial autonomy and a more rigorous financial control and economy. "Gokhale was perhaps the first in India to emphasise that government expenditure and income should be directed to set right deficiencies in the working of the economic system."[11]

MOHANDAS KARAMCHAND GANDHI (1869-1948)

    M.K. Gandhi was neither an economist nor a politician. His was a socialist plan based on non-violence, truth, love and sympathy. Gandhi wanted to have an ideal society of his own imagination. His ideas on economics are a part and parcel of his philosophical, political and sociological ideals. Gandhi was essentially concerned with the free growth of human beings, emancipation of the downtrodden and exploited masses. The economic ideas of Gandhi are scattered in his various writings. The major economic ideas of Gandhi are briefly discussed below.

Welfare Economy

    Gandhi was in favour of the maximisation of social welfare. The welfare is not in the material sense of the term but it is more of spiritual nature. His concept of welfare is based on the growth of the totality of human personality. It is against the classical notion of *homo-economicus* or economic man. Gandhi wanted reduction in inequalities and the free growth of human beings. To Gandhi, wealth does not mean welfare. Gandhi was in favour of the satisfaction of the basic human wants like food, clothing and shelter. He was against the concentration and acquisition of wealth beyond the point of necessity. He was dreaming of a socialist type of society where the basic demands of the people would be met. Gandhi thought that sometimes it is necessary to voluntarily reduce the wants.

    The basis of economic activities should be, according to Gandhi, moral and ethical considerations. In fact, Gandhian economics is very much interlinked with ethics. His economics was pragmatic but not amoral.

Village Reorganisation and Agricultural Development

    Gandhi was in favour of self-sufficient villages. He wanted to use such technique of cultivation which will not deplete our soil. The use of fertiliser

---

11. P.K. Gopala Krishnan, *Development of Economic Ideas in India*, 1959, p. 140.

must not spoil the soil. He was against the use of artificial fertilisers. For irrigation, he preferred well irrigation to large hydro-electric projects, as these will lead to exploitation. Gandhi was against the individual ownership of land. He thought that it is better to have communal ownership of land for balanced cultivation. Land should belong to the cultivators. The surplus produce on the land must be distributed to the rest of the communities. Gandhi said that India lives in villages. Therefore, the development of India depends on the development of villages. Every village has to be a self-contained republic. Every village has to grow the articles for its own consumption. Every village must have all the amenities and facilities such as school, theatre, water supply, public hall and so on. He wanted the revival of the ancient village system. He evolved the system of village Sarvodaya. The problems of villages must be solved properly so that poverty is eradicated and people can be happy and self-reliant. Gandhi laid emphasis on the revival of village industries like soap-making, paper-making, hand-grinding, khadi and hand-pounding. The village will serve as a part of a decentralised economy.

Gandhi wanted the abolition of *zamindari* system without any compensation. He did not favour individual or peasant farming, but advocated the need for collective effort in this direction.

Industrial Development and Industrial Economy

In villages, there are village industries and cottage industries. In the case of village industries, production, consumption and distribution are confined within the villages. In the case of cottage industries, the articles may be produced for the country as a whole and even for foreign countries. Gandhi found the possibilities of exploitation in the case of cottage industries but not in the case of village industries. Human development is more possible in village industries. In large-scale industries, human initiative is destroyed and there is a sense of *alienation*. The large-scale industries bring out things convenient to life. Gandhi says that this makes the consumer lazy. Khadi industries are based on the ideas of non-violence and truth, though mill-made products are cheaper than khadi products. Large-scale production through machinery involves the danger of violence and untruth. Therefore, such a type of production should not be allowed. Moreover, the capitalist method of production also involves the possibilities of clash between labour and capital. Khadi industry is the symbol of unity, freedom and equality. Khadi implies the decentralisation of production and distribution of the necessary products.

Large-scale industries are profit-oriented. Therefore, they are bad for the society because they lead to concentration of wealth and power in a few hands. They violate the basic tenet of Gandhian economics.

Decentralisation

Gandhi wanted decentralised pattern of development because such a attern is better normally and spiritually. Decentralised industries can play

a crucial role in the development of a country like India with least disturbance and dislocation. The small industries and village industries can serve
the purpose of decentralisation. The centralised industries are generally
large-scale industries. These industries are anti-democratic and lead to
regimentation. Village industries are highly democratic and also conducive
to the growth of happiness between labour and capital. However, some industries are by nature large scale. They cannot be avoided. In that case,
Gandhi advocated state control over such industries. These industries
should be under strict control.

Gandhi advocated decentralisation because it can avoid violence. He
suggested delocalisation of production as against concentration in particular areas. He observed that village industries can be mechanised
gradually.

Large-scale industries are sometimes found to be wasteful. These industries are unrelated to the rest of the economy. Gandhi thought that by
and large the people should try to use the indigenous power and material
for the development of the economy. Power has to be used in small-scale
and cottage industries very cautiously, lest it should generate exploitation.
Cows, bullocks, horses, etc., give not only power but also manure. They are
helpful for not only ploughing the land but also for manure.

Gandhi was not in favour of industrialisation, because it does not help
the growth of personality : it simply favours material progress. The end of
life is not material progress. He wanted de-centralisation from the initial
stage of industrial development. He advocated nationalisation of some
basic and key industries. Gandhian pattern of decentralisation is to correct
the evils of centralised economy.

Use of Machinery

Gandhi was against the use of machinery. "It is machinery that has impoverished India," said Gandhi. Indian handicrafts were destroyed by the
use of machinery. Machinery makes labourer slaves. It produces horrible
working conditions. It displaces human labour and increases unemployment. Gandhi says that it is criminal to displace labour by the introduction
of power-driven machinery. It is wrong to think that machinery saves
labour. Machinery improves the lot of a few persons only but it deteriorates
the conditions of the common people who are unemployed and exploited.
Small-scale type of family industries help to grow employment and output
more than the large-scale industries. Under large-scale industries, employment is always lower to which Gandhi objected. The employment differences between these two types of industries can be shown in the following
diagram which shows that large-scale industries have the possibility of
generation of more unemployment.

Gandhi was perhaps influenced by the labour-absorptive power of
cottage and village type of industries. This thinking was rational in the
perspective of the existence of a large number of surplus labour in India. In

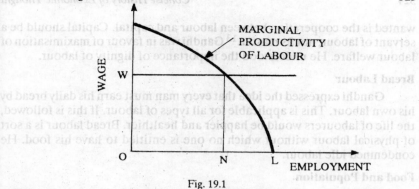

Fig. 19.1

the above diagram, *ON* is the amount of employment generated by the large-scale industries which want to maximise profit ; but a family type industry which wants to maximise output and employment can generate *OL* amount of employment. Thus, if employment generation is regarded as an objective function, Gandhi's advocacy for village-type industries seems to be on a rational ground.

Gandhi does not find any necessity of industrialisation in any country. Gandhi seems to be opposed to machinery because machines establish "their own mastery over man and make him their slave." He was reasonable enough to say that machinery is permissible if it does not deprive masses of man of the opportunity of labour, increases his efficiency and does not make people slave. He was in favour of the use of electricity in the village. He hated machinery because it creates conflict between labour and capital. Machinery also encroaches upon the individuality of the labourers. But Gandhi was not against the use of all machinery. He was against the craze for the labour-saving machinery. He welcomed that type of machinery which helped the workers and which worked as servants. Machanisation was good particularly for labour-deficit countries. It is bad for labour-surplus economies.

On Labour

Labour has a very crucial role to play in an economy. Gandhi favoured the formation of trade unions in different production places. The actions of the trade union should be based on non-violence, arbitration and truth. The trade unions will safeguard the rights and interests of their members. The trade unions will share the functions of the state. He favoured strike.[12] He himself was the leader of many strikes. But he pointed out that the cause of strike must be just. He advocated the participation of labour in management. He advocated economic equality in factories, shortening of the hours of work and more leisure. He was in favour of equal pay for equal work. He observed that if the distinction between labour and capital is eliminated, the world would be a much happier place to live in. What he wanted is the cooperation between labour and capital. Capital should be a servant of labour, not its master.[13] Gandhi was in favour of maximisation of labour welfare. He understood the importance of dignity of labour.

Bread Labour

Gandhi expressed the idea that every man must earn his daily bread by his own labour. This is applicable for all types of labour. If this is followed, the life of labourers would be happier and healthier. Bread labour is a sort of physical labour without which no one is entitled to have his food. He condemned idle labour.

Food and Population

Gandhi was convinced that the food problem in India was a genuine problem. He requested the business people not to undertake speculative activities in foodgrains. He suggested a number of measures for solving the food problem in the country, such as the extension of cultivation, reduction in demand for food, removal of black-marketing, spread of irrigation facilities, and so on. In 1947, Gandhi requested the government to introduce decontrol in foodgrains. He was of the opinion that control on foodgrains will lead to corruption and inflation.

Gandhi favoured the natural way of controlling population through self-control or *Brahmacharya*. He did not advocate the use of contraceptives. He wanted to propagate sex education. According to him, till 1947, India was not overpopulated, because there was enough possibility of increasing the food supply for the growing population.[14]

Trusteeship Doctrine

Gandhi was against the concentration and misuse of wealth. He said that the rich people who have accumulated wealth should distribute it for maximising the welfare of the rest of the community. The wealth really belongs to the entire community. The rich people should consider themselves to be the trustees. The capitalists are like thieves.[15] However, no force should be used to get rid of their wealth. Their wealth should be used properly through their consent as trustees. The capitalists should act as only the trustees of the accumulated wealth. The poor workers, under trusteeship, will consider the capitalists as their benefactors, and would place every faith in their good actions. In such a case, the labour welfare can be maximised. The rich people should not use their wealth arbitrarily but for the benefit of others. Trusteeship is a means of transforming the capitalist order of society into a socialist one. Under the trusteeship scheme, the rich people will keep for them only that much of wealth which is essential for a good standard of living.[16] The rest would be meant for others in the society.

---

13. D.G. Tendulkar, *Mahatma,* Vol.VI, p. 365.
14. M.K. Gandhi, *India of My Dreams,* p. 238.
15. J.B. Kripalani, *Gandhian Thought,* p. 8.
16. *Harijan,* 25 August, 1940.

Trusteeship will eliminate economic inequalities between the rich people and the poor people.

Evaluation

Gandhi is regarded as a utopian socialist. He was not a theoretical economist. There is no place for capital accumulation in his schema. Gandhi never thought of the process of accumulation of surplus for economic development. His was a model of simple reproduction. The development of agriculture suggested by Gandhi has to be based on some sort of industrial development, the type of which Gandhi has never clarified. Be that as it may, Gandhian economics is the economics of bare self-sufficiency. He disfavours an acquisitive society, and materialistic conception of development. He was right in emphasising labour-intensive method of production for a labour-surplus economy like India's. His scheme of development is also relevant for a capital-poor and inflation-biased economy as India is. To some extent, Gandhian economics seems to be relevant for the developing economies of our times, and also for those economies which are fed up with the excess of materialism and lack of human values and relations. The spirit of Gandhian economics seems to be still alive today in the form of a low-aspiration model of development, as proposed by Mellor and others.

Part Six

Metamorphosis of Economic Doctrines |

20

Development of Economic Theories

I. DEVELOPMENT OF THE THEORY OF UTILITY

The analysis of value and price in terms of utility was first analysed by the Scholastic writers. But these writers lacked a marginal apparatus. The utility theory went on developing right from the times of Adam Smith-Galiani. Soon, the theory reached its peak level of achievement. In the development of the theory of utility, Genovesi occupied a place of distinction. The paradox of value (*i.e.*, why useless diamonds are valued more highly than useful water) was explained by many writers, including John Law, in terms of exchange values. Bernoulli side by the side developed the famous marginal utility of income analysis. However, many writers referred to the element of utility as a matter of course. Bentham formulated explicitly Gossen's law of satiable wants. Adam Smith and all the English classical writers, with the exception of Senior, did not realise the possibilities of utility approach to the explanation of the phenomenon of economic value. But this attitude was applicable to Ricardo, as Schumpeter observes. However, the step taken by Senior did not constitute a definite step in advance. Gossen and Dupuit did much for the development of the theory of utility. Walras, Lloyed and Jennings also developed a similar analysis of utility. The marginal utility concept was clearly present with all these three writers and so are the arguments about how wants and utility are related to value. This argument became very famous after half a century. Dupuit distinguished between marginal and total utility, and could explain consumer's surplus. Gossen, however, was the first writer to formulate the fundamental principle of utility (Law of Equimarginal Utility):

$$\frac{MU_1}{P_1} = \frac{MU_2}{P_2} = \frac{MU_3}{P_3} \cdots \cdots \frac{MU_n}{P_n}$$

Walras, Jevons and Menger restated Gossen's or Bentham's or Bernoulli's Law of Satiable Wants. In doing so, they all treated utility as a psychological phenomenon which can be felt by introspection, and they observed that the utility of every commodity to the possessor depends on the stock of that commodity alone. It is a fact that some of the most prominent exponents of marginal utility analysis were utilitarians, *e.g.,* Gossen, Jevons and Edgeworth. While explaining utility, some writers mixed up economics with hedonics. Marshall discarded the link between utility and utilitarianism, excepting the development of the idea of disutility which he borrowed from Jevons. Be that as it may, utility theory of value is entirely independent of any hedonistic postulate of philosophy.

The early Austrians believed that utility was related to psychology. Among others, Menger, Bohm-Bawerk and Marshall realised that utility is a psychological phenomenon and is related to introspection. Marshall, however, pointed out that although utility is not directly measurable, it can indirectly be measured by the sacrifices in terms of money. Jevons denied that utility was cardinally measurable. Marshall assumed that the marginal utility of money remains constant.

Gossen formulated in 1854 the *Law of Diminishing Marginal Utility*. According to Jevons, this can be called Gossen's first law. Gossen's second law was the Law of Equimarginal Utility. Marshall thought that consumer's equilibrium is obtained at the point where $MU_A = P_A$ However, soon, reaction against this formulation started gaining momentum. It was demonstrated that it was not possible to quantitatively measure cardinal utility. A theory developed with the idea that satisfaction can be compared and arranged according to choice, and consumer's behaviour can be explained in terms of his preference or ranking for different combinations of commodities. This attempt is known as introspective ordinalism.

Long, long ago, Pareto made an attempt to develop the idea of ordinal utility. But he could not be quite consistent. Further advance in the direction was made by Johnson and Slutsky. In 1934, the job was done completely by Hicks and Allen. According to them, a consumer has a scale of preference and an indifference map from which indifference curves for the consumer can be drawn and, his equilibrium can be found out. Pareto called this analysis an index function. Every point on the indifference curve will mean separate combinations of two goods, but it will represent equal satisfaction with every other. Hence, the consumer need not measure utility cardinally. Indifference curve was first discovered by Edgeworth. A higher indifference curve would mean higher satisfaction. This implication was realised by Irving Fisher. The indifference curve technique replaces utility by preference and marginal utility by the marginal rate of substitution. It is free from the obstacle put by the assumption of constant marginal utility of money. It also requires fewer assumptions, and can separate of income effect and substitution effects, and can also explain Giffen's Paradox. But indifference curve analysis is like the old wine in a new bottle. We do not find much of an improvement in the indifference curve analysis as compared to utility analysis.

As against the introspective ordinal utility analysis of Hicks and Allen, Samuelson has developed a behaviourist utility analysis which goes by the name of *Revealed Preference Theory*. This has been called by Hick *Direct Consistency Test* under strong ordering. This theory is based on two conditions: *(i)* direct consistency and transitivity. Direct consistency means that if $A > B$ under one situation, B is not preferred to A under any other situation. The theory is based on the actual consumer behaviour where choice reveals preference. It does not require the restrictive assumption that all income must be spent. The theorem establishes that positive income elasticity means negative price elasticity of demand. The theory only takes into account positive income elasticity of demand. It cannot enunciate the demand theorem when income effect or income elasticity is negative. It cannot isolate the substitution effect from income effect. The theory is conditional.

The earlier theories of utility did not take into account the situations involving risky choices. The modern theory of utility considers risk, uncertainty and gambling. This theory has been developed in the post-war period, and is also called the Bernoulli Utility Theory. Bernoulli observed that utility resulting from any small increase in wealth will be inversely proportional to the quantity of goods previously possessed. In other words, the marginal utility of money diminishes as income increases. According to Bernoulli, rational decisions in the case of risky choices would be made on the basis of expectation of total utility rather than mathematical expectation of monetary value. The modern theory of utility sets up a method of measuring utility under certain conditions. It brings out the possibility of increasing marginal utility of money, and it provides logical ground for making certain types of rational decisions. The credit for the method of measuring utility goes to von Neumann and Morgenstern (N-M) who developed their ideas in the work entitled: *The Theory of Games and Economic Behaviours.* The N-M method is concerned with the calculation of expected utility. The N-M utility convention or equation is :

$$U(L) = P \times U(A) + (1-P) \times U(B).$$

Where, $U(L)$ = Utility of lottery tickets, P = Probability,

$$U(A) = \text{Utility of prize } A, \text{ and } U(B) = \text{Utility of prize } B$$

Why does a man indulge both in insurance and gambling ? The answer has been provided by Friedman and Savage hypothesis which is an extension of N-M method. It states that marginal utility of money income diminishes for income below some levels, then it increases and again diminishes for all income above that level. Whereas Friedman and Savage point out that utility is a function of the level of income, Markowitz maintains that it is a function of change in the level of income. The N-M cardinal utility is meant to be used in making predictions. However, for all practical purposes, the N-M theory is ordinal. It is cardinal only in name and is not additive in neo-classical cardinal utility.

II. DEVELOPMENT OF THE THEORY OF VALUE

Over the last two hundred years, value theory has developed between the extremes of scarcity, utility and labour. The philosophical concept of value as developed in the past involved materialism and idealism. Value, in the context of materialism, is an objective matter. However, the chasm between the subjective and objective estimates of value has never been satisfactorily bridged. A confusion on the subject of value and the market equivalent of value (*i.e.*, price) still persists in the history of economic analysis. While some opine that these are basically different, others maintain that they are synonymous.

According to Aquinas, although the utility of a commodity changes very often, yet it has little bearing on the objective estimate of value. He observes that the value of an article in the long run is determined by the quantity of labour necessary to produce it. Following Aquinas, the trend of emphasis shifted from labour away to utility as the basis of value. Buridan and Beil, in the 13th and 14th centuries, pointed out that the ability of a commodity to satisfy human needs was the basis of value. Similar view was also maintained Nicholas Barbon. In the 17th century, William Petty subscribed to the view that land and labour should simultaneously be considered for the purpose of estimation of value. Land, in fact, is the mother, and labour is the father, so to say. But at another place, he observed that the cost of a day's food is a better measure of value for an adult than a day's labour. But Locke held the opposite view. According Locke, land as such had no value, and labour, therefore, was mainly responsible for the creation of value. He also observed that demand and supply may affect value in the short period, but in the long run, labour alone determines value. Locke observes that water which is abundant in supply has no value in exchange but diamond, which has no use, commands high prices. Thus, John Locke, for the first time, used the diamond-water paradox to explain exchange value. However, Adam Smith is wrongly credited for this.

Turgot put emphasis on utility as the criterion of value. But in the explanation of market price, Turgot very much emphasised the importance of demand and supply. Be that as it may, the foundation of the classical theory of value was laid by Cantillon. Cantillon observed that the intrinsic value of a commodity is the measure of the quantity and quality of labour that enters into its production. And market price, which is determined by demand and supply, does not always reflect intrinsic value.

Adam Smith's *Wealth of Nations* came out twenty years after the publication of Cantillon's *Essay*. Smith distinguished between value-in-use and value-in-exchange. These two values are not always equal, because commodities having value-in-use may be abundant in supply and may have no value-in-exchange. Value-in-exchange depends upon the labour that is required to acquire it. The labour is the real price and the money value is the nominal price. However, excepting in the simplest society, labour cost is not the only cost which sets up the real price. He realised the difficulties in the application of labour theory of value. He observed that labour-content of a commodity cannot always be calculated in quantitative terms. Smith admitted that market value may well be below or above the normal value set by the cost of production; but he said that natural order will make adjustments in such a way that these two values would be equal except in monopolies and other critical situations which may temporarily or permanently keep the market value above the normal value.

Ricardo considered long-term or normal value. He took into account both scarcity and quantity of labour influencing value. In the case of non-reproducible objects, scarcity determined value. But such objects are very limited, and they need not be considered in value theory. Most of the commodities can be produced with the help of labour, and labour cost then becomes the basis of value. Capital being stored-up or dead labour, and rent being payment for the superiority of land over the poorest quality land under cultivation, it is understandable that only labour contributes to value. But later on, Ricardo became dissatisfied with his labour theory of value. This was evident in the successive editions of his *Principles*.

Nassau Senior did not approve of Ricardo's labour theory of value. To senior, scarcity was a fundamental aspect of value. But he added that cost of production also influenced value. Thus, Senior became the forerunner of the theory of value which later on was developed by the noe-classical school, particularly by Marshall.

John Stuart Mill's analysis of value was heavily based on Samuel Bailey's treatment of value which was used against the Ricardian theory of value. Mill divided all commodities into three categories: *(i)* those absolutely limited in supply, *(ii)* those which can be increased by the application of labour, and *(iii)* those which can be increased only at increasing cost. For the first category of commodities, value depends on demand and supply, for the second category, value depends on cost of production, but supply and demand remain still important; and for the third category of commodities, cost of production, again, determines value.

Marshall's main contribution to the value theory was his synthesis between the utility and the cost of production theories of value. Marshall explained that neither demand nor supply was important exclusively for value theory. But both these forces had equal influence on value. A pair of scissors does not cut with either the upper blade or the lower blade alone, but with both together. Marshall remarked that in the short period, value is entirely influenced by demand, whereas in the long period, value is influenced by the supply.

Karl Marx, like many others, deviated from the classical labour theory of value. Marx improved upon Ricardian theory of value. The socialist writers used labour theory of value to prove their contention that profit, rent and interest are unjustifiable charges upon the true values which are created solely by labour.

Lauderdale clearly explained the relation of utility to value, and analysed what we call today elasticity of demand. Lloyd first used the concept of diminishing utility and marginal utility. Value to him was a state of mind which could be observed at the point of separation between satisfied and unsatisfied wants.

According to Gossen, value is representative of two things: satisfaction in consumption and cost of production. Value is determined at a point where marginal utility and marginal disutility balance each other. Jevons worked in line with Gossen. Jevons emphasised the infinite nature of human wants, and the idea of marginal utility which determined exchange value. Walras harmonised cost of production and utility theories of value. Value is considered as the total utility of a given commodity. But the exchange value of a commodity can be determined by a comparison of the marginal utility of a commodity with that of another.

The Austrian school provided the philosophical slant to the analysis of value. According to the economists belonging to this school, *e.g.*, Menger, Weiser and Bohm-Bawerk, value is a subjective phenomenon. Menger completely ignored objective considerations. Weiser believed that value arose only out of utility. He observed that cost of production really is a matter of utility. Bohm-Bawerk also subscribed to the marginal utility theory of value. He said that the power of one good to satisfy wants gives it a power to acquire other goods in exchange for it.

The extension of the classical ideas of value has been made by the socialist writers, *e.g.*, Thompson, Bray, Gray and Mars. The theory of surplus value and labour theory of value are implicit in the writings of the socialists. Labour creates value over and above what is paid to him as wage. The extra value which is created by labour and which is pocketed up by the capitalists is called the surplus value.

However, it is difficult to find the sole crucial factor which influences such a complicated phenomenon as value. The conceptualisation of value was the product of the world in which a particular school of thought grew up, or a particular economist lived.

III. DEVELOPMENT OF THE THEORY OF DISTRIBUTION

Functional distribution is concerned with the payment of remuneration to land, labour, capital and organisation in the form of rent, wage, interest and profit. Relative simplicity of economic life in ancient times provides a reasonable explanation for the lack of sufficient interest in the field of distribution. Similarly, in the Middle Ages, the self-sufficiency in feudal estate and rigidity of class structure made the question of distribution non-existent. During the period of mercantilism, the expansion of trade had little effect on the general growth of the theory of distribution. Only national distribution mattered and it was influenced by politics.

The physiocrats thought that since wealth emerges from one source, agriculture, it is necessary to have an elaborate theory of distribution. The physiocratic idea of distribution can be seen from Quesnay's *Tableau Economique*. In Quesnay's system, agriculturists are the only productive class, landlords partly productive and manufacturing class is sterile. If the annual return is 100 units, 40 units are used by the primary sectors to meet the expenses of the next year's production, and 40 units are paid to the landlords and 20 units go to the manufacturing class as a payment for the purchase of manufactured goods. Now, out of 40, the landlords pay 20 to the agricultural sector for the purchase of food, and 20 to the merchant class. The sterile class now has an income of 40, which is entirely paid to the agricultural class for the purchase of food and raw materials. Thus, the agricultural sector receives the entire income of all classes, and this is used for increasing the real production. This process goes on indefinitely to the benefit of all classes. This shows that agriculture and mining are the only productive occupations. However, the physiocratic scheme of distribution was a paternalistic idea and was unrealistic in many ways. But it directed the attention of the economists to the important aspects of distribution of wealth.

Adam Smith's idea of distribution was much influenced by the physiocrats. However, Smith paid more attention to production rather than to distribution. Adam Smith thought the society consisted of three classes. The return to each class is not a matter of equity but of natural law. The laws of market regulated distribution in the Smithian system. However, in the matter of distribution, Smith was a pessimist. He observed the genesis of class conflict in distribution. The contribution of each factor to the value of the produce determines its relative return. J.B. Say improved Smith's idea of distribution by introducing the concept of entrepreneur who was solely responsible for distribution to take place.

According to Ricardo, the main problem in political economy is the discovery of laws which govern distributive shares. His theory is based on marginal principle and surplus principle. The former explains the share of rent, whereas the latter explains the division of residue between wages and profit. The whole economy is divided into two sectors—agriculture and industry.

Ricardian theory of distribution can be explained with the help of a diagram (see the diagram earlier in Chapter 4 on *Ricardo*). In the Ricardian system, rent is the difference between the average product and the marginal product. The wage level is at the subsistence. Therefore, profit is the residue. With higher accumulation, population and employment increase in agriculture, and wage fund also increases. But due to diminishing returns, marginal productivity of labour decreases. The share of rent increases but profit rate decreases $\left(\dfrac{\text{Profit}}{\text{Wage fund}} \right)$ With greater accumulation, wage increases for various reasons. Increased wage leads to fall in profit. Fall in profit will fall to zero, and stationary state sets in.

Marxian theory of distribution is based on Ricardian surplus principle. The total produce, according to Marx, is distributed between the owners and the wage-earners. Marx did not take into account diminishing returns. He made no distinction between rent and profit. He said that wage rate is always decided at the subsistence level. Marx did not believe in the Malthusian theory of population and criticised the Ricardian direct relationship between wage rate and population. In the Marxian scheme, the capitalist sector expands due to constant competition. Marx says that monopoly capitalism faces realisation crisis due to maldistribution of income. Profit under capitalism becomes the source of weakness. Workers are exploited, underconsumption develops and capitalism faces crises. The falling rate of profit takes place due to the organic composition of capital.

Sismondi observed that all income arises from one source, i.e., labour. If income is not properly distributed, overproduction takes place. Inequality in income distribution, according to Sismondi, is caused by ownership of land and capital in a few hands.

Mill remarked that distribution depends on man-made laws. Rent, to him, was unearned increment. Profit and interest are derived from abstinence, productivity of labour and stored-up labour. Wage influences profit in a reverse way; and wage itself is dependent on the wage fund. Distribution, according to John Stuart Mill, is affected by historical processes. Mill observes that since distribution is guided by man-made laws, there is sufficient scope for reform in order to bring about more equitable distribution.

Robertus thought that the aim of distribution is to assure to everybody the product of his labour. He wanted the suppression of private property and unearned income. He pointed out that the programme of distribution can be accomplished by the gradual establishment of state socialism. The Fabian socialists content that wealth is social and it should be equitably distributed by the state surpluses for society as a whole. Robert Owen and Warbase wanted to bring an era of equitable distribution through cooperative movement. However, unlike Ricardo and Smith, Carey and Bastiat presented an optimistic picture of distribution.

According to the scheme of the Austrian school, the process of distribution is based on the power of each factor of production to impute value to the final product. Weiser says that factor payment is determined by the value produced by the marginal unit of land, labour and capital.

The distribution theory of Marshall is based on marginal productivities of factors of production. Demand and supply also play an important role. Demand is determined by the entrepreneur's estimate of the value of land, labour and capital, whereas supply is determined by costs of producing factors. His analysis rests on the notion that the return to each factor depends on the price it can command. J.B. Clark also based his theory of distribution on marginal productivity of factors. The neo-classical theory of distribution is based on the marginal principle. Wicksteed opined that the share of the factors is determined by their marginal productivities. He said the total product is equal to the sum of amount of factors, each multiplied by its marginal product, provided constant returns to scale are in existence. This is generally known as Euler's theorem. Marginal productivity theory of distribution, however, has many loopholes. And in recent years, there has been a growing tendency to scrap the theory in favour of a more realistic bargaining theory. The modern theory of distribution has taken into account both demand for and the supply of factors.

Keyes did not build up any theory of distribution; but with the help of Keynesian tools, one can build up a theory of distribution, as has been done by Kaldor. The principle of multiplier can be utilised to determine the relation between prices and wages, if the level of employment and output is taken as given.

In the neo-classical theory, monopoly profit was considered as a distinct form of revenue. The modern theories of imperfect competition emphasise that monopoly profit is not an isolated phenomenon; profit generally contains an element of monopoly revenue. Kalecki builds up a theory of distribution where the degree of monopoly power determines the share between wages and profit. The higher the degree of monopoly power, the lower is the wage and the higher is the profit. The degree of monopoly power is defined as the ratio of prime cost to the price. However, the degree of monopoly power is the essential feature of capitalism. The transition from capitalism to communism will experience the destruction of inequality in income distribution: from each according to his ability and to each according to his needs. This, however, goes against the widely accepted notion of distribution that each factor receives an income which is equivalent to its contribution.

It is necessary to trace the historical development of the different components of the theory of distribution. These are briefly discussed below.

THEORY OF WAGES

1. Subsistence Theory of Wages. This theory was first formulated by the physiocrats. Lassalle called it the Iron Law of Wages, because the subsistence cost was primarily fixed and it was something like a natural law. This theory of wage was maintained by the classical economists including Adam Smith, Ricardo and others. Karl Marx also used this theory of wage as the basis of his theory of surplus value.

2. Wage Fund Theory. This theory was popularised by the classical writers like Adam Smith, John Stuart Mill and others. According to this theory, wages depended on the demand for and the supply of labour. It pointed out that a particular proportion of capital of the economy was devoted for the wage payment. Thus, the wage fund was actually utilised for the payment of wages, and it regulated the demand for labour. Wage fund itself was regulated by the tempo of capital accumulation. The higher the capital accumulation, the larger was the size of the wage fund.

3. Residual Claimant Theory. This theory maintains that wage is a residual factor. After every factor of production is paid, whatever remains is paid to the worker. This theory was proposed by an American economist named Walker. It was also explained by Jevons, among others.

4. Marginal Productivity Theory. This theory which says that wage is equal to the marginal productivity of labour was formulated by the Neo-classical writers and also by the marginal economists.

5. Discounted Marginal Productivity Theory. According to this theory, wage is equal to the marginal productivity of labour minus the amount of discount on account of the advances made to the workers. The workers take advances from the employers. Therefore, the employers charge a discount which is equivalent to the current rate of interest. This charge is made because the advance is given much before the workers produce goods for the employers. This theory was put forward by F.W.Taussig originally.

6. Demand and Supply Theory. This theory is regarded as the modern theory of wage. According to this theory, wage is determined by the interaction of demand and supply of labour in the market. This idea was popular among the classical and also among the neo-classical writers.

THEORY OF PROFIT

1. Rent Theory of Profit. This theory, among others, was proposed by Nassau Senior and also by John Stuart Mill. According to this theory, profit is due to the superior talent of the business people. Walker also considered profit as a form of rent or surplus.

2. Dynamic Theory of Profit. According to J.B. Clark, profit arises only in a dynamic society where population, capital stock and technique are all changing. If the society is static, it cannot generate any profit.

3. Risk Theory of Profit. This theory was put forward by F.B. Hawley in 1907. According to him, profit is mainly a reward for risk-taking. Since business involves risk, it also involves gain. No risk, no gain.

4. Uncertainty Theory of Profit. This theory of profit is due to Knight who said that profit arises because of uncertainty. If the world is certain, there is no chance of profit. The uncertainty is the risk which cannot be measured.

THEORY OF INTEREST

1. Productivity Theory of Interest. The physiocrats believed that interest is justified on the capital which is productive. This idea, however, continued for a long time.

2. Loanable Fund Theory of Interest. This theory was propounded by Knut Wicksell. It was subsequently refined by others and used by the classical economists. According to this theory, rate of interest is determined by the demand for and the supply of loanable funds.

3. Abstinence Theory of Interest. According to this theory, rate of interest is reward for abstinence or waiting. This theory was popularised by Senior and Cairnes.

4. Agio Theory of Interest. This theory is also known as the Psychological theory. It was first proposed by John Rae. The theory was refined further by Bohm-Bawerk. This theory says that since people prefer present goods to future goods, there is always a premium for the production of present goods. The premium is the rate of interest which is paid to the people who are parting with their savings.

5. Time Preference Theory of Interest. This theory is also most similar to the *Agio theory*. This theory was propounded by Irving Fisher. The theory maintains that it is the time preference which is the crucial factor for the generation of interest. Since the people prefer present enjoyment to future enjoyment, the supplier of money must be compensated. This compensation is the interest. Interest is really the payment for waiting.

THEORY OF RENT

(For the History of the Development of the Theory of Rent, see below.)

IV. DEVELOPMENT OF THE THEORY OF RENT

The earliest known modern discussion on rent is from William Petty of the 17th century. According to him, rent is the surplus over and above the cost of production and the cost of maintenance of labourers. Values of land and the amounts of rent tended to increase directly with the growth of population, according to Petty.

The physiocrats, particularly Turgot, considered origin of rent in the same way as the origin of value. Rent arises from land itself. After deducting from the produce, the subsistence cost of labour, cost of materials for production and the cost of new supply of seeds, whatever remains is the *produit net* or net product which is equal to perspective yield and the prices offered by others for using the land. If competition is very keen, rent will be equivalent to the total surplus but if competition is not so keen, the producer can have some surplus for himself.

Adam Smith more or less shared the views of physiocrats as regards the origin of rent. Smith thought that rent is a kind of fee to encourage the owner to use his land productively. According to Smith, rent arises out of monopoly in land and out of unjust exaction from the value created by labour. J.B. Say was of the opinion that rent is produced by the supply and demand for the products of the land which set a price in such a way that a surplus always remains after meeting the cost of production. Secondly, rent is an interest payment for improving the land and making it ready for cultivation.

Many of the ideas of Malthus and Ricardo on rent were already conceived of by James Anderson, but his writings did not come to the attention of prominent economists. Malthus agreed with the physiocrats that rent was the surplus after deducting all expenditures. Malthus said that since the growth of population outstrips the growth of food supply, different types of land are cultivated for meeting the demand for food; and the difference in the productivity of the best land over the poorer constituted a surplus which might be considered as rent.

Ricardo's ideas on rent are similar to those of Malthus, but the former's theory is more comprehensive and systematic. According to Ricardo, "rent is that portion of the produce of the earth which is paid to the landlord for the use of the original and indestructible powers of the soil." When different grades of land are cultivated, the difference between the produce of more fertile land and less fertile land generates rent. Marginal land cannot produce any rent. Rent as a surplus arises out of intra-marginal land. The laws of supply and demand, and cost of production on the marginal land determined the price of the produce. Rent, according to Ricardo, does not enter into price fixation. Ricardo assumes that rent is the difference between average product and marginal product.

Rent may arise also out of diminishing returns. Beyond a certain point, application of more capital and labour to land produces a proportionately less return. This principle was discussed by Edward West elaborately.

A theory of rent similar to that of Ricardo was developed at the same time in Germany by Von Thunen. He maintained that some amount of capital is always utilised on farms. Rent is the residue after the deduction of interest on capital, costs of production and transportation charges. However, Carey and Bastiat vehemently criticised the Ricardian theory of rent. To Bastiat, rent is a payment for the labour and capital expense involved in making the land suitable for cultivation. A number of economists including Senior, Mill, Say, Walker, Menger and Marshall did not find any reason to confine the rent analysis to land only. The tendency was to extend the idea of rent to cover any differential surplus regardless of source. In fact, Senior defined rent as "all revenue earned without sacrifice."

Changes in the theory of rent were introduced by the Austrian school and by Walras. Bohm-Bawerk's concept of time preference and the introduction of the concept of margin, made the rent of national agents equivalent to the discounted value of marginal product. The productivity theory of rent was developed between 1873 and 1914. But the Austrian and Walrasian theories could not gain much ground due to the overwhelming victory of Ricardian differential cost theory of rent. The productivity theory could not specifically demarcate between natural and unnatural agents, and also could not emphasise the aspect which was treated elaborately by the Ricardian theory.

Marshall has shown how rent, quasi-rent are parts of the same totality. He brings into focus the fact that any factor can earn rent if its supply is fixed in the short and long run and is less than its demand at zero price. The rent arising out of specificity of a factor in the short run, is called quasi-rent by Marshall.

The theory of rent as a differential ability or entrepreneurial gain has been advanced by Mill, Walker, Baily and Mangoldt.

The modern theory of rent has been put forward by Joan Robinson and others as a generalised theory. According to the modern theory, rent is the difference between actual earnings and transfer earnings. These earnings are influenced by demand and supply forces. If a factor of production does not have any alternative use, its transfer earnings would be zero, and all its return would be rent. The modern theory is capable of explaining the differential rent by classifying different categories of a factor of production and calculating actual and transfer earnings in each case. In a dynamic economy, the supply of factors cannot be quickly adjusted to the changing demand conditions; therefore, almost every factor will have a rent element in its earnings.

V. DEVELOPMENT OF THE THEORY OF CAPITAL

Capital is generally regarded as accumulation of wealth which can be used in production. Capital is a factor of production. The theory of capital is a recent development. The word 'capital' was not used in the English language prior to the year 1600. The word 'stock' was used in lieu of the word 'capital' in early writings. Adam Smith used the word 'stock' in his *Wealth of Nations* to mean the supply of tools, goods, equipment and money. But Smith's use of the term 'capital' was not very clear. He pointed out that capital was that portion of man's stock from which revenues could be earned.

Physiocrats can be credited for the first use of the idea of capital. Turgot's use of the idea of circulating capital was a clear recognition of capital as a factor of production. However, Adam Smith was the first economist to give an analytical role to capital in production. He realised the importance of capital fully in the analysis of production. He expressed that division of labour itself is dependent on the availability of capital. Capital, according to him, also determines the magnitude of employment in a country. In the pursuit of self-interest, capital grows out of savings.

In 1804, Lauderdale pointed out that Smith's explanation of capital is not sufficient. Lauderdale observed that capital itself is productive, and is an independent factor of production. He said that capital could also be substituted for labour. He showed that industry and labour were limited by capital, and that a country could very well be oversupplied with capital.

Von Hermann defined capital as "all producers of income which have durability and exchange value." He classified capital into two types: use capital and industrial capital. Industrial capital was further classified into loan capital and productive capital. His contribution to the theory of capital was that land, being a durable source of income, was capital. To Hermann, capital had a separate entity. According to him, total capital is never destroyed, but it is replenished out of the income which it produced.

To Ricardo, capital was stored-up labour. His idea was completely in line with his labour theory of value. But the price of a commodity is also influenced by waiting time. This idea was given a more through treatment by

Nassau Senior. He is credited with the formation of the abstinence theory of capital. According to him, without productive equipments, the productivity in the economy cannot be increased. But to make productive tools, it is necessary to abstain from consumption of some of the resources at present. He scribed the word *abstinence* to capital. Capital was wealth produced by labour to be used in the production of more wealth.

John Stuart Mill discussed the classical idea of capital. His idea of capital is similar to the Ricardian concept which considered capital as stored-up labour. The basis of Mill's conception of capital can be traced back to the days prior to Adam Smith. He considered capital as the maintenance for labourers during the period of activity. This essentially smacks of the idea of his wage-fund theory. Mill used the earliest ideas of capital as stock.

Bastiat defined capital as stored-up labour and showed how the value of capital was constantly diminishing. Von Thunen added to the theory of capital the diminishing productivity concept which he applied in the case of rent and wage. His analysis of capital was much in the same style as his analysis of land and labour.

Bohm-Bawerk's ideas on capital are much outstanding in the analysis of the theory of capital. He defined capital as a "group of products which serve as a means to the acquisition of goods." He had treated capital as the *produced means of production.* Capital is the result rather than the cause of profitable matters of production. Capital, according to him, is an intermediate product of nature and labour. He believes that goods in the present are of more value than the same goods in the future. Present goods had greater value because capital was productive. Human beings fail to calculate properly their future wants. Bohm-Bawerk assumes that future values at the present time are less than the present values. This is known as the *time preference* concept. The value of capital has to be judged by its ability to make up the loss between present and future consumption of goods.

Karl Marx says that by appropriating surplus value which is solely created by labour, employers are able to purchase additional means of production. This process is continued by incorporating living labour with their dead substance and the employers convert materialised and dead labour into capital. Marx regards capital as a means for exploiting labour. As capital increases in the hands of employers, the working class is increasingly impoverished. However, Marx did not condemn capital as such, but what he condemned was the private ownership of capital. Marxian concept of capital was similar to the Ricardian concept of stored-up labour.

Keynes has challenged many of the older ideas on capital. He, however, shared the old idea that the supply of capital may be larger than what a community can productively put to use. This condition will arise if there are underconsumption, low-effective demand and contraction of investment opportunity. The tendency on the part of the community to save more and more is ultimately responsible for such a situation as secular stagnation. Keynes said that waiting and abstinence upon which Senior and Bohm-Bawerk had placed so much emphasis, had no factual foundation, since waiting or abstinence cannot in itself produce value.

Capital plays an important part in the teachings of the socialist writers. Sismondi complained about the effects of capital. He contended that capital should serve a social purpose, such as creating a new demand for labour or putting goods within the reach of consumers. If this purpose is not achieved, capital at least should not displace producers—native or foreign. However, he concluded that economic life was a war created by machines against men.

The modern theory of capital has had a definite conceptualisation and broader perspective. Capital recently is considered not merely as a stock, but it is also analysed in terms of flows. The economists of the present century are not only concerned with non-human capital as such but also concerned with human capital—its problems, influence and growth. Capital formation aspect is given a prominent role in the study of economic development of underdeveloped countries, and capital as a factor has been assigned a key position in the growth models which are designed for studying the growth possibilities of lagging areas. Capital theory is being integrated with monetary theory in recent years. The recent trend is the application of capital theory to monetary theory—the effort to work out the theory of money in terms of the theory of capital, regarding money as an asset, and the choice as to how much money to hold as a problem which can be solved with the concepts of the theory of capital. Friedman's application to monetary theory of the fundamental principle of capital theory—that income is the return on capital, and capital the present value of income, is perhaps the most outstanding development in monetary theory after Keynes' *General Theory*.

VI. DEVELOPMENT OF THE THEORY OF TAXATION

The earliest and the most prevalent form of government's interference on individuals and business enterprises is taxation. Increase in public expenditure along with wars, depression and economic development have brought the question of taxation to the mind of everyone. In the 12th and 13th centuries, the revenues of the government came from the estates. But heavy expenditure, extravagance and luxurious spending compelled the government to levy taxes.

The mercantilists believed that taxes should be paid according to the benefits received from the state. Petty observed that men should contribute taxes according to their riches or estates. But people were reluctant to pay taxes, because of the inconvenience of the time of payment, scarcity of money, etc. Petty gave an economic justification for taxation. He said that taxes did not change the economic position of a nation because the money which is taken by the state is returned to the society. Taxes are not harmful as long as they are spent on domestic product. One of the major difficulties in making taxes equitable and proportional was in the lack of proper knowledge concerning the exact number of people and their wealth. Petty said that the basement of currency was in fact a very inequitable system of taxation, falling most heavily upon the creditors of the state and upon the fixed income group. According to him, each person should be taxed in proportion to his enjoyment or expenditure which he thinks to be just. Export and import duties are approved if they are reasonably and selectively imposed. An import duty should be just high enough to keep the foreign product away from domestic consumption. Import duties on luxury goods should be excessive. Poll taxes were unfair but taxes on monopolies were sound. Petty first systematically treated the problem of taxation.

Like Petty, Hume was also against all arbitrary taxes because they were unequal and costly to collect. If industries are too heavily taxed, the earning of the industry reduces. According to him, tax on luxury goods is a good form of taxation. Von Justi had important views on taxation. Most of the views of Adam Smith on taxation were already expressed by Justi. According to him, taxes should be such as to be paid willingly; taxes should not restrict industry and commerce; taxes should fall relatively equally; taxes should be levied on persons and objects which made collection possible; tax collections should not require many officials; the amount of taxes and the time of payment should be in accordance with the convenience of the tax-payers.

Roscher said that the king had certain rights. He had the right to line up his people, to own property which had no owner, to own newly-discovered property, to receive fines and to share booty. The state could receive compensation for its services and authorisation.

Much of physiocratic system is concerned with taxation. It said that agriculture can only produce *produit net* (surplus). Therefore, only agriculture should be taxed. Quesnay calculated that the amount of taxes should be (approximately) 33% of the total income from agriculture. If the tax is shifted from the landlord class to any other class, it would reduce the working capital of farm or industry which would reduce the income of the nation. Tax (single) on agriculture set a natural value upon the tax and prevented arbitrary taxation. A single tax on agriculture (*impot unique*) provided an ample source of direct taxation, and many of the physiocrats distributed indirect taxation. The single tax was an aspect of natural order in the society.

Montesquieu, a contemporary of physiocrats, relied heavily on progressive taxation. He said that the necessaries of life should not be taxed; but on consumption above the necessaries, a graduated scale of taxation should be set. Luxuries should be heavily taxed.

Adam Smith expressed his ideas on taxation through some canons which, of course, were not original to smith, but which were already discussed by Justi. Adam Smith had the following canons of taxation: (1) canon of ability, (2) canon of certainty, (3) canon of convenience and (4) canon of economy. He acknowledged the fact that all taxes should be derived from income but observed that tax on wages and profit was difficult, and would affect industry and trade. Like physiocrats, he held the idea that a tax on rent was a good tax. He said that taxes on lands, cultivated by the owners, should be lower than the taxes on land owned by absentee landlords.

Thomas Paine observed that taxes on house and windows, etc., should be abolished. Taxes should be paid for increasing public goods and social benefit. Instead of indirect tax, he said that the principle of luxury taxation should be applied to incomes. He proposed a system of graduated taxes on income.

The classical economists were preoccupied with the question of incidence of taxation. According to Ricardo, taxes are a portion of the produce of land and labour of the country, placed at the disposal of the government; and are always paid out of capital or from the revenue of the country. Taxes paid from revenue were better than taxes paid from capital—the latter destroyed the productive efficiency. On incidence, Ricardo made the following observations: tax on raw materials falls on consumers but will diminish profit, land tax falls on landlords, taxes on profit fall on consumers and on wages fall on capitalists. Taxes on houses are partly paid by the occupier and partly by the landlord. However, the Recardian theory of rent became the basis for the revival of the single tax system. Smith and Ricardo both looked upon taxation on the basis of humanitarian philosophy. They advocated a more equitable distribution of wealth through taxation. They hated indirect taxation as it fell on the poor.

John Stuart Mill advocated changes in taxation in order to bring about social reform. He suggested a limitation upon the amount which anyone might inherit through inheritance. He suggested the confiscation of the unearned income in land values, and gradual nationalisation of land through a tax on increase in valuation. Inheritance tax was formally mentioned by Bentham, then by Thomas Paine and later on by J.S. Mill.

Saint Simon attempted to use inheritance as a means of transferring ownership from individuals to the state. The state should spend the amount collected from inheritance for increasing capital and productivity in the economy.

Marxian theory of taxation is not original. He suggested several types of taxation in *The Communist Manifesto*. First, the abolition of all private property in land; second, graduated income tax; third, abolition of all inheritance.

The theory of taxation has been made elaborate in recent years by a number of economists, *e.g.*, Seligman, Ursula Hicks, Due, Musgrave, etc. The amount of taxation in every country has increased considerably. Such an increase has two purposes—to bring about an equality in the distribution of income and wealth and to collect money for meeting mounting state expenditure. Taxes are increasing in both depth and range and a number of taxes have been and are being devised, *e.g.*, payroll taxes, processing taxes, undistributed profit tax, expenditure tax, wealth tax, gift and a host of other taxes. In underdeveloped countries taxes are designed more and more to regulate the economy and to feed the process of capital formation. The introduction of a number of indirect taxes in recent years in different countries could not, however, be avoided. The modern trend is to diversify the tax structure by suitably adjusting the income and substitution effects of taxes.

VII. DEVELOPMENT OF THE THEORY OF MONEY, CREDIT AND BANKING

Adam Smith observed that money originated as a counterpart of specialisation. It arose to remove the inconvenience of the barter system which had many disadvantages and limitations. However, money was explained in ancient times in terms of mortality. The Mosaic code forbade the lending of money at interest. Wealth gained by trade was thought to be unstable and tainted. But when trade increased, the restrictions went away. When trade and commerce increased, money became indispensable as a medium of exchange and as a standard of value, both for the present and future.

Aristotle believed that to lend money at interest was wrong. This was so because money could not reproduce itself. Aristotle realised first that money was a commodity, and as such, it was subject to all fluctuations in value as all other commodities. But Aristotle believed that the value of money was more constant. Money had no natural value, but its value is created by law. Money is a danger to Aristotle, because its possession leads to speculation. In thomas Aquinas, one can find the influence of religious teaching. Money and trade were necessary, but were spiritually dangerous since they led to the search for wealth for its own sake. Like Aristotle, Aquinas believed that money was barren and interest was an unjust payment. Prices were the money expressions for fair value, or as Aquinas put it, the value of a man's labour according to his station in life.

In spite of opposition and legal restrictions, trade increased considerably, and as a consequence of it, the demand for money, as early as in the 13th century. In the Middle Ages, the growth of trade and commerce led to the rapid growth of money lending institutions and of bills of exchange. Lack of a common unit made the function of the money-changer important. Two types of money were in circulation—one having full gold value and the other having part of the gold value. The people began to hold good money and spend bad money. As Gresham stated: bad money drives good money out of circulation. But although Gresham did not originate this principle, yet it was commonly known as Gresham's Law.

Mercantilism thought wealth consisted of money. The mercantilist writers pointed the importance of money in trade, commerce, defence and development. They thought that more money circulation increased the price level and stimulated trade. Money was also considered the sinews of war. However, John Law pointed out that the state, instead of depending upon favourable balance of trade to maintain its supply of money, might keep the supply of bullion intact, and issue paper money for domestic transactions. He created a bank in France for the issue of paper money and was responsible for bringing a period of unprecedented inflation. Similarly, Vanderlint was in favour of increased circulation of paper currency, and Misselden was in favour of rising prices for the growth of trade.

Petty advocated that the creation of a bank can make up the deficiencies by means of credit. He thought that quantity of money in circulation affected prices. Hume's exposition of the fallacies of bullionist proposition and his advocacy of automatic regulation of the flow of money is even now important. Hume believed that there is a direct and equal relationship between the quantity of money and the price level.

Adam Smith thought money as a medium of exchange and as a measure of value; but he did not think that money had any value in itself. Money being a commodity, the regulation of it had to be done on the basis of necessity. If a greater quantity of money is available than what is required by domestic trade, the excess would be used for making purchases abroad. He thought that the value of paper money was an aid to economic development. Ricardo believed that monetary instability was the effect of poorly-regulated paper currency. He believed that paper money should be substituted for coin but observed that the amount of paper currency should be reduced to conform to the quantity of specie. Ricardo believed that the value of money is also influenced by its cost of production. He suggested 100% gold reserve for the issue of bank notes, and was in favour of state regulation of banking policy. J.S. Mill had observed that the value of money could be affected both by its quantity with rapidity of circulation, and by its cost of production. Mill said that their law of supply and demand operated more quickly on money than on any other commodity.

The idea on the quantity theory of money, i.e., the effect of money circulation on the price level, was considered by Bodin, Locke, Hume etc. Irving Fisher is the best exponent, in modern times, of the quantity theory. His equation is $PT = MV + M'V'$ (P = price, M = quantity of metal money, V = Velocity of metal money, M' = volume of bank deposits, V' = its velocity, T = transaction). This means that the price level is equal to the quantity of money and bank deposit multiplied by their velocities, divided by the number of transactions. Gustav Cassel explained the recent price changes in terms of quantity of money. He believed that fluctuations in gold supply also led to the fluctuations in the price level. Changes in prices were in direct ratio to the variation of the additional gold supply.

In classical economics, money was only a medium of exchange; it had no other important function. Money was a *veil*. The real factors were more important than the monetary factors. But Keynes observed that money is not a veil; it has a positive role to play. It had no substitute, and it is a link between the past and the present. Money has an important liquidity function and has always a market. Keynes did not accept the fact that quantity of money had a direct bearing on the price level. He said that higher money supply lowers the rate of interest which increases investment and consequently income, output and employment increase, and prices increase as a result of increase in the cost of production. He emphasised more on the dynamic role and the store of value function of money. Keynes integrated the theory of money with the theory of value, whereas in classical economics, these were kept separate.

In recent years Prof. Milton Friedman reformulated the quantity theory of money. Quantity theory, according to him, is a theory of the demand for money, and not of output, money income or prices. Since money is a capital good, its demand is a problem in capital theory. His application to the monetary theory of the basic principle of capital theory is the most important development in monetary theory since Keynes's *General Theory*.

Petty and North both advocated the formation of the Bank of England. Bank of England was formed (1694) to lend money to the government ; but the ideas of note issue and commercial credit were scarcely known in the 17th century. The function of the Amsterdam Exchange Bank was mainly the local manufacture of international coinage. The immediate effect of the organisation of the Bank of England was the stabilisation of public finance; but the long-run effect was serious inflation. Ricardo outlined the accurate conservative banking practices of his time. But uncertain economic conditions and continuous warfare upset the normal banking procedures. There arose a controversy regarding money, credit and currency. The currency school advocated the adherence to a metallic standard of paper money; whereas the banking school believed that both paper money and credit can be regulated without governmental interference by economic processes themselves. But government regulation continued after all.

An important deviation from the classical theory of money appeared in the writings of the historical school. German economists denied that the value of money was related to the use value of the metal of which it was made. They believed that the value of money was an act of the state. The classical economists believed in the automatic monetary control but the recent states are in favour of managed currency.

The socialist ideas on money were different. Owen wanted to get rid of profit, and this, he said, could be done by eliminating metallic money. He wanted to introduce labour notes expressing labour hours as the unit of currency which could be exchanged for purchasing commodities. Proudhon was in favour of establishing an exchange bank for issuing paper money. His idea of an exchange bank has been incorporated into modern cooperative and credit societies.

In the Marxian theory of money, two things are important: *(i)* the use of money as capital, *(ii)* the relationship of money to the working of labour theory of value and surplus labour. Marx did not condemn money; but in the way which Marx proposed, there was no necessity of money or credit. Since the state owned and managed all industries, there was no need for credit.

In the early days of the USSR, Lenin, however, found that the absence of money was really an obstacle. Therefore, at the time of New Economic Policy (NEP), money was reintroduced. The use of money in recent years has increased rather than decreased.

An attempt to do away with money was made through the introduction of scrip payment and social credit during the Great Depression of the thirties. But these schemes were devised as a temporary adjustment to meet an emergency and credit. As a measuring rod, *i.e., numeraire,* the use of money can perhaps never be discontinued.

VIII. DEVELOPMENT OF THE THEORY OF FOREIGN TRADE

Trade never ceased in the static period of the Middle Ages. In the 15th, 16th, 17th centuries, trade was carried on mainly in the form of monopoly. Mercantilism placed great emphasis on trade and commerce. The mercantilist philosophy was to maximise export and minimise import, and thereby to procure silver, gold and other precious metals through favourable balance of trade. Under mercantilism, trade and commerce received the favours of the government, while agriculture was left alone to seek its own survival. Colonies were treated as markets, and duties on imports, restrictions to the export of gold and great trading monopolies were the features of every nation which followed mercantilism. Misselden, a great exponent of mercantilism, believed that once the trade balance between two nations is known, it was the duty of the government to take proper measures for securing a favourable balance of trade. The best mercantilist ideas can be found in Thomas Mun's writings. The main points of economic programme of mercantilism, according to Mun, can be described as below:

(i) Wastelands should be cultivated so that the imports of certain commodities can be curtailed.

(ii) The imports of foreign wares can be curtailed, if people refrain from their consumption.

   (iii) England can supply wares to foreign countries at high rates, if
          they cannot get them elsewhere, and at low rates, if they can
          get them elsewhere.
   (iv)   Commodities should be supplied by England's own ships.
    (v)   More should be exported; the poor should be employed.
   (vi)   Fishing industry should develop in the adjacent seas.
   (vii) England should be developed into a distributing centre.
   (viii) England should develop trade relations with far-off countries.
   (ix)   In certain cases, it is beneficial to export money.
    (x)   Manufactures of foreign materials should be allowed to be ex-
          ported free.
   (xi)   England must make the best of its own in the matter of foreign
          trade.

However, apart from Mun, Petty emphasised the monetary aspect of foreign trade, and Child stressed the need to lower the rate of interest. However, Coke, Barbon and Davenant criticised the mercantilist doctrine. Mercantilism was opposed to free trade and was in favour of protection, while Petty, Locke and North laid the foundations for the revolutionary doctrine of free trade.

Quesnay considered commerce as unproductive. The gain made by the merchants was at the cost of agriculture which alone could produce wealth. Physiocrats thought that mere exchange of wealth was not the same as the creation of wealth. According to physiocrats, foreign trade is a liability and protection is against the natural order, and, therefore, free trade should be utilised as a matter of policy.

Hume denied that the wealth of nations was dependent upon the accumulation of bullion. Hume supported the idea of territorial division of labour and opposed any artificial barriers to trade.

Adam Smith was a great exponent of free trade doctrine. But his ideas were not new. A large part of *The Wealth of Nations* is devoted to an attack upon the principle of mercantilism. He showed how each nation would be far better-off economically by concentrating on the thing it could do best. Free competition in foreign trade is best for the individuals as well as for the nations. But Smith did not think absolute free trade position to be pragmatic. He said that in times of necessity, government might regulate foreign trade. However, Smith had the idea that the opportunities for trade were practically unlimited, if government privileges and legal restrictions were removed. J.B. Say remarked that trade was really an exchange of goods for goods: every supply of goods gave rise to demand. Trade could be increased if supply of goods increased in nations, and an over-supply of goods is generally impossible.

Ricardo developed the theory of comparative cost in the matter of foreign trade. He stated that a nation would do its best to produce the articles for trade in which it has comparative advantage. He said that imports could be sometimes profitable to a nation even though the nation could produce the imported articles at a lower cost at home, provided the same amount of labour could produce more value in the export front than is sacrificed by importing the dearer commodities. J.S. Mill said that the values of export must be equal to the values of import. Therefore, comparative cost method of exchange is limited. Ricardo and Mill held that complete specialisation may not always be attained by a country.

Bastiat advocated the adoption of free trade as a government policy. But Von Thunen had serious doubt, like Adam Smith, about an absolute free trade position. However, all the classical economists did not support free trade.

The important economists who were against free trade policy were List, Muller and Rae. List supported protection on the basis of his theories of economic nationalism and of productive power. He said that protection should never be granted to agriculture, but should be granted to those industries which are infant and which are necessary for national development. He never suggested protection as a permanent economic policy.

Ohlin in 1933 made the basis of modern theory of international trade. He depended on the general equilibrium theory to deal with exchange between different regions within a single country, or between different countries. According to Ohlin, the immediate cause of inter-regional trade is the inequality in the relative commodity prices. Differences in the relative scarcities of the factors of production give rise to dissimilar scales of relative commodity prices. The relative price differences are translated into absolute price differences upon the establishment of a rate of exchange. However, the rate of exchange and the value of inter-regional commodity trade are determined by reciprocal demand.

Be that as it may, international trade not only tends to equalise commodity prices, but also factors prices; and inter-regional mobility of factors of production also tends to bring about an equalisation of factor prices.

However, foreign trade is a two-way traffic. One country cannot always try to generate foreign trade surplus at the cost of other nations. This idea is expressed in modern times through the dictum of "beggar-thy-neighbour-policy," which ultimately leads to retaliation. An important aspect of modern discussion on foreign trade is carried on in terms of trade between developed and underdeveloped nations. While the developed countries are interested in maintaining the level of employment and in searching out markets in underdeveloped countries, the backward countries are interested in achieving development and higher level of income and employment. The lagging nations are increasingly engaged in export-promotion and import-substitution for capital formation. Underdeveloped nations are deriving a lot of advantage from foreign trade and aid. But Myrdal and Prebisch demonstrate that foreign trade is going more and more against the backward nations. International trade is producing strong *backwash effect* on underdeveloped countries. The colonial heritage is still generating unfavourable circular causation against the low-income countries. Thus, the trend, as has been predicted by Mydral, is towards a new theory of international trade for the under-developed countries.

Part Seven

Post Script

21
Some Topical Notes

(I) : A NOTE ON THE MEANING OF POLITICAL ECONOMY

The term, political economy, was first used by Antonine Montchrestien (1575-1621). After Antonine, Sir James Stuart elaborated the meaning and nature of political economy in his book, *Inquiry into the Principles of Political Economy (1767)*. In the beginning of the classical period, Adam Smith analysed the meaning and nature of political economy in his book, *Wealth of Nations* (book IV) which was published in 1776. According to Adam Smith, political economy describes the actual working of the economy (positive aspect) and the also the way the economy should work (normative aspect). However, as a matter of fact, political economy consists of more of prescription than of description. It analyses the economic effects of political actions and political effects of economic actions.

Political economy signifies the rule of state management. What *economy* is to family, political economy is to state. In the past, the term political economy was virtually equivalent to public administration. Adam Smith referred to political economy as a branch of the system of civil government. It was essentially concerned with public policy. Political economy in the olden days, was generally understood to include both analysis and policy prescription, and Lord Robbins does not, therefore, consider political economy as scientific economics. Schumpeter explained political economy as an exposition of a comprehensive set of economic policies that its author advocates on the strength of certain unifying normative principles. In modern times, however, political economy is conceptualised as a subject studying *power relations,* particularly with respect to distribution problem.

Political economy came to assume the role of an independent discipline in the 17th century, but it became more prominent since the time of 18th century enlightenment. In the 17th century, a shift of emphasis was evident from the process of circulation (of money and commodities) to the process of production. With the abandonment of treating circulation as the principal source of wealth, ways were opened for the development of political economy in a new manner. The true scientific definition of political economy was provided by Karl Marx and Friedrich Engels. According to them, the process of production is a contradictory unity of two relations :

(i) relation between man and nature. This relationship is such that man
through nature tries to fulfil the human needs, *(ii)* the relations of production. This latter relation constitutes the subject matter of political
economy. Political economy studies production relations in terms of their
inter connections with the contemporary development of productive forces, as dictated by history.

Thus, political economy can be regarded as a subject which studies
the social relations that evolve between different classes of people in the
course of production, distribution, exchange and consumption. In a sense,
political economy is a class science or a science dealing with class relations.
Marxian political economy discovered contradictions in capitalism, which
would be responsible for its decay. Political economy uncovers the true nature of class relations and conflicts. To Lenin, political economy is the
science of the developing historical systems of social production. Leninist
political economy is dialectical materialism which is concerned with the
development of a society. Classical political economy, particularly Marxian
political economy, analyses the growth and decay of capitalism and also the
laws governing the new social order. However, it should be noted that
political economy studies not only the capitalist system but other systems
too. According to Engels, political economy is the science of laws governing the production and the exchange of the material means of subsistence
in human society. The idea is the same as of Adam Smith and Ricardo.
Smith, however, emphasised production aspect of the economy, and Ricardo distribution, but both of them studied the problem of surplus for the
purpose of economic growth. In fact, the main question concerning the
classical political economy was the question of economic growth (the
wealth of nations). In analysing the process of production and distribution,
the classical economists discovered class conflict in the society.

Marx and Engels developed a historical approach to the study of
political economy. Such an analysis purported to reveal the laws of
economic life. These economic laws express the essential aspects of
production relations and their inter-connection with the productive forces.
The economic laws are objective in character and work independently of
human volition and will. As against the historical laws, economic laws are
not historical in character. These laws will be different under different
socio-economic conditions and under different modes of production.
Economic laws are specific to one particular social formation and express
the essence of relations of the given mode of production. Marxian political
economy provides different economic laws to deal with different socio-
economic conditions. Political economy studies the effects of various
socio-econo-political changes on the production and distribution systems
of an economy. In such a system of study, economics is not separated from
politics and vice versa.

Sometimes, political economy is wrongly defined as the study of relations between man and nature. However, these relations are studied by a

number of other subjects. It is also not a science of scarce things. In fact, it is not the scarcity of goods that characterises the contemporary economic system, rather, it is the relative over-production which leads to enormous unproductive consumption that slows down growth and gives rise to militarisation of the economy. A considerable proportion of our resources is being devoted to the production of destructive weapons. With the development of social production, the scarce goods can be made easily reproducible. This may lead to progress and the growth of wealth of nations. But the main bottleneck is the absence of suitable production relations.

A given mode of distribution, often, depends on the given mode of production. Distribution depends on the social relations under which production takes place and, also on the social forms of production i.e., who owns the means of production. As a matter of fact, production, distribution, exchange and consumption are different parts of a single whole that is social reproduction. Political economy views the social reproduction as an integrated form of production, distribution, exchange and consumption, and seeks to provide solution to the contemporary problem.

Political economy emphasises interdependence of production, technical and institutional structures. Unlike the old paradigm, it does not emphasize market so much as the structure and the working of a system and its failure. It studies the factors that are responsible for the working or breakdown of the system. It, thus, analyses the system of production and of social relations surrounding production. The new vision of political economy deals with the question of introducing certain new changes which often alter the parameters of the system or even the level of consciousness of the society. In the new paradigm, unlike the old, markets are not supposed to be naturally stable.

Political economy is very wide in scope as it deals with political, economic, social, cultural and ethical factors. The new vision of political economy adopts a picture of the relation between production and distribution, which is quite distinct from the one that ruled the economist's roost since the marginal revolution. It observes that factors of production do not receive their rewards on the basis of their marginal productivities and that all factors are not treated on equal footing. Thus, there is scope for injustice, exploitation and class struggle. This was neglected by neo-classical economics which predicted a harmony of interests among the various classes. As a matter of fact, Marxian political economy maintains that property and power are essential elements in class struggle. This vision of political economy takes into account the importance of ideological influence on actions and policies. However, whereas the Marxian political economy emphasises the ownership of means of production as the source of power, Chicago school of political economy puts more faith on the ability to control as the source of power.

According to the new paradigm of political economy (Marxian Political Economy), distributions should not be regarded as the species of exchange. It maintains that capital goods rather than capital contributes to production. The orthodox economists altogether ignored the fact of technological interdependences and institutional relationships. In the analysis of political economy, income distribution interacts with all economic variables, not just with factor market. Political economy takes into account market power, financial prowess, state machinery, ability to use laws, bargaining strength and so on in analysing the responsiveness of the market and hence, in the matter of wage and price adjustments. The orthodox economics makes a mistake by treating income distribution as a form of exchange, and hence, it misinterprets the way the system works.

Orthodox economics (neo-classical economics) tries to show that market allocates scarce resources according to relative efficiency; political economics tries to show that market distributes income according to relative power. Orthodox economics neglects the nexus between capital and social class, and between social class and economic power. Political economy is clearly more realistic and more capable of handling questions connected with property, social class formation and social valuation and development. It is concerned more with development than with growth, more with distribution than with production and more with disequilibrium than with equilibrium.

Needless to add, for successful theorising in economics, one needs an integration of human behaviour with product behaviour. It is exactly here that political economy comes to play its decisive role. It provides the key to development by taking into account the social and economic relations in production. It is not sufficient to know to how much to produce but it is more important to know what to produce and how to produce. It is also necessary to know the socio-politico-economic factors that are associated with production. This is helpful for comprehending the contemporary problems and finding out their solutions. Owing to its comprehensive nature of studying and identifying a problem, it is found to be more appropriate for tackling many of our contemporary ills and issues. This is the reason why after its prolonged hibernation during the period of neoclassical economics, it is being resurrected in our times. The present day economics has been witnessing a complete resurrection and revival of political economy (See Edward Nell's Paper in Robin Blackburn (Ed.), *Ideology in Social Science,* Fontana, 1975).

(II) : SALIENT FEATURES OF CLASSICAL POLITICAL ECONOMY

Political Economy is concerned with the study of economic effects of political actions and political effects of economic actions. Political economy consists of both normative and positive analyses. Classical economics is based on the study of political economic aspects of a country. Adam Smith's book analyses the working of an economic system in such a way that certain policy prescriptions can be made for the improvement of the economy. Almost all the classical economists analysed the political economy but there were minute differences in their analyses. However, in spite of the differences, certain common pattern can be noticed in their writings.[1]

The classical political economy was concerned mainly with the question of *economic growth*. The classical question can be formulated in terms of the wealth of nations. In fact, Adam Smith's *Wealth of Nations* is an essay on economic growth and development. All the classical economists agreed on the necessity of generation of *surplus* for the purpose of economic development. The Mercantilist writers also emphasised the need for the generation of surplus for the purpose of economic growth. However, the Mercantilist's thought that surplus could be generated by exporting more and importing less and also by buying in the cheapest market and selling in the dearest market. In the same way, the Physiocrats also thought of generating surplus from the agricultural sector which was the only productive sector, according to them. Since the classical economists were concerned with the problem of generation of surplus, they paid their attention to the problem of accumulation.

Adam Smith concentrated on the problem of material or real basis of production through which surplus can be generated in the economy. For this purpose, Smith relied much on the division of labour, both internal as well as international. According to Smith, free trade can be very helpful for the accumulation of surplus for development.

According to Ricardo, surplus is originated in production. The fact that surplus is originated in production has remained the principal basis of classical political economy. However,Marx observed that while surplus originated in production, it could be realised through circulation. The classical political economy is production-oriented : it neglected the demand side (consumption). The production aspect of the economy, as Marx pointed out, was analysed in a systematic manner by the Physiocrats, who depicted the interdependence in the economic system. Adam Smith emphasised that production can be regarded as the permanent source of surplus and commerce cannot certainly supplant the place of production. In his system *profit,* apart from *rent,* was a distinct type of surplus. The productivity of labour and capital provides the basic source for the generation of surplus and the employment of labour.

Income Distribution and Class Conflict

The distribution of surplus became very important with Ricardo. In fact, Ricardo pointed out that the basic purpose of political economy is to analyse the distributive shares. Ricardo was concerned with the study of

1. See, B.N. Ghosh, *Political Economy : A Marxist Approach,* Macmillan, 1990, and Krishna Bhardwaj, *Classical Political Economy and Rise to Dominance of Supply and Demand Theories,* Universities Press, Hyderabad, 1986.

relation between different distributive shares. In his analysis of distribution, Ricardo found the genesis of class conflict. Firstly, he recognised the conflict between the landlord and the rest of the society. This conflict has to be understood with reference to Corn Laws. When the price of corn was very high in England, Ricardo suggested the import of corn in order to reduce its price in the domestic market. This suggestion of Ricardo was not accepted by the landlord class because that will tantamount to reduction in rent (rent depends on price). This debate dominated the British Parliament around 1815. The divergence of the interests on the issue of import of corn was an example of class antagonism. It was not a conflict between rich and the poor but between the land-owning class and the land-less class. In course of this debate, the views of Ricardo regarding value, distribution and accumulation became very clear. Ricardo put forward the view that rent does not enter into price rather price determines rent. He was of the opinion that if rent is taxed, production will not be affected. While Ricardo was against the rentier class, Malthus was a pro-rentier. Malthus himself was a landlord. Ricardo made it very clear in his *Essay on Profit* that the interest of the landlord class was essentially opposed to the interest of the rest of the society. Secondly, Ricardo analysed the class conflict between the capitalists and the labourers. This was explained by him through his theory of distribution where he showed that whatever increases wages will decrease profit. The inverse relationship between wage and profit is the basic starting point for capital-labour conflict. The rising cost of production of corn led to higher wages (money wages) and as a result, there would be a tendency for the rate of profit to fall. When the price of corn rose, the landlords gain because they receive higher rents, but the capitalists will lose, as the rate of profit will fall. The position of the labourer will also not be very comfortable because although the money wages go up, the real wage remains constant, but there is the possibility of shrinkage of employment consequent on the adverse effect on accumulation. The question of class conflict became one of the central points in the classical political economy, particularly with the later classical writers. The more complete analysis of class conflict was provided by Karl Marx in his analysis of capitalist economy.

Theory of Value

In the process of analysis of *surplus,* the classical writers confronted the question of relative price or exchange value. Adam Smith analysed relative price for the quantification of surplus and also for comparison of the magnitudes of surplus over different time periods and for different countries. Smith observed that market prices are too inadequate to measure the *real* magnitude of surplus. He was pre-occupied for finding an invariant standard. In this connection, he suggested two methods: labour-embodied method and labour-commanded method. The proper method of measurement must have a strict relation to exchange value. According to him, for a crude state of society, where labour is the only factor of production, labour embodied measure can be a satisfactory method. However, for a civilised society where output is produced by many factors of production, he recommended the use of labour-commanded measure as the correct method.

Ricardo criticised Adam Smith on this point. He said that it was not an invariable standard. Therefore, the question of labour measure could not be settled very satisfactorily by Adam Smith. But Smith analysed the three components of value, namely, wage, profit and rent as appropriate constituents for a multi-sector economy. It becomes pretty clear from Adam Smith's value analysis that Smith never used labour-commanded as a cause of value : it is always used as a measure. In Smith's schema, labour is not the only source or determinant of value. However, there appears apparently a confusion between the cause of value and the measure of value in Smith's analysis.

Ricardo was much more deeply concerned with the question of determination of exchange value. He observed that labour-embodied measure is the nearest approximation to truth for measuring the exchange value. He resolved the whole cost of production (natural price) into labour terms. Ricardo had, as Stigler says, a 93% labour theory of value. Ricardo, unlike Smith, did not include rent in the cost of production. Ricardo ultimately devised the labour-content measure for converting and measuring all commodities in terms of the common labour-content units. Ricardo, however, pointed out that relative price can be influenced by the changes in the distribution of income (i.e. in wages and profits).

Political Economy is the study of the nature and causes of wealth; but Ricardo thought that it should be regarded as an inquiry into the laws which govern the distribution of national product among different classes. Thus, while Smith emphasised production, Ricardo emphasised distribution as the more significant aspect of political economy. Ricardo found two inverse relations in distribution : *(i)* given wages, rent and profit are inversely related and *(ii)* wages and profits are also inversely related. Malthus opposed Ricardo by saying that in a multi-commodity system, where many factors are responsible for the determination of profit, no such inverse relations as Ricardo formulated, could hold good, and hence, class conflict is not so inevitable. Given the technique of production, price rise may allow the rise of all factor income.

When wages change, prices change and profits also change. But what governs the changes in relative prices when wages change? The answer lies in the theory of value. Ricardo adhered to the labour-embodied theory of value. Ricardo wanted to show that in a competitive economy where there is a tendency towards equality of rate of wage and also equality of rate of profit, *(i)* surplus was located in production and not in circulation and *(ii)* class conflict was inevitable. Malthus agreed to differ from both these views of Ricardo.

Marx carried forward the classical theories of value and distribution but with distinctly different notions, although they were based on the classical *surplus approach.* Marx was concerned more with the form and manner in which surplus is generated, appropriated and distributed under different modes of production. He analysed the competitive capitalist mode of production and the class conflict between labour and capital, and predicted that owing to the inherent contradictions in capitalism, it will ultimately break down. In a capitalist economy, wages are taken as determined by historical and social forces and surplus is distributed in such a way as to yield the same rate of profit. It is to be noted that Marx found that labour values differed from prices under capitalism. Therefore, he sought to transform the values into prices of production (Transformation problem).

There is no gain-saying the fact that classical political economy was essentially based on the labour theory of value but why? *(i)* Because measure of value and *(ii)* all means of production could be reduced to labour units.

In the classical political economy, social output levels and techniques of production are given. There is explicit predominance of production relations pervading all through, and competition brings about uniformity in the rate of real wage and in the rate of profit. Once the level of real wage is specified, the rate of price and of profit can be uniquely determined.

The classicals made two distinctions in the value domain : *(i)* absolute value and relative value and *(ii)* natural price and normal price. The pricing process was dichotomised. Absolute price was determined in the money market independently of product market and relative price was determined in the product market independent of money market. These two prices were separated and also the markets. This was an invalid dichotomy which Patinkin has tried to remove by introducing *real balance effect* and the process of *Tatonnement.* The natural price is long run cost-determined. The relative price and the market price are determined in the product market through the influence of demand and supply. The theory of demand and supply could not be elaborated by the classical political economy. It became the burden of the neoclassical economics to develop this theory in greater detail.

The basic features of classical political economy can now be presented in a summarised form :

Firstly, according to the classical economists, the basic problem in an economy is the removal of poverty. Therefore, it is necessary to initiate the process of economic growth so that the wealth of the nation can be increased. For economic growth, it is necessary to generate *surplus.* The accumulated surplus can be invested for increasing employment, income and output of a nation.

Secondly, the classical political economy is concerned with aggregative economics or what is called *macroeconomics,* like the study of income, output and employment situation of the economy. It studies the macro dynamic aspects of different variables like, profit, rent, wage and so on inter-temporally. These variables are studied with reference to economic progress.

Thirdly, in the classical system, *value concept* has been brought in to convert the heterogenous goods that compose the entire system into something that is homogeneous. A measure of value becomes essential, and value is conceived as a magnitude and not simply as a ratio. It is essential to know the *equivalence* so that the values of the aggregate production of commodities can be precisely known.

Fourthly, the classical political economy takes into account the existence of *different classes in the society,* like working class, capitalist class, rentier class and so on. The main objective of the classical theory of distribution is to show how the total output is distributed among these classes. The classical economists also demonstrated the possibilities of class conflict between : *(i)* labour and capital, and *(ii)* Landlords and the rest of the society, particularly, the peasants.

Lastly, the classical political economy can be regarded as a set of *policy-oriented economic doctrine.* It formulated definite policies against trade restrictions, against corn laws and so on.

However, it must be admitted that any good system of economic theory is ultimately concerned with the formulation of a suitable set of pragmatic policies. The classical political economy was not an exception in this regard.

(III) : SALIENT FEATURES OF NEOCLASSICAL ECONOMICS

Neoclassical economics came into being in 1870s. Its founders were Carl Menger, Wieser, Bohm Bawerk, Jevons, Walras, Clark, Marshall and Pigou. It was started as a reaction to classical Ricardinism and Marxism.[2] It formulated certain rules for the optimal regime for managing capitalist enterprises under competition and determine the principles of economic equilibrium in this system. Neoclassical economics is concerned with micro perspective of the economy, and as such, is interested in the *relative prices.* It aims at maximising various objective functions for various groups of people, e.g., consumers, producers and so on. Neoclassical economics tried to analyse profit maximization and the like through the method of general equilibrium. Neoclassical economics is based on a number assumptions, the important among which are the following :

(i) Individual consumer maximises utility;

(ii) Individual producer maximises profit;

2. See, B.N. Ghosh, *Political Economy : A Marxist Approach,* Macmillan, 1990,; Krishna Bhardwaj, Op. Cit., ; Rowthron's Paper in *Social Scientist* (1973), and Resnick and Wolff's Paper in *Monthly Review,* Dec., 1984.

(iii) Man maximises his pleasures and minimises pain (hedonism). People try to buy in the cheapest market and sell in the dearest market (economic man : *homoeconomicus).*

(iv) Value is a subjective phenomenon based on the concept of marginal utility.

(v) There is full employment in the labour market.

(vi) Money is 'Veil'. It does not serve any real purpose; it is simply a medium of exchange.

(vii) The incomes of the factors of production are equal to their respective marginal productivities. So, there is no exploitation or class conflict. There is complete harmony of interests among different classes of people.

(viii) There are constant returns to scale.

(ix) Human beings are rational and have the endowments to produce the required things

Neoclassical economists assumed the idealist form of a pure economy regardless of the social form or mode of production. In such a pure economy, everybody pursued his self-centered interests to maximise the objective functions. The market is free and fully competitive and the institutions are also free in every respect. Market imperfections are identified and removed. According to the neoclassicals, the classical labour theory of value was one-sided and Marxian solution to transform values into prices was not satisfactory[3]. Therefore, they put forward an alternative approach to value based on the novel theory of *marginal utility*. Thus, value was regarded as a subjective category. The same principle of *margin* was extended for the determination of factor prices. It was stated to by J.B. Clark that marginal productivity of a factor determines its remuneration. Marginal apparatus was extensively used by the neo-classical writers.

The neo-classical theory of value and price formation found its fullest expression in the writings of Alfred Marshall who was the leader of this school. The neoclassical theory advanced a theory of general equilibrium which stated that the mechanism of free competition was supposed to ensure not only the just distribution of income but also an optimal allocation of resources. Neoclassical economics advocated the supremacy of *market* and free competition. The theory served as the basis for the internal stability of the capitalist system. Marshall's real contribution was to make a synthesis between the supply-side theory of value put forward by the classicists and the demand side theory of value put forward by the marginalists. So, the neoclassical period witnessed the emergence of *Demand-Supply Theory of Value* (K. Bharadwaj).

---

3. It must be stated that both Ricardo and Marx found that prices do not always equal values, and both of them confronted with difficulties in translating propositions relating to labour values to those in terms of prices. Sraffa tried to bypass the problem through the construction of an invariant standard in terms of which the distributive relations can be directly known even without facing the complications of price variations. (See, Krishna Bhardwaj, Op. Cit., p. 21, fn. 26).

The neo-classical theory working through the forces of demand and supply had a few far-reaching implications, e.g. : *(i)* opportunity for justice through the operation of impersonal market forces *(ii)* possibility of pursuing self-interest unobstructed *(iii)* the concept of class was relegated to the background, and individuals emerged as free decision-making units *(iv)* different distributive classes were considered as symmetrical and equal. All these suggested not simply the reconstruction but truly speaking, a radical re-orientation of classical political economy. The pivotal role of the classical concept of surplus was replaced by the focal significance of pricing or analysis of relative prices. The classical notion of absolute value was completely abandoned. The discussion of the concept of surplus was placed in the theory of welfare economics. Neoclassical theory brought a symmetry among the distributive classes. It also introduced a symmetry between demand and supply by giving them a balanced treatment for the determination of value. Neoclassical economics, thus, appeared to be in many ways the economics of symmetry (K. Bhardwaj). The new theory found a harmonious cooperation among the various distributive classes. The theory of price subsumed the theory of distribution in the sense that both product and factor prices were explained by the same construct, demand and supply (the Marshallian cross). The general theory of relative prices became a significant signal for all the economic activities.

Neoclassicism is essentially a subjectivist or individualist approach. Society is explained in terms of the constituent individuals. In this system, production is regarded as a natural process or social process of transforming inputs into outputs which are exchanged freely in the market. There is the primacy of market.

As has already been pointed out, neoclassical economics is equilibrium economics which will ensure stability and full employment. It is a self-regulating system. Deviations from equilibrium can, of course, create instability and unemployment. In the matter of production function analysis with reference to equilibrium, the neoclassical theory assumes constant returns to scale and uniformly diminishing marginal productivity of factors of production. All these will ensure an unique equilibrium position which will ensure factor income according to marginal productivity. This factor income or reward is equal to the disutility or sacrifice made by the factor in the production process.

Neoclassical economics postulates that it is not necessary for the workers to organise themselves at work place to improve their economic positions. Redistribution of wealth and income can be done by means of fiscal instruments like taxation. But distribution should not destroy incentives and state action should not jeopardise individual freedom.

Critical Appraisal

(1) In the neoclassical theory, relations among social classes do not enter the analysis of production. Production is regarded simply as the out-

come of market decision of individual producers. This view is not realistic. They have neglected social relations and class relations.

(2) The neoclassical theory could not provide a theoretical basis for building up a coherent account of the broad movements of the real economy.

(3) Neoclassical theory is micro-based theory; it neglected the consideration for macroeconomic analyses. Problems of macro categories were simply explained away as deviations from equilibrium.

(4) Marginal technique used by the neoclassicals has had many defects. It is indeed very difficult to correctly calculate the marginal productivity of a factor.

(5) It cannot offer any satisfactory explanation for capitalist crisis.

(6) The equilibrium technique does not take into account the institutional framework, the social relations and the like. It is, therefore, divorced from reality. The theory assumed a pure economy regardless of social form.

(7) All the assumptions of the neoclassical economics can be regarded as unrealistic and heroic.

(8) It does not explain individuals in terms of society, but the other way round.

(9) It neglects the fact that in a capitalist society, factors are not paid according to their marginal productivities. Many factors are paid less. Hence, there is the element of exploitation, and therefore, class harmony becomes a distant possibility.

(10) Neoclassical theory depicts the model of a self-centered homo-economicus always trying to maximise his gains. This model of man is neither theoretically true nor empirically encountered at all times.

(11) Human nature alone is the essence of the story. The story is one-sided and reductionist in nature.

Since 1930s, the dominant position of neoclassicism was seriously undermined with the development of Keynesianism which advocated state interference for the regulation of the economy and for bringing about full employment without inflation (internal balance) in capitalistic economies. However, attempts were made to combine neoclassicism and Keynesianism for solving the various economic problems. This combination is generally described as *Neoclassical Synthesis*. Neoclassical synthesis provides that Govt. policies can ensure full employment without inflation.

Since 1950s, the neoclassical economists focused their attention to the area of macrodynamics which was so long pre-empted by the Keynesian school. They advanced, as they claimed, the more realistic version of the theory of economic growth. They proceeded from production function characterising the link between expenditure of economic resources and the output of products. The neoclassical theory of growth was expected to prove that capitalist economy is inherently stable and it can easily ward off disequilibrium.

In 1960s, the neoclassical offensive against Keynesianism gained momentum. It was found that Keynesian prescriptions boosted worldwide inflation and crisis. The capitalist economies became more destabilised. In the meantime, Milton Friedman, revived the neoclassical monetary theory by showing that all economic activities are money-supply oriented. Monetarists believe that capitalist economies are inherently stable and that a steady growth rate of money supply must be ensured in an economy. Monetarism castigated Keynesianism which brought about indiscipline in money supply rule for implementing the Keynesian policy framework. Monetarists urge that there must be a limit to state's social expenditure. In fact, according to the new neo-classical theory (Monetarism), the state regulation must be strictly limited over the economy. The govt. interference must be primarily restricted to the sphere of credit and monetary policy. However, it has been noticed that like Keynesianism, neoclassicism has had certain inherent limitations and contradictions. For instance, their growth theory has been facing a crisis. In fact, the concept of growth in terms of quantity cannot ensure the desired and better quality of life. Thus, both Keynesianism and neoclassicism have led to failures in many fronts. The present era is indeed a limbo and is confronting a regime of crisis in economic theory.

(IV) : RICARDIAN THEORY OF VALUE AND MARXIAN THEORY OF VALUE : A COMPARATIVE ESTIMATE

Marxian theory of value is developed along the classical line, but in many important respects, Marxian theory of value differed from the Ricardian theory of value. However, it should be noted that both Ricardo and Marx upheld the labour theory of value in the classical tradition.

Ricardo observed that in the case of ordinary reproducible commodities, value depends on the amount of labour necessary to produce them. If a commodity is produced by labour and capital, Ricardo would say that since capital can be converted to labour (Capital is dead labour or stored-up labour), value would ultimately depend on the labour-content of the commodity. In the Ricardian formulation, rent does not enter into price. Ricardo was concerned with the theory of price. He used the labour embodied theory of value because it leads to the nearest approximation to truth for measuring the relative value. Ricardo was considering relative price and he had real cost theory of value.

According to Ricardo, wage-price changes will not much affect the relative values but they may affect the normal price or *absolute value* : However, he noted that a change in the fixed capital-labour ratio will change the value. Similarly, value may be different if the fixed capital differs in turn-over rates. Ricardo very clearly appreciated the importance of time element in the theory of value. A change in the relative value is dependent on : *(i)* labour-content and *(ii)* time taken for production.

Capital cost (Profit) will have only a marginal effect on the relative value. Under perfect competition, profit tends to be the same in all industries. Similarly, labour quality differences are already adjusted by the market forces in a free economy. Then, the real difference in value is really made by the difference in labour-contents of commodities. Ricardo, thus, had an empirical labour theory of value, which is considered by Stigler as 93% labour theory of value. In fact, Ricardo found labour as both a cause and a measure of value.

Ricardo needed an invariable measure of value for finding out the relative price (or exchange value). In his analysis of value, skill differentials of labour did not pose any difficulty to Ricardo. Ricardo did not make any distinction between value-producing abstract labour and use-value producing concrete labour, and also between individual labour and socially-necessary labour. Ricardo's concept of labour was a kind of ordinary labour. He did not grasp the distinction between labour and labour-power, and hence, he does not explain profit through surplus value. Ricardo was unable to show where the uniform rate of profit came from and how to calculate it. He seems to have forgotten the fact that constant capital (fixed capital) plays a crucial role in the determination of profit. Ricardo, after all, was interested in the analysis of quantitative exchange problem.

Marx, unlike Ricardo, was not considering a theory of price; but he was analysing a theory of value. Marxian theory of value, commonly known also as a labour theory of value, expresses a social relation in a capitalistic economy. A basic form of this relation is commodity. Marx's quantitative value analysis is concerned with the determination of exchange, value, whereas his qualitative value analysis is concerned with the analysis of social relation. To Marx, value is the objectification of abstract labour. Marx was eager to find out the existing production relations through his value analysis. Value is measured by the abstract labour-content in units of time which is on an average necessary to produce a commodity (*i.e.* socially necessary labour or average labour). The social relation is expressed through the act of exchange. Value is not something intrinsic to a single commodity.

According to Marx, means of production cannot create values. The contribution of capital (means of production) is reckoned in value and it is equivalent to depreciation of capital (wear and tear). The means of production simply transfer the value already created by labour. The value of the raw materials, likewise, is immediately transferred to the product produced by them. Value is created by labour. The value of a commodity consists of the labour time required to produce it. Labour power is a commodity to Marx. The value of a commodity consists of constant capital used (c) plus variable capital used (v) and surplus value (s). Thus, value is equal to $(C+V+S)$. In other words, value will consist of the depreciation of capital used plus wage paid to labour plus the extra value created by labour (surplus value) during his employment over and above his wage in a particular period of production.

In the Marxian schema, price which is equivalent to cost of production plus profit may not always be equal to value. They are equal only under an ideal situation. The extent of variation between value and price will depend basically on the organic composition of capital (c/v) or capital per worker. The subject is analysed in detail by Marx in his Transformation Problem.

We can now attempt a comparative estimate of Ricardo's and Marx's value theories. Both Ricardo and Marx analysed labour theory of value and accepted labour as the principal cause of value. Both writers explained the possibility of deviation of price from value. But such a deviation was empirically insignificant to Ricardo but not to Marx. Ricardo played down the chasm between value and price. Marx explained it away elaborately. While Ricardo considered labour embodied in a commodity without qualification, Marx explained value in terms of average labour-embodied in a commodity. Ricardo did not consider the variation of skill among the labourers. Marx was giving more importance to socially necessary labour. Both Ricardo and Marx adopted labour quantity theory of exchange value. However, the introduction of the concept of socially necessary labour by Marx was by itself an improvement over the Ricardian theory of value which did not account for the skill differentials of labour.

Marx made a distinction between labour whose quantity can be measured in hours and labour power whose value is given by the quantity of labour required to produce wage goods. These goods and their real value are essential elements in Ricardian analysis. But Ricardo did not identify this real value with the real value of commodity labour power. In his analysis of exploitation, Marx used the concept of commodity labour power in a fashion which was completely unknown to Ricardo. Marx's analysis was more pointed, purposeful and analytical as compared to Ricardo's.

Ricardo was explaining a theory of relative price but Marx was considering the theory of value. While Ricardo put more emphasis on the labour theory of value, Marx put more emphasis on the value theory of labour. To Marx, labour quantity not only regulated value but it was the essence of value. To Ricardo, labour quantity was a hypothesis helpful to explain actual relative prices. While Ricardo put emphasis on the relative price, Marx was more keen to analyse absolute value. Ricardo never made absolute value the centre-piece of his analysis. For Ricardo, relative prices and relative values were the same things, but for Marx, they were different things. Time element was very crucial for Ricardo's analysis of relative price, but it was not so with Marx.

Marx explained production relations in terms of his value analysis. Ricardian value analysis is divorced from the production relations. Ricardo's theory is more formal and metaphysical, Marx's theory of value is more practical and dialectical. Marx's purpose was to analyse qualitative exchange problem i.e. social relations which underlie the market phenomena, but Ricardo wanted to explain the exchange problem as it takes place in the market. The implication of Marxian analysis of value is, thus, more deep-rooted and far-flung than that of Ricardo's analysis.

The essential points of similarities and distinctions between Ricardian and Marxian theories of value are summarised in the following chart.

	Ricardo's theory of value	*Marx's theory of value*
1.	Labour theory of value.	Labour theory of value.
2.	Labour is the cause of value.	Labour is the cause of value.
3.	Labour alone creates value.	Labour alone creates value.
4.	Value and price deviate; but the deviation is empirically insignificant.	Value and price deviate and the deviation may be significant (explained away through Transformation Problem).
5.	Explains Relative Value (relative price); absolute value not important.	Explains primarily absolute value.
6.	Social relation or production relation is not taken into account.	Social relation and production relations are explained through value.
7.	Relative price and relative value are the same.	Relative values are different from relative price.
8.	Time element is very crucial to relative value.	Not so.
9.	Explains value of commodities	Explains price.
10.	Explains labour theory of value.	Explains value theory of labour.
11.	Considered ordinary labour without skill variation.	Considered socially necessary labour (average labour).
12.	Labour power is not a commodity.	Labour power is a commodity
13.	Concerned with invariable measure of value.	Not concerned with invariable measure of value.
14.	Value is divorced from production relations.	Value and production relations are intimately connected.
15.	Value analysis is formal.	Value analysis is dialectical.
16.	Ricardo does not distinguish between absolute labour and concrete labour, and between individual labour and socially necessary labour.	Marx does make these distinctions.
17.	Ricardo does not grasp the distinction between labour and labour power. Hence, he does not explain profit through surplus value.	Marx makes this crucial difference formal.
18.	Ricardo was unable to show where the uniform rate of profit comes from and how to calculate it?	Marx is able to explain them.
19.	Ricardo forgets the role of constant (fixed) capital in the determination of profit.	Marx recognises its role.
20.	The cost of capital is profit.	The cost of capital is its wear and tear (depreciation).
21.	Commodities exchange in proportion to their respective embodied labour time.	Commodities exchange in proportion to their respective embodied socially necessary labour time.

22.	Ricardo was interested in quantitative exchange.	Marx explains mainly qualitative exchange problem i.e. social relations.
23.	Ricardo explains quantitative value.	Marx explains mainly quantitative and qualitative value problems.

Thus, from the above analysis, it becomes pretty clear that Marx's analysis of value was more broad-based, analytical, objective and realistic. It was more cautious and pragmatic. It could explain commodity values as well as social relations involved in the production process. It explains not only the labour theory of value but also the value theory of labour and their social implications. It is in this sense that Marx's theory can be looked upon as a distinct improvement over the Ricardian Theory of Value.

(V) : A NOTE ON PIERO SRAFFA'S PRODUCTION OF COMMODITIES BY MEANS OF COMMODITIES

P. Sraffa published a book; *Production of Commodities by Means of Commodities : Prelude to a Critique of Economic Theory* in 1960. In this book, Sraffa has tried to improve upon the classical theory of value by considering a standard commodity (average commodity), with which Ricardo was primarily concerned. Thus, Sraffa has given a new dimension to the value analysis and also to the theory of distribution. With the help of the standard commodity, it is possible to analyse the distribution of national product between wage and profit without disturbing the value of the national product.

Sraffa's book contains all the characteristics of Ricardian touches. The presentation of the book is a kind of "Ricardo in modern dress". Like Ricardo, Sraffa has also searched for a standard of value independent of demand and unaffected by alteration in the distribution pattern of the total product between wages and profits. Sraffa has given emphasis on the *standard commodity* as the yardstick of value. Sraffa has demonstrated that relative prices depend only on the technical conditions of production of *standard commodity* and on no other factor.

Sraffa's work is designed to solve the traditional problem of value. It can be regarded as an attack on the marginal analysis. The subtitle of the book is : *Prelude to a Critique of Economic Theory*. The book can be regarded as an attempt to rehabilitate the classical approach to certain crucial problems relating to value and distribution.

Sraffa assumes an economic system in which the nature of the return to scale is not relevant. Production goes on without any change in scale or factor proportions. Sraffa shows that for an economy in which any number of (K) different commodities is produced, a set of K production equations in price terms can be arranged in which the number of independent equations is equal to the number of unknowns. In this way, the prices of the K commodities and the average rate of profits, can all be determined. In Sraffa's system, wage is assumed to be a variable. If the wage is known, the rate of profits and all the prices will be determined. The movements in the relative prices of any two products, consequent upon a change in wages, depend not only on the proportion of labour and capital but also on the proportions by which the capital has been produced and also on the proportions by which the means of production (capitals) of those means of production have been produced and also on the proportions by which the means of production (capitals) of these means of production have been produced. The ratio of the value of a border-line industry's (standard industry) net product to the value of its means of production would always remain the same, irrespective of changes in the wage level. This ratio must be equal to the average rate of profits which would prevail over the economy as a whole, if wages were zero (*i.e.*, maximum profits). This is the basic condition of an *invariant* industry. It is possible to find out, according to Sraffa, a sort of composite industry in which the ratio of the net product to means of production will remain invariable in spite of changes in wage level. The *composite industry* can be regarded as the *standard industry*. The standard industry would fulfil the basic condition of invariance.

It is well-known that a change in the division of surplus between wages and profits will also change the relative prices. We need to know the prices so that we can know the value of the surplus to be divided. This was the problem which concerned Ricardo. Sraffa provides a solution. He isolates those basic commodities which enter into production. In this way, he constructs a standard of value in the form of a composite commodity into which every particular item enters as means of production, in the same proportion as it appears as output. In Sraffa's system production of commodities is done by means of commodities. He has removed the assumption of technically-determined physical real wage. He demonstrates that there is no such thing as a quantity of capital which exists independently of the rate of profit. In the Marxist fashion, Sraffa observed that all commodities are required for further production of commodities in the endless cycle of a self-maintaining system. In order to determine wages, he introduces a measure of value which is called *standard commodity* which is produced under a standard system in which the various commodities are produced in the same proportion as they enter the aggregate means of production. The standard commodity is used to measure the net income. A standard commodity can stand independently by itself. It consists of a self-replacing set of basic commodities in which every commodity enters for the purpose of production. Sraffa has observed that it is the interdependence of commodity production which determines the standard measure of value in terms of commodities. The standard measure of value which was the wage good in the Ricardian system, does not find its favour with the Sraffian system. In the Sraffian system, the standard commodity is produced with the average capital-labour ratio of the economy. Thus, a change in wages and profits will not change the value of the standard commodity.

Sraffa maintains that the relationship between wages and profits is not simply limited to the standard system but it can be extended to the actual economic system. In such a system, once the wage is given, the rate of profits can also be determined. In this way, Sraffa concludes that for the economy as a whole, the rate of profit is determined as soon as we know the ratio of net product to the means of production in the standard industry and also the proportion of the net product of the standard industry going to wages. In other words, if the wage of the standard industry is given, the average rate of profits of the economy depends on the ratio of net product to the means of production of the standard industry. (Or 'R' ratio)

Sraffa has widely used the simple relation between wage and profit to explain a number of difficult problems. Finally, Sraffa brings into his analysis the role of *land*, and arranges a more complex system of equations in which, if wages are given, the prices, profit and rents are all determined. Sraffa considers what is left of fixed capital at the end of the production year as a kind of joint-product of the industry in which it is used. He also makes a distinction between the basic and non-basic products. A basic product enters into the production of all commodities, and a non-basic product does not.

Sraffa wanted to rehabilitate the classical labour theory of value. As Sraffa observed, in a particular type of industry whose conditions of production represent a sort of *social average,* the average rate of profits is determined by the ratio of surplus value to the means of production in that type of industry. This type of industry represents, according to Karl Marx, the *organic composition of capital* which is equal to the social average. Thus, there is a striking similarity between the Marxian relation and the analysis of Sraffa. Sraffa's ratio of the value of the net product of the standard industry to the value of its means of production, is equal to the ratio of the labour-embodied in its means of production. In other words, Sraffa is postulating the same relation between the average rate of profits and the production condition in his standard industry as Marx was postulating between the average rate of profit and the production conditions in his industry of average organic composition of capital (social average). Both Sraffa and Marx have observed that wages being given, the average rate of profit (therefore, the deviations of the price ratios from embodied-labour ratios) are governed by the ratio of direct to indirect labour in the industry whose production conditions represent an average. In the case of Marx, the organic composition of capital in an average industry is equal to the social average. However, Marx's result was only provisional and approximate, as he had abstracted from considering the effect of change in wage on price of capital employed in average industry. Sraffa demonstrates that exactly the same result can be obtained without any abstraction, provided we use the concept of *standard industry.* Needless to say, Sraffa's standard industry defines the average conditions of production in such a way as to get the same result which Marx was trying to get. Thus, in a sense, Sraffa has really corroborated the Marxian value analysis. This point is also maintained by Steedman in his book, *Marx after Sraffa.*

Be that as it may, a number of criticisms can be levelled against Piero Sraffa's analysis. Firstly, the sub-title of this book, *Prelude to a Critique of Economic Theory,* appears to be a misnomer because the book does not really furnish any critique to economic theory whether past or present. Secondly, Sraffa has neglected the problem of factor substitution and changes in the scale of operations. Thirdly, Sraffa's analysis has altogether brushed aside the role of capital in production process. Fourthly, Sraffa has not used the traditional method of price determination by considering demand, supply and the cost of the production. Lastly, Sraffa, in practice, has not been able to find out any standard commodity which he was theoretically trying to achieve. Sraffa has really hunted the Heffalump of standard commodity in vain. His attempts in this direction have not been quite successful. In spite of all this, it should be noted that the book provided the starting point of a new school which set out to criticise the logical foundations of neo-classical economics, and to reconstruct those of Marxist economics, by posing an alternative theory of distribution based on class struggle over the level of wages and profits. The book has indeed established Marx more strongly than ever before.

VI : RICARDIAN ECONOMICS AND SRAFFIAN ANALYSIS : A NOTE

In his book, *Production of Commodities by Means of Commodities,* Piero Sraffa has tried to find the *standard* commodity. This standard commodity can serve as an invariable measure of value. In fact, Ricardo always wanted to have such an invariable standard for his value analysis. Basic inputs are essential for standard commodity. The basic inputs enter into the production of all commodities and are the basis on which price, wage and profit relations are calculated. Sraffa has defined standard commodity in terms of the system of basics. A standard commodity is the composite commodity. If this bundle of commodities (basic commodity) is used as inputs, it will reproduce itself in the same proportion as outputs, but the scale would be larger. In a one-commodity world, the one commodity is the standard commodity. For instance, if corn is used to produce corn, then corn can be regarded as the standard commodity.

With the help of the use of standard commodity, the many-commodity economy can be reduced to one-commodity economy. In case the standard commodity is used as a *numeraire,* it can be shown that an inverse relationship exists between the level of wages and the rate of profit. Thus, Ricardo's fundamental theorem of distribution is found to be valid. However, it should be noted that the standard commodity is defined purely in terms of the basic inputs *excluding* labour. Labour is regarded as a separate input which is paid wage in accordance with the distribution of net produce. When the standard commodity is used as a *numeraire,* the variation in relative prices due to uneven layering of labour can be eliminated.

Both Ricardo and Sraffa *(i)* find a relationship between past labour and present labour. This leads to a change in prices when wages change, and *(ii)* both try to have a theory of *average commodity*. However, Ricardo did not have anything in his system as Sraffian *standard commodity*.

For Ricardo, commodities are produced by labour, and labour is the sole source of value. The labour expended on a commodity is the past labour (capital) as well as present labour. Ricardo's dated labour can only extend back one period. For Sraffa, commodities are produced by commodities, and these commodities have been produced by other commodities and so on back in time indefinitely. Sraffa's dated labour, therefore, can extend back indefinitely. This difference between Ricardo and Sraffa on the theories of labour is indeed very vital. And it produces sharp difference in their solutions to the search for an invariable measure of value.

Ricardo did not want to have a theoretical invariable standard : he was interested in an accurate empirical approximation. Sraffa's standard commodity finds only a theoretical solution : it has no empirical counterpart. Such a *standard commodity* is an empirical Heffalump and it cannot be found in the real universe of discourse.

Theoretically, Sraffian system solves the price problem that troubled Ricardo. But Sraffian system is not consistent with the heart of Ricardian system. Sraffa attempts to displace the role played by labour in Ricardian value theory and substitutes instead an analysis of use value, inputs, technical coefficients and commodities.

However, the concept of *standard commodity* serves mainly two important purposes : (i) it simplifies the distributional relation between capital and labour in terms of the division of net production, and (ii) it provides a commodity with uniform layering of dated labour. In fact, Ricardo was also concerned with these two purposes. He was very much concerned with distributional relations and he analysed their evolution through the development of productivity in a single-commodity corn-economy.

But Ricardo's analysis of corn economy is a simplified Sraffian economy in which the only basic is corn. Ricardo regarded corn as a special case of a composite commodity. Ricardo never extended the use of this special case too far.

It must be noted at the end that Ricardo's system was distinctly different from the Sraffian system. Ricardo's life long purpose was to identify value, measured by labour time, as the source of exchange value. Sraffa attempts to identity exchange value with a physical system of use values in which the standard commodity reduces the economy to the simplest form of physical production. Since Ricardian system is different from Sraffian system, the *standard commodity* approach does not really salvage the Ricardian value analysis (See also the discussion on Sraffa's book in this chapter).

VII : MARXIAN LABOUR THEORY OF VALUE AND SRAFFIAN ANALYSIS : A NOTE

After the publication of Ian Steedman's *Marx After Sraffa* (London, 1977), the necessity of labour theory of value in understanding some of the basic features of capitalist economies is being questioned. It must be noted that Sraffa has implicitly presupposed capitalist relations in production. The use of wage as a share of *net product* is simply an analytical convenience.

In the simple case of an exchange economy, there is *simple reproduction,* just enough to maintain itself. There is no *surplus product.* All the products are necessary inputs in production. In such a case, the exchange ratios of all commodities become determinate. We can take any one commodity as the *standard commodity.* The relative values of other commodities can be expressed in terms of this standard commodity. Thus, we can estimate the total value of production in terms of this single commodity. If we assume that *(i)* all productions, require labour and *(ii)* total labour is unity, then, we can know as to what fraction of total social labour has been used to each line of production. In such a situation, relative labour values of the commodities necessarily become equal to their exchange ratios. This is so because the total social labour produced the total social product and all products are used in specified quantities in production. We can now know the commodity exchange ratios without knowing anything about labour at all. The ratios are determined by the fixed production requirements of a commodity economy where there is no *surplus production.* Thus, labour theory of value is not necessary for determining the exchange ratios (relative price).

All the difference is made by the existence of *surplus product.* The existence of surplus may lead to a change in the exchange ratios. Sraffa mentions a situation where the entire surplus product goes to the workers who wholly spend it on increased consumption. In such a case, the consumption of labour is explicitly indicated as commodities (consumption beyond subsistence). Here, the exchange ratios directly derived from the production structure equal the social labour content. The situation here is the same as the earlier case: labour theory of value is not necessary for knowing the relative value.

A change in the division of surplus between capitalists and workers will change the relative prices. However, a change in wages and profits will not change the value of *standard commodity* because this is produced with average capital-labour ratio of the economy. In such a system, when the wage is given, the rate of profit can be determined. The average rate of profit is determined by the ratio of surplus value to the means of production in a standard industry. In Marx's terminology, the organic composition of capital here is a *social average.* Both Sraffa and Marx did speak about the same type of standard industry (or average organic composition of capital). But Marx abstracted from considering the effect of wage change on the price of capital employed in average industry. Sraffa got the same result as Marx's by using his concept of *standard industry*. But Sraffa did not make any abstraction. Sraffa was able to establish the Marxian postulate without facing the problem of translating propositions relating to labour values to those in terms of prices. Sraffa's invariant standard could explain the distributive relations directly. However, Steedman demonstrated that after Sraffa, Marx has emerged as a stronger value theorist than ever before (See, also the discussion of Sraffa's book in this chapter).

VIII : CLASSICAL MODEL OF ECONOMIC GROWTH : A MATHEMATICAL NOTE

In the classical model, development is a race between technological progress and population growth.[4] The technological progress depends on capital accumulation which, in turn, depends on the rate of profit. Capital accumulation, needless to say, permits increasing mechanisation and greater division of labour. The classical model of growth can be represented in terms of the following inter-related propositions :

Proposition 1 : Production Function

It shows that output (O) is a function of the size of labour force (L), the stock of capital (Q). The amount of land available (supply of known resources) and the level of technology (T). Thus, classical production function can be written as :

$$O = f(L, K, Q, T) \qquad \text{......... (i)}$$

The production function was of *linear and homogeneous type*. This means that if the quantities of all inputs are doubled, production of output will also exactly double. However, the classical economists were wise enough to think that the supply of land cannot be doubled. The supply of land remains fixed.

Proposition 2: Capital Accumulation Permits Technological Progress

The classical economists believed that technology is capital-absorbing, and capital accumulation requires saving. Thus, "work hard and save more" was their basic policy prescription for economic growth. Saving was ultimately converted to investment (I) for the accumulation of capital on which will depend the level of technology. Thus,

$$T = T(I) \qquad \text{......... (ii)}$$

Proposition 3 : Investment Depends on Profits

Net investment can be done by the utilistion of profit made by the capitalists. The purpose of investment is also to earn more and more profits. Thus,

$$I = dQ = I(R) \qquad \text{......... (iii)}$$

---

4. See, Benjamin Higgins, *Economic Development*, 1959, pp. 87 ff.

(R is the return on the fixed factors of production or profits. dQ represents the increase in the stock of capital).

Proposition 4 : Profits Depend on Labour Supply and the Level of Technology

Needless to say, technological progress can offset the diminishing returns and increase the level of profits. Labour supply and population growth change together in the same direction. With the increase in population, diminishing returns on land would necessitate the use of more labour. This will raise the labour cost and reduce profits. However, the tendency of diminishing returns can be offset by introducing improved technology. Thus, the fourth classical proposition can be written as :

$$R = R(T, L)$$ .... (iv)

Proposition 5 : The Size of the Labour Force Depends on the Size of Wage Bill (Wage Fund)

In the classical system. other things remaining the same, when wage fund increases, wage rate goes up, families are expanded and labour force is increased temporarily. In the long run, however, an expanded labour force will bring down wages to subsistence. Ordinarily, in the short run, there is a direct nexus between the size of the labour force and the size of the wage fund. Thus,

$$L = L(W)$$ .... (v)

Proposition 6 : Wage Bill (Wage Fund) Depends on the Level of Investment

Wage fund is built up by saving and put into effective use through investment. Wage fund is the available money for hiring labour. But the size of the wage fund itself depends on net saving, and therefore, on net investment. Thus,

$$W = W(I)$$ .... (vi)

Proposition 7 : Total Output Equals Profits Plus Wages

This shows that total national income is equal to the value of all goods and services produced, and this amount is divided between labourers and capitalists. Thus,

$$O = R + W$$ .... (vii)

We have thus the determinate classical model of growth : There are seven equations and seven unknowns.

It becomes clear from the above set of equations that profit is the prime mover in the classical model of growth. Thus,

$$(\uparrow) \quad dR \to dI \to dQ \to dT, \qquad dW \to dL \to dR \quad (\downarrow)$$

An increase in profit, brings about an increase in investment, capital stock and technology. All this will raise wage fund, population growth, and labour costs, which in turn, will reduce profit. Reduced profit will reduce investment, retard technical progress, diminish wage fund and slow down population growth. In the classical model of growth, the end result is *stagnation*. In fact, in the classical schema, *stationary state* is the inevitable eventuality of a mature capitalist economy.

SELECT BIBLIOGRAPHY

Aiyangar, Ramaswamy, *Aspects of Ancient Indian Economic Thought*, Benaras Hindu University, Varanasi, 1965.

Ayres, C.E., *The Theory of Economic Progress*, Schocken Books, New York, 1962.

Bell, John Fred, *A History of Economic Thought*, The Ronald Press, 1953.

Blaug, Mark, *Ricardian Economics*, Yale University Press, 1958.

Blaug, Mark, *Economic Theory in Retrospect*, Cambridge University Press.

Blaug, Mark, *Great Economists Before Keynes*, Wheatsheaf Books, London, 1986.

Brahmananda, P.R., *Explorations in the Theory of New Classical Political Economy*, Allied Publishers, Delhi, 1974.

Dasgupta, A.K., *Epochs in Economic Theory*, Oxford Univ. Press, Delhi, 1985.

Datta, Bhabatosh, *The Evolution of Economic Thinking in India*, Federation Hall Society, Calcutta, 1962.

Dutt, R.C., *The Economic History of India*, Routledge and Kegan Paul, 1956.

Ekelund, Robert and Hebert, R., *History of Economic Theory and Method*, McGraw Hill, Japan, 1985.

Ferfuson, J.M., *Landmarks of Economic Thought*, Green and Co., 1937.

Ganguly, B.N., *Indian Economic Thought, Nineteenth Century Perspective*, Tata McGraw Hill, N.Delhi, 1977.

Gherity, J.A. (Ed.), *Economic Thought : A Historical Anthology*, Random House, New York, 1965.

Ghosh, Rama(Ed.), *Development of Economic Thought and Theories*, Deep & Deep, 1989.

Ghosh, B.N., *Principles of Economic Science*, Vikas Publication, Delhi, 1984.

Ghosh, B.N., *Political Economy : A Marxist Approach*, Macmillan, 1990.

Gide, Charles and Rist, Charles, *A History of Economic Doctrines* (2nd Edn.), George G. Harap & Co.

Gokhale, B.G., *Indian Thought Through the Ages*, New York, 1961.

Gopalkrishna, P.K., *Development of Economic Ideas in India*, People's Publishing House, Sept. 1959.

Gray, Alexander, *The Development of Economic Doctrines*, Longmans, Green & Co., New York, 1933.

Gray, A., *The Socialist Tradition*, London, 1954.

Haney, Lewis H., *History of Economic Thought* (4th Edn.), Macmillan, 1949.

Hecksher, E., *Mercantilism*, 2 Vols., 1935.

Heimann, Edward, *History of Economic Doctrines*, Oxford University Press, New York, 1964.

Homan, P.T., *Contemporary Economic Thought*, Harper & Brothers, NewYork, 1928.

Huchison, T.W., *A Review of Economic Doctrines*, Oxford, 1953.

Ingram, J.K., *History of Political Economy*, A & C Black Ltd., London, 1913.

Kapp, K.W. and L.L. Kapp (Ed.), *History of Economic Thought*, Barnes and Nobles, New York, 1963.

Lekachman, Robert, *A History of Economic Ideas*, Harper & Bros., 1959.

Madan, G.R., *Economic Thinking in India*, S. Chand Co., 1966, Delhi.
McConnel, J.W., *Ideas of Great Economists*, Barnes and Nobles Books, New York, 1980.
Mehring, Franz, *Karl Marx : His Life and Work*, Covici Friede, 1936.
Monroe, Arthur (Ed.), *Early Economic Thought*, Cambridge, Mass., Harvard University Press, 1924.

Neff, Frank A., *Economic Doctrines*, McGraw Hill Books, 1950.
Newman, P.C., *The Development of Economic Thought*, Prentice Hall, 1952.

Oswald, St. Clair, *A Key to Ricardo*, Augustus M. Kelley, New York, 1965.

Patterson, S. Howard (Ed.), *Readings in the History of Economic Thought*, Holt, Rinehart and Winston, New York, 1970.

Roll, Eric, *A History of Economic Thought*, Faber and Faber, 1940.
Rubin, I.I., *History of Economic Thought* (Translated), 1979.

Schumpeter, Joseph A., *Ten Great Economists*, Oxford University Press, London, 1951.
Schumpeter, J.A., *History of Economic Analysis*, Oxford University Press, New York, 1959.
Scott, William A., *The Development of Economic Thought*, Appleton Century-Croft, 1933.
Sen, B.C., *Economics in Kautilya*, Sanskrit College, Calcutta, 1967.
Singh, V.B., *From Naoroji to Nehru*, Macmillan, Delhi, 1975.
Spiegel, Henry William, *The Growth of Economic Thought*, Prentice Hall, 1971.
Spiegel, H.W. (Ed.), *The Development of Economic Thought*, John Wiley and Sons, 1952.
Sraffa, P. and Dobb, M. (Ed.), *Works and Correspondence of David Ricardo*, Vol.I.
Stigler, George J., *Production and Distribution Theories*, Macmillan, New York, 1941.
Sweezy, Paul, *The Theory of Capitalist Development*, Monthly Review Press, New York, 1947.

Taylor, O.H., *A History of Economic Thought*, McGraw Hill Book Co., 1960.

Whittaker, Edmund, *Schools and Streams of Economic Thought*, Rand McNally, 1960.